CICERO: THE ASCENDING YEARS

CICERO

THE ASCENDING YEARS

THOMAS N. MITCHELL

New Haven and London
Yale University Press
1979

Designed by Sally Harris
and set in IBM Press Roman type.
Printed in the United States of America by
Vail-Ballou Press, Binghamton, New York.

Published in Great Britain, Europe, Africa, and
Asia (except Japan) by Yale University Press,
Ltd., London. Distributed in Australia and
New Zealand by Book & Film Services, Artarmon,
N.S.W., Australia; and in Japan by Harper & Row,
Publishers, Tokyo Office.

Library of Congress Cataloging in Publication Data

Mitchell, Thomas N., 1939–
  Cicero, the ascending years.

  Bibliography: p.
  Includes index.
  1. Cicero, Marcus Tullius. 2. Statesmen–
Rome–Biography. 3. Orators.–Rome–Biography.
I. Title.
DG260.C53M57   937'.05'0924 [B]   78-31188
ISBN 0–300–02277–8

178358

CONTENTS

PREFACE

The importance of the study of Cicero's political life and thought needs little illustration. His career spans the final half-century of the Roman Republic, a period of abiding interest in the history of government. In the course of it, the republican constitution, which in a long process of growth and adjustment to the political demands of the various segments of the society had identified basic principles of political freedom and democratic government, and under which Rome had achieved military supremacy in the Mediterranean and a high level of stability and prosperity, collapsed under the stress of changing social, economic, and political conditions and gave way to an opposing philosophy of government—autocracy. This development, commonly known as the Roman Revolution, makes a dramatic story of decline and fall and provides the material for an instructive study of the forces and circumstances that can steer a free society toward dictatorship and overthrow institutions cherished for centuries.

Cicero was at the center of Roman political life throughout all the internal crises of the final decades of the Republic, and his well-documented career and his frequent expressions of his political views provide valuable insights into the causes of the Roman Revolution. The importance of his political life and thought lies not in the impact he had on the course of events, but in the fact that to a large extent he epitomizes the political mentality of the conservative leaders of the late Republic and reveals in his efforts to preserve the status quo and in his reflections on politics, political institutions, and the tensions and divisions that brought five civil wars in his lifetime, the goals and perceptions of the proponents of traditional republicanism and their inadequacy in the face of rapid change and serious unrest. Nowhere else can the nature of the Roman republican ideal, or the reasons for the failure of its adherents to understand and correct its deficiencies, be as plainly seen.

There is, of course, no shortage of political biographies of Cicero. The present book differs from them, however, in several important respects. It concentrates on the first two-thirds of Cicero's life, the period least well documented in the ancient sources and least discussed in modern biographies. Specifically, it examines Cicero's political heritage, including the figures who shaped his thinking in his early years, and the way his ideas evolved and affected his political conduct during the most active and successful phases of his career—his years as a candidate and his term as Rome's chief magistrate in 63.

The relatively narrow range of the book makes possible a thorough exploration of the scattered and sometimes ambiguous evidence for Cicero's ascending years in Roman politics and a full discussion of the complex political conditions and events with which he had to deal and which often crucially shaped or circumscribed his political responses. The result, I hope, is a more complete and fully documented account of Cicero's political life and thought in the most significant and revealing stages of his career and a more extensive discussion of the political background of his statesmanship than can be found in standard biographies.

My debts are many. The book was written during two sabbatical leaves made possible by grants from the American Council of Learned Societies and Swarthmore College. The second of these leaves was spent at Trinity College, Dublin, where I was warmly received and generously assisted in varied ways by Professors D. E. W. Wormell and W. B. Stanford. I had the good fortune to have Russell Meiggs as a colleague at Swarthmore College during the academic years 1974–75 and 1977–78. He was always ready to read a chapter or discuss a problem, and many sections of this book have benefited from his wide knowledge and sound judgment. Professor R. E. A. Palmer was a frequent source of reference throughout the years of research and writing, and he read the entire manuscript on its completion. I would like to extend particular thanks to him for the many ways in which he helped to make this a better book. The entire manuscript was also read by Professor D. R. Shackleton Bailey, and his detailed critique of it saved me from several errors and some faulty argument. I am grateful to have had the benefit of his unique expertise. To my Swarthmore colleagues Helen North and Martin Ostwald a special acknowledgment is due. I owe much to their help and encouragement and, above all, to their scholarly example. Finally, I owe a deep debt of gratitude to my wife, Lynn, and I dedicate this book to her in recognition of her patient support, unending willingness to listen, valuable criticism, and many hours cheerfully spent in the tiresome task of proofreading.

LIST OF ABBREVIATIONS

Abh Leipz	*Abhandlungen der sächsischen Akademie der Wissenschaften, Leipzig*
AC	*L'antiquité classique*
AHR	*American Historical Review*
AJP	*American Journal of Philology*
ANRW	*Aufstieg und Niedergang der römischen Welt*
ASNP	*Annali della R. Scuola Normale Superiore de Pisa, Sezione di Lettere*
BJ	*Bonner Jahrbücher*
CAH	*Cambridge Ancient History*
CJ	*Classical Journal*
CM	*Classica et Mediaevalia*
CP	*Classical Philology*
CQ	*Classical Quarterly*
CR	*Classical Review*
CSCA	*California Studies in Classical Antiquity*
CW	*Classical World*
DUJ	*Durham University Journal*
HSCP	*Harvard Studies in Classical Philology*

Jahrb Cl Phil	*Jahrbücher für classische Philologie*
JRS	*Journal of Roman Studies*
Mem Ist Lomb	*Memorie del Reale Instituto Lombardo di scienze, lettere ed arti, Milan*
Mn	*Mnemosyne*
NRS	*Nuova Rivista Storica*
PCPS	*Proceedings of the Cambridge Philological Society*
PP	*La Parola del Passato*
RAL	*Rendiconti della Classe di Scienze morali, storiche e filologiche dell' Accademia dei Lincei*
RE	*Real-Encyclopädie der classischen Altertumswissenschaft*
REL	*Revue des études latines*
RH	*Revue historique*
RhM	*Rheinisches Museum für Philologie*
Riv Fil	*Rivista di Filologia e d'Istruzione Classica*
TAPA	*Transactions and Proceedings of the American Philological Association*
WS	*Wiener Studien*
ZSS	*Zeitschrift der Savigny-Stiftung für Rechtsgeschichte romanistische Abteilung*

1: CICERO'S POLITICAL HERITAGE

The material for a study of Cicero's political life comes almost entirely
from his own pen and is abundant, diverse, and sometimes overwhelming in its detail. This wealth of evidence is, however, primarily concerned with his later years and the thinking of his mature statesmanship.
It provides only scattered and allusive references to his early life and
serves, in fact, to highlight the poverty of our information on this crucial period, which is obscured not only by the absence of a contemporary
record from Cicero himself, but by the fact that it coincides with the
shadowy decade of the nineties and the turbulence and confusion of
the Social War and the civil conflicts of the eighties. Yet it was during
these two decades that Cicero made his place in Roman political society,
forged the links so vital in a system where political success was grounded
on a broad network of personal connections with men of *dignitas* and
opes, made some basic decisions about his political sympathies and
affiliations, and gave notice by the men he cultivated and the patrons
he acquired of the political path he was likely to follow.

The scanty evidence for those early years has been often assembled
and welded into a familiar story of his parentage, background, and
education, but, divorced from detailed study of the men and events
which touched his life and shaped his thinking, it is a threadbare tale,
inadequate for an understanding of his place and prospects in Roman
politics when he contemplated his first campaign for public office at
the age of thirty. Fresh investigations of the period in the last two
decades and the diligent application of the prosopographical method

have done much to illuminate this mysterious and poorly documented era in republican history. Though agreement is still lacking and results have been sometimes vitiated by excessive ingenuity and refusal to accept the limitations of prosopographical evidence, the major figures, issues, and political patterns of the nineties and eighties have nonetheless emerged in sharper focus. The picture of Cicero's early life has become clearer in consequence, calling for a fresh look at some old assumptions.

The Family and Its Connections

Cicero was born in Arpinum, a town about seventy miles southeast of Rome which had received the full Roman franchise only in 188. But Cicero's family, which was old and distinguished and had long been a major force in Arpinum's affairs, was not unknown in Rome or in its great consular houses.[1] Cicero's *novitas* and its implications for his political sympathies and actions can be easily exaggerated, a tendency encouraged by the frequency of his own allusions to his lack of noble ancestry. His sensitivity on this issue coupled with a considerable vanity led him frequently to assail aristocratic emphasis on birth and to extol his own achievements, attributing them solely to exceptional *virtus* and *industria.* His political shrewdness further led him to publicize his ties to the powerful *equester ordo* and to invite comparison with another Arpinate parvenu, the popular hero Marius, with whom he had almost nothing in common except his birthplace.[2] But the Roman *nobilitas*, for all its class consciousness, was never closed to outsiders who had the favor of the right families, and Cicero was unusually privileged in this regard. He was technically a *novus homo*, and his newness was a serious handicap in a society remarkably partial to high birth, and a target for the *invidia* of *nobiles* who could not match his success; but some of the more formidable barriers to his political advancement had already been

1. *Leg.* 2.3. *Hic enim orti stirpe antiquissima sumus, hic sacra, hic genus, hic maiorum multa vestigia.*
2. *Man.* 2.4. *Cluent.* 152. *Cael.* 4. *Rab. Post.* 15. *Q.F.* 1.1.6, 35. *Fam.* 3.10. *Scaur.* 4. *Fam.* 13.9. *Sest.* 136. *Leg. Agr.* 2.100. *Sulla* 5.23. *Quir.* 19–20. *Leg.* 2.6. *Planc.* 17–20. It was customary for Roman statesmen to stress the degree to which they had increased the *dignitas* of their family, a practice exemplified by Scaurus and Sulla. Cf. E. Badian, *Lucius Sulla, the Deadly Reformer* (Sydney 1970), 5.

surmounted by his family's *amicitia* with several of Rome's most distinguished consular families.[3]

The Tullii Cicerones had attracted the attention of Rome's ruling oligarchy at least as early as 115, when Cicero's grandfather energetically and successfully resisted an attempt by his brother-in-law Gratidius to introduce a ballot law at Arpinum. This confrontation represented more than a squabble between small-town politicians and had ramifications reaching far beyond Arpinum. It has been plausibly argued that Marius, praetor in 115, and already identified as a foe of the *nobilitas*, was backing the bill.[4] He was a close friend and *adfinis* of Gratidius, had himself successfully introduced a ballot law at Rome over the senate's opposition as tribune in 119, and had a strong personal motive for seeing such legislation enacted at Arpinum, in that he had been rejected for office there before entering Roman politics, shut out, it would appear, by the *potentia* of a local aristocracy hostile to his peasant background.[5]

The dispute was finally referred to Rome. The circumstances of its referral to the capital must remain uncertain, though it is tempting to see the Roman *nobilitas* moving in to thwart a Marian enterprise. What is certain is that Cicero's grandfather found a champion in the consul Aemilius Scaurus and won his commendation, and doubtless that of the powerful Metelli, Scaurus's close associates, for his vigorous stand against *populares* and in defense of a key safeguard of aristocratic dominance.

Municipal families of this stamp could be useful props both in Italy and in Rome for dynastic noble houses, and their promotion in Roman politics was a common consequence of association with *principes* of the capital. There are indications that contact persisted between the Tullii Cicerones and Scaurus, particularly in Cicero's allusions to the latter, which reflect admiration, affection, and a sense of indebtedness.[6]

3. Cf. E. Badian, "Marius and the Nobles" *DUJ* 56 (1964), 141. C. Nicolet, "Arpinum, Aemilius Scaurus et les Tullii Cicerones" *REL* 45 (1967), 276–304. *Com. Pet.* 4.

4. Nicolet, *REL* 45 (1967), 292. For a different view of Marius's political standing at this time cf. P. Bicknell, "Marius, the Metelli, and the *Lex Maria Tabellaria*" *Latomus* 28 (1969), 327–48.

5. *Leg.* 3.38. Plutarch, *Marius* 4.2. Val. Max. 6.9.14. Cf. J. Van Ooteghem, *Caius Marius* (Brussels 1964).

6. Asconius 22, Clark. *Q.F.* 2.16.3. *Font.* 38. *De Or.* 1.214. *Sest.* 101. *Rab.* 21, 26. For more tenuous links between Scaurus and Cicero's family cf. Nicolet, *REL* 45 (1967), 297 ff.

Cicero's father did not enter public life, but Cicero implies that the reason was ill health, not lack of ambition or opportunity.[7] He was a scholarly man, the inspiration for Cicero's insistence on *doctrina* as a prerequisite for *prudentia* and *eloquentia*, with the erudition and literary bent which were much in favor with many prominent figures of the nineties.[8] His broad culture and that of his brother, which betoken a high-level liberal education, and the extent of the acquaintance of both with leading aristocrats, suggest early and extensive contact with Rome, and Cicero's father may have acquired and used his house on the fashionable Carinae well before the educational welfare of his sons prompted a move to the city.[9] In any event it is well attested that he took an active part in the life of the capital in the nineties and cemented ties with several of its consular families.

He had a close relationship with Cato's father, the brother-in-law of Livius Drusus and a stalwart optimate whose career was cut short by a premature death.[10] In the *De Oratore* he is presented by C. Caesar Strabo, uterine brother of the Elder Catulus, as a *familiaris* of all the interlocutors. Cicero sometimes stretches truth in his dialogues in the interests of mood or personal aggrandizement, but this statement, at least in the cases of M. Antonius, L. Crassus, and Scaevola the Augur, is fully substantiated elsewhere.[11]

The family had secured the favor of Antonius at least as early as 102 when the latter was accompanied to his Cilician command against the pirates by Cicero's uncle Lucius. Lucius spent two years with Antonius, returned with him to Rome, and remained his friend and admirer.[12] Cicero's father's marriage helped pave the way for *amicitia* with Crassus. The sister of his wife, Helvia, was married to C. Aculeo, whom Crassus

7. *Leg.* 2.3. *Off.* 1.71.

8. *Leg.* 2.3. *De Or.* 2.2. For the interest of Antonius, Crassus, Catulus the Elder, and Scaurus in learning and literature cf. *De Or.* 2.1–8. *Arch.* 6. *N.D.* 1.79. *Brut.* 112.

9. Cicero calls Lucius *humanissimus* in *De Or.* 2.3. It seems probable that he and Cicero's father received some of their education in Rome. For the house on the Carinae cf. Plutarch, *Cicero* 8. *Q.F.* 2.3.7.

10. *Fam.* 15.4.13. *Brut.* 222. Gellius 13.20.14. Cf. *Off.* 3.65–66.

11. *De Or.* 2.265. It should be stressed that Cicero's concern with truth and historical accuracy in his dialogues is, in general, remarkable. Cf. *De Or.* 2.9. *Brut.* 218–19. *Att.* 6.1.8; 12.20; 12.23; 13.21; 13.31; 13.30; 13.32; 13.33; 13.6; 13.4; 13.5; 12.5b.

12. *De Or.* 2.2. Cf. U. Scholz, *Der Redner M. Antonius* (Erlangen 1963).

had living in his house and whom "of all men he loved the most." Cicero testifies to the familiarity of both his father and Lucius with Crassus by classing them with Aculeo as expert witnesses to the orator's learning and intellectual abilities.[13] Links with Scaevola the Augur were probably established through the association with Crassus, Scaevola's son-in-law. Whatever the basis of their connection, when Cicero assumed the *toga virilis* about the end of 91, his father was able to place him under the tutelage of the prestigious consular and Rome's leading expert on civil law.[14]

The social structure of the late Republic did not preclude such close friendships between *nobiles* and men of equestrian rank. The family of Atticus presents another well-documented example.[15] Atticus's father closely resembles Cicero's. He was moderately wealthy, devoted to learning, and a careful supervisor of the education of his son, who studied with Cicero under Scaevola. The family moved in the best social and political circles. Friendly relations with the Luculli and Hortensii can be documented, as can a marriage connection with P. Sulpicius Rufus. Atticus did not choose to follow in Cicero's footsteps; but he clearly could have, and with every prospect of success, as is indicated by the fact that he attracted the attention of Sulla, who made a strong but vain attempt to involve him in public life. He never sought to change his equestrian status, yet he remained an influential force in politics, was courted by its major figures, and ultimately found himself the father-in-law of Agrippa and the close friend of Augustus, with a granddaughter betrothed to Tiberius.[16] The drawbacks of equestrian origin could be largely eliminated by those whose ability and personality enabled them to utilize *amicitia*, an institution which freely crossed class boundaries.

The established position of the Tullii Cicerones in Roman society by

13. *De Or.* 1.191; 2.2.

14. *Leg.* 1.13. *Brut.* 303. *Am.* 1. Cf. E. Ciaceri, *Cicerone e i suoi tempi* (Milan 1939), 1.14 ff.

15. L. Aelius Stilo Praeconinus is another example of an *eques* who enjoyed the close friendship of the most notable aristocratic families of the nineties. *Brut.* 169, 205–07. Suetonius, *De Gramm.* 2.

16. Nepos, *Att.* 1–5, 12, 19. *Leg.* 1.13. *Att.* 4.16.3. For Atticus's interest and influence in Roman politics cf. Nepos, *Att.* 4.4. *Att.* 4.14.2; 2.11.1; 5.21.3; 5.9.2; 2.1.4; 2.22.4. For his friendly relations with Hortensius, Pompey, the Manlii Torquati, the Metellus brothers Celer and Nepos, Brutus, and other *nobiles* cf. D. R. Shackleton Bailey, *Cicero's Letters to Atticus* (Cambridge 1965), 1.3 ff.

90 B.C. is further illustrated by Cicero's references to his youth and to his patrons and teachers. He and his brother Quintus received their early education at the house of Crassus in the company of the sons of Aculeo, who lived there. This was an unusually close and privileged relationship with an influential consular house, and it extended even to the distinguished women of the family, Mucia, wife of Crassus, her sister, and their mother, Laelia. Further, it would appear that Crassus personally supervised the curriculum of the Ciceros and chose their teachers.[17] One of these can be named, the Greek poet Archias, who came to Rome before the turn of the century, lived at the house of the Luculli, and was warmly patronized by all the prominent *boni*, including Crassus.[18] Later, as an *adulescentulus*, Cicero had frequent contact with Antonius, who instructed him in a variety of subjects. He was also a frequent visitor at another house, that of L. Aelius Stilo, an *eques* but an influential insider, a devoted friend of Metellus Numidicus, and an erudite speechwriter who could number among his clients Metellus Celer, Q. Servilius Caepio, Q. Pompeius Rufus, and C. Aurelius Cotta.[19] The friendship of such a man was an obvious boon to an aspiring newcomer, and it provides another indication of the scope of Cicero's contacts with influential figures. After 91 came his study of civil law, and his association with Scaevola the Augur and later with Scaevola Pontifex, cousin of the Augur and close political ally of Crassus.[20]

Conspicuously absent from Cicero's references to those with whom he was closely connected in the nineties is the name of Gaius Marius, his fellow townsman and *adfinis*, who is commonly presented as a major political asset to Cicero and the man who helped him establish his early contacts with prominent *nobiles*.[21] Cicero's relationship to Marius was indirect, through the Gratidii, the family of his paternal grandmother. The Marii and Gratidii had many ties, and political cooperation between them was close and consistent. That *adfinitas* similarly

17. *De Or.* 2.2 ff. *Cumque . . . et ea disceremus, quae Crasso placerent, et ab his doctoribus, quibus ille uteretur, erudiremur . . . Brut.* 211 tells of Cicero's contact with the women of the family.

18. *Arch.* 1, 6.

19. *Brut.* 169, 205–07. Suetonius, *De Gramm.* 2.

20. *Am.* 1. *Leg.* 1.13. *Brut.* 206. *Att.* 4.16.3. Scaevola Pontifex was Crassus's colleague in all the offices except the tribunate and censorship. *Brut.* 161.

21. Cf. Badian, *DUJ* 56 (1964), 143. D. Stockton, *Cicero. A Political Biography* (Oxford 1971), 5.

resulted in political friendship between either of them and the Tullii Cicerones, however, has no foundations in the available evidence.

Gratidius, brother-in-law of Cicero's grandfather, married a sister of Marius and later strengthened this link by surrendering a son of the marriage for adoption by Marius's brother Marcus.[22] Gratidius first appears in our sources as the sponsor, most probably in collaboration with Marius, of secret voting legislation at Arpinum, a move which, as already noted, brought him into collision with Cicero's grandfather and Aemilius Scaurus. Nothing in his subsequent career is likely to have erased his differences with either of these conservatives. He is next heard of as the prosecutor of Flavius Fimbria, consul of 104, who stood trial for extortion in late 103 or early 102 and was acquitted despite the efforts of Scaurus, who testified against him. That Gratidius was in league with Scaurus in this trial is highly unlikely. Fimbria, whose son was later one of Marius's most militant and trusted adherents, was almost certainly himself a friend of the general. Though a *novus homo*, he had defeated Catulus for the consulship of 104, in a year when Marius's recent triumph over Jugurtha dragged many of his supporters into office. His enmity with Scaurus, at this time a bitter enemy of Marius, also denotes a Marian connection. In brief, a Marian consular, under heavy attack from Marius's leading optimate foe, secured acquittal in a prosecution conducted by Marius's brother-in-law. There can be little doubt that Gratidius was a collusive prosecutor, ranged not with Scaurus but once more against him, pursuing a consistent course as an ally of Marius and watchdog of his interests. Soon afterwards he died in Cilicia while serving as a *praefectus* of Antonius.[23]

One of Gratidius's sons fell victim to Sulla in 88 when he was sent by Marius after passage of the *Lex Sulpicia* to take command of the legions in Campania.[24] The other, Marius Gratidianus, had a longer and more spectacular career as an aggressive partisan of his uncle and of Cinna. Tribune in 87, he fled from Rome with Cinna, was one of the commanders who helped him and Marius fight their way back, and was the man chiefly responsible for the death of the Elder Catulus. As praetor in 85 he demonstrated an unscrupulous opportunism by claiming sole

22. *Brut.* 168. *Schol. Bern.* 62, Usener.
23. *Brut.* 168. *Font.* 24. Val. Max. 8.5.2. Cf. L. A. Thompson, "Pompeius Strabo and the Trial of Albucius" *Latomus* 28 (1969), 1038.
24. Val. Max. 9.7.1. Orosius 5.19.4. Plutarch, *Marius* 35.4.

credit for a joint agreement by praetors and tribunes to remove from circulation a debased coinage which had been issued amid a shortage of silver in 91. He held a second praetorship, probably in 84, and was killed in 82 by his brother-in-law, Catiline, who wished to demonstrate his newly found loyalty to Sulla by the elimination of a particularly hated foe of the victorious general.[25]

Cicero's comments on the Gratidii are sparse and mainly concerned with Gratidianus, but they are sufficient to indicate that relations between the two families, which were visibly strained when their links were firmest, did not improve with the next generation. Cicero repeatedly condemns the manner of Catulus's death, expresses disapproval of the praetorship of Gratidianus, and in general identifies the latter with that variety of *popularis* which, in Cicero's thinking, was particularly vicious, thriving on sedition and unruly assemblies.[26]

The record of coolness or antagonism between the Tullii Cicerones and the Gratidii, their one link to the family of Marius, invalidates any assumption of political friendship between Marius and Cicero which is based solely on *adfinitas*. Yet, when *adfinitas* is laid aside, little else can be found connecting Marius to Cicero in the nineties.

Cicero's references to the general are numerous, are spread throughout his writings, and come from different periods of his life. Nowhere, however, does he claim a close personal relationship or imply that he ever enjoyed Marius's active patronage or benefited from his prestige and influence. Even when he speaks glowingly of his fellow townsman and seeks to identify with him and emphasize a parallelism in their experiences, he claims no closer association than that he saw him and heard him speak.[27] Noteworthy too is the absence of Marius's son from Cicero's lists of his contemporary friends and fellow students.[28] Finally, our evidence for Cicero's military service fails to uncover the

25. *Schol. Bern.* 62, Usener. Diodorus 38.4. *Brut.* 223. *Leg.* 3.36. *Com. Pet.* 10. Asconius 84, Clark. *Off.* 3.81. Pliny, *NH* 33.132; 34.27. Livy, *Per.* 88.

26. *Brut.* 168, 223, 307. *Leg.* 3.36. *De Or.* 3.9. *N.D.* 3.80. *Tusc.* 5.55–56. *Off.* 3.81.

27. *Quir.* 19–20. *Par. St.* 16. Cf. T. F. Carney, "Cicero's Picture of Marius" *WS* 73 (1960), 83–122.

28. Cicero makes many allusions to his youthful friends and fellow students. They included Atticus, Pupius Piso, Q. Pompeius Bithynicus, Servius Sulpicius Rufus, Q. Aelius Tubero. *Leg.* 1.13. *Brut.* 151, 240. *Fin.* 4.73; 5.1 ff. *Lig.* 21. Cato should, perhaps, also be included. *Fam.* 15.4; 13.16.

slightest trace of Marius's favor, though here, if anywhere, he would have extended a helping hand and had the opportunity to do so.

Although Cicero was eligible for military service in 90 when Marius held a command in the Social War, he did not enter the army until 89, and when he did enter his *contubernalis* was L. Aelius Tubero, whose family traditions make it unlikely that he was a favorite of Marius, and his first general was Sulla, Marius's archenemy. Cicero served with both Sulla and Pompeius Strabo in this year, but the two surviving allusions to his soldiering make it certain that he served first with Sulla. He recalls from his service with the latter a victory near Nola which must be dated in the first half of 89, and, besides, Sulla's campaign in this year ended relatively early, since he returned to Rome to stand for the consulship of 88. Pompeius's campaign, on the other hand, continued almost to the end of 89, and the incident which Cicero describes from it, a peace parley between Pompeius and the Marsic leader Vettius Scato, most probably took place in the latter half of the year when, according to Livy's Epitome, the Marsi were suing for terms following defeats by Pompeius's *legatus* Cinna and the praetor Metellus Pius.[29]

Pompeius, unlike Sulla, may have been a friend of Marius, but if he was this brought no special benefit to Cicero, as is indicated by the absence of his name from Pompeius's *consilium*, the younger membership of which has been preserved in an inscription commemorating the granting of citizenship by Pompeius to some Spanish horsemen serving at Asculum. The *consilium* contains several contemporaries of Cicero, many of them later firmly attached to the Marian cause, and the absence of Cicero is strong evidence that his early career was neither helped nor moulded by Marius and owed nothing to the general's active patronage.[30]

29. *Lig.* 21. *Div.* 1.72. *Phil.* 12.27. Plutarch, *Cicero* 3.1. Livy, *Per.* 76. Cf. Appian, *BC* 1.50. There seems to be no likelihood that Cicero's service under Sulla could have been in 88. Sulla did campaign in Campania early in 88, but there is no indication that he won any major victories in that period. Besides, Cicero does not call Sulla consul in his reference in the *De Divinatione*, though he is careful to give that title to Strabo when he alludes to his service with the latter. Cicero also states very clearly in the *Brutus* that he regularly attended the daily *contiones* of Sulpicius in the early part of 88. He is guilty of distortion by omission in the *Brutus*, but it is unlikely that he told any barefaced lies.

30. For Pompeius's relationship with Marius cf. E. Badian, *Studies in Greek and Roman History* (New York 1964), 54. The inscription, *ILLRP* 515, has been analyzed in detail by C. Cichorius, *Römische Studien* (Leipzig-Berlin 1922), 130–

The Politics of Cicero's Patrons

The foregoing review of Cicero's earliest associations with Rome's ruling aristocracy reveals that his youth was dominated by a group of influential *consulares*, most of whom belonged to the inner ranks of the *nobilitas*. Cicero's connection with them had been building over two generations, and their obvious importance in terms of his political thinking and his place in the political spectrum at the outset of his career invites a closer study of their political attitudes and actions, particularly in the nineties.

L. Licinius Crassus had the most direct and extensive influence on Cicero's education and overall development. He is often presented as typical of many post-Gracchan politicians, a shaky conservative who curried popular favor in his youth, then drifted toward the *boni* as success increased his stake in the preservation of the status quo.[31] This model, created to explain minor vagaries from other facile categorizations, does not fit the figure of Crassus, whose one brush with popular causes was his involvement in the establishment of a Roman colony at Narbo c. 115 and his advocacy of the project in a speech critical of senatorial policy. It seems certain that the man behind the scheme was Domitius Ahenobarbus, who had secured the region in the years following his consulship in 122 and whose son was appointed, along with Crassus, to supervise the colony's foundation. Domitius was no *popularis.* His family had earlier been friendly with the Scipios; he had cooperated closely in the Gallic campaign with Fabius Allobrogicus, nephew of Aemilianus, and in 115 he worked with a Metellus in an extremely active censorship and agreed to the selection of Aemilius Scaurus as *princeps senatus.* Other such colonies were founded in the

---

85. His account of Cicero's military service unduly stretches the evidence, however, and has a totally unacceptable chronology. Cf. E. Badian, *"Quaestiones Variae" Historia* 18 (1969), 454. For additional comments on the membership of Pompeius's *consilium* cf. E. S. Gruen, *Roman Politics and the Criminal Courts* (Cambridge, Mass. 1968), 243. E. Badian, "Two More Roman Non-Entities" *Phoenix* 35 (1971), 142. N. Criniti, *L'Epigrafe di Asculum di Cn. Pompeo Strabone* (Milan 1970). On Pompeius cf. M. Gelzer, "Cn. Pompeius Strabo und der Aufstieg seines Sohnes Magnus" *Kleine Schriften* 2 (Wiesbaden 1963), 126. H. B. Mattingly, "The *Consilium* of Cn. Pompeius Strabo in 89 B.C." *Athenaeum* 53 (1975), 262–66.

31. Cf. Badian, *Studies,* 43. Crassus's parentage remains obscure. Little is known of the family's activities in the 120s. Cf. F. Münzer, *RE* 25, 247.

same period on the initiative of powerful *nobiles*, and they in no way represented an onslaught on senatorial political or economic interests.[32] Crassus's association with the founding of Narbo is no proof of radical leanings, and it was only some time later when the senate moved to cancel the undertaking that he delivered his well-known anti-senatorial speech. As one of the colony's founders he could hardly have acted otherwise.[33]

Crassus had begun his public career several years earlier with a brilliant prosecution in 119 of C. Papirius Carbo, an active Gracchan when tribune in 130 who, during his consulship ten years later, in an apparent volte-face, had defended Opimius, the high-handed executioner of numerous Gracchani. The political implications of Carbo's trial and conviction are obscured by the scantiness of our information on the decade following the death of C. Gracchus, a period which, like the nineties, saw relative calm after violent turmoil and failed to engage the interest of our sources. The political alignments of those years are further complicated by the senate's skillful maneuvering in its confrontation with Gracchus to minimize the repercussions of its policy of violence. Livius Drusus had earlier isolated much of Gracchus's popular support; in 121 individual defections were encouraged by promises of generous rewards and key figures like Carbo were neutralized by swift political advancement.[34] There resulted some strange alliances, which were unlikely, however, to outlast the crisis which had created them, and it is clear that Carbo's purchased defection affected neither his long-term standing with the *nobilitas* nor his reputation as a seditious *popularis.*The oligarchs predictably deserted him in 119, more than willing to witness the downfall of a former foe whom they had

32. The date of the colony's foundation is uncertain. Cf. H. B. Mattingly, "The Foundations of Narbo Martius" *Hommages Grenier* (1962), 3.1159–71. Guido Clemente, *I Romani nella Gallia meridionale* (Bologna 1974), 77 ff. B. Levick, "Cicero, Brutus 43.159 ff. and the Foundation of Narbo Martius" *CQ* 31 (1971), 170–79. E. Badian, *Roman Imperialism in the Late Republic* (Oxford 1968), 98. For the political sympathies of the Domitii cf. H. H. Scullard, *Roman Politics 220–150 B.C.* (Oxford 1950), 116, 208. Cicero stresses the strategic importance of the colony in *Font.* 43. For other such colonies in this period cf. E. T. Salmon, *Roman Colonization* (London 1969), 121.

33. *Brut.* 160. *Cluent.* 140. It is significant that his detractors in seeking to embarrass Crassus with charges of inconsistency had nothing besides this speech with which to taunt him.

34. The number of Gracchani who defected is impressive. Cf. Gruen, *Roman Politics*, 98.

been forced by unhappy circumstances temporarily to conciliate. The apparent completeness of his isolation, coupled with the fact that Crassus's attack emphasized his anti-senatorial activities and alleged involvement in the death of Scipio Africanus, suggest that the prosecution was approved if not instigated by the now triumphant oligarchy, and Crassus emerges from the trial as an eloquent youthful champion of the *boni* and an opponent of radical agitators.[35]

It was about this time too that he became the son-in-law of Q. Mucius Scaevola Augur and formed an unbroken lifelong friendship with this distinguished family.[36] Scaevola's background was conservative and his career shows consistent support of senatorial interests and adherence to traditional republicanism. An eminent jurist, friend and follower of Panaetius, he became a favored son-in-law of Panaetius's intimate, the influential *consularis* C. Laelius, who secured him an augurate at an early age.[37] There is no account of his political allegiance in the 120s, but there is no reason to believe that it differed sharply from that of other prominent adherents of Scipio who vigorously continued the latter's policy of opposition to Gracchan programs. C. Fannius, another son-in-law of Laelius and consul in 122; Livius Drusus, tribune in 122, who was married to a Cornelia and whose father was probably a relative of Scipio and his consular colleague in 147; Aelius Tubero, a nephew of Scipio; Fabius Allobrogicus, another nephew and consul in 121; Rutilius Rufus, a Scipionic protégé—all of these men show a record of resistance or hostility to Gaius Gracchus.[38] That Scaevola had similar

35. On Carbo and his trial cf. Val. Max. 6.2.3. *De Or.* 1.40; 2.106; 3.74. *Brut.* 103, 159. *Mil.* 8. *Am.* 41, 96. *Fam.* 9.21.3. *Off.* 2.47. *Leg.* 3.35. In this last passage Cicero calls Carbo *seditiosus atque improbus civis* and explicitly states that the *boni* refused to protect him, though he had deserted to them. Carbo's suicide further illustrates his desperation and the completeness of his isolation, and belies theories that his trial was engineered by Gracchani or *equites*, or resulted from factional strife within the *nobilitas*. Cf. Badian, *Studies,* 43. D. C. Earl, "Sallust and the Senate's Numidian Policy" *Latomus* 24 (1965), 535. Gruen, *Roman Politics*, 107.

36. Crassus was married by 119. Lucilius 2.86.

37. *De Or.* 1.43, 45, 75. *Brut.* 101, 212. *Am.* 1 ff.

38. For Fannius cf. *Brut.* 99. Plutarch, *Gaius Gracchus* 8 ff. H. C. Boren "Livius Drusus, T.P. 122, and His Anti-Gracchan Program" *CJ* 52 (1956), 36. Gruen, *Roman Politics,* 92. For Drusus cf. Seneca, *Ad Marc.* 16.4. F. Münzer, *Römische Adelsparteien und Adelsfamilien* (Stuttgart 1920). For Tubero cf. *Brut.* 117. For Fabius Allobrogicus cf. Plutarch, *Gaius Gracchus* 6. For Rutilius Rufus cf. *Brut.* 114. *Off.* 3.10. He was married to a sister of Livius Drusus, Val. Max. 8.13.6.

sympathies is indicated by Cicero's portrayal of him as a denouncer of the Gracchi and by his election to the praetorship and his governorship of Asia in 120 at the height of the triumph of the oligarchy. In connection with that governorship he scornfully rejected a request by Septumuleius, a Gracchan turncoat bought by Opimius, for a prefecture. This action is sometimes advanced as a sign of Gracchan leanings, but in light of our other evidence it more likely reflects the prevailing contempt and hostility of the *nobilitas* toward purchased Gracchan renegades evidenced by the case of Carbo, than sympathy for the cause that Septumuleius had abandoned.[39]

After his governorship of Asia, Scaevola weathered a prosecution for extortion initiated by a personal enemy, T. Albucius. He then went on to win the consulship of 117 and to become an influential *consularis*, and, like many former Scipionic associates, a friend of the Metelli, the most powerful noble family of the last two decades of the second century.[40] Crassus was allied with an established figure within the ruling oligarchy.

The orator's own career indicates an ever closer association with the Metelli and adherence to the notion of aristocratic rule and senatorial supremacy. His main activity during the 110s lay in the courts, and the two cases about which there is specific information both signal a conservative drift. In 113 he made a celebrated though unsuccessful defense of the Vestal Licinia, charged together with an Aemilia and a Marcia

---

Pliny *NH* 7.158. The only major Scipionic associate who sided with the Gracchi was C. Porcius Cato, a nephew of Scipio. *Am.* 39. He may have soon repented, however. At least he survived the onslaughts on Gracchani and became consul in 114.

39. *De Or.* 1.38; 2.269. The only indication of any link between Scaevola and the Gracchan cause is the fact that one of his daughters may have married Acilius Glabrio, author of the *Lex Acilia. Brut.* 238. Cf. E. Badian, "*Lex Acilia Repetundarum*" *AJP* 75 (1954), 374–84. It is far from certain, however, that Glabrio's father-in-law was the Augur and not the consul of 133 as stated by the scholiast on *Verr.* 1.55. Besides, the political allegiance of Glabrio is, in some respects, mysterious. His son married a daughter of Scaurus. *Verr.* 1.52.

40. *De Or.* 2.281; 3.171. *Brut.* 102. *Fin.* 1.8–9. Scaevola's consulship in 117 as colleague of Metellus Diadematus at a time when the Metelli were particularly influential, is a strong indication that he had the family's friendship. For other Scipionic associates who show links with the Metelli cf. Gruen, *Roman Politics*, 116 ff. His efforts to construct rival factions centered around the Metelli and more extreme survivors of the old Scipionic group are, however, farfetched and unconvincing.

with *incestum*, and risked the disfavor of an outraged *populus* which was striking in superstitious fear at three of Rome's most distinguished families.[41] About the same time he collaborated with the *princeps senatus*, Aemilius Scaurus, in defense of L. Calpurnius Piso Caesoninus, consul in 112, and gained his acquittal.[42]

Scaurus was a patrician, though his immediate family was poor and undistinguished. A man of unusual *severitas* and determination, he was soon to remedy both of these conditions, amassing great wealth and rising to a political preeminence which lasted twenty-five years.[43] He reached the consulship in 115, and in the same year he was appointed *princeps senatus*, a position he held until his death in 89. Though he had outstanding political virtues, he lacked the benefits of distinguished parentage, was renowned neither as a soldier nor as an orator, and must have had powerful patronage to win the highest political offices.[44] The likelihood is that his benefactors were the Metelli, who had a member in the consulship and censorship in 115 and were partial to talented aspiring politicians who needed connections. Scaurus may have won their favor at the same time as Marius, whom they befriended at the start of the decade, and who, like Scaurus, had overcome poverty and demonstrated similar qualities of political *virtus* and *industria.* There is evidence that Marius and Scaurus were closely associated in that period and had cooperated in their common pursuit of wealth.[45] Soon, however, their careers were to diverge sharply and permanently. Marius

41. *Brut.* 160. Plutarch *RQ* 83. Orosius 5.15.20. The political implications of the trial are discussed by Gruen, *Roman Politics*, 127 ff.

42. *De Or.* 2.265, 285. Cf. P. Fraccaro, *Opuscula* 2 (Pavia 1957), 139–40.

43. Val. Max. 4.4.11. *Vir. Ill.* 72. Pliny, *NH* 36.116. Sallust, *Jug.* 15. *De Or.* 2.283. For his personality cf. *Off.* 1.108.

44. For his political virtues cf. *Mur.* 16. Asconius 22, Clark. His oratorical ability is discussed in *Brut.* 110. *De Or.* 1.214.

45. The business association between Marius and Scaurus alluded to in Pliny's obscure description of the latter as *Mariani sodalicii rapinarum provincialium sinus* most reasonably belongs to their early careers before political differences had developed and while both were actively accumulating wealth. Both spent time in Spain in their early careers, and it is possible that they were there together. Pliny, *NH* 36.116. *Vir. Ill.* 72. Val. Max. 8.15.7. Plutarch, *Marius* 3.4. On the meaning of Pliny's phrase cf. Fraccaro, *Opuscula* 2, 139–40. G. Bloch, "M. Aemilius Scaurus" *Mélanges d'histoire ancienne* 25 (1909), 36–38. E. S. Gruen, "Political Prosecutions in the 90's B.C." *Historia* 15 (1966), 58. T. F. Carney, "Marius' Choice of Battlefield in the Campaign of 100" *Athenaeum* 36 (1958), 235-37. A. Passerini, "C. Mario come uomo politico" *Athenaeum* 12 (1934), 16.

broke with his patrons to court the extra-senatorial elements given power and political awareness by the Gracchi and to seek success by exploiting their prejudices and conflicts of interest with the *nobilitas*. Scaurus, perhaps bound by his patrician background, worked within the traditional power structure to become a masterly manipulator of *amicitia* and *auctoritas*, Cicero's ideal optimate, model of *constantia*, defender of ancestral practice, wooing *equites* and people to support, not attack, aristocratic government, and relentlessly opposing all revolutionaries from the Gracchi to Varius.[46] Crassus's collaboration with him in the trial of Piso foreshadowed another lifelong association between the orator and a powerful conservative.

Crassus went on to hold his first public office, the quaestorship, in 109, and followed it with the tribunate in 107, the year of Marius's first consulship, when the *nobilitas* was under heavy attack and tribunes were busy capitalizing on popular dissatisfactions. Crassus was careful to steer clear of any association with attempts to discredit the aristocracy, and the following year he came forward as a committed partisan of the ruling oligarchy with a powerful speech on behalf of the *lex iudiciaria* of Servilius Caepio. It was a model encomium of senatorial rule and an indictment of the senate's traducers, notably Memmius, tribune of 111, bitter foe of the *nobilitas*, particularly of Scaurus.[47]

By the end of the century Crassus was squarely in the camp of the traditionalists and an eloquent spokesman for senatorial interests. He is listed with Scaurus and the Metelli among the foremost enemies of Marius, and he was a leading figure in the senate's forceful suppression of Saturninus.[48] By then he had also formed a close political partnership

46. *Sest.* 101, 137. *Verr.* 1.52. *Rab.* 21, 26. *De Or.* 1.214. Asconius 22, Clark. Scaurus's durability in an era fatal to many leading *nobiles* is quite remarkable. His deep conservatism is beyond question, but that he was a flexible, practical politician who understood compromise and the need to cultivate the extra-senatorial elements in the wake of the Gracchi also seems clear. His election as a *quaesitor* in the Mamilian commission in 109 illustrates his high standing with senate and people. His background, business interests, and the large contracts of his censorship (*Vir. Ill.* 72. Strabo 5.1.11) undoubtedly won him many friends among the *equites*. Cf. A. R. Hands, "Sallust and *Dissimulatio*" *JRS* 49 (1959), 56–60. R. Syme, *Sallust* (Berkeley 1964), 165. P. Fraccaro, *Opuscula* 2 (1957), 125 ff.

47. *De Or.* 1.45; 2.365; 3.75. *Brut.* 160–61, 296–98. *Par. St.* 41. *De Or.* 1.225; 2.240, 267. *Cluent.* 140. For the enmity between Scaurus and Memmius cf. Sallust, *Jug.* 32. *De Or.* 2.283. *Font.* 24.

48. *Prov. Cons.* 19. *De Or.* 3.68. *Rab.* 26.

with Q. Mucius Scaevola Pontifex, cousin of his father-in-law, son of the consul of 133, a noted jurist in the tradition of the Mucii Scaevolae, and a formidable orator. He and Crassus were quaestors together in 109; he presided as tribune at the *contio* at which Crassus delivered his famous speech for the *Lex Servilia* in 106, and was later the orator's colleague in the aedileship c. 100, the praetorship c. 98, and the consulship in 95. The two men possessed the essential ingredients of perfect *amicitia* listed by Cicero: similarity in *mores, studia*, and political views, and a spirit of cooperation instead of rivalry in their political careers.[49]

The evidence for the political activity and aspirations of Crassus and the other figures prominent in Cicero's early life becomes more tenuous in the nineties and its interpretation more controversial. Most of the decade was free of major foreign and domestic upheavals, and was neglected by our sources, forcing modern historians to rely more heavily than usual on the fruits of prosopographical research. The evidence of criminal trials, of lists of magistrates, of family histories—including marriage connections, adoptions, *clientelae*, new and traditional friendships, and political bias—has been painstakingly assembled in recent studies. The effort has uncovered valuable information and inspired fresh thinking on the workings of late republican politics, but it has also produced the inevitable tendency of the prosopographical approach to impose order and consistency on a welter of scattered data whose significance is frequently ambiguous or inexplicable, the product of shifting private interests and ambitions rather than political ideology or affiliation.

The most outstanding recent work on the nineties has been done by Badian and Gruen, both of whom interpret the major political events as a power struggle between rival senatorial factions. Gruen has woven a similar pattern for preceding decades, rival factions of *nobiles* reverting to a habitual preoccupation with their own power whenever the threat to the position of the aristocracy as a whole was absent.[50]

Badian's groupings for the nineties consist of the Metelli and their associates and Marius and his following of *nobiles*. Gruen also believes

49. *Brut.* 145–50, 161. *De Or.* 1.180; 2.221–23. *Am.* 20, 33 ff., 65, 74, 82.
50. Badian, *Studies,* 34, 157; *Foreign Clientelae* (Oxford 1958), 210; "Q. Mucius Scaevola and the Province of Asia" *Athenaeum* 34 (1956), 104–23. Gruen, *Roman Politics,* 185–214; *Historia* 15 (1966), 32–64.

in the existence of a powerful Metellan clique but argues that Marius courted rather than opposed it, the challenges to the *factio* coming from a new alliance headed by men like Domitius Ahenobarbus and Cassius Longinus, consuls of 96. Apart from this disagreement on the precise composition and leadership of the factions, both present them as closely knit and—despite some disclaimers—essentially static groupings, the criminal courts their chief battleground and their favorite arena for the resolution of political disputes.

This whole notion of defined, cohesive, and relatively stable factions in late republican politics has been strongly and rightly challenged. It is a concept which finds no support in writers such as Sallust and Cicero. Its assumptions of family solidarity and of total and long-term allegiance to the goals and policies of a group or individual impose a restraint on personal independence and attribute a rigidity and permanence to political *amicitia* contradicted by other evidence on Roman political practices. It ignores the complexity of Roman personal relationships, the many bonds and forms of *familiaritas* which were independent of political allegiance but affected political actions. *Gratia* and a host of similar private concerns were often more significant in directing a politician's behavior than *causa* or *partes* and precluded rigid or wide-ranging political alliances.[51]

Reliance on the evidence of trials for the construction of political alignments and trends evokes additional objections. A similar procedure applied to similar data from the better documented Ciceronian age would result in serious distortions and make nonsense of many of the political developments of that era. Personal considerations were a still more crucial factor in the courts than in the *comitia* or *curia*. A criminal trial, whatever its political implications, involved the honor, property, and safety of an individual. It gave scope for the indulgence of

51. For the role of *gratia* cf. *Planc.* 80–81. *Att.* 9.7.3. *beneficium sequor . . . non causam. Fam.* 8.11 and Cicero's relationship with Matius as depicted in *Fam.* 11.27 provide examples of the individuality of Roman politicians and the overriding importance of private concerns in determining their behavior toward one another. Cf. J. Hellegouarc'h, *Vocabulaire latin des relations et des partis politiques sous la république* (Paris 1963). M. Gelzer, *The Roman Nobility*, trans. R. Seager (Oxford 1969). P. A. Brunt, "*Amicitia* in the Late Roman Republic" *PCPS* 11 (1965), 1–20. C. Meier, "Review of Badian, *Foreign Clientelae*" *BJ* 161 (1961), 503–14; "Review of Carney, *A Biography of C. Marius*" *Gnomon* 36 (1964), 64–70; *Res Publica Amissa* (Wiesbaden 1966). D. R. Shackleton Bailey, "The Roman Nobility in the Second Civil War" *CQ* 10 (1960), 253–67.

inimicitiae; it made basic demands on the *fides* of *amici* of all descriptions. The array of accusers and defenders that resulted, often odd combinations from the political standpoint, provides reliable evidence of the friends and enemies of the accused, but, in the absence of other information, allows few conclusions about the relationships of these friends and enemies with one another.[52]

The existence of groups in Roman politics cannot, of course, be denied entirely. It is clear that dynastic noble houses supplemented the private *opes* of the family with alliances formed through marriage connections, adoptions, patronage of promising younger politicians, and straightforward political compacts. Occasionally such a house acquired a temporary ascendency through an unusually prestigious member or members. Sometimes too a political issue could draw men of similar views together. Needless to say, alongside such power-building and political alliances there existed rival power-builders and counteralliances, with the possibility of bitter feuds and deep divisions.

But these kinds of political association are a far cry from the idea of formal, continuous factions. In most cases the cooperation existed for reasons of private gain or short-term political objectives. Even when men were bound more firmly by kinship, *beneficia*, and general compatibility of political philosophy, it was a totally unstructured relationship and imposed no limitations on the individual's freedom to choose his own friends and enemies, do his own political thinking, and pursue in his own way his sacred duty to maintain or enhance the *dignitas* of his family. The concern of Roman *nobiles* with family prestige and their birthright to distinction was incompatible with subordination of personal ends to the welfare and objectives of any group. Their individualism is exemplified by the difficulty of tracing consistent relationships of friendship or enmity, and by the diverse character of the lists of magistrates, which seldom show any pattern that suggests neat factional divisions, unless one forgets many names, admits a plurality of factions or a fluidity of membership which renders the terminology meaningless.[53]

52. The trials of Murena in 63, Sestius in 56, and Scaurus in 54 provide examples of the hazards of constructing political groupings on the evidence of trials. Cf. *Sulla* 49. *Fam.* 8.6; 8.8. Brunt, *PCPS* 11 (1965), 12 ff.

53. For the importance of *dignitas* cf. *Planc.* 51. *Att.* 4.18.1. *Sest.* 48, 128. *Mur.* 76. *Phil.* 10.20; 13.7. Caesar, *BC* 1.9. The consular lists for the nineties and

As a consequence of the excessive emphasis on factionalism, inter-necine senatorial conflicts, occasionally blunted or interrupted by a popular movement requiring a temporary unity, tend to emerge as the central theme of Roman politics between the Gracchi and Sulla. The strife for honors, *dignitas*, and influence surely continued within the *nobilitas*, but it was almost constantly overshadowed by a more basic concern to maintain the aristocracy as a whole in a stable position of power in the face of growing threats arising from the changing conditions of an expanding state and empire.

After the Gracchi, the proponents of oligarchic rule—and they included the bulk of the *nobilitas*—were constantly on the defensive. The people had been given an awareness of their political importance and a distrust of the *nobilitas*. The *equites* had secured political leverage which guaranteed interference with any senatorial policy unlikely to serve the interests of financiers. Basic constitutional and social issues, all of them in some measure a challenge to the privileged position of the aristocracy, had been raised: agrarian reform, grain doles, the secret ballot, the power of tribunes, the senate's control of judicial procedures and of the standing courts, the enfranchisement of the Italians. Some had merely been aired, some had been resolved to the detriment of the oligarchy, all of them would survive as part of a continuing struggle between the traditional ruling class, grimly defending the status quo, and those who for various reasons advocated change and, in pursuit of their various goals, were prepared to exploit the class tensions which were the major legacy of the Gracchi.

Impoverished noble families which had faded into obscurity, new men, those whose *opes* and connections were insufficient to guarantee success by traditional routes, the occasional genuine reformer, most of whom in earlier days would have had to rest content with the lower offices and the senate's backbenches, now had a new weaponry which could be used in varying degrees to achieve advancement or more altruistic objectives. The extent and manner of the challenge to

---

for other periods such as the 120s reveal no trace of the existence of continuous, cohesive groupings. It is noteworthy that even such close and long-lasting friendship and political cooperation as existed between Crassus and Scaevola Pontifex had important limitations. They appeared on opposite sides in the courts, and it was Scaevola who blocked Crassus's demand for a triumph in 95. *De Or.* 1.180; 2.140, 221. *Brut.* 195. *Inv.* 2.111. *Pis.* 62. Asconius 15, Clark.

the status quo would depend on the ends sought and the measure of dissatisfaction with traditional republicanism. Men like Cn. Domitius Ahenobarbus and L. Marcius Philippus, who were basically conservative, might make popular gestures to increase their political leverage, but they had no wish to diminish senatorial influence. More committed *populares* such as Marius, Memmius, and Mamilius, sometimes joined by declining noble houses anxious to revive a former greatness, would exploit to the full the dissatisfactions of the *equites* or the people but had no interest in radical constitutional or social reform, while determined foes of the senate such as Saturninus and Glaucia would not hesitate to go to the extreme of violence to effect radical change and their own aggrandizement.

The emphasis of post-Gracchan politics had shifted considerably. Narrow oligarchic competition and dissension were frequently eclipsed by the threat which the varied assortment of challengers and occasional large-scale popular movements and their lingering tensions posed to the great majority of the aristocracy. That is not to deny that Roman politics remained many-sided. The reaction against such neat dichotomies as *optimates* and *populares* is as valid as the objections to schematic factional divisions. The challenges to senatorial supremacy did not eliminate internal senatorial clashes and rivalries; they continue to complicate the picture, but they are no longer its dominant feature.

The nineties brought a lull in the series of onslaughts on the status quo and its guardians, but the pressures on the Roman oligarchy continued. The forceful suppression of Saturninus and his followers in 100 had removed a threat of anarchy and temporarily arrested the forces of radical change, but the enactments of the preceding years and the controversies that had built into violent confrontation could not be eradicated as quickly and summarily as their authors. There was a new standing court dealing with the vaguely defined charge of *maiestas* and manned by equestrian juries. The court provided a permanent machinery for the kind of attack which had been launched against *nobiles* in the trials before the Mamilian Commission in 109 and before the people in 103, and it conferred additional political power on the *equites*, a power which, unrestrained by responsibility for the country's government, was a serious limitation on the independence of those who carried that responsibility.

A new dimension had also been added to the agrarian question by

Saturninus's proposal, backed by Marius, for large-scale settlement of veterans, including allies as well as citizens, in colonies in Gaul, Sicily, Macedonia, and Achaea, a scheme which would have provided enormous *clientelae* spread throughout the empire for its authors. The senate's resistance to this proposal had not only created new and dangerous enemies in the veterans but had further worsened the uneasy relations between Rome and her Italian allies. Looming over the unsettled domestic scene was the threat of a major foreign war with Mithridates, which could quickly revive the demagoguery, class tensions, and extended military commands which had seriously threatened oligarchic control in the Jugurthine and Germanic wars.

It is gratuituous to assume that the *nobilitas* was so devoid of foresight that it remained oblivious to these problems or was so preoccupied with private hates and rivalries that it subordinated them to factional interests. If the ambiguous and frequently conflicting evidence of the trials is not allowed to cloud more explicit testimony, the political activity of the nineties reveals a basic political unity within the senate and a continuous and overriding concern to consolidate the senate's position and perpetuate oligarchic government and the system that guaranteed it.

Among the chief architects of this policy were Crassus and the other *nobiles* with whom Cicero and his family were closely associated: M. Antonius, Scaurus, and Scaevola Pontifex. Antonius was consul in 99, the crucial year following the senate's resort to violence against Saturninus. Although later in the decade he was incontestably a close friend and political ally of Crassus and a prominent leader of the *boni*, some recent studies have argued that at the beginning of the century and in his earlier career he was allied with Marius rather than with the conservative *nobiles*.[54] The question has considerable importance for any interpretation of the politics of the nineties and deserves detailed comment.

Antonius was of undistinguished family but a brilliant orator who rose to the highest offices with an ease that calls to mind the success of

54. Cf. Badian, *Studies*, 46; *Roman Imperialism*, 52. T. F. Carney, *A Biography of Marius* (Assen 1961), 47. For a contrary opinion cf. Scholz, *Der Redner M. Antonius.* E. S. Gruen, "The *Lex Varia*" *JRS* 55 (1965), 67; *Historia* 15 (1966), 39. Antonius's later friendship with Crassus and the *boni* is attested in *De Or.* 1.24; 2.88. *Brut.* 115. *Planc.* 33. He was prosecuted before the Varian commission in 90. *Tusc.* 2.57.

Cicero a generation later. Though his career before the praetorship is poorly documented, the indications are that, like Cicero, he concentrated during this stage on the courts, an orthodox and time-honored route to political distinction. He reached the quaestorship in 113 and, after successfully defending himself on a charge of *incestum* in the trial of the Vestals, served in Asia.[55] On his return, following a familar pattern, he prosecuted Cn. Carbo, consul of 113 and brother of the Carbo whom Crassus had prosecuted in 119. This trial ended similarly in the suicide of the defendant. Antonius had chosen his case with skill. Carbo was unpopular with the public because of a serious military defeat in his consulship at the hands of the Cimbri, and like his brother he was no favorite of the *nobilitas.* Cicero describes them both as trouble-makers and their downfall as a boon to the state.[56]

Following this prosecution, Antonius became an active advocate for the defense; Cicero relates that, in contrast to Crassus, he was always willing to undertake a case. Two of these cases from the second century are mentioned in the *De Oratore*, his defense of Marcius Rex, who was probably the consul of 118, and of Mallius Maximus, consul of 105, who was accused of *perduellio* by Saturninus in 103.[57] No record of his political oratory and no direct, conclusive information about his political activity and associations in this period survive, but his forensic activity, particularly his defense of Mallius, undertaken when he was a candidate for the praetorship, indicates that he was not aligned with the radical *populares*, who were Marius's chief allies before 100.

Antonius was praetor in 102, and was appointed to an extraordinary command against the pirates in Cilicia. That his selection was due to the influence of Marius seems most unlikely. It was a special commission assigned by the senate, where Marius never had significant influence, particularly not at this period. It was extremely difficult for a military commander, however powerful, to maintain an effective following in the senate and control its administrative decisions during prolonged service abroad, and Marius had spent little time in Rome since

55. Cf. E. S. Gruen, "M. Antonius and the Trial of the Vestal Virgins" *RhM* 111 (1968), 59–63. T. F. Carney, "The Picture of Marius in Valerius Maximus" *RhM* 105 (1962), 289–337. Antonius was apparently *quaestor pro praetore* in Asia. Cf. T. R. S. Broughton, *The Magistrates of the Roman Republic* (New York 1951–52), 1.539.

56. *Off.* 2. 48–49. *Fam.* 9.21.3. Apuleius, *Apol.* 66.

57. *Brut.* 207. *De Or.* 2.125.

109. Besides, his overall power in 103 and early 102 had receded along with the Germanic threat. He had had to exert himself to win reelection to the consulship for 102, accept a leading conservative, Catulus, as his colleague, and watch two Metelli, one his foremost enemy, sweep into the powerful censorship.[58] The senate and its conservative *principes* still had a tight hold on the reins of government in 102, and when they finally moved to confront the long-standing pirate threat, one may be sure that they assigned the task to a safe and trusted commander.[59]

Antonius returned to Italy in 100 and won a triumph and the consulship for 99. His achievements had been less than spectacular, and the honor accorded them again indicates a close association with the potentates of the senate, an association further confirmed by his actions in the consulship.[60] Remnants of Saturninus's followers were still active in

58. On Antonius's Cilician command cf. T. R. S. Broughton, "Notes on Roman Magistrates" *TAPA* 77 (1946), 35 ff. D. Magie, *Roman Rule in Asia Minor* (Princeton 1950), 283 ff., 1161 ff. Another measure against the pirates was seemingly enacted c. 100, the famous "Pirate Law" recovered from the monument of Aemilius Paullus at Delphi (*SEG* 3.378). Cf. M. Hassall, M. Crawford, and J. Reynolds, "Rome and the Eastern Provinces at the End of the Second Century B.C." *JRS* 64 (1974), 195–220. Badian's contention that Catulus attached himself to Marius in 103 (*Studies*, 38) is untenable. Marius was regarded by the *boni* at this period as an enemy. *Prov. Cons.* 19. One need only recall Cicero's reluctance in 59 to accept any favors from Caesar for fear of criticism from the *boni* (*Att.* 2.5.1), and the resentment against him in 56 when he sided with the triumvirs (*Prov. Cons.* 18, 26, 40, 44. *Fam.* 1.8.2; 1.9.17), and in the forties when he appeared to lean toward Caesar (*Att.* 8.16.1; 8.11b.3; 13.13.2; 13.20.4. *Fam.* 7.3.6; 9.2.2), to realize the hostility Catulus would have incurred if he had defected to Marius in 103. There is no trace of such hostility. Cicero groups him with Scaurus, Antonius, Crassus, and the Scaevolae in his list of the participants in the suppression of Saturninus, separating the six of them as a group of preeminent statesmen. Their common political virtues clearly imply common political sympathies and goals. Plutarch reports that Catulus was highly respected by the *nobilitas* (*Marius* 14), and his reputation for integrity was proverbial. (*De Or.* 2.173). Any favor extended to him by Marius more reasonably signifies a unilateral gesture of conciliation by the general toward a powerful and hostile oligarchy than a desertion of the *bonae partes* by a staunch conservative.

59. Antonius took with him to Cicilia his *perfamiliaris* M. Gratidius, Marius's kinsman and loyal adherent, a fact often adduced to support the notion that Marius and Antonius were political allies. The perils of forging links between Roman politicians on the basis of common friendships or enmities have already been discussed. Cicero's friendship with Caesar's devoted follower Matius did not make him Caesar's friend or political supporter. The friendship of Antonius and Gratidius was as likely a product of their strong mutual interest in oratory (*Brut.* 168) as of their political beliefs and allegiances.

60. The importance of the support of the *boni* in obtaining a triumph can be

99, eager to capitalize on any public resentment of senatorial high-handedness in the suppression of their leader and to promote afresh his legislative program. The tribune Titius was in the forefront of the lingering agitation, and, as one of several attempts to rekindle the popular movement, he tried to reopen the land question which the senate had speedily shelved in 100 by annulment of Saturninus's agrarian bill. Antonius resisted Titius at every turn and continued his opposition into the following year when he helped secure condemnation of the turbulent tribune.[61] Antonius's behavior cannot be presented as an extension of Marius's decision in 100 to suppress his former allies. Marius may have welcomed the downfall of Saturninus, whose growing power and extremism were as menacing to him as to the senate, but he cannot have welcomed cancellation of the land law nor the continuing opposition to similar legislation. Saturninus's bill was crucial to Marius, for it would have enabled him not only to provide his veterans with the rewards they expected, and which their African counterparts had received, but it would have allowed him to extend his patronage and influence by conferring citizenship on large numbers of Italians. These benefits to Marius and to the bill's sponsors led to fierce opposition to the measure in the senate in 100 and to its speedy cancellation after Saturninus's death; Antonius's actions in 99 were a continuation of the efforts of the *boni* to bar their opponents from this road to *potentia.*[62]

------

illustrated by Cicero's maneuvering to secure this honor in 50. The attitude of Pompey and Caesar mattered less than that of the leading *optimates.* Cf. *Fam.* 15.4; 15.10; 15.13; 15.5; 8.11. *Att.* 7.2.6–7; 7.3.2. Further, in Cicero's description of Saturninus's suppression, Antonius is associated with Scaurus, Crassus, the Scaevolae, and Catulus in a very special way. Cf. note 58. Badian (*Studies*, 47) finds it significant that Saturninus and Glaucia, who caused the death of the consular candidate, Memmius, did not interfere with the candidacy of Antonius. But the latter stood *in absentia* while waiting outside Rome with an army, a circumstance sufficient to discourage a violent challenge. Memmius was a far more vulnerable target.

61. *Schol. Bob.* 95, Stangl. Sources for Titius's legislation are listed in Broughton, *MRR*, 2.2. For the role of Antonius cf. *De Or.* 2.48, 253, 265; 3.10. His behavior in 99 is consistent with Cicero's description of his part in the suppression of Saturninus in 100. *Rab.* 26.

62. There can be no doubt that Saturninus's land legislation of 100 was cancelled. *Balb.* 48 is explicit on this point. The prosecutor of Matrinius argued that a grant of citizenship by Marius under the law of Saturninus had no validity since (1) the bill's provisions regarding colonies had never been implemented and (2)

Antonius went on to hold the censorship of 97. The only actions recorded from his term in that office are the expulsion of the tribune Duronius from the senate for abrogation of a sumptuary law and the reappointment of Aemilius Scaurus as *princeps senatus*. [63]

Two other aspects of his behavior in the early years of the first century have been advanced as indicators of political friendship with Marius—his failure to promote the recall of Metellus Numidicus in 99 and his appearance alongside Marius in defense of Aquillius c. 97. Legislation for the recall of Metellus had been introduced by the tribunes Q. Pompeius Rufus and C. Porcius Cato following the suppression of Saturninus, but it had been vetoed by the tribune Furius, backed by Marius. [64] The effort was not repeated until 98, and it would appear that the *boni* as a whole considered it imprudent to force this issue in the tense aftermath of the violence of 100. Antonius's public inaction has been given prominence by Cicero's mention of it, but it should be noted that Cicero's comment, whose primary purpose was to show that the *boni* had displayed greater zeal in his cause than in that of other well-known political exiles, in no way implies that Antonius's lesser zeal in the case of Metellus was the result of enmity and political differences. The same relative inaction is attributed to Antonius's colleague A. Postumius Albinus, who was hardly a Marian, and to the

---

the law itself had been cancelled (*re ipsa sublata*). Cicero apparently agreed with the prosecutor's contention, and he makes it clear that Marius's client had a poor case and was saved only by his patron's *auctoritas*. Cf. E. Gabba, "Ricerche su alcuni punti di storia Mariana" *Athenaeum* 29 (1951), 12–24; "Review of Badian, *Foreign Clientelae*" *RFIC* 37 (1959), 196. E. Badian, "From the Gracchi to Sulla (1940–1959)" *Historia* 11 (1962), 219. Passerini, *Athenaeum* 12 (1934), 109–43. There is no specific information on the substance of Titius's land law, but it seems likely that it pursued the objectives of the preceding year. Cf. Carney, *RhM* 105 (1962), 314.

63. Sources in Broughton, *MRR*, 2.6. Badian's theory (*Studies*, 48; *Roman Imperialism*, 104) that Antonius and Flaccus enrolled large numbers of Italians as part of Marius's strategy to increase his strength with the voters, a move which gave rise to the *Lex Licinia Mucia*, has no support in the ancient sources and has not won widespread acceptance. Cf. P. A. Brunt, "Italian Aims at the Time of the Social War" *JRS* 55 (1965), 106. Gruen, *Historia* 15 (1966), 40. It is worth noting that the friendship between Antonius and Crassus, who are presented by Badian as directly opposed to one another on the citizenship issue, went back at least as far as 96 and seems never to have been broken. *De Or.* 2.89.

64. The date of this bill and Furius's tribunate is disputed. The evidence would seem to favor 100. Cf. E. Gabba, *Appiani Bellorum Civilium Liber Primus* (Florence 1958), 110–11. Gruen, *Historia* 15 (1966), 33.

stalwart optimate Opimius, who likewise found it prudent in a closely analogous situation in 121 not to press immediately for the recall of C. Gracchus's victim, Popillius Laenas.[65] Both Popillius and Metellus were recalled in due course, when the repercussions of civil violence had receded.

The trial of Aquillius has also been given prominence by allusions to it in the writings of Cicero, though none of them suggest that it had political significance. Aquillius had been Marius's colleague in the consulship in 101, and he had subsequently governed Sicily and ended the slave war there, returning to Rome to celebrate an *ovatio* before the end of 99. He was accused of extortion, a charge faced by a large number of returning governors, who could generally gather support from diverse elements of a sympathetic aristocracy.[66] I have already emphasized the limitations of the evidence of such trials for constructing political alignments. No contemporary historian found Aquillius's prosecution worthy of mention, and it would doubtless have shared the fate of countless other such cases which deservedly went unrecorded were it not that Cicero found in Antonius's speech for the defense an unusually fine example of effective emotional pleading.[67]

In summary, the record of Antonius's early career and of his behavior in the highest offices points throughout to the conservative outlook and conservative connections attested in Cicero's presentation of him in the *De Oratore*. Arguments to the contrary must not only rely on equivocal evidence and dubious assumptions, but must accept the unlikely conclusion that he did a dramatic volte-face in his declining years and was warmly welcomed by an oligarchy notoriously unreceptive to renegades.

Antonius's consulship laid the groundwork for a return to smooth senatorial government. The following year allowed bolder steps in the

65. *Quir.* 11. This passage does not state that Antonius did nothing, merely that he did not publicly promote Metellus's recall as the consuls had done in Cicero's case in 57. Gabba, *App. BC Lib. Prim.* 110, dates Metellus's recall to 99 and he is followed by Badian (*Studies*, 171), but *Schol. Bob.* 176, Stangl, Diodorus 36.16, and the above passage from Cicero all point to 98.

66. Sources for Aquillius's governorship in Broughton, *MRR*, 2.2. For the frequency of extortion trials and the complex factors that determined lineups for prosecution and defense cf. *Fam.* 8.6; 15.14; 8.8. *Q.F.* 1.3.5. Cf. also n. 52, above.

67. *De Or.* 2.124, 188, 195. The Livian Epitomator clearly states: *Cicero eius rei solus auctor* (70).

senate's drive to reestablish its supremacy. The two most prominent survivors of the radical movement, Titius and Decianus, tribunes in 99, were prosecuted and convicted. Metellus was recalled with great fanfare, and the *Lex Caecilia Didia* was enacted by the two conservative consuls, Caecilius Metellus Nepos and T. Didius. The law prescribed a definite interval between the promulgation of a bill and its voting and forbade the inclusion of unrelated measures within a single bill. It was designed to guard against sudden legislation, and to prevent the formation of powerful coalitions behind omnibus bills which could combine diverse provisions designed to lure various political elements. [68]

In 97 the senate turned its attention to the impending trouble in the East. Mithridates was ordered to evacuate Cappadocia and Paphlagonia, and an embassy headed by Scaurus was dispatched to convey the senate's command. In the following year Sulla, who as praetor in 97 had received a command in Cilicia similar to that of Antonius in 102 and was probably by this time considered a safe conservative, was entrusted with the task of installing Ariobarzanes on the throne of Cappadocia. A decision was also taken to reform the administration of Asia, and the province, normally governed by praetors, was allotted to Scaevola Pontifex, consul of 95, who was assigned the distinguished consular and legal expert Rutilius Rufus as his *legatus*. [69]

The reasons for these decisions seem clear enough. The oligarchy was determined to seize the initiative in the developing crisis in the East and by forceful action handled by safe, competent, and distinguished leaders to prevent a recurrence of the popular discontent that had marked the Jugurthine and Germanic wars and seriously weakened senatorial control. Reorganization of the province of Asia, which was most directly

68. Sources in Broughton, *MRR*, 2.4–5. Cf. A. Michels, *The Calendar of the Roman Republic* (Princeton 1967), 41. It is noteworthy that the two landmark bills of this decade bear the names of consuls, not tribunes, another indication of the temper of the *nobilitas.*

69. Badian's articles on the date of Sulla's praetorship and Cilician command (*Studies*, 157), and of Scaevola's proconsulship (*Athenaeum* 34 [1956], 105), have convincingly eliminated many chronological uncertainties from this period, and their conclusions are accepted here. Sulla's election to the praetorship in 98, a year of optimate supremacy, and his eastern commissions at a time when this area was of particular concern to the senate suggest that he was a trusted adherent of the *boni* in this period. Badian's dating of Scaevola's proconsulship has been challenged, but not convincingly, by B. A. Marshall, "The Date of Q. Mucius Scaevola's Governorship of Asia" *Athenaeum* 54 (1976), 117–30.

exposed to attack from Mithridates, and which had long been a victim of deplorable misgovernment and the unchecked greed of the *publicani*, was a necessary part of that strategy, and necessary too if the senate was ever to assert its governing authority over the class that posed the most serious continuing threat to its supremacy. That the oligarchy was aware of the likelihood of a confrontation with the *equites* over the reorganization of Asia and had decided to face it, is clear from its unusual efforts to disarm potential attackers by selecting two *consulares* with impeccable credentials for the task of revising a *lex provinciae* and by passing a senatorial decree in 94 that formally validated their enactments and approved them as an exemplary guide for successors.[70]

Finally, the problem of the rights of the Italians was confronted in 95. The political partnership of Crassus and Scaevola carried them both into the consulship for that year, and they proceeded to enact a reactionary bill, the *Lex Licinia Mucia*, which established an investigation into the exercise of citizen rights by non-Romans and ordered the withdrawal of such rights in cases of illegal usurpation.[71] It was a clear pronouncement on the attitude of the *nobilitas* toward extension of the franchise.

It was also consistent with the overall policy of the senate discernible in every major political decision of the first half of the nineties. Under the conservative leadership of men like Scaurus, Rutilius, Antonius, Crassus, and the Mucii Scaevolae, it was moving with energy, though not always with foresight, to reinstate and fortify traditional republicanism. Temporarily its efforts were seemingly unhampered by serious internal division or external challenge. The popular movement lacked leaders and issues, and the rivalries and enmities within the *nobilitas* do not appear to have hindered political cooperation on the crucial questions. No sign survives of major political strife within the senate or at electoral and legislative *comitia* which would justify the factionalism and internal power struggles which have been constructed on the evidence of trials. The figures in the consular lists most likely to have had

70. Val. Max. 8.6. The term *equites* is used in this discussion, as frequently by Cicero, to designate the business class, the order's main component.

71. On this bill cf. E. Gabba, "Politica e cultura in Roma agli inizi del I secolo a.C." *Athenaeum* 31 (1953), 260. R. W. Husband, "On the Expulsion of Foreigners from Rome" *CP* 11 (1916), 321.

personal and political differences with the more conservative *nobiles* are Domitius Ahenobarbus and Cassius Longinus, consuls of 96, yet it was under their presidency that the senate made its most important decisions concerning the East and that the *comitia* elected Crassus and Scaevola to the consulship.

It is more difficult still to discern an opposition faction of *nobiles* led by Marius, to whom the political conditions of the nineties were decidedly unfavorable. He had risen to power by exploiting popular prejudices against the *nobilitas*, and by the aid of a succession of foreign wars in which his military skill and resolution, heightened by aristocratic incompetence and indecision, had won him enormous influence with the public. Seeking to maintain that influence in peacetime and to force recognition of his preeminence from the *nobilitas*, he allied himself with the radical *populares*, failing to see the conflict between their revolutionary goals and his own pursuit of high position within the status quo. Forced to draw back from a self-defeating extremism, he found himself in uncomfortable isolation. He had lost the support of the remnants of the radical movement; the *nobiles* who had joined his bandwagon in the second century had done so from weakness or for reasons of temporary expediency, and there was little chance of a real rapprochement with the conservative *boni* whom he had so deeply offended.[72] He still had formidable resources in his popularity as a military hero, his connections with the *equites*, his immense wealth and *clientelae*, which included large numbers of veterans among the citizenry and the Italians; but since he lacked the will to establish an ascendancy by force and an issue around which to rally the people or the *equites*, he was not in a position to challenge the senate and had insufficient connections to be an effective force within it.

The whole course of events in the earlier part of the nineties illustrates the decline in his power and the senate's determination to prevent any revival of it. The land legislation so important to his interests was blocked; Metellus was recalled over his opposition; he did not seek the censorship in 97 or 92, a coveted office for ex-consuls; he did not receive a command in the East, though he had carefully angled for one

72. Cf. *Prov. Cons.* 19. *Brut.* 175 alludes to the *petitionis angustias* caused by Marius's monopoly of the consulship; the families whose ambitions he had thwarted would not readily forgive.

by his trip to Asia Minor in 98 and his meeting with Mithridates, a move which may well have helped spur the senate to resolute action in 97 and 96 to insure that the eastern crisis was placed in safer hands.[73] He did win the augurship in 98, which is testimony to his popularity with the public, but this election, which involved seventeen tribes chosen by lot and lacked the preparatory canvassing and opportunities for the use of aristocratic influence present in normal elections, is no indication of how Marius would have fared before the regular *comitia centuriata.*[74] The *nobilitas* could not afford to ignore a man of his stature and resources, who, given the right circumstances, could recover his ascendancy of the last years of the second century, but these circumstances were absent in the nineties, and it is misleading to portray him as a dominant figure in the political developments of that period.

About the middle of the decade occurred two trials, the prosecutions of Norbanus and Caepio, with which two of Cicero's patrons, Antonius and Crassus, were closely connected, and largely on the basis of which deep factional rifts have been discerned within the *nobilitas* and presented as the primary motivating force in the political activity of the nineties. Norbanus was tribune in 103, and during that year he had engaged in riotous conduct at the trial of the Elder Caepio, consul of 106. For this he was charged with *maiestas* by P. Sulpicius Rufus, was defended by Antonius and acquitted. The date of the trial is not stated, but it was later than 97, and, because of its obvious connections with the case of Caepio, which took place in 95, has been plausibly assigned to the same year.[75] Caepio, son of the consul of 106, was similarly charged with *maiestas* for violent opposition to the grain law of Saturninus in 103. His *accusator* is unknown. Crassus appeared for the defense, and once again the verdict was acquittal.[76]

73. For a full discussion of Marius's trip to Asia c.f. T. J. Luce, "Marius and the Mithridatic Command" *Historia* 19 (1970), 161–94.

74. The election by seventeen tribes, established by Domitius Ahenobarbus for all priesthoods in 104, was a difficult procedure for the oligarchy to control and was favored by *populares.* Rullus prescribed it as the method of election for the *decemviri* who were to administer his agrarian bill (*Leg. Agr.* 2.16). Under it Caesar defeated two leading *optimates*, Catulus and Servilius Isauricus, for the position of Pontifex Maximus in 63 (Plutarch, *Caesar* 7. Suetonius, *Julius* 13). Ordinarily a year's canvassing preceded a major election, giving full scope for the utilization of the *opes* of the *nobilitas. Fam.* 10.25.2.

75. *De Or.* 2.89, 107, 197. *Off.* 2.49. Val. Max. 8.5.2. *Part. Or.* 104. Cf. Badian, *Studies*, 34. Gruen, *Historia* 15 (1966), 32.

76. *Brut.* 162, 169. *Ad Herenn.* 1.21.

The similarities between the cases make a connection probable, and the nature of the charges suggests political overtones, but the importance attributed to these trials in some modern analyses, and the conclusion that bitter factional divisions underlay them, go far beyond the evidence.

Sulpicius, prosecutor of Norbanus, was an ambitious and talented young orator, friend and pupil of Crassus, and to all appearances imbued with his ideals and headed for similar success.[77] It is hardly surprising that he followed the example of his mentor, and decided to launch his public career with a prosecution. Norbanus provided an inviting target. The downfall of a prominent survivor of the anti-senatorial movement of the late second century would be welcomed by the *nobilitas* and would no longer be likely to provoke a popular protest. That Sulpicius was encouraged by Crassus and Scaurus need not be doubted. The latter, who had actually suffered physical injury in the disturbances caused by Norbanus, was a key prosecution witness. It is entirely possible that other *boni* who wished to erase all relics of their discomfiture in 103 were also backing the prosecution.[78]

That the case involved Marius or any group of *nobiles* opposed to Sulpicius and his backers, however, is nowhere attested. Marius had not been personally implicated in the prosecution of the Elder Caepio, and it is unlikely that he had the friendship of the radical Norbanus after his break with the *populares* in 100. If he had aided Antonius in the defense, surely this would be stated in the lengthy account of the trial in the *De Oratore*, where so much is made of his appearance for Aquillius.

Antonius certainly did not at this time belong to any faction hostile to Norbanus's accusers, nor was his decision to undertake the defense motivated by political considerations. He was a friend and former teacher of Sulpicius, and it was he who had sent the young orator about a year earlier to Crassus for further instruction, a gesture which indicates that he was also a friend of the latter at least as early as 96. His political association with the conservatives generally has already been

77. *De Or.* 1.25, 97, 136; 2.89; 3.47. *Off.* 2.49. *Brut.* 203.
78. *De Or.* 2.197, 203. Cicero relates that the *boni viri* filled the forum (*De Or.* 2.198), an indication of their interest in the case. The earlier prosecutions of Titius, Decianus, and the renegade Furius, whom the aristocracy did not try to save, reveal the eagerness of the *boni* to eradicate remnants of the popular movement.

demonstrated, and it is evidenced again by a reaction of surprised disapproval which his appearance for Norbanus aroused among the *boni* and by his repeated efforts to justify himself on purely personal grounds of *necessitudo* with a former comrade and quaestor.[79] It was an acceptable plea in a system partial to the claims of *amicitia*, particularly when it came from Antonius, whose readiness to defend was well known and who, more than any of his contemporaries, drew a sharp distinction between his forensic and political activity. Its genuineness was obviously believed by Sulpicius and his supporters, with whom Antonius continued to maintain a close personal and political friendship.[80]

No record survives of the *accusator* of Caepio nor of his motives or backers and little is known about the trial in general, but the most obvious conclusion is that it was a retaliatory action by friends or sympathizers of Norbanus against a political adherent of his prosecutors who was closely associated with the events of 103 and had engaged in similar unruly behavior in the optimate cause. This notion gains support from the fact that Crassus, who in contrast to Antonius carefully chose his cases, undertook the defense, and in the course of it delivered an unusually extended eulogy of Caepio, elaborate enough to merit independent publication.[81] One may safely assume that he used his eloquence

79. *De Or.* 2.89, 198, 202. Cf. M. Gelzer, "Die angebliche politische Tendenz in der dem C. Herennius gewidmeten Rhetorik" *Kleine Schriften* 1 (Wiesbaden 1962), 218. On the bonds between quaestors and commanders cf. L. A. Thompson, "The Relationship between Provincial Quaestors and Their Commanders-in-Chief" *Historia* 11 (1962), 339–55.

80. *De Or.* 2.124. *Brut.* 207. *Cluent.* 140. It should be noted that it was relatively common for friends to find themselves on opposite sides in the courts, an experience that in no way affected their friendship. Cf. the famous case of Manius Curius in which Crassus and Scaevola Pontifex faced each other. *De Or.* 1.180; 2.140, 221. *Brut.* 195. *Caec.* 53, 69. Antonius and Crassus were similarly on opposite sides in the case of M. Gratidianus late in the nineties. *De Or.* 1.178. *Off.* 3.67. Cicero describes his opponents in the trials of Cornelius and Cluentius as *amici. Brut.* 271.

81. It is sometimes suggested that Crassus's defense was perfunctory, an idea based on a dubious emendation of the following text of Cicero: *Est etiam L. Crassi in consulatu pro Q. Caepione defensione iuncta, non brevis ut laudatio ut oratio autem brevis. Brut.* 162. The lack of a subject in the first clause is difficult, and *defensiuncula* is a common emendation for *defensione iuncta*. The word, however, is nowhere found in extant Latin, and the text as it stands is far from unintelligible, indicating that Crassus published independently a digressive eulogy on Caepio which had formed part of his speech in the latter's defense. Lengthy digressions were not uncommon in Roman forensic speeches. Cf. Cicero's excursus on *optimates* and *populares* in the *Pro Sestio.*

to glorify Caepio's resistance to seditious demagoguery, and to decry the activities of the last years of the second century.

It would appear that Sulpicius's quest for forensic glory had escalated into a skirmish between the oligarchy and surviving radical elements, and that the most eloquent spokesman of the *boni* had taken advantage of the public platform provided by a criminal trial to extol his brand of government and defame the aims and methods of its extremist opponents.

About the same time Crassus gave his daughter, who was a granddaughter of Scaevola the Augur, in marriage to the son of Marius.[82] This surprising development, which linked the Mucii Scaevolae as well as Crassus to Marius, took place about the same time that Scaevola Pontifex began his governorship of Asia, and it may well be that the marriage was an attempt by Crassus and the Scaevolae to neutralize Marius in any confrontation that might develop with the *publicani* over the proposed reorganization of Asia by offering him an alliance that would lift him out of the impotence of isolation in which he had languished for the preceding five years.

In any event, the marriage heralded no change in the political sympathies of Crassus and effected no lasting rapprochement between him or his political circle and Marius. When the *equites* convicted Rutilius of extortion in 92 in retaliation for the curtailment of their activities in Asia, Marius seems to have sided with them against an old *inimicus*, taking advantage once more of domestic division and a serious challenge to senatorial rule.[83]

82. The date of the marriage is uncertain, but Marius and Crassus were *adfines* by the time of the trial of Matrinius, which probably took place soon after passage of the *Lex Licinia Mucia*. Cf. Badian, *Studies*, 44. Gelzer, *Kleine Schriften*, 1.214.

83. There is no sign that the relationship ever warmed. Crassus did not defend Matrinius (*Balb.* 49. Cf. Badian, *Historia* 18 [1969], 491); he attacked Claudius Marcellus, an old associate of Marius (*Font.* 24. Val. Max. 8.5.3); his edict against Latin rhetors in 92 most probably affected Marius's close friend Plotius Gallus (*Arch.* 20). Cicero's lack of contact with Marius in the nineties also suggests that the general was never close to Cicero's chief patron. For Marius's enmity with Rutilius cf. Plutarch, *Marius* 28.5, and for his role in the trial cf. Dio, fr. 97.3. Another indication of positive antagonism between Marius and the *boni* in the late nineties is the fact that, probably in late 91, the senate permitted the Numidian Bocchus to erect on the Capitol a group of statues representing the surrender of Jugurtha to Sulla (Plutarch, *Marius* 32; *Sulla* 6). Scaevola's escape from prosecution was not necessarily due to Marius's influence. He did come under attack

The condemnation of Rutilius produced widespread anger and consternation among the *nobilitas*. Matters were not improved by the indictment soon afterwards of Scaurus on charges related to his activities in Asia Minor, and, though this time the verdict was acquittal, the vulnerability of the ruling oligarchy and the impossibility of government under intimidation from an interest group with significant political power but no accountability for its use, stood revealed.[84] Reaction came in the form of an elaborate legislative program formulated under the direction of Scaurus and Crassus and introduced, fittingly enough, by Livius Drusus, a nephew of the exiled Rutilius, a tribune in 91, and son of the tribune who had helped the senate outmaneuver C. Gracchus in 122. The Younger Drusus was likewise well known as a champion of the senate, was a dour and determined politician and a close friend of Crassus and of the orator's disciples Sulpicius and Cotta.[85]

Repeating the example of his father, the Younger Drusus first attempted to conciliate the public and undermine the strength of his opponents by proposing agrarian and colonial bills and a *lex frumentaria*. He then introduced his *lex iudiciaria*, which was designed to deprive the *equites* of their exclusive control of the major criminal courts, though the details of his proposed reorganization of the judicial system remain in dispute. All of these measures were apparently passed, though not without disturbances and the use of strong-arm tactics by the obstinate and militant Drusus. Finally, he offered a proposal to enfranchise the Italians, but this does not appear ever to have reached the voting stage and coincided with a dramatic decline in Drusus's support, culminating in annulment of all his legislation by the senate late in 91.[86]

---

from the *publicani* (*Fam.* 1.9.26. *Planc.* 33), but he had spent a far shorter time in Asia than Rutilius and most likely had not aroused the same degree of hostility.

84. For the effects of the trial and the reaction of the *optimates* cf. *Brut.* 115. *De Or.* 1.230. *Font.* 38. *Pis.* 95. Asconius 21, Clark. *Off.* 2.75.

85. *Dom.* 50. Asconius 21, Clark. For Drusus's background, personality, and associates cf. *Cluent.* 153. *De Or.* 1.24, 97. Asconius 69, Clark. *Mil.* 16, 20. *Rab.* 21. *Off.* 1.108. *Planc.* 33. *N.D.* 3.80.

86. Sources in Broughton, *MRR*, 2.21. Cf. R. Thomsen, "Das Jahr 91 v. Chr. und seine Voraussetzungen" *CM* 5 (1942), 13–47. E. Gabba, "Osservazioni sulla lege giudiziaria di M. Livio Druso (91 a.C.)" *PP* 11 (1956), 363–72; "M. Livio Druso e le riforme di Silla" *ASNP* 33 (1964), 1–15. Meier, *Res Publica Amissa,* 211. U. Ewins, "*Ne Quis Iudicio Circumveniatur*" *JRS* 50 (1960), 94–107.

The citizenship bill is a puzzling feature in a program which the evidence, both documentary and circumstantial, clearly indicates was inspired by Rutilius's conviction and its disturbing implications, was undertaken on the senate's behalf and with the backing of its leaders, and was primarily concerned with elimination of equestrian control over the lives and property of government officials.[87] It is difficult to find any vital connection between Italian enfranchisement and the judicial reform contemplated by Drusus and his backers or any independent motive which would explain oligarchic sponsorship of such a proposal in 91. These facts, coupled with the bill's ultimate failure and disastrous consequences for Drusus's other measures, suggest that it was not an integral part of the original legislative package, but an additional later move by the ambitious and headstrong tribune, independently taken and for reasons independent of his own initial goal and that of his sponsors.

It is important to note that until late in 91 Drusus had the support not only of his *consiliarii* Crassus and Scaurus but of the oligarchy as a whole, which continued to manifest the basic political unity in evidence throughout the decade. His chief opposition in the senate came from the consul Philippus and from Servilius Caepio. Both had private reasons for opposing Drusus and his friends, but, whatever their motives, they were seemingly acting on their own, were not the leaders of any defined or sizable opposition within the *nobilitas*, and were in fact bitter enemies of one another.[88] Philippus was undoubtedly a formidable opponent and had substantial obstructive power as consul, but,

---

Badian, *Foreign Clientelae*, 216. Gruen, *Roman Politics,* 206. Brunt, *JRS* 55 (1965), 90–109. E. J. Weinrib, "The Judiciary Law of M. Livius Drusus (tr. pl. 91 B.C.)" *Historia* 19 (1970), 414–43. A. Bernardi, "La Guerra Sociale e le lotte dei partiti in Roma" *NRS* 28–29 (1944–45), 60–99. B. P. Seleckij, "Der Gesetzentwurf Drusus' des Jüngeren zur Gewährung der Bürgerrechte für die Italiker im Lichte der Schriften Ciceros (Q.fr.1.1; Att. 2.16)" *Klio* 58 (1976), 425–37. A. R. Hands, "Livius Drusus and the Courts" *Phoenix* 26 (1972), 268–74.

87. There can be no doubt that initially Drusus was acting as the senate's instrument and that the primary goal of his tribunate was judicial reform. Cf. *De Or.* 1.24. *Mil.* 16, 20. *Off.* 2.75. *Brut.* 222. Asconius 69, Clark. Velleius 2.13.2. Livy, *Per.* 70–71. Diodorus 37.10. Appian, *BC* 1.35, is the only ancient source which makes Italian enfranchisement the central concern of Drusus's program, but his main interest was the story of the Social War and he tended as a result to magnify the issues most directly related to it, and to obscure all else.

88. *Cluent.* 153. *De Or.* 1.24. *Prov. Cons.* 21. Florus 2.17. *Vir. Ill.* 66. Val. Max. 9.5.2. Cf. Gruen, *Historia* 15 (1966), 50. Badian, *Studies*, 40.

though he was able to pressure Drusus into extremist and divisive behavior and doubtless had some following among senators unhappy with the judiciary law, he was not able through most of the year to overcome the tribune's solid oligarchic backing, and was actually censured by the senate in September for publicly criticizing its support of Drusus.[89]

The breadth and earnestness of that support and its sudden evaporation late in 91 almost defy explanation, if citizenship for the allies was an original and advertised objective of Drusus's program. Hindsight may reveal the justice and inevitability of Italian enfranchisement and the mounting passions and frustrations which were approaching the stage of violence by 91, but there is no evidence that the Roman oligarchy had similar insight or that any development had taken place since 95 to reveal the necessity for a radical change of policy. Even if the likelihood of rebellion had been obvious, it is improbable that the senate would have allowed itself to be coerced by a threat of force into unwanted change of such dimensions.

The Livian Epitomator presents the citizenship bill as a device to secure Italian support for the other legislation of 91, and this view has been adopted and expanded by some modern historians who argue that the measure was designed to win a vast new *clientela* for the oligarchy which could continue to be used to maintain an easy dominance over the *equites.*[90]

The explanation has serious difficulties. The agrarian, colonial, and grain bills, designed specifically to woo the favor of the *plebs*, were unlikely to need the cooperation of the Italians to pass the *concilium plebis.* These proposals represented an elaborate and costly bid for the support of that assembly on the judicial issue, and it would hardly have seemed necessary to offer a far-reaching concession to the nonvoting allies as well, and it is clear, in fact, that Drusus did not initially enjoy the support or goodwill of the Italians.[91]

89. *Vir. Ill.* 66.10 states that some senators were unhappy with the judiciary law, as does Appian, *BC* 1.35. The censure of Philippus is described by Cicero in *De Or.* 3.2 ff.

90. Livy, *Per.* 71. Florus presents a similar view, but Livy was his chief source. Cf. Badian, *Foreign Clientelae,* 216. Weinrib, *Historia* 19 (1970), 440.

91. Livy's account is contradicted by Appian, who states that the Italians as a whole feared the land law and that the Etruscans and Umbrians came to Rome to aid Philippus in achieving its annulment. *BC* 1.36. On the meaning

Nor is it reasonable to suppose that the oligarchs suddenly saw in the allies in 91 a hitherto unnoticed prop for their tottering supremacy. They had always viewed expansion of the citizenry as a serious threat to their ability to control the *comitia*, and that they continued to do so is amply demonstrated by their attempts to minimize the power of the new voters after the Social War and by their resistance to Sulpicius in 88. As for the *equites*, Italian enfranchisement, regardless of who bestowed it, would be far more likely to increase their strength than the senate's, since the vast majority of the new citizens, particularly the Italian *provinciales*, would be linked to them by common interests and a common social status and would transform the *ordo* into a far more formidable counterforce to the senate both in Rome and in the provinces.[92]

The same difficulties face the contention that Drusus's *consiliarii* Crassus and Scaurus inspired or favored the citizenship bill. Their antipathy toward the Italians had been clearly and recently revealed, and there is nothing to suggest a change in their attitude. Asconius explicitly states that Scaurus's concern was with judicial reform, and none of Cicero's allusions to their role as Drusus's advisors connects them with the citizenship proposal.[93] Crassus's career shows few liberal tendencies, and the indications are that his conservatism continued to the end. In his last public office as censor in 92, he and his colleague Domitius Ahenobarbus had issued an edict banning Latin rhetors from Rome. Whether or not the victims of the ban were Latins, the measure showed hostility to new influences and to expansion of political opportunity, and it reflected the reactionary thinking which made a massive influx

---

of 'Ιταλιῶται in Appian cf. J. Göhler, *Rom und Italien* (Breslau 1939), 76 ff. R. Syme, "Review of Schur, *Zeitalter des Marius und Sulla*" *JRS* 34 (1944), 106. Y. Shochat, "The *Lex Agraria* of 133 B.C. and the Italian Allies" *Athenaeum* 48 (1970), 25–45. D. Kontchalovsky, "Recherches sur l'histoire du mouvement agraire des Gracques" *RH* 153 (1926), 161–86. M. Gelzer, "Review of F. Taeger, *Tiberius Gracchus*" *Kleine Schriften* 2.73. Past history had shown the perils of championing the Italians. A citizenship bill was an unlikely weapon with which to seek influence over the Roman legislative assembly. Cf. n. 97, below.

92. This was the effect of enfranchisement on the *ordo equester* after the Social War, and it forced Sulla to take drastic measures to end the conflict between *equites* and senate. Cf. Badian, *Roman Imperialism*, 63.

93. Crassus had sponsored the *Lex Licinia Mucia*. For Scaurus's attitude toward the Italians cf. *De Or.* 2.257. For their role as Drusus's *consiliarii* cf. Asconius 21, Clark. *Dom.* 50.

of new citizens culturally and politically unacceptable to the aristocracy.[94]

Crassus's famous "swan-song" speech, which was delivered in the senate on September 13, less than a week before his death, and which supported Drusus's move to censure Philippus for attacking the senate at a *contio*, tells nothing of his stand on the Italian question. His condemnation of Philippus's policies and his anger at the continuing efforts of a prominent *nobilis* to thwart the will of the senate were unrelated to the citizenship issue. As Badian has demonstrated, what Philippus was seeking at this time with ever-increasing determination was invalidation of the legislation already passed, and he was actually rallying Italian support for that purpose.[95] The political atmosphere at Rome was heating rapidly by the time of Crassus's death, but the controversy was still centering on Drusus's earlier measures, and the senate was still firmly committed to them. In the final analysis, our sources contain no record of Crassus's stand on the citizenship bill and no definite proof that it had been formally promulgated or become a center of controversy before his death.

Finally, the dramatic political shift which took place at Rome toward the end of 91 would seem to point to a late espousal of the Italian cause by Drusus. Soon after Crassus's final speech and the senate's rebuke of Philippus, that body broke with Drusus, sided with the consul, and abandoned its urgent goal of judicial reform by annuling all of Drusus's laws. The death of Crassus is an insufficient explanation of this remarkable development. Scaurus, who had been equally involved in the formulation of Drusus's proposals and had equal influence in the senate, was still alive, and Cicero's statement that Philippus was suddenly reconciled with all his greatest enemies clearly indicates that Drusus's backers were not forced to capitulate, but rather that they abruptly abandoned the tribune and their hopes in him, and cooperated in the cancellation of his laws.[96]

94. Sources in Broughton, *MRR*, 2.17. Aulus Gellius 15.11.2 quotes the edict as does Suetonius, *Rhet.* 2.1. Cf. Gabba, *Athenaeum* 31 (1953), 269.

95. *De Or.* 3.2ff. Cf. Appian *BC* 1.36. Badian, *Foreign Clientelae*, 217.

96. Sources in Broughton, *MRR*, 2.21. Cicero speaks of Philippus's reconciliation with his enemies in *Prov. Cons.* 21. Drusus was not the only one to take a sudden political fall in late 91. His close associate, C. Aurelius Cotta, who was flourishing politically before the death of Crassus, shortly afterwards failed to gain election to the tribunate, an office he had been considered certain to win. A

A reversal so complete, which meant forsaking a crucial objective, was not occasioned merely by disenchantment with Drusus's personality or methods. The senate was not particular about the means to its ends, and one may safely assume that its abandonment of Drusus and of its goal of judicial reform coincided with the emergence of an irreconcilable conflict between its objectives and his. A sudden new move by Drusus to enfranchise the Italians seems the obvious and only adequate explanation of such a conflict. It also seems the only explanation of Drusus's sharply improved relations with the allies in the later part of 91. Earlier they had reacted unfavorably to his program, and some had actively aided Philippus in opposition to him, yet toward the end of his tribunate they viewed him as their champion and were outraged to the point of rebellion by his murder.[97]

These various strands of evidence point repeatedly to the conclusion that the Italian question was a later intrusion on an internal political

----

few months later he was exiled by the Varian commission. Cicero relates that another close friend of Drusus, P. Sulpicius Rufus, was also a target of the *invidia* which first defeated and later exiled Cotta, though it was not manifested so directly. *De Or.* 3.11. This sudden *invidia* points again to a new development after the death of Crassus which cost not only Drusus, but also his closest associates, who very likely continued to support him, their political following. None of the senate's *principes*, however, were convicted by the Varian commission. Their connection with Drusus obviously could not be shown to have extended to sympathy for the cause of the Italians.

97. No convincing explanation of Drusus's shifting relations with the Italians and of the active opposition to him from the Etruscans and Umbrians has been offered by those who believe that enfranchisement was an integral part of his original program. In light of the bitter fighting of the following years, it is hard to accept that even the Etruscans and Umbrians would have jeopardized the citizenship bill because of uncertain fears about their holdings of public land. Brunt's suggestion (*JRS* 55 [1965], 95) that Drusus's influence and consequently the hope of enfranchisement were already gone by the time the Etruscans and Umbrians demonstrated at Rome against the land law is based on the unlikely premise that Philippus would not have proposed annulment of Drusus's laws if the tribune still had strong senatorial backing. Drusus's unquestionable earlier support from the *nobilitas* had not deterred the determined consul from seeking to turn the senate against him. It seems likely too that there was a sharp change in Drusus's standing with the Roman *plebs* toward the end of his tribunate. The *invidia* experienced by Cotta and Sulpicius, which came, in part at least, from the general public, is one indication of a popular reaction against Drusus. The fact that the tribune's murder brought no public outcry is another. Once again a new proposal to enfranchise the Italians appears to be the only explanation for what seems like another sudden shift in the political lineup of late 91. Such proposals in the past had invariably alienated the Roman *plebs*, and the Varian

conflict initially unconnected with it. It resurfaced at this particular time most probably as a result of Drusus's agrarian legislation, an unwanted side effect which had followed similar legislation in the days of Tiberius Gracchus. It came to overshadow more basic concerns because of its explosiveness and a chronic tendency of Roman politicians to exploit it for their own advantage. Philippus tried to capitalize on allied fears of land losses to frustrate all of the initial designs of Drusus, and the latter, repeating a familiar pattern, attempted to upstage his prime antagonist by outbidding him for Italian support.[98] There followed the dramatic realignments. Drusus had underestimated the abiding opposition of the oligarchy to large-scale extension of the franchise and, when with characteristic obstinacy he refused to be deterred by it, the senate sided with his adversary and consented to annulment of his earlier legislation, a step which would help to negate the influence it had gained him and pave the way for invalidation of the citizenship bill if he repeated earlier high-handed methods to secure its passage. Drusus was forced to yield and soon afterwards was murdered. The senate did not investigate his death, a measure of how completely one of the brightest hopes of the oligarchy had fallen from grace.[99]

But the Italian question had been raised, used, and shelved once too often, and a decade marked by relative quiet and harmony ended in

---

commission established in 90, which certainly had popular support at the beginning and which represented an angry backlash against Drusus's concessionary attitude toward the allies, indicates that popular feeling on this issue had not changed and makes it highly unlikely that the Roman *plebs* had ever looked with approval on Drusus's proposal for Italian enfranchisement.

98. Diodorus (37.11) records an oath of loyalty to Drusus taken by the Italians, which, if genuine, is another strong indication that Drusus's advocacy of enfranchisement was an independent venture and designed to build his personal power. On the genuineness of the oath cf. L. R. Taylor, *Party Politics in the Age of Caesar* (Berkeley 1964), 46. One need not, of course, deny that Drusus also had more altruistic motives. He was a trusted friend of at least one important Italian leader. Plutarch, *Cato Min.* 2.1–2. Val. Max. 3.1.2. *Vir. Ill.* 80.1.

99. There are signs that the senate, as usual, tried to dissuade Drusus. Val. Max. 9.5.2. Velleius 2.13. *Orator* 213. Cicero comments on the senate's failure to investigate Drusus's death in *Mil.* 16. Another indication that the senate's *principes* changed their minds about Drusus and approved the cancellation of his laws is the fact that Cicero praises that action, though elsewhere he speaks highly of Drusus's initial goals and his dedication to the optimate cause. *Leg.* 2.14, 31. *Vat.* 23. *De Or.* 1.24. *Mil.* 16.

disastrous war and bitter division between senate and *equites*. A sustained and remarkably unified effort by the oligarchy to restore strong senatorial rule had failed, partly because of aristocratic shortsightedness and inflexibility, partly because of a system which fostered conflict by subjecting the government to checks and pressures from a class which owed no accounting to anyone, and whose primary concern was not the public interest but its own.

This lengthy review of the political history of the nineties has been necessitated by the controversial nature of the evidence and by the degree to which an understanding of the political sympathies and aspirations of the men most closely associated with Cicero's early life and education is linked to its interpretation. Scaurus, Antonius, Crassus, and the Mucii Scaevolae emerge as leading spokesmen of the conservative *nobilitas* in the nineties and the dominating influence in the formulation of senatorial policy. Their political behavior and the senatorial decisions they shaped or accepted reveal a frequently narrow conservatism preoccupied with preserving aristocratic control of the Roman state and reestablishing a dominant senate, a necessary machinery for oligarchic rule. This thinking is repeatedly exemplified throughout the decade in the opposition to agrarian reform that might significantly affect the distribution of wealth and upset the economic balance or bestow political benefits on individuals; in the opposition to extension of the franchise and to cultural and educational innovations which might endanger aristocratic holds on the citizenry; in the efforts to impede or suppress popular politicians and any form of political action which lacked senatorial sponsorship or approval; in the efforts to minimize and counteract the preeminence of Marius; in the efforts to free the governing class from the restraints imposed by the judicial power of the *equites.*

In brief, Cicero's patrons epitomized traditional republicanism, committed by ideology and self-interest to the conservative interpretation of the ancestral constitution. Their political position, outlook, and relationship to one another were in many ways similar to those of Catulus, Cato, Lucullus, and Hortensius in the sixties. Distinguished and influential, bound by a common political philosophy and various ties of *amicitia*, they formed the principal guardians of the *via optimas* and the chief obstacles to major economic, social, and political change.

The Influence of His Patrons on Cicero

The impact of his early mentors on Cicero was deep and permanent. He testified to its importance at the end of his life when he affirmed the need for close associations between young men and prominent elder statesmen and stressed the lasting effects of such relationships both in shaping the political thinking and social conscience of an *adulescens* and in gaining him recognition with the public and identification as a disciple of the moral and political doctrines of his patrons.[100] Elsewhere too he frequently reveals the abiding influence of his early mentors on his political sympathies and beliefs by his repeated expressions of admiration for their characters and abilities and by his unvarying approval of their statesmanship.

Crassus in particular continued throughout Cicero's life to provide a source of inspiration and a model for imitation. There were striking similarities between their political talents and intellectual attainments, and Cicero felt a close identification with the orator, tending to view him as an idealized version of himself. He saw in him a rare and admirable combination of wide learning, great eloquence, and practical political wisdom. Crassus had been carefully educated under his father's supervision, had later continued his studies in Asia and Athens, had developed a deep interest in *doctrina*, and, to Cicero's mind, had attained the ideal skills of the civilian statesman by applying his learning to produce a richer eloquence and to sharpen his political understanding and foresight. In addition, he had exercised these abilities with the greatest industry, and, aided by his forensic labors and the *privata officia* rendered through them, won fame and the favor of honest men and a commanding position of influence in the state.[101] Cicero believed that he himself had similar talents, similar skill and zeal in their exercise, similar springs of political influence. He recognized the parallels, stressed them, and even sought to create others.[102]

100. *Off.* 1.122; 2.46. Cf. *Cael.* 9 ff.

101. *De Or.* 2.1–4, 6; 3.7, 74–77, 131–36. *Brut.* 143, 159. *Off.* 2.47.

102. Cf. *Rep.* 1.13. *Leg.* 3.14. *Brut.* 321–22. *Orator* 11 ff. *De Or.* 1.1 ff. *Arch.* 12 ff. *Cael.* 6. *Sulla* 5. *Man.* 1 ff. Cicero attributes to Crassus not only his own thinking on rhetorical and philosophical subjects, but also such personal characteristics as his own tendency to get very nervous before speaking. *De Or.* 1.121. *Div. In Caec.* 41. *Cluent.* 57. *Deiot.* 1. He also emphasizes other common features, such as the lifelong friendship of each of them with a distinguished lawyer. *Brut.* 150–56. Cf. E. Rawson, "Lucius Crassus and Cicero" *PCPS* 17 (1971), 75–88.

He was eager to identify and to be identified with the great orator and conservative statesman, and Crassus's high *auctoritas* and ultimate position as a distinguished *consularis* and *censorius* directing the decisions of a dominant senate represented the peak of his own ambition. He never achieved that objective; it was no longer attainable in the turmoil and changed power structure of Cicero's later life, but it remained his cherished goal, as did restoration of the system and the political circumstances which would have made it possible.[103]

Cicero's close affinity with Crassus, his unqualified admiration for his political abilities and wisdom, and his deep desire to emulate his achievement produced, as a natural consequence, acceptance and approval of his political methods, loyalties, and ideals. Cicero invariably speaks in praise or defense of Crassus's political actions and the thinking that inspired them. He commends his prosecution of Carbo; he describes his speech for the *Lex Servilia* as a masterly defense of the senate's *auctoritas* and a model for himself from boyhood; he incorporates a senatorial resolution sponsored by Crassus in 92, making presidents of assemblies responsible for maintaining order, into his ideal constitution; he extols the orator's eloquent castigation of Philippus; he even approves the *Lex Licinia Mucia* and finds a laudable motive for the ban against Latin rhetors. Charges of inconsistency against his patron he brushes aside as the necessary adjustments of the skillful orator and politician to the needs of the moment.[104] In his native ability, in his training, industry and moral character, in his prestige and influence, and in his courageous use of them in defense of the ancestral constitution, Crassus came close to Cicero's concept of the ideal statesman of the Republic.[105]

The political abilities and achievements of Scaurus and Antonius evoked similar responses in Cicero, though his comments on them are fewer and his affinity with them less pronounced. As in the case of Crassus, their political skills were similar to Cicero's own, and both exemplified, as Cicero believed he did himself, the power of political

103. Cf. *Att.* 4.2.6. *Fam.* 1.8.4; 1.9.2. *Q.F.* 3.6.4. *Fam.* 4.13.2; 4.6.2; 5.15.3. *Att.* 13.10.1. *Brut.* 7–9.

104. *Fam.* 9.21.3. *Brut.* 103, 159. *Off.* 2.47. *Brut.* 164, 296–98. *Cluent.* 140. *Leg.* 3.42. *De Or.* 3.2 ff., 39. In *Off.* 3.47 Cicero appears to approve the *Lex Licinia Mucia*, though in his speech for Cornelius he reports the common view that it was detrimental to the state. Asconius 67, Clark.

105. Cf. *Sest.* 99, 101, 137–39. *De Or.* 2.5; 3.59–60. *Leg.* 3.14.

virtus, when combined with energy and determination and exercised in the interests of decent citizens, to achieve the highest political success unaided by inherited *dignitas* or the benefits of military glory. Cicero acknowledged the inspiration he drew from the career of Scaurus in particular, and the encouragement it gave him to follow a similar political path.[106] The behavior of both men in public office and their use of political power he similarly lauded as an example and inspiration. They devoted their efforts to the defense of the *respublica* and faced the dangers of resistance to *improbi* and *seditiosi.* Cicero was fond of describing his own endeavors and performance as a leader in similar terms.[107]

Scaevola the Augur and Scaevola Pontifex represented a somewhat different order of politician. Less forceful as orators, their success and influence depended more on family prestige and connections and on their reputations for integrity and learning in law.[108] Cicero, the *novus homo* whose interest and main hope for political distinction lay in eloquence, and who saw limited value for the politician in legal expertise, could perhaps identify with them less closely than with the other counselors of his youth, but he was no less deeply influenced by their political behavior and beliefs, and he showed the same tendency to find in their statesmanship the true elements of political virtue.

He cites the Augur, who in the several crises of his later life never allowed age or physical infirmity to interfere with his duties as a leading senator, as a model of the watchful energy which should mark all *consulares*, and on which depended the safety of the state and the prestige and influence of the senate as its principal guardian. Scaevola Pontifex, who was Cicero's chief political mentor throughout much of the eighties, had a far more direct and profound impact on Cicero's political life. In his reactions to the civil dissensions which plagued the eighties, Cicero closely followed the pontiff's lead in avoiding involvement in civil war or in the government of Cinna, and more than thirty years later, in 49, with an explicit appeal to Scaevola's example, he was

106. *De Or.* 2.4–6. *Sest.* 136–37. *Brut.* 242. Asconius 22–23, Clark. Cf. *Leg. Agr.* 2.3. *Planc.* 62. *Cluent.* 111. *Mur.* 17.
107. *Rab.* 21, 26. *De Or.* 1.214. *Sest.* 101. *De Or.* 1.3. *Leg. Agr.* 1.23 ff. *Sulla* 28. *Quir.* 19. *Phil.* 2.1. *Cat.* 4.22.
108. *Brut.* 102, 212. *Leg.* 2.47, 49–52. *Att.* 4.16.3. *Brut.* 115, 145, 148, 152, 194. *N.D.* 3.80. *Off.* 3.62. *De Or.* 1.180. *Verr.* 2.2.27.

to adopt a similar course in what he believed were closely similar circumstances. The Pontifex was also his model and standard of reference in his governorship of Cilicia. He followed his Asian edict closely, and his chief concern throughout his tenure was to rival Scaevola's reputation for fair dealing and incorruptibility.[109]

In all his references to these five statesmen, references which span most of his life and all phases of his political career, can be detected a special regard and respect for them as men and citizens and a strong sympathy with their political aspirations and their efforts to achieve them. In his allusions to their qualities are constant echoes of the language he employs in reflections on the ideal statesman.[110] In a striking passage in the *Pro Rabirio* he separates all five, together with the Elder Catulus, from his list of deceased participants in the suppression of Saturninus for special mention as the men who far excelled all others in ability and judgment. His explicit approval of their statesmanship is matched by consistent disapproval or unsympathetic presentation of the men and movements with which they came in conflict. The Papirii Carbones, the Memmii, Saturninus, Glaucia, Norbanus, Titius, the Younger Caepio, Philippus, the Mamilian commission and its condemnation of Bestia and Opimius, the prosecution of the Elder Caepio, the attacks on Metellus Numidicus, the conviction of Rutilius, the Varian commission, all of these men and events Cicero criticizes directly or indirectly.[111]

But nowhere perhaps can Cicero's affinity with his early patrons and with the optimate cause they championed be better illustrated than in his attitude toward Marius, an attitude born of conflicting loyalties whose resolution is a significant index of Cicero's most basic political sympathies. Marius had pursued success, often with scant regard for the

109. *Rab.* 21, 26. *Phil.* 8.31. *Att.* 8.3.6. *Rosc. Am.* 33, 136. *Att.* 6.1. 4, 15; 5.17.5. *Fam.* 15.4.14. Cf. ch. 2, pp. 88–100.

110. *Ingenium, virtus, consilium, prudentia, sapientia, doctrina, eloquentia, dignitas, auctoritas, temperantia, industria, constantia, vigilantia*: these are the terms most frequently on Cicero's lips in his allusions to these five statesmen. Cf. *Rab.* 26. *De Or.* 2.1 ff. *Par. St.* 41. *De Or.* 3.7. *Font.* 24. *Leg.* 3.42. *Pis.* 62. *Div. In Caec.* 25. *Verr.* 1.52. *De Or.* 1.214. Asconius 22, Clark. *Verr.* 2.2.27. *N.D.* 3.80. *Phil.* 8.31. *Rosc. Am.* 33.

111. *Rab.* 26. *Fam.* 9.21.3. *Brut.* 103. *Off.* 2.47. *Brut.* 136. *Brut.* 224. *Rab.* 18, 22 ff. *Leg.* 2.14. *De Or.* 2.124. *De Or.* 2.48. *Brut.* 223. *De Or.* 1.24. *Att.* 8.3.6. *Brut.* 127–28. *Tusc.* 5.14. *Brut.* 135. *Sen.* 25. *Quir.* 6. *Dom.* 87. *Sest.* 101. *De Or.* 1.230. *Brut.* 115. *Font.* 38. *N.D.* 3.81. *Sest.* 101.

sensibilities and prerogatives of the Roman oligarchy, and his relationship with its *principes*, to whom Cicero owed loyalty and gratitude, had fluctuated between open hostility and uneasy truce. Nonetheless he had strong claims on the goodwill and good opinion of Cicero. Though he had done little personally to advance the latter's career, he was an *adfinis*, a fellow townsman, and a *novus homo* who had dramatically illustrated that a *municeps* of humble origin had the right to aspire to the highest political success at Rome. Besides, it was often politically expedient for Cicero to sing the praises of Marius, to publicize his links to him, and to invite comparison with a man who had been a close and consistent friend of the *equites* and who, by the time Cicero was seeking the highest offices at Rome, had been reinstated as a folk hero and a champion of the people.[112]

Cicero's portrait of his fellow Arpinate reflects the many and sometimes conflicting considerations that shaped it. His references to the general are numerous, the bulk of them favorable, many extremely so. Much of Cicero's praise, however, is unrelated to Marius's political behavior, or else it is the product of the special needs of the occasion or of a sympathy based on parallel experiences in their careers. Cicero's direct judgments on Marius the statesman are few, but they clearly reveal that, despite the bonds of kinship and fellow feeling and the promptings of political expediency, he could not accept his kinsman's political methods nor in general approve his political attitudes or actions.

The most frequent subjects of Cicero's complimentary allusions to Marius are the latter's military skill and success. Cicero seldom misses an opportunity to extol the glory and the benefits of the triumphs over Jugurtha, the Cimbri, and the Teutones, and he consistently ranks Marius with the most celebrated commanders of Roman history.[113] There is no reason to deny that Cicero had a genuine admiration for the military genius of Marius and for the *vis* and *virtus* which underlay it,

112. The funeral of Marius's widow in 69, at which Caesar delivered the eulogy and displayed, amid great popular enthusiasm, effigies of Marius and his son, is an indication of how the memory of Marius was revered among the masses. Suetonius, *Julius* 6. Plutarch, *Caesar* 5. Cf. *Leg. Agr.* 3.6 ff. The influence of the pseudo-Marius in 44 also illustrates Marius's popularity. Cf. *Att.* 12.49.1. *Phil.* 1.5. Carney, *WS* 73 (1960), 122.

113. *Verr.* 2.5.25. *Font.* 36, 43. *Man.* 47, 60. *Cat.* 4.21. *Sulla* 23. *Arch.* 5. *Prov. Cons.* 32. His provincial governorship is also praised. *Verr.* 2.3.209.

but in evaluating the significance of this form of praise it is important to note that Cicero attributed limited value to military skill in political leaders, had serious reservations about the notion of a soldier-statesman, and found the true measure of a leader's performance not in his record on the battlefield but in his achievements as a *togatus* in senate and forum.[114] Furthermore, it was good policy and a practice of Cicero's to champion popular military heroes, and his encomia on Roman commanders in his speeches—where all his plaudits on Marius's generalship occur—tended to have an inflated quality which often bore no relationship to his true opinion of the individuals concerned as leaders of the *respublica.*[115]

Cicero also speaks approvingly of Marius in the speeches as a precursor of himself in opening high political office to every citizen of ability and ambition. The approval was largely genuine, but it was not a product of any shared political ideology. Despite the long and close association of his family with distinguished consular houses, Cicero remained self-conscious about his lack of noble ancestry, easily stung by spiteful allusions to his lineage, and inclined to see envy and resentment as the source of his every disagreement with a *nobilis.* His sensitivity produced frequent attacks on rigid notions of hereditary excellence and on claims that high office was the birthright of a few. It also brought regard and sympathy for all new men who had battled similar prejudices and helped break down the *claustra nobilitatis*, as well as a tendency to magnify their merits and achievements as a demonstration of the irrelevance of birth. It is not surprising therefore that Marius, who whatever his political attitudes and ideals had made his way from the humblest circumstances to seven consulships and a legendary name, was frequently appealed to by Cicero as a refutation of aristocratic claims to superiority. It is not surprising either that in his public oratory Cicero was willing to couple Marius's achievement with his own and to draw whatever favor and honor he could from the association.[116]

114. *Cat.* 4.21. *Marc.* 28–29. *Off.* 1.74, 76 ff. *Sest.* 99.
115. Cf. his praise of Caesar, *Prov. Cons.* 32 ff. Though he thought highly of Pompey when he delivered his speech for the Manilian law, Cicero admits he made full use of rhetorical ornament in glorifying the general. *Orator* 102.
116. *Verr.* 2.5.180. *Mur.* 17. *Sulla* 23. *Att.* 4.5.1; 4.1.8; 4.2.5. *Fam.* 1.7.2; 1.9.15; 5.12.4; 3.7.5. Cicero praises many other *novi homines* besides Marius for their efforts and success in the face of class prejudice, though he would not necessarily approve their political ideals.

Cicero objected to political exclusivism, a natural consequence of the circumstances of his birth, but his feelings on this issue had no wide-ranging influence on his overall political ideology, and his commendation of new men who successfully withstood the class prejudices of the Roman oligarchy no more implies a wider sympathy with their political thinking than it does a wider hostility to the principles and objectives of oligarchic government.

His repeated condemnation of the outlawry of Marius provides another example of partiality for the general which had little to do with his estimate of the latter's merits as a statesman. Cicero's sympathy for Marius's fate becomes prominent only after his own exile and would seem to have been largely generated by fellow feeling derived from what he came to see as closely similar experiences. He liked to compare his own banishment to the calamities of a long succession of eminent exiled statesmen in Greek and Roman history, but it was in Marius's case that he found the closest parallels. Both were new men from the same town; as consuls both had delivered the state from the most serious dangers; and both had fallen victim to the fickleness and ingratitude characteristic of civil dissension. Cicero also found in Marius's fortitude in the face of undeserved misfortune a badly needed source of strength and encouragement, which further increased his sympathy and regard. His political loneliness and disenchantment with his political allies, the *boni*, which reached a peak during his exile and in the years following, was yet another factor predisposing him at this time to friendly feelings for his fellow Arpinate.[117] His empathy with the general in these years has often been emphasized and is well attested in the speeches of the fifties, and particularly in the *De Divinatione*, where he relates that Marius was in his dreams and often on his mind throughout his exile.[118]

It is possible that it was also in this period that he wrote his poem the *Marius*, though there is insufficient evidence to allow any certainty about this issue. The period was, however, one of poetic activity during

117. *Cat.* 3.24. *Quir.* 7, 19–20. *Sen.* 38. *Pis.* 43. *Planc.* 26. *De Or.* 3.8. *Rep.* 1.6. *Fin.* 2.105. *Par. St.* 16. *Div.* 1.59; 2.140. *Att.* 4.1.8; 4.2.5. *Fam.* 1.9.15–17.
118. *Div.* 1.59; 2.140. Cf. Carney, *WS* 73 (1960), 83. G. B. Lavery, "Cicero's *Philarchia* and Marius" *Greece and Rome* 18 (1971), 133–42. M. Rambaud, *Cicéron et l'histoire romaine* (Paris 1953), 33–35. R. Gnauk, *Die Bedeutung des Marius und Cato Maior für Cicero* (Berlin 1936).

which Cicero produced the *De Temporibus Suis*, which dealt with his own exile and recall. The passage from his poem on Marius quoted in the *De Divinatione* indicates that the latter's exile figured prominently in that work. This thematic connection is significant in view of the fact that Cicero's other writings indicate that his reflections on his own banishment were often linked to observations on Marius's exile and other aspects of the latter's career and character, and it makes plausible the suggestion that both poems were composed together in this period of Cicero's greatest regard for his fellow townsman.[119]

While there are signs of emotional bonds between Cicero and Marius in the mid-fifties, their strength and particularly their political significance can easily be exaggerated. Many of the complimentary references and comparisons are coupled with outright condemnation of Marius's behavior on his return from exile and serve more to highlight Cicero's more glorious homecoming and more selfless and patriotic response to similar injustice than to exalt the memory of the general. Besides, Cicero's position on Marius's banishment was basically a condemnation of the behavior of the latter's enemies in this particular instance and was independent of his opinion of Marius's own political stance. His attitude was indeed closely similar to that of his patron Scaevola the Augur and, it would appear, many other *nobiles*, who found it an abomination that a man who had saved the state should be declared its enemy by the summary act of a senatorial decree. Such a stand was far removed from any approval of Marius's politics or of his actions and aspirations in 88.[120]

In fact, only one positive action of Marius's domestic statesmanship wins explicit praise from Cicero—his response to the ultimate decree in 100 and his forceful suppression of Saturninus. The approval is hardly surprising since on this occasion Marius acted in full cooperation with the *nobilitas*. The warmth of Cicero's praise and his occasional association of Marius with men like Nasica and Opimius as a stalwart foe of *seditiosi* lose much of their significance when one considers that this high acclaim occurs only in speeches and chiefly in contexts where

119. The only other references to the *Marius* in Cicero occur in *Leg.* 1.1 ff. and *Att.* 12.49.1. Neither helps to date the poem. Cf. H. W. Benario, "Cicero's *Marius* and Caesar" *CP* 52 (1957), 177–81.

120. Val. Max. 3.8.5. Cicero certainly did not approve of the activities of Sulpicius in 88. *De Or.* 3.11. *Har. Resp.* 41, 43. *Vat.* 23. *Leg.* 3.20.

Cicero's chief concern was to defend the ultimate decree and the violence it unleashed and to dramatize the unhesitating use of it by a champion of the people.[121] His sincerity is further impugned by other less flattering references which show Marius backing these same *seditiosi*, particularly in their attacks on Metellus Numidicus, for whose exile Cicero holds Marius responsible in the same way he holds Caesar responsible for his own.[122]

Cicero's other direct judgments on Marius's domestic political actions are uniformly unfavorable and are mostly found in his theoretical writings, where they could be stated with less political risk. They are relatively few in number but touch on several highpoints of Marius's career. His ballot law of 119 is implicitly criticized as an unacceptable limitation on the workings of *auctoritas*, and Cicero would repeal it together with the other laws that sought to eliminate all modes of aristocratic influence on voters; his demagogic attacks on Metellus Numidicus in 108 are condemned as a violation of good faith and justice; his role in the exile of Metellus, though not directly censured, is emphasized, and Cicero elsewhere indicates his disapproval of the treatment of Metellus; his return from exile by force of arms and the cruel massacre which followed are repeatedly denounced, and the death of Catulus is specifically, and as a special reproach, laid to his charge.[123]

In summary, while Cicero's portrait of Marius is far more favorable than the biased tradition handed down in the memoirs of Marius's enemies, most of the praise contained in it is divorced from Marius's political activity at Rome or is inspired by political expediency or emotional bonds rather than genuine political sympathy and accord. Both by what he said and by what he left unsaid Cicero indicates that he found little to commend and much to deplore in Marius's domestic statesmanship. The limited extent of his praise and the import of his criticisms are highlighted when contrasted with the unvarying enthusiasm and admiring approval with which he describes the skills, goals, and methods of his optimate patrons and his debt to their inspiration and example. He pays no tributes to the political wisdom of Marius; he found him *calidissimus* rather than *sapientissimus*. Marius's principal skills were military and did not greatly impress Cicero, who asserts that

121. *Rab.* 27, 30. *Cat.* 3.15. *Har. Resp.* 51. *Mil.* 8. *Planc.* 88.
122. *Sest.* 37. *Pis.* 20. Cf. *Sest.* 41, 52. *Sen.* 32.
123. *Leg.* 3.38. *Off.* 3.79. *Cat.* 3.24. *Sen.* 38. *Quir.* 7, 20. *Har. Resp.* 54. *Sest.* 50. *Phil.* 11.1. *De Or.* 3.8. *Tusc.* 5.56. *N.D.* 3.80.

even as a boy he thought just as highly of the civilian skills of Scaurus, and it was the political road traveled by the latter that he sought to follow.[124] With the single exception of the suppression of Saturninus, Marius's political behavior is never cited as a model of good statesmanship or political virtue, and his political clashes with the *nobilitas* are passed over in prudent silence or treated with veiled disapproval or outright condemnation.

It would appear that Cicero owed little more to Marius's influence and inspiration than he did to his active patronage. His own political instincts and his loyalty to the goals and tenets of his conservative patrons prevailed over bonds of kinship and fellow feeling, and prevented any lasting sense of political fellowship with a man whose reach for success had too often ignored the interests of the *respublica* and its ruling oligarchy.

The conclusions of this examination of Cicero's heritage and early associations at Rome can be stated briefly. When Cicero entered the forum at the beginning of the eighties he emerged from a background steeped in the social and political thinking of a conservative aristocracy which was dedicated to the preservation of the social, economic, and political conditions that had secured it wealth, privilege, and firm control of the state. He came of a conservative and ambitious family which belonged to the gentry of a country town where class consciousness and elitism were no less pronounced than in the capital. His early education at the house of Crassus, his close association with him and with other conservative *principes* of the *nobilitas*, and his military service as the *contubernalis* of a Tubero continued an unbroken succession of conservative influences that deeply and permanently affected his life and thinking, as is illustrated by his consistent admiration for the mentors of his youth, by his approval of their values, ideals, and accomplishments, and by his desire to imitate them. This background also secured him the firm friendship of distinguished consular houses, and when he began to appear in the forum it was as the protégé of the prestigious *consularis*, Scaevola the Augur, and later of the equally prestigious Scaevola Pontifex. As he stood on the threshold of his public life, his heritage and his connections bound him closely to the *via optimas* and identified him in the public mind as a protégé and disciple of its principal champions.

124. *Att.* 10.8.7. *Off.* 1.76.

2: CICERO'S APPRENTICESHIP

Cicero gives an account of his life in the eighties in the *Brutus*, in which he presents himself as mainly an observer of political events, concentrating his energies on acquiring *doctrina*, on developing his rhetorical skills, and on familiarizing himself with the art of politics by close observation of its leading practitioners. He pursued his legal studies with the Scaevolae, studied philosophy with Philo the Academician in 88 and a little later with Diodotus the Stoic, who took up residence at his house. He listened to the rhetorician Molo of Rhodes in 87 and again in 81, and throughout the period he wrote, read, and practiced declamation daily, most often in the company of Pupius Piso and Quintus Pompeius. In addition he was a frequent visitor to the forum to hear and observe the leading politicians at trials and *contiones*. Determined to perfect his rhetorical skills before making his debut as a pleader, it was only after Sulla's victory and the restoration of stable government in 81 that he undertook his first case. In 80, his first criminal case, his defense of Roscius, won him high acclaim and established him as one of Rome's leading advocates.[1]

The incompleteness of the picture has often been observed. Cicero was concerned in the *Brutus* to present a portrait of an orator in the making and emphasized what contributed to that end and omitted what did not. There is no word of his military service and little indication of

1. *Brut.* 304–12. Cf. A. E. Douglas, *M. Tulli Ciceronis Brutus* (Oxford 1966), 221. Badian, *Historia* 18 (1969), 454. M. Gelzer, *Cicero. Ein Biographischer Versuch* (Wiesbaden 1969), 19–28.

his political stance or sympathies amid the convoluted political developments of a decade marked by recurring violence and civil war. Yet the
stage at which Cicero had arrived by the eighties was normally one of great
importance and high political activity in the careers of ambitious *iuvenes.*
Young men in their early twenties who were not on military service
were generally busy in the courts and frequently involved in electoral
contests and political controversies. Long years of silent, passive apprenticeship were unheard of in Cicero's day, as he himself testifies in his
speech for Caelius.[2]

A *iuvenis* of Cicero's promise and distinguished connections cannot
have remained an anonymous, detached observer in Roman politics
throughout the eighties, during which two of his most eminent patrons,
Antonius and Scaevola Pontifex, with whom he was in close association
in this decade, fell victims to proscriptions. His avoidance of forensic
engagements and his general quiescence cannot be disputed, but they
must be viewed as a calculated response to political conditions, not as
a concern to burst on the political scene as a fully fledged Demosthenes.
He was already on the public scene by the eighties and cannot have
avoided confronting hard political choices in the tangled political aftermath of the breakdown of law and constitutionality in 88 and 87. What
he did or did not do in this period, the thinking that inspired his political posture, his overall reaction to the repeated civil disturbances, and
his judgments on the men who led them and on the clashes of ideology
and self-interest that provoked them are all matters of vital importance
to an understanding of his place in the political spectrum and of his
political outlook and affiliations as he moved further along the road
toward his first candidacy. It is the purpose of the following pages to
piece together the evidence for these questions, questions that Cicero
chose largely to ignore in his account in the *Brutus.* Fortunately, his
comments on the decade elsewhere are sufficiently numerous, are
spread widely enough over different stages of his career, and show sufficient consistency to allow reasonably confident conclusions to be
drawn concerning his political attitudes and sympathies during his
unusually lengthy apprenticeship.

2. *Cael.* 9 ff. On the importance of *iuvenes* in politics cf. T. N. Mitchell,
"Cicero, Pompey, and the Rise of the First Triumvirate" *Traditio* 29 (1973), 7 ff.
Plutarch (*Cicero* 3 and *Brut.* 307) provides indications that Cicero's dedication to
learning was not unconnected with politics.

Cicero and the Crisis of 88

A summary of events must precede discussion of Cicero's response to them. The tribunate of Drusus in 91 struck a damaging blow at the position and prestige of the ruling oligarchy. It had raised and then dashed the hopes of many and had sharpened the divisions within Roman politics, but, worst of all, it appeared or could be made to appear as the primary cause of the allied revolt which quickly followed the death of Drusus, beginning with the murder of a Roman commander and the Roman citizens of Asculum and spreading to threaten the very existence of Rome itself. Reaction was swift, and characteristic of widespread popular indignation and discontent. A special tribunal was established by a law of the tribune Varius early in 90 to try on a charge of *maiestas* those whose conduct could be argued to have helped or encouraged the Italians to resort to an armed conflict with Rome. The law, which bears similarity to the *Lex Mamilia* of 109, reflected popular wrath against the *nobilitas*, as is clearly attested by Asconius, and should not be presented as an equestrian scheme for vengeance or a move by a *factio* of *nobiles* around Philippus or Caepio to press home its attacks on the *factio* which had supported Drusus. The bill undoubtedly drew support from particular enemies of its political victims, but the *invidia* which underlay it was that of a *populus* traditionally unsympathetic to Italian claims, outraged by the resort to armed insurrection, and eager to strike at sympathizers of the rebels.[3] Cicero and Asconius both imply that the number of prosecutions was large and the convictions many. It is probable that the closest and youngest associates of Drusus suffered heavily.[4] None of the senate's *principes* is mentioned

3. Asconius 22, Clark. Val. Max. 8.6.4. Appian, *BC* 1.37. Cf. Badian, *Historia* 18 (1969), 447 ff. Gruen, *JRS* 55 (1965), 59 ff. R. Seager, "*Lex Varia de Maiestate" Historia* 16 (1967), 37–43. Fraccaro, *Opuscula*, 2.144. Gabba, *App. BC Lib. Prim.,* 124. T. Mommsen, *Römisches Strafrecht* (Leipzig 1899), 198. The traditional view of the Varian court as a *quaestio extraordinaria* whose sole purpose was to try those accused of encouraging the Italians to revolt has been convincingly defended by Badian. The objections to the thesis that it was a general *maiestas* law, superseding the *Lex Appuleia*, seem overwhelming.

4. *Brut.* 304 ff. Asconius 73–74, Clark. Those whose convictions are recorded include: C. Aurelius Cotta, a *sodalis* of Drusus (*Brut.* 303 ff. *N.D.* 3.80. *De Or.* 1.25; 3.11); L. Calpurnius Bestia, an adherent of Scaurus and probably son of the consul of 111 (Appian, *BC* 1.37; cf. G. Bloch, *Mélanges d'histoire ancienne* 25 [1909], 70–72); probably L. Memmius, a *consiliarius* of Drusus (Sisenna fr. 44. *Brut.* 304). Sulpicius probably escaped because he was a *legatus* in 90. *Brut.* 304.

among the convicted, however, and the oligarchy gradually recovered its ascendancy during 90, aided by the seriousness of the war and the atmosphere of crisis, conditions generally favorable to acceptance of the senate's leadership.

The oligarchy exploited these conditions with skill, and it managed not only by prudent compromise to contain the war and turn the tide in Rome's favor, but in the process to outmaneuver its domestic enemies and to achieve its long-standing goal of judicial reform. As the revolt spread quickly in 90 and the seriousness of the threat became apparent, the senate took advantage of the mood of concern to declare a *iustitium*, having first carefully aired the proposal at a series of *contiones* and having obviously obtained a favorable reaction. All legal activity, including the Varian trials, was suspended. The burgeoning popular resentment against the aristocracy had been arrested.[5]

In the same year a law of the consul L. Julius Caesar bestowed citizenship on all allied communities which had not revolted or which had stopped fighting. Though it was apparently accompanied by other measures designed to minimize the political effects of the concession, it did curtail and fragment the insurrection.[6] By 89 the senate felt

---

De Or. 3.11. Another younger politician who was very likely a victim of the Varian court was Cornelius Scipio Nasica, son-in-law of L. Licinius Crassus. *De Or.* 3.8. *Brut.* 211. Antonius and Scaurus were also accused, but both were apparently acquitted. *Tusc. Disp.* 2.57. Asconius 22, Clark. Val. Max. 3.7.8. *Vir. Ill.* 72.11. Cf. Gruen, *JRS* 55 (1965), 59 ff.

5. Asconius 73–74, Clark. Cicero (*Brut.* 304–05), relates that only one court was active in 90, the Varian, *ceteris propter bellum intermissis*, and he does not mention anywhere that the Varian court was suspended. The apparent conflict between Asconius and Cicero is not difficult to resolve, however. Cicero's statement that the courts were interrupted is a very different thing from saying they were formally suspended by a *iustitium*, and there is no reason to suppose that such a ban on public business was instituted at the beginning of the war and the Varian court then somehow established despite the ban. The evidence of Asconius that a *iustitium* was declared later in the war and that it suspended the Varian court can stand. Cicero's failure to mention suspension of the Varian court is not surprising in view of the many other omissions of important facts in the sketchy account in the *Brutus.*

6. The details of the citizenship bills of 90 and 89 are controversial. Cf. G. Niccolini, "Le leggi *de civitate Romana* durante la guerra sociale" *RAL* S.8.1 (1946), 110 ff. Brunt, *JRS* 55 (1965), 107. E. Gabba, "Le origini della guerra sociale e la vita politica romana dopo l'89 a.C." *Athenaeum* 32 (1954), 41 ff., 293 ff. A. N. Sherwin-White, *The Roman Citizenship* (Oxford 1939), 126–35. A. Biscardi, "La questione italica e la tribu sopprannumerarie" *PP* 6 (1951), 241–56.

secure enough to end the *iustitium* and to attempt passage of a judiciary bill which prescribed that jurymen were to be elected by the tribes without regard to status, each tribe selecting fifteen of its members for the panel. The bill's democratic flavor was an obvious play for popular support, which was simultaneously courted by the optimate praetor, A. Sempronius Asellio, who used his judicial powers for the benefit of debtors, an attempt not only to conciliate the public but to drive a wedge between it and the *equites*. The senate was using the same strategy as in 91, but its lures to the masses were more skillfully chosen in 89. The judiciary bill, introduced by the tribune Plautius, passed. Its significance was immediately evident. Varius found himself prosecuted and condemned by the very court he had himself established to exploit the public anger against the *nobilitas*. The oligarchy had neatly turned the tables.[7]

Matters continued to go smoothly for the aristocracy throughout 89. The war was virtually brought to an end, and without elevating to alarming preeminence any military figure unsympathetic to the senate. Marius had been kept out of the limelight, and, for whatever reason, had not participated at all in the military action of 89.[8] Pompeius Strabo, consular commander of a formidable army in Picenum, a new man of great ambition, impressive military ability, and ambiguous political loyalties, did achieve considerable distinction and was eager to capitalize on it, but his plans for power were forestalled when his bid for a second consulship was foiled, and the office was secured by two trusted *optimates*, Cornelius Sulla and Pompeius Rufus.[9]

7. Asconius 79, Clark. Cicero's remarks (*Brut.* 305) imply that Varius's trial took place early in 89, and it seems certain that he was convicted by a jury selected in accordance with the *Lex Plotia*. Cf. Badian, *Historia* 18 (1969), 465. G. Bloch and J. Carcopino, *Histoire romaine* 2 (Paris 1940), 400. H. Last, *CAH* 9 (Cambridge 1932), 196. Gruen (*JRS* 55 [1965], 68) takes a contrary position. On Asellio cf. T. Frank, *An Economic Survey of Ancient Rome* 1 (Baltimore 1959), 268. Badian, *Historia* 18 (1969), 475 ff. Gabba, *App. BC Lib. Prim.,* 159.

8. Plutarch, *Marius* 33. Marius's retirement from the war in 89 was probably involuntary. Traditional explanations of a voluntary withdrawal as a result of pique, sympathy for the Italians, or a desire to concentrate on securing an eastern command are inadequate when one considers his vigorous campaign in 90, his need to prove his military capabilities at an advanced age, and the fact that war with Mithridates cannot have seemed very likely early in 89. Cf. Carney, *A Biography of Marius*, 52. Passerini, *Athenaeum* 12 (1934), 358 ff.

9. Velleius 2.21 is the only source which reports that Pompeius Strabo sought a second consulship, but it seems a likely story. There is other evidence that

Sulla's early political affiliations continue to be debated, but his dispatch to Cilicia as praetor and subsequent commission in Cappadocia strongly indicate that, at least as early as 97, he had found favor with the leadership of the senate. Confirmation of continued friendship with the *boni* is provided by the senate's action c. 91, when, to Marius's indignation, it permitted the Numidian Bocchus to dedicate on the Capitol statues representing a famous Sullan coup—the surrender of Jugurtha. In 89 Sulla was favored once more by the senate when he was placed in command of the southern theater in the Social War, while both consuls operated in the north. His election to the consulship immediately afterwards and a marriage to Metella, the widow of Scaurus, brought him to the fore and marked him at the beginning of 88 as the principal leader and the brightest hope of the conservative *nobilitas.* [10]

Pompeius Rufus was also firmly allied to the traditionalists. As tribune in 99 he had declared his political allegiance when he sponsored with Porcius Cato a bill to recall Metellus Numidicus. His known connections in the nineties point to unbroken association with the *boni.* He was an intimate friend of Sulpicius Rufus before the latter's tribunate, and there is evidence also of friendly relations with Crassus. In 90 he was prosecuted before the Varian commission, but he successfully defended himself. The trial connects him with the backers of Drusus, who came from the ranks of the *boni*, and his acquittal links him particularly to the conservative *principes* of the senate, placing him in the company of Antonius and Scaurus, who had fared similarly before Varius's court, and suggesting that, like most of the leading conservatives, he had stopped short of supporting the citizenship bill and shared the reactionary outlook of the hard-line oligarchs rather

---

Strabo wanted power and that the senate wanted to keep it from him. It would appear that efforts were made to relieve him of his command in 88, efforts which he resisted. Val. Max. 9.7. ext. 2. Sulla, on gaining control of Rome, lost no time in making use of an unusual but incontestable method of abrogating his *imperium*, a *lex* whereby command of his army was bestowed on Pompeius Rufus. Strabo reacted by engineering Rufus's murder. Appian, *BC* 1.63. Livy, *Per.* 77. If Badian ("The Date of Pompey's First Triumph" *Hermes* 83 [1955], 110 ff.) is right in applying the fragment from Sallust (*Hist.* 2.21, Maur.) to Pompeius Strabo, this is further evidence of the latter's ambition and of the senate's determination to thwart it. Cf. E. Badian, "Servilius and Pompey's First Triumph" *Hermes* 89 (1961), 254 ff. On the question of a prosecution of Pompeius in this period cf. Badian, *Historia* 18 (1969), 470 ff.

10. Plutarch, *Sulla* 6; *Marius* 32. Livy, *Per.* 75. Appian, *BC* 1.50–52.

than the more liberal thinking of Drusus and his younger associates. Finally, by the time of his consulship he had become an *adfinis* of the new favorite of the *boni*—Sulla. His son had married Sulla's daughter, the second important marriage alliance in or around 89 cementing ties between the leading elements of the oligarchy.[11]

The *nobilitas* had won notable political successes in 89, and, as Sulla and Pompeius entered office in 88, strong oligarchic government seemed, to all appearances, to have been reinstated; there were few signs of the troubles immediately ahead, in which violence would escalate from the brawling of hirelings and extremist partisans that had marked earlier disturbances to full-scale civil war, shattering the traditional power structure and transforming forever the character of Roman politics.

Hindsight reveals, however, the many threats to stability latent in 88 and the tenuous basis of the revival of oligarchic ascendancy. A serious crisis had rallied the public behind tradtional leaders and protectors, but this was a temporary phenomenon and did not bring with it, nor was it utilized to achieve, any lasting solution to the most serious problems of the preceding decade. Hostility continued between the ruling class and the *ordo equester*, and the financiers who dominated that *ordo* remained a potent political force and a constant threat to smooth government even without formal political power. The Italian question was also far from settled. The determination of the *nobilitas* to curtail the political power of the new citizens by restricting them to certain tribes had created a new source of grievance and the likelihood of further conflict. New threats to stability and peace had also developed. The tradition of violence in Roman politics was stronger than ever in the wake of Drusus's forceful tactics, his subsequent murder, and another political killing in 89, when the praetor Asellio was assassinated for his concessions to debtors. In addition, Italy now held camps of professional soldiers, accustomed to fighting former comrades and more truly in the service of their generals than of the state, while the prospect of a new and major foreign war was sharpening tensions and rivalries within the ruling class itself.

11. *Am.* 2. *De Or.* 1.168. *Brut.* 304. Orosius 5.17.11. Livy, *Per.* 77. Appian, *BC* 1.56. Velleius 2.18.6. The date of the marriage alliance cannot be determined exactly, but Badian has pointed out that a son of the marriage who was tribune in 52 is unlikely to have been born much before 87 (*Lucius Sulla*, 13).

The internal history of 88 was shaped by the interaction of these various factors. It is complex and controversial, the difficulties increased by the failure of our sources to provide a clear chronology of events. The earlier part of the year was dominated by the activities of the tribune Sulpicius Rufus, a promising young optimate and a brilliant orator, disciple of Antonius and Crassus, prosecutor of Norbanus, close friend of Pompeius Rufus, Cotta, and Drusus, who in the course of his tribunate abandoned his former friends and political associates and by his violent methods unleashed in civil war the tensions and hostilities that had been building in Roman politics for decades.[12]

Sulpicius entered office as a friend of the *boni*, a fact attested by Cicero and Asconius and demonstrated by his early opposition to a popular move to recall political exiles who had not received a proper legal hearing.[13] The key to an understanding of his subsequent behavior, and of the motivations that underlay his methods and the dramatic switch in his political allegiance, lies in the first major controversy of his tribunate, his confrontation with C. Julius Caesar Strabo, who, in his desire to obtain command of an impending war with Mithridates, was illegally seeking the consulship without having been praetor. Sulpicius, in collaboration with a fellow tribune, Antistius, argued the case against acceptance of Caesar's *professio*. The tribunes had a good case and made it well, but apparently they failed to persuade their audience. Caesar continued to be a candidate and Sulpicius resorted to force to stop him, aided by Marius, who was also seeking the eastern command and was eager to eliminate a formidable rival. Neither Caesar nor Marius,

---

12. *De Or.* 1.25, 97; 2.88, 197; 3.11, 47. *Am.* 2. *Brut.* 203. *Off.* 2.49. Cf. F. Münzer, *RE* 7 (2), 843. Gruen, *JRS* 55 (1965), 72 ff. Badian, *Historia* 18 (1969), 481 ff. A. W. Lintott, "The Tribunate of P. Sulpicius Rufus" *CQ* 21 (1971), 442 ff. C. Meier, *Res Publica Amissa*, 216. G. Bloch and J. Carcopino, *Histoire romaine* 2, 392 ff. E. Valgiglio, *Silla e la crisi repubblicana* (Florence 1956), 7. L. Pareti, *Storia di Roma* 3 (Turin 1953), 556. Carney, *WS* 73 (1960), 109. Luce, *Historia* 19 (1970), 161. T. N. Mitchell, "The Volte-Face of P. Sulpicius Rufus in 88" *CP* 70 (1975), 197–204.

13. Asconius 64, Clark. *Har. Resp.* 43. *De Or.* 3.11. *Ad Herenn.* 2.45. *Am.* 2. The identity of the exiles in question remains in doubt, but it can be stated that, aside from certain followers of Saturninus, there are no *exules* in our records of the nineties who could have been the subject of the proposal which Sulpicius first opposed but later sponsored. Cf. Lintott, *CQ* 21 (1971), 453. Gruen, *JRS* 55 (1965), 72. Badian, *Historia* 18 (1969), 487.

however, obtained his objective; the command against Mithridates went to Sulla.[14]

Recent arguments have urged that the controversy concerned the consulship of 88 and should be dated to December 89, the first weeks of Sulpicius's tribunate.[15] But such a view must presuppose that the consular elections for 88 were postponed to the very last weeks of the preceding year, a contention unsupported by any ancient source and difficult to justify. Although Pompeius Strabo, sole consul after the death of his colleague, Porcius Cato, in the earlier part of 89, was engaged in military operations, notably the siege of Asculum, until late November, there is no reason to believe that he was unable to come to Rome to hold elections before that date. An unfinished war in Campania and the siege of Nola did not keep Sulla from departing relatively early to seek the consulship, and there is no evidence that Pompeius's military operations were so intensive or critical as to require his constant presence and necessitate postponement to so late a date of the consular elections, which were of vital importance, particularly in troubled times. Besides, it is wholly improbable that Pompeius, who was himself most likely angling for the consulship of 88 and who had no special regard for the *boni* and had connections with Marius, was the man who presided over the decision to accept the *petitio extraordinaria* of a staunch optimate. Further, if Marius had sought and lost the consulship of 88 to Sulla, a corollary of the view that places his confrontation with Caesar in 89, it would not have escaped mention in the memoirs of Sulla and of Marius's other enemies and would have been known to Plutarch.

It also seems unlikely that war with Mithridates was an accepted fact even by late 89 or that the senate had by that time decided to commit a consular expedition to Asia in 88. The political machinations of Mithridates in Asia in 90 and 89 were similar to his expansionist schemes earlier in the nineties and drew a similar response from the

14. *Phil.* 11.11. *Brut.* 227. *Har. Resp.* 43. Asconius 25, Clark. Quintilian 6.3.75. Diodorus 37.2.12. It seems certain that Caesar began his quest for the consulship with a request for exemption from the *Leges Annales,* and that the request was adjudicated and decided in Caesar's favor. It is also clear that it was Sulpicius, and not Caesar, who initiated the violence surrounding this episode. Cf. Mitchell, *CP* 70 (1975), 199–200.

15. Badian, *Foreign Clientelae,* 230; *Studies,* 51; *Historia* 18 (1969), 487. Luce, *Historia* 19 (1970), 190.

Roman senate. An embassy was dispatched in 89, headed by the *consularis* Manius Aquillius, to cooperate with the governor of Asia in restoring the pro-Roman kings to Bithynia and Cappadocia. Such embassies were a standard and generally successful tool of the senate's foreign diplomacy in the late Republic, and it is unlikely that any additional action against Mithridates was contemplated or expected to be necessary. It is certainly inconceivable that the senate, in view of its traditional aversion to major military involvements abroad, its continuing preoccupation with the Social War, and its failure to take any steps to strengthen its meager forces in Asia, planned, sought, or expected in 89 a full-scale war with the Pontic king. Nor can the inevitability of such a war have become evident at Rome before the spring of 88, when Mithridates repulsed an attack from Nicomedes, king of Bithynia, and, goaded by numerous provocations from Aquillius, swept through Asia Minor, slaughtering the Roman population.

Conferral of the Asian command on a consul of 88 does not invalidate this reasoning and mark 89 as the year of the senate's decision to make war on Mithridates, for the indications are that Asia was not allotted to Sulla until long after he had entered office and was not therefore one of the consular *provinciae* designated by the senate before the elections in the preceding year. Several of the ancient sources reveal that Sulla left home early in his consulship, not, however, to prepare for an expedition to the East, but to conduct military operations in Campania, particularly the siege of Nola.[16] It is therefore apparent that his original *provincia* for 88 was not Asia but once again the southern theater of the Social War, where fighting with the Samnites and Lucanians continued. In fact, Sulla's activities at the beginning of 88 substantiate the view that a major war with Mithridates was not yet envisaged at that date and confirm the conclusion that Caesar's bid for the consulship, which all agree was inspired by a desire to direct such a war, must be placed in 88, after the full dimensions of the Mithridatic crisis had unfolded. When war and a consular expedition did become certain and led to a rowdy contest for the consulship of 87, the senate, perhaps alarmed at the violence of Sulpicius and Marius and fearful that the latter might regain a position of leadership, or concerned

16. Diodorus 37.2.13. Plutarch, *Sulla* 7.2. Velleius 2.18.4. Appian (*BC* 1.55; *Mith.* 22) indicates that the allotment of Asia to Sulla only took place after news reached Rome of Mithridates' invasion of that province.

to confront Mithridates with a trusted general of proven ability as soon as possible, revised its allocation of consular provinces for 88, thus enabling Sulla to secure the eastern command.[17]

No more is heard of the candidacy of Caesar, but the political repercussions of the controversy he had stirred continued. The affair profoundly affected the political loyalties of Sulpicius, and, in consequence, subsequent events in 88. Its full impact on the tribune's political stance has sometimes been obscured by a tendency to ignore the personal and independent nature of his involvement and to view his behavior and the whole incident in terms of factional loyalties and maneuverings. But there is no justification for assuming that when Sulpicius first stood in opposition to Caesar's illegal candidacy he was acting in the interests of any group or individual, or had any motivation other than an objection on principle to opportunism and excessive ambition which sought to bypass laws specifically designed to curb the impatient reach for unusual distinction and influence. The objection was deeply rooted in the oligarchic mentality, which was inalterably opposed to individual preeminence, and ordinarily the *nobilitas* as a whole would have shared Sulpicius's concern, but on this occasion, anxious no doubt to pit a strong optimate candidate against Marius, the *principes civitatis* were willing to bend a principle and allow Caesar to stand. That decision, however, involved handing a political defeat to a proud aristocrat, and Sulpicius, stung by the fact that a body whose leadership contained his closest political associates and whose chairman was probably his intimate friend, Pompeius Rufus, refused to take his side and the side of the law, turned to demagoguery to vindicate his cause and his *dignitas.* [18]

Cicero explicitly states that the dispute with Caesar was the turning point in Sulpicius's career, analogous to the senate's refusal to ratify the Numantine treaty in the career of Tiberius Gracchus, to the killing of the latter in the career of his brother Gaius, and to the transfer of administration of the corn supply to Scaurus in the career of Saturninus.

17. There is no reason to believe that the senate was not entitled to reallocate consular provinces in emergencies after the consuls had been elected or had entered office. Cf. Badian, *Athenaeum* 34 (1956), 115 n. 4.

18. If, as seems most likely, Sulla was absent in Campania when the Caesar controversy first erupted, the task of presiding over adjudication of Caesar's request for exemption from the *Leges Annales* would have fallen to Pompeius. This would also help to explain why Sulpicius's anger at his former political associates was directed particularly at Pompeius. *Am.* 2. Cf. *De Or.* 3.11.

Sulpicius, who had similarly started out as an optimate, was similarly led by proud resentment at the behavior of the oligarchy into furious resistance to his former associates and to their methods of government.[19]

Worse was to follow, as Sulpicius's blend of idealism, pride, and obstinacy brought him into deeper conflict with the *boni* and moved him to more extreme behavior to overcome their opposition. Following in the footsteps of his friend Drusus, whose liberal attitude toward the allies he had probably fully supported, he introduced a measure to give full equality of political rights to the Italians and to another category of second-class citizens, the freedmen, by enrolling them in all the tribes. The proposal brought predictable opposition from the *boni* and from the Roman populace; Sulpicius resorted to force; the oligarchy countered with one of its more drastic obstructionist devices, the *iustitium.* But Sulpicius, his capacity for violent intimidation reinforced by an alliance with Marius, who commanded the support of the *equites,* refused to observe the ban on public business. In a resulting clash both consuls almost lost their lives; Sulla was forced to lift the *iustitium,* Sulpicius deposed Pompeius, passed his bill on the enrollment of citizens, and fulfilled his bargain with Marius by conferring on him the command against Mithridates.[20] Sulla managed, however, to get to the army in Campania and persuaded it to march on Rome. He quickly overcame the feeble resistance of Marius and Sulpicius, had them and their leading supporters declared *hostes,* and had the legislation of Sulpicius annulled. After restoring order he sent the army back to Campania.

The political quarrels of 88 had resurrected once again a power struggle

19. *Har. Resp.* 41–44. The key sentence is: "Sulpicium ab optima causa profectum Gaioque Julio consulatum contra leges petenti resistentem longius quam voluit popularis aura provexit." The present participle *resistentem* indicates that it was in the course of his resistance to Caesar that the *popularis aura,* here clearly meaning demagoguery aimed against the senate, took hold of Sulpicius. This was the incident that turned him, in high-spirited anger at the course of events *(animi virilis dolor),* from the *optima causa* in whose service he had begun his political career and tribunate. Cf. Lintott, *CQ* 21 (1971), 453 ff. For a different interpretation of this passage cf. Badian, *Historia* 18 (1969), 481.

20. Sources in Broughton, *MRR,* 2.41. The exact point at which Sulpicius made his compact with Marius is difficult to determine, but that he resorted to such drastic trafficking before the need for it became apparent seems unlikely. Cf. Badian, *Foreign Clientelae,* 232.

of fundamental importance, pitting the ruling oligarchy against an able and unruly tribune intent on ignoring constitutional checks on his power, on bypassing the policy-making prerogatives of the senate, and on enacting in its despite, by a coalition of extra-senatorial elements and a measure of forceful intimidation, significant political change. Sulla's drastic recourse to military action had summarily ended this challenge to oligarchic control, but it had added a frightening new dimension to violence in politics and had pointed the way to a new weaponry which could be used as readily to attack as to defend the status quo. The fundamental issues involved in the momentous civil upheavals of this initial stage of Cicero's public life give his statements on the strife and on the protagonists, Sulpicius and Sulla, particular value as an indicator of his early political leanings and basic political tenets.

His comments on Sulpicius and his statesmanship are extensive and represent the testimony of an expert witness. He knew Sulpicius personally; since the latter was a friend and follower of Crassus and a friend and *adfinis* of Atticus they moved in the same circles. But Cicero was also drawn to Sulpicius by the fact that he was an exciting and highly acclaimed orator and a stylish political performer believed to be headed for great political success. Cicero was an eager observer of such men at the beginning of the eighties, and he regularly attended the daily *contiones* of Sulpicius in 88.[21]

His reaction to the tribune's political course in that year is unequivocal. He greatly admired his ability, but he saw it as a misdirected talent seeking to charm the wise into error and the right-minded into wrong thinking. He pondered Sulpicius's volte-face in breaking with the *boni* and resorting to demagogic methods, and found insufficient justification for it; he had allowed himself to be led by private hate and prideful resentment into reckless and seditious behavior to the great detriment of the state. He repeatedly classes him with the Gracchi and Saturninus; the political sins of these four tribunes were essentially the same, as were the resultant dangers to the state, and consisted not so much in the substance of their programs, about which Cicero says little, as in the fact that they defected from the cause and policies of the senate

21. *Brut.* 205, 306. *De Or.* 1.25, 97. Nepos, *Att.* 2.

and by seditious attacks on the authority and *dignitas* of its leaders, the *boni*, threatened the *status reipublicae.* [22]

Cicero viewed the forceful elimination of the Gracchi and Saturninus as actions of the highest patriotism, heroized those responsible, and defended the extreme and extralegal methods to which they had resorted. His references to the death of Sulpicius leave no doubt that he similarly approved and considered necessary and justifiable the drastic and unprecedented measures which led to that tribune's forceful suppression and murder. He describes his killing as the penalty of rashness; he had compelled the *respublica* to use the sword against him. When he lists the orators who died in 88 and 87, he remarks that Catulus, Antonius, and Caesar Strabo were cruelly killed, but the note of sympathy is pointedly absent in his reference to Sulpicius, whose death he simply reports by the noncommittal *occiderat.* [23]

Consistent with these sentiments is the fact that, though Cicero was an outspoken critic of many aspects of Sulla's political behavior in the eighties, he never explicitly disapproves the latter's first march on Rome, apart from some pious denunciations in the *Philippics* of all who had ever brought civil war, delivered while he was himself in the process of diligently promoting one. Elsewhere Sulla's resort to arms is presented as an act of the *respublica*, a tendentious formula also used to describe the violence initiated by Scipio Nasica in 133. [24]

Cicero's only objection to Sulla's conduct in 88 was the latter's failure to minimize the civil strife and its wounds: Sulla gave vent to private indignation, drove out whom he wished, killed whom he could. Cicero particularly disapproved the outlawry of Marius. Not all of his reasons were based on legal and political considerations, as already noted, but there can be no doubt that he had objections on such grounds to Sulla's high-handed insistence on vengeance and on summary annihilation of leading citizens and high-ranking magistrates. [25] Such action was unprecedented, smacked of tyranny, and went far beyond the bounds of prudence and the needs of the *respublica.* The backers and

22. *Leg.* 3.20. *Har. Resp.* 41, 43–44. *Am.* 2. *De Or.* 3.11. *Vat.* 23. Asconius 80, Clark.

23. *Brut.* 307. *De Or.* 3.11. *Leg.* 3.20–21. *Cat.* 1.3, 29; 4.4, 13. *Dom.* 82, 91, 102. *Har. Resp.* 41–43. *Mil.* 8–14, 72. *De Or.* 1.38. *Brut.* 103–04, 212. *Tusc.* 4.51. *Am.* 37. *Off.* 1.76, 109; 2.43. *Rab.* passim.

24. *Phil.* 13.1. *Brut.* 103. *Leg.* 3.21.

25. *Phil.* 14.23. *Cat.* 3.24. Cf. pp. 48 ff., above.

beneficiaries of Sulpicius's activities were in a different category from the tribune who had instigated the violence and divided the state. Even the backers of Tiberius Gracchus had received a form of trial. Besides, many of Sulpicius's supporters were figures of note and influence. A Marius or a Brutus could not be summarily dismissed as a *seditiosus* or an *improbus* and arbitrarily marked for destruction without the most serious risk of further division and a popular reaction against the senate.

But Cicero's criticism of Sulla's arrogant and vengeful use of victory and of his unnecessary and imprudent drive to purge all his political foes implies no disapproval of the drastic measures taken to end Sulpicius's tribunate, nor should it be equated with high concern for the rule of law or the rights of citizens. Cicero was no legalist in matters pertaining to the survival of traditional republicanism; he viewed unrestricted force as a necessary and legitimate tool of government in dealing with violent dissenters, and he urged its use when the welfare of the state dictated it. He argued that violence legitimized a violent response and that, in such circumstances, the laws fell silent so as not to endanger by their restrictions the law-abiding. Throughout most of his public life he preached a doctrine of *summa severitas* against *seditiosi*, to be administered summarily by senate and magistrates. He vigorously defended the *senatus consultum ultimum* as a constitutional weapon for the implementation of such a doctrine, and he did so before his personal interests dictated such a stand. He also defended and advocated a more dangerous and extreme expedient—extralegal action in the interests of the *respublica* by individual magistrates and, under extreme conditions, by leading private citizens, when time or circumstances made procurement of senatorial authorization impractical or impossible.

Cicero's policy toward those who threatened the status quo was directed by the belief that the survival of his brand of republicanism represented the highest law and that violent dissidents who sought to destroy it forfeited their rights as citizens and should be viewed and treated as *hostes*. These beliefs are most clearly illustrated in the correspondence of 44 and 43, in which he exults over the murder of Caesar, laments that Antony was left alive, extols Dolabella's arbitrary killing of large numbers of citizens and slaves demonstrating their grief at Caesar's death, organizes armed resistance to a consul, urges individual holders of *imperium* to act without waiting for senatorial direction,

and castigates Brutus for leniency and for being concerned in a dangerous emergency about the rights of citizens and the constitutional powers
of senate and people.[26]

His readiness to violate public law in the fight against the Antonii was
not an uncharacteristic ruthlessness born of hate and failure, as is sometimes alleged, but was totally consistent with every major pronouncement of his public life on the rights and duties of the *principes civitatis*
in dealing with those who threatened by force and civil discord the
peaceful operation of the traditional mode of government.[27] He did
display a contrasting attitude toward powerful enemies of the senate,
particularly in the fifties and, it should be noted, throughout most of
44, while Antony's position was unchallengeable, but his doctrine of
compromise and coexistence in these situations was not a contradiction
of the hard-line stand on *seditiosi* discussed above. Both positions were
founded on a single concern, both were products of the same practical
determination to preserve the *vetus respublica* by whatever means
necessary. His policy of appeasement applied only to that category of
internal crisis in which the *potentia* of the opposition and the dimensions of the dispute made the risks of violence unacceptable. In such
cases Cicero was as willing to relax the law in accommodating his adversaries as he was willing to overstep it in suppressing them where such a
course seemed feasible and expedient.[28]

His remarks on the death of Sulpicius and on the events surrounding
it fit the pattern of his thinking in all the internal crises of his career
and leave little reason to doubt that, whatever his misgivings about
Sulla's cruelty in victory, he approved his drastic resort to military
force to free the state from the domination of a turbulent tribune.
There is also little reason to doubt that these remarks, though they
are later than the events to which they allude, accurately reflect his

26. *Leg.* 3.8. *Mil.* 8, 11. *Rab.* 1–5, 20–28. *Dom.* 91. *Sest.* 86. *Cat.* 1.2–4, 28–29;
2.3; 4.10, 12–13. *Tusc.* 4.51. *Phil.* 1.5; 11.28. *Att.* 14.15.1; 14.17a.1, 7. *Fam.*
10.16.2; 11.7.2; 12.7.2; 12.28.1. *Ad Brut.* 1.2.5; 1.3.3; 1.4.2; 1.15.3, 10–11;
2.5.5. Cf. H. Siber, *"Provocatio" ZSS* (1942), 376–91.

27. Cf. the manifesto on the rights and duties of *principes* in *Sest.* 99–140 and
Leg. 3.8.

28. *Att.* 2.9.1; 2.21.1–2. *Balb.* 60–61. *Planc.* 91–94. *Fam.* 1.9.21. He also
believed that Caesar should have been accommodated in 49. *Att.* 7.15.3; 7.18.2;
8.8.1; 8.11d.6; 9.4.2; 9.10.3. *Fam.* 4.1.1; 5.21.2; 6.6.4; 7.3.5; 15.15.1; 16.11.2;
16.12.2. *Phil.* 2.23–24.

reaction and sympathies at the time when these events took place. They are not confined to a single period of his career, nor to circumstances which called for the bias they exhibit, but come from different periods and varied contexts, show complete self-consistency, and are in full accord with one of the most deeply rooted and loudly proclaimed dogmas of Cicero's political creed. They are also in accord with the conservative aristocratic traditions to which he was so consistently exposed in his childhood and in the nineties, reflecting the oligarchic mentality, the arbitrariness and repressive instinct of those who believe in the inherent right of a preeminent few to rule the state and to make the crucial decisions regarding its safety and welfare. Finally, they would seem to be in accord with the sentiments of the conservative *nobilitas* in 88, to which Cicero was still firmly linked in that period as a protégé of the Mucii Scaevolae.

To the historian looking back, Sulla's march on Rome appears as a disastrous precedent, the end of all hope for the survival of the traditional order. In his action two major threats to peaceful constitutional government of independent but more or less parallel development— the proletarian client army, a legacy of the military reforms of Marius, and the habit of violence in political disputes, increasingly in evidence since 133—merged to insure that from that point onwards force would be the real determinant of the course of political events. In consequence, the evils of military intervention in Roman politics are traced to Sulla, and he tends to emerge as the prototype of the power-hungry general, using a loyal army to ride roughshod over the law and the constitution in a drive for personal ascendancy.

But hindsight has often blurred a picture by allowing the nature and significance of an act to be obscured or distorted by its consequences. There was a great deal more at stake in the governmental crisis of 88 than Sulla's claims and aspirations, and, while his ruthlessness and the keenness of his ambition need not be denied, his march on Rome cannot be presented as a mere expression of them, with the corollary judgment that his action dismayed and alienated the oligarchy. Such a view runs counter to most of the available evidence and ignores the seriousness of Sulpicius's challenge to senatorial control, the often demonstrated readiness of the senate in the face of such challenges to condone and authorize the most extreme, primitive, and despotic methods to defend its supremacy, the immediate political benefits which Sulla's action bestowed on its position, and the lengths to which it was later willing to go to retain these benefits.

Cicero reveals the bitterness and antagonism with which the *boni* as a whole, including such figures as Scaevola the Augur, viewed the activities of Sulpicius in his tribunate. They were astounded and outraged at his desertion of the optimate cause. They saw him as a traitor to his friends and to his heritage, and as a *seditiosus* of the stamp of the Gracchi and Saturninus.[29] Specific allusions to the role and thinking of the *boni* in the events leading to the forceful termination of his tribunate are more difficult to find. Cicero has no direct comment on their reaction, and in the accounts of the ancient historians the towering figures of Sulla and Marius and their rivalry and ambitions dominate the picture, overshadowing the wider issues and interests involved and obscuring even the fact that Sulpicius's original goals and the roots of the political turmoil they generated initially bore no relation whatever to the ambitions of these two generals.[30]

But one significant fact does emerge. Sulla's resort to the army was immediately and wholeheartedly supported by his colleague, Pompeius Rufus, a confirmed optimate and, despite personal injury in the conflict with Sulpicius, an unlikely adherent of a revolutionary maneuver abhorrent to the conservative *nobilitas.* The march on Rome became therefore a joint action of two consuls who were both committed partisans of the oligarchy and whose action was directed against a man whom, on Cicero's testimony, that oligarchy viewed not only as a dangerous opponent but as a hated renegade. A strong presumption of aristocratic support for the consuls is created by these facts and would seem to be confirmed by an important passage in Asconius, which states that, since Sulpicius's pernicious undertakings precipitated Rome's first civil war, his forceful suppression by the arms of the consuls was seen as a legitimate act.[31]

Evidence of antagonism or disaffection provoked by Sulla's resort to military force is confined to a single statement in Appian that the

29. *Am.* 2. *De Or.* 3.11. Asconius 80, Clark.

30. The biographer Plutarch naturally concentrates on the figures whose lives he is recording. Appian (*BC* 1.55) makes Marius the central figure in the events of 88 and presents Sulpicius's program as a Marian scheme to secure the eastern command and to increase Marius's power with the voters by distributing the Italians over the thirty-five tribes.

31. Appian, *BC* 1.57. Asconius 64, Clark. Note the tense of *visus est.* Asconius

ἄρχοντες of the army in Campania, with the exception of one quaestor, deserted him, refusing to participate in a military action against their country. The significance of this statement, which is not recorded in any other source, is hard to decide because of the vagueness of the term ἄρχοντες and the difficulty of determining with certainty the precise rank and social status of the individuals to whom it refers. Since the ἄρχοντες are mentioned in this passage in close conjunction with a quaestor, the word would seem to denote officials of a similar level, and a common translation is "senior officers," and a common inference is that these officers belonged to the *nobilitas* and that their action reflected fundamental aristocratic objections to Sulla's radical maneuver in leading an army against Rome.[32]

But a later use of ἄρχοντες by Appian in a similar context, when he describes Cinna's plea for support in 87 to the officers and men of part of this same army, reveals a different significance for the term. He relates that Cinna attempted to win over both the ἄρχοντες and the men of senatorial rank who were present, and that the former responded favorably and were instrumental in getting the rank and file to swear allegiance to the deposed consul. Here the term, which in the earlier passage seemed to signify high-level officers of senatorial rank, clearly denotes junior officers below the rank of senator, since the men to whom it refers are carefully distinguished from members of the senatorial class. Whatever the explanation of this apparent discrepancy, it is obvious that Appian's use of terminology in these statements is careless and imprecise, a fact which greatly impairs the value of his testimony and renders tentative any conclusion based solely upon it.[33]

But even if Appian's statement on the men who deserted Sulla indisputably identified them as the highest ranking officers, this would not justify equating their attitudes and reactions with those of the ruling

---

is reporting not his own opinion, but how Sulpicius's suppression was viewed at the time it took place. Cf. *Har. Resp.* 43, which Asconius echoes in his description of Sulpicius's progression *ab initiis bonarum actionum ad perditas.* Cf. Meier, *Res Publica Amissa,* 224.

32. Appian, *BC* 1.57. Cf. Plutarch, *Sulla* 9.2. Cf. Badian, *Studies,* 216. Gabba, *App. BC Lib. Prim.,* 166; "Ricerche sull' esercito professionale romano da Mario ad Augusto" *Athenaeum* 29 (1951), 188, 206.

33. Appian, *BC* 1.65. Velleius 2.20 supports the idea that the ἄρχοντες of this passage of Appian were tribunes and centurions. The commander of the army, Appius Claudius, did not follow Cinna. Livy, *Per.* 79. *Dom.* 83.

oligarchy. Prior to the eruption of the Mithridatic crisis, which did not occur before the spring of 88, the commission of the Campanian legions promised little in the way of fame or fortune and is unlikely to have attracted many leading *nobiles.* The one figure of distinguished lineage who can confidently be associated with the Campanian operation in 88, L. Licinius Lucullus, a member of one of Rome's most influential optimate families, the Metelli, significantly sided with Sulla.[34] It is hardly reasonable to conclude that the opposite reaction of nameless officers, whose social distinction must remain highly questionable, was more nearly representative of the thinking of Rome's conservative aristocracy.

All other signs of aristocratic disenchantment with Sulla's behavior in 88 concern not his march on Rome, but his vengeful high-handedness in dealing with his defeated foes, particularly Marius.[35] Plutarch indicates that the senate as a whole was privately distressed by Sulla's impolitic treatment of the general, and Valerius Maximus reports that Scaevola the Augur openly opposed Sulla's demand that the senate declare Marius a *hostis.* These indications of disapproval echo criticisms of Cicero, whose testimony leaves no doubt that Sulla displayed an extremism and an insolence in the aftermath of victory that offended many of the *boni.* But Cicero's overall comments on 88 also reveal, as already indicated, the limited nature of this displeasure with Sulla's conduct. It implies no repudiation of Sulla's resort to an army to quell Sulpicius, indicates no basic conflict of interest or policy between Sulla and the senate, and it must not be allowed to obscure the senate's stake in the elimination of Sulpicius and the extent to which Sulla's victory was the victory of the oligarchy.[36]

34. It is worth noting that there is a pronounced tendency in Appian to present, with the wisdom of hindsight, Sulla's march on Rome as a radical and ruinous expedient, the first of a series of lamentable military interventions in politics. Cf. *BC* 1.58,60; 5.17. The motivation he attributes to the ἄρχοντες who deserted Sulla, namely that they would not lead an army against their country, is in line with this prejudice, and its veracity is suspect.

35. Appian (*BC* 1.57) and Plutarch (*Sulla* 9.2) mention embassies to Sulla urging him to desist. The indications are, however, that these embassies did not represent a genuine senatorial effort to stop Sulla. Plutarch explicitly indicates that the senate acted under compulsion from Marius and Sulpicius, and Appian, though anxious to emphasize the extremism of Sulla, also acknowledges that at least some of the embassies were dispatched by Marius and Sulpicius in an effort to buy time. Cf. Badian, *Foreign Clientelae,* 235. Gabba, *App. BC Lib. Prim.,* 167. Passerini, *Athenaeum* 12 (1934), 369 ff.

36. Plutarch, *Sulla* 10. Val. Max. 3.8.5. Cf. pp. 65 ff. and R. A. Bauman, "The *Hostis* Declarations of 88 and 87 B.C." *Athenaeum* 52 (1974), 270–93.

Sulpicius had put together a formidable alliance in 88 which included not only Marius but also the *equites*, whose relations with the senate had gone steadily downhill since 100 and who for the first time were willing to stand against the establishment in support of the extreme and dangerously disruptive course of a violent tribune.[37] Against this coalition obstructive devices proved useless; a single violent clash demonstrated the superiority of Sulpicius's forces; both consuls almost lost their lives, were publicly humiliated and rendered helpless, and Pompeius was actually deposed. In the words of Asconius, Sulpicius had violently taken possession of the state.[38]

These were the circumstances under which Sulla, declaring that he was acting to liberate the state from those who were tyrannizing it— the standard aristocratic *apologia* for supralegal governmental action against unruly dissenters—resorted to the legions, and, in view of the proven superiority of Sulpicius's forces in the city, it is unlikely that his action outraged or dismayed a hard-pressed oligarchy which had many times before displayed a ruthless extremism in defense of its interests.[39]

On previous occasions, when faced with rebellious politicians who refused to be restrained by constitutional curbs on their power and who leaned toward violence, the senate had not hesitated to cause armed forces to be assembled in Rome to reestablish its control and eliminate its unruly challengers. By its action in 133, and by its usurpation of special emergency powers through the *senatus consultum ultimum* and free exercise of them in 121 and 100, it had consecrated the use of massive and unrestricted force as a legitimate and patriotic response to the activities of intractable *seditiosi* well before 88.

Sulla's coup de main was not different in kind from expedients previously conceived and sanctioned by the senate and executed by earlier consuls in far less extreme conditions of civil disorder. The dimensions

37. On equestrian support for Sulpicius cf. Plutarch, *Sulla* 8; *Marius* 35. The *equites* had shied away from revolutionary violence in the past. They had deserted both Gaius Gracchus and Saturninus at the end. Plutarch, *Gaius Gracchus* 14.4. *Rab.* 20. A handful of aristocratic names also appears among Sulpicius's supporters. Appian, *BC* 1.60. *Brut.* 168.

38. Appian, *BC* 1.55–56. Plutarch, *Sulla* 8; *Marius* 35. Velleius 2.18. Livy, *Per.* 77. Asconius 64, Clark.

39. Appian, *BC* 1.57. Cf. Plutarch, *Gaius Gracchus* 14.3. Cf. C. Wirszubski, *Libertas as a Political Idea at Rome* (Cambridge 1960), 100 ff.

of the violence and the division which it set in motion were greater than
in earlier domestic conflicts, but that was a measure of the strength of
the coalition Sulpicius had succeeded in forming against the senate.
Regular legions were used in place of militiamen assembled for the
occasion; but there was no manpower in Rome available to the state
in 88 capable of resisting Sulpicius and his allies, and the resort to a
regular army under these conditions was an extension, but not a contra-
vention, of the senate's doctrine, embodied in the *consultum ultimum*,
that in extreme emergencies armed forces could be formally organized
by the government and used within the city for the summary elimination of citizens threatening the *respublica*. [40]

No *consultum ultimum* backed the action of the consuls in 88, but
the senate's failure to resort to this *perfugium et praesidium salutis* in
the near anarchy of that year was surely due only to the fact that no
opportunity can have existed for the passage of such a decree after
Sulpicius's triumph in forcing an end to the *iustitium* had placed him
in firm control of political affairs in the city. The senate's inaction
following this victory of Sulpicius's forces reflects its helplessness, not
a reluctance to invoke the use of supralegal force against the tribune,
and its response to Sulla's employment of such force was hardly governed by the absence of a decree that it undoubtedly would have
passed had it been given the opportunity to do so.

Serious legal questions were, of course, raised by Sulla's lack of senatorial authorization and also by the unprecedented nature of his
action not only in leading an army on Rome but an army of whose
command he had been deprived by popular decree. But the legal ramifications of his behavior are largely irrelevant to a consideration of the
oligarchy's reaction to it. In violent civil strife, which presupposes a
serious breakdown of orderly government and legal procedures, the
boundaries of the legal and the right are notoriously difficult to define
and are inevitably seen differently by the different sides. Besides, the
Roman *nobilitas* was particularly adept at molding and interpreting the

40. Cf. Sallust, *Catiline* 29.2–3. G. Plaumann, "Das sogennante *senatus consultum ultimum*" *Klio* 13 (1913), 321–86. A. W. Lintott, *Violence in Republican
Rome* (Oxford 1968), 149 ff. T. N. Mitchell, "Cicero and the *Senatus Consultum
Ultimum*" *Historia* 20 (1971), 47–61. B. R. Katz, "The First Fruits of Sulla's
March" *AC* 44 (1975), 100–25. In 52 B.C. the senate authorized Pompey to do
precisely what Sulla had done in 88, namely to lead professional troops into the
city of Rome to suppress seditious citizens. Sources in Broughton, *MRR*, 2.234.

law in its own interests, and the record of its behavior in the various internal conflicts of the late Republic provides no grounds for supposing that its attitude toward Sulla was significantly affected by high-principled dedication to the rule of law.[41]

Nor is it justifiable to construct hypothetical oligarchic objections on grounds that Sulla's action was a dynastic move for personal power and an alarming illustration of a proletarian client army being used to further the private ambitions of its commander.[42] Sulla was undoubtedly serving his own interests in forcefully toppling Sulpicius and his laws, but he was also serving the interests of the oligarchy as a whole, and in important ways. His victory not only relieved the senate of the domination of Sulpicius and the prospect of a revival of the ascendancy of Marius, but also made possible the cancellation of the Sulpician laws, whose offensiveness to the oligarchy was dramatically illustrated in 87 when the consul Cinna was forcibly ejected from the city by his conservative colleague and deprived of his office by the senate for his efforts to resurrect the Sulpician program.

Besides, in marching on Rome Sulla was seeking no new powers which the senate had not already gladly bestowed upon him, nor did he use his victory to fortify his personal position. The army was sent back to Campania as soon as the suppression of the Sulpician movement was accomplished. Its occupation of Rome resulted in no extraordinary power for Sulla and in no diminution of the freedom, prerogatives, and privileges of the aristocracy, and all subsequent actions of Sulla in 88 were designed to entrench the senate's supremacy, not his own.[43]

As for the dangers of the precedent established by Sulla's use of the legions in a civil dispute and the ominous implications of their response to his appeal, there is no evidence that the oligarchy was greatly disturbed by either. The story of the civil conflicts of the late Republic

41. The legal maneuvering in 44 and 43 and the disregard by the senate of the plebiscite which had bestowed the Gallic provinces on Antony illustrate the willingness of the conservative *nobilitas*, when threatened, to ignore, violate, or manipulate the law as its interests dictated.

42. Cf. Badian, *Lucius Sulla*, 16. Gruen, *Roman Politics*, 228.

43. Sulla's legislation in 88 is hard to disentangle from his later enactments, but no facet of any of his legislative programs threatened oligarchic interests, though admittedly his concern was not simply to protect those interests. Cf. E. Gabba, "Il ceto equestre e il Senato di Silla" *Athenaeum* 34 (1956), 124 ff.; "Review of Valgiglio, *Silla e la crisi repubblicana*" *Athenaeum* 35 (1957), 138–41.

reveals many imprudent and unprecedented remedies sanctioned by the oligarchy for short-term gain without consideration of the long-range risks.[44] Besides, the extent of the aristocracy's appreciation of the nature and gravity of the military threat, inherent in the gradual emergence of a predominantly proletarian army and first exemplified in Sulla's hold on the loyalty of the Campanian legions, is questionable. It was far from self-evident that a preponderance of poorer citizens in the armed forces would seriously undermine the loyalty of Rome's armies to the state and render them liable to easy manipulation by popular commanders, nor can the Sullan experience in the peculiar circumstances of 88 have been sufficient to reveal the true nature and dimensions of so complex a problem.

Half a century later the roots of the military danger had revealed themselves, and they became a subject of frequent analysis in the writings of historians; but it is not possible to demonstrate a similar awareness among Sulla's contemporaries, and it is anachronistic to attribute to them an insight derived from the succession of military interventions, or the threat of them, which dominated the post-Sullan history of the Republic.[45] At no time during that period was any effort made to attack the military problem at its source by changing the recruiting practices and reducing the dependence of the soldiers on their commanders. Even Sulla's reforms reveal an imperfect understanding of the most fundamental aspects of the military threat; he attempted to keep military leaders loyal and subordinate to the senate, but he made no alterations in the basic military system and, in consequence, essentially changed nothing.[46]

In brief, Sulla's march on Rome was not viewed by the oligarchy as a revolutionary and dynastic action which threatened the very foundations of the *respublica*, but as a necessary and defensible counterstroke

44. The crises of 133, 52, 50, and 43 provide many examples. Cf. a statement of Cicero (*Man.* 60): "Non dicam hoc loco maiores nostros semper in pace consuetudini, in bello utilitati paruisse, semper ad novos casus temporum novorum consiliorum rationes accommodasse."

45. Sallust, *Jug.* 86.2. Appian, *BC* 5.17. Plutarch, *Sulla* 12.8–9.

46. Cf. Gabba, "Le origini dell' esercito professionale in Roma" *Athenaeum* 27 (1949), 173–209; *Athenaeum* 29 (1951), 171 ff. P. A. Brunt, *Italian Manpower 225 B.C.-a.d. 14* (Oxford 1971). J. Harmand, *L'armée et le soldat à Rome de 107 à 50 avant notre ère* (Paris 1967). R. E. Smith, *Service in the Post-Marian Army* (Manchester 1958).

against such a threat arising from the lawless and seditious behavior of a recalcitrant tribune. The interests of the *boni*, as they saw them, were being seriously jeopardized by Sulpicius, and they accepted and approved the violence necessary to suppress their enemy, just as they had accepted and approved earlier unprecedented acts of force by government officials against the dissenters and reformers.

Their sentiments were fully shared by Cicero. In this the first confrontation between traditionalists and reformers following his entry into the forum, he shows the impact of his conservative heritage and connections on his political reactions. There is no indication in any of his comments that either his admiration for Sulpicius's oratorical and political skills, or their mutual connection with Crassus, or any goodwill which Cicero may have felt toward Marius lured him into any degree of sympathy for Sulpicius's position, or that any youthful idealism was stirred by the equity of the proposal to grant full political equality to the Italians. Cicero's statements reflect only a basic commitment to the traditions and institutions of the *vetus respublica*, and a ruthless hostility toward those who, for whatever reason, sought to defy or overthrow them.

Cicero and Cinna

Early in 87 Sulla left Italy for Epirus to take command of the war against Mithridates. Even before his departure there were signs that his forceful suppression of the Sulpician movement and his constitutional enactments designed to curb future opponents of the senate had neither silenced political dissent nor disarmed the dissenters. Friends of Sulla fared badly at the elections for 87; his colleague and supporter Pompeius Rufus, who had been given command of the army of Pompeius Strabo, was murdered by the soldiers with the suspected connivance of Strabo; Sulla himself faced mounting and overt hostility from influential friends of those he had exiled, and, after he left the city to join his army, he was actually summoned to stand trial by a tribune, Vergilius, whose action was allegedly instigated by the consul Cinna and whose charges were presumably connected with the murder of Sulpicius and the outlawry of his chief backers. The tribunician indictment was an unprecedented legal procedure against a holder of *imperium* and of dubious legal force, and it was most likely conceived primarily as a propagandist weapon with which to publicize the government's despotic handling of the crisis of 88. Sulla naturally declined to provide his enemies with a forum for further airing of charges of tyranny and violation of citizens' rights by obeying the summons, and he proceeded on his way to a more critical confrontation with the forces of Mithridates.[47]

There quickly followed an all-out attack on the settlement of his consulship. Cinna, backed by the friends of the exiles and by Italian leaders, proposed anew Sulpicius's bill to distribute the new citizens throughout the thirty-five tribes. The sequel repeated the pattern of earlier legislative controversies. An attempt was made to obstruct passage of the measure, this time by tribunician veto. Cinna attempted to override the veto by force. A major battle ensued in which the conservative forces, led by the consul Octavius, proved superior. Cinna was forced to flee from Rome with six tribunes who had supported him, and he was immediately deprived of his office by senatorial decree.

The Italians, however, were willing to continue the fight, and Cinna quickly mobilized a large army, including the legion which Sulla had left behind to continue the siege of Nola. He was joined by Marius, who, on learning of the new situation, had returned to Italy and raised a force in Etruria. Together they marched on Rome and, after some hard fighting, gained control of the city.[48]

47. Appian, *BC* 1.64. Plutarch, *Sulla* 9.4. *Brut.* 179. Cicero calls Sulla *imperator*, meaning he had already left the city and assumed his proconsular *imperium*. This is the first recorded instance of a tribunician indictment of a promagistrate. It is uncertain whether Sulla had immunity under the *Lex Memmia* (Val. Max. 3.7.9). Weinrib ("The Prosecution of Roman Magistrates" *Phoenix* 22 [1968], 32-56) argues that the law did not apply to *iudicia populi*, but there is no hard evidence to prove this, and an indication that it did apply, or at least that its application was not ruled out by the terms of the law, is the failure of the tribune Antistius to prosecute Caesar in 58 after he was *paludatus* (Suetonius, *Julius* 23.11). But even if Sulla did not have immunity under the *Lex Memmia*, he was not legally bound to answer a tribunician summons delivered after he left Rome, since tribunician jurisdiction did not extend beyond the city. Cf. Weinrib, *Phoenix* 22 (1968), 40-41. When Appius Claudius, commander of the legion left behind by Sulla, was similarly indicted by a tribune in 87, he similarly refused to appear, an action which, on Cicero's testimony, did not make him an outlaw in the eyes of the sane. *Dom.* 83. Cf. Badian, *Studies*, 224. J.P.V.D. Balsdon, "Review of Badian, *Studies in Greek and Roman History*" *JRS* 55 (1965), 231.

48. Appian, *BC* 1.64. Velleius 2.20. Livy, *Per.* 79. *Phil.* 8.7. *Sest.* 77. *Cat.* 3.24. Florus 2.9.9. *Vir. Ill.* 69. Plutarch, *Sertorius* 4-5. It would seem that a bill to recall Marius and the other exiles was to follow the franchise law.

There resulted a series of executions formally agreed upon by the victors and clearly designed to eliminate their most prominent and inveterate enemies. Fourteen of the proscribed are listed in the sources, among them six *consulares*, many of them prominent conservative leaders of the nineties. Others were exiled. Sulla's legislation was repealed, those he had outlawed were restored, he was himself declared a *hostis*, his property was confiscated, and all funds and supplies for his army were cut off. Cinna and Marius were elected consuls for 86, but the latter died in January, leaving Cinna in a position of single dominance.[49]

The *Cinnae dominatio* spanned the next two and a half years, a controversial era vilified by a hostile ancient tradition heavily influenced by Sulla's memoirs, a tradition sometimes uncritically accepted by modern scholarship, sometimes scornfully rejected in impatient overreaction against flagrant bias.[50] As often, there is a measure of justification for both reactions, but the goals and actions of Cinna's government cannot be reduced to simple judgments of praise or blame.

The regime was undoubtedly a despotism; Cinna had unchallengeable power and he used it, however moderately and astutely, to maintain firm control of the government. His election to four successive consulships in the absence of a military crisis which demanded his leadership, was without precedent or justification under the law, the illegality compounded by the fact that he had the same colleague, C. Papirius Carbo, in 85 and 84. Rome's chief magistracy was controlled and manipulated during the Cinnan years to perpetuate the supremacy of an individual; the traditional electoral processes, a cornerstone of republicanism and oligarchic preeminence, were no longer functioning. The legislative *comitia* and the courts similarly declined in importance. Only one law, the *Lex Valeria* of 86, a measure for the relief of debt, and only one trial, the prosecution of Pompey, are recorded for this period. The

49. The six *consulares* were Q. Catulus, M. Antonius, P. Crassus, L. Julius Caesar, Cn. Octavius, and L. Cornelius Merula. A full list of sources is provided by Broughton, *MRR*, 2.46. On the termination of funds and supplies to Sulla cf. Appian, *Mith.* 54. Pausanias 9.7.5.

50. Cf. H. Bennett, *Cinna and His Times* (Menasha, Wisc. 1923), 6–35. J. Van Ooteghem, *Caius Marius* (Brussels 1964), 303 ff. C. Lanzani, *Mario e Silla* (Catania 1915), 15–145. Badian, *Studies*, 221 ff. Gruen, *Roman Politics*, 230 ff. Carney, *Marius*, 60–70. C. M. Bulst, *"Cinnanum Tempus" Historia* 13 (1964), 307–37. Valgiglio, *Silla,* 33 ff. Balsdon, *JRS* 55 (1965), 231. B. R. Katz, "Studies on the Period of Cinna and Sulla" *AC* 45 (1976), 497–549.

vetus respublica still stood in theory, and there are no indications that Cinna had plans to transform it, but all facets of its political life were tightly regulated, with little room for meaningful operation of its institutions.[51]

On the other hand, Cinna's rule bestowed substantial benefits on Rome and cannot be dismissed as an intemperate, lawless tyranny. It brought stability and peace to a society badly scarred by the Social War and the domestic conflicts that followed it. It resulted in the integration of the Italians into the Roman state on an equitable basis; it restored a measure of economic soundness to a tottering economy and made strong efforts to establish harmony between all political elements. Cinna came to power with the aid of the Italians and the coalition which had formed around Sulpicius; but, after the initial elimination of his more intractable optimate foes, he worked hard to gain broad aristocratic support. Like Caesar, Cinna the patrician was partial to high birth and to the notion of hereditary excellence and was interested in ruling with the goodwill of the oligarchy, not in its despite. No prosecutions, no harassment of *nobiles* are recorded after the initial reprisals in the wake of victory, and recent prosopographical studies of the period indicate that Cinna succeeded in winning the active cooperation of some distinguished *nobiles* and the acquiescence of others.[52]

The principal obstacle to his goal of a strong, broadly based government under his own leadership was, of course, Sulla. The latter had survived attempts to cripple his army through lack of supplies, and by the middle of 86 he was in control of Greece and supplying himself from the wealth of Greek temples and from spoils collected in Attica and Boeotia. A second effort was made in 86 to counteract his military strength by dispatching an army to Asia under the consul Valerius Flaccus. Flaccus's mission was not to fight Sulla but to urge him to submit to the senate and to cooperate with the consular army, and, if he refused, to forestall him in defeating Mithridates and to secure the fruits of such a victory for the Cinnan forces. Sulla naturally

51. Cf. *Brut.* 227, 308, 311. Livy, *Per.* 79–83. Plutarch, *Pompey* 4. Appian, *BC* 1.77. Gruen, *Roman Politics*, 244. Bennett, *Cinna*, 64 ff. Balsdon, *JRS* 55 (1965), 231.
52. Cf. Bulst, *Historia* 13 (1964), 334 ff. Badian, *Studies*, 222 ff. Gruen, *Roman Politics*, 240 ff. Meier, *Res Publica Amissa*, 225 ff. For Caesar's attitude toward *nobiles* cf. *Fam.* 4.8.2; 6.5.3; 6.6.8–10.

declined to be drawn from his position of strength into virtual surrender to Cinna's regime, and Flaccus's enterprise not only failed but
produced the opposite of the desired effect. The consul was murdered
by his own troops toward the end of 86. His *legatus*, Fimbria, who
took over command, won some notable successes against Mithridates,
but he was outmaneuvred by Sulla, who frustrated all his efforts by
concluding peace with the king in the middle of 85. As a result, Fimbria's army, which was far inferior to Sulla's, deserted to the latter.[53]

Even before this development had greatly increased Sulla's capacity
to challenge Cinna militarily, the likelihood of a violent confrontation
between the two men was high. Basic ideological differences as well as
personal enmity and rivalry were precipitating a collision. Cinna had
revived Sulpicius's voting rights bill, which Sulla had so determinedly
opposed; he had recalled the men on whose banishment Sulla had
insisted; he had set aside all of Sulla's constitutional arrangements and
had tried to isolate and force the proconsul into submission by having
him declared a *hostis* and by closing off his supplies. Sulla never con-
cealed the fact that he was determined to reverse these developments
and to exact satisfaction for the several affronts to his *dignitas*, and
there is little to indicate that Cinna anticipated reconciliation or was
ready to make any important concessions to accommodate his rival.
The senate, faced with the prospect of another major civil war, which
was certain, whatever the outcome, to bring large-scale devastation and
the cruelty and arrogance characteristic of victory in domestic conflicts,
was anxious for a peaceful settlement; but senatorial efforts at media-
tion in a crisis which, after the fashion of embittered civil disputes
involving military forces, was being inevitably impelled toward the
arbitrament of arms, made very little headway.[54]

After Fimbria's fall, Cinna and his colleague Carbo pressed efforts
to build their military strength in Italy, ignoring a senatorial directive
to suspend recruiting. The urgency of their position increased the
arbitrariness of their rule, which in turn increased the hostility and

53. Sources in Broughton, *MRR*, 2.53, 59. Cf. Bennett, *Cinna*, 45–46. Badian,
Studies, 223–24. Meier, *Res Publica Amissa*, 233–34.
54. Velleius 2.24.4. *Phil.* 12.27 reveals the basic ideological concerns under-
lying this crisis. The senate's efforts for peace in 85 and 84 are recorded by
Appian, *BC* 1.77 ff. Livy, *Per.* 83–84. Cf. B. Frier, "Sulla's Propaganda: The
Collapse of the Cinnan Republic" *AJP* 92 (1971), 585–604.

resistance to it. Cinna was killed by mutinous soldiers early in 84, and Carbo, who continued preparations for war and high-handed methods of government, encountered growing opposition from many sides, from the tribunes, the senate, the cities of Italy. When Sulla landed at Brundisium in late 84 or early 83, the *flos nobilitatis*, including many who had cooperated with and benefited from Cinna's regime, rallied to his support. By the end of 82 he was securely in control of Rome. A reign of terror against his enemies ensued, foreshadowed by his conduct in 88 but conducted on this occasion without any pretense of legality. At the same time he assumed dictatorial powers for the purpose of reconstituting the *respublica*, and during 81 he enacted a program of reform designed to restore the senate to a stable position of power unhampered by the judicial, legislative, and military pressures which had repeatedly disabled senatorial government in the preceding decades. At the end of 80 Sulla retired from public life.[55]

His retirement marked the end of eight years of upheaval and uncertainty, described by Cicero as a period when the state was disfigured in all its aspects, when the old order of things was in disarray, and when elder statesmen despaired of the *respublica*.[56] It was an uneasy and perplexing interval for Roman politicians, who had to move in the treacherous, changeful world of raw power politics and in the shadow of an impending war, a war whose outcome was uncertain, whose causes were personal enmities and ambitions as well as political ideology, and whose consequences as a result were likely, whoever the victor, to harm rather than to help the state. Choices were complicated, the paths of public and private expediency alike obscure.

Cicero's reactions to the successive crises of those years and his views on the men and issues behind them are of obvious importance in any consideration of his early political life and thought. Direct evidence for his actual political posture in the period is scanty, confined to brief remarks in the *Brutus* and the *Pro Roscio*. His highly elliptical account of his early life in the *Brutus* has been cited already. Carefully tailored

55. Sources in Broughton, *MRR*, 2.60–78. Cf. Lanzani, *Mario e Silla*. Valgiglio, *Silla*. J. Carcopino, *Sylla ou la monarchie manquée* (Paris 1931). Gabba, *App. BC Lib. Prim.,* 206–81. Meier, *Res Publica Amissa,* 222–66. Badian, *Lucius Sulla.* J.P.V.D. Balsdon, "Sulla Felix" *JRS* 41 (1951), 1–10. B. Twyman, "The Date of Sulla's Abdication and the Chronology of the First Book of Appian's Civil Wars" *Athenaeum* 54 (1976), 77–97.

56. *De Or.* 1.3; 3.8. *Fam.* 2.16.6. *Font.* 6.

to magnify his tireless strivings as a student for flawless eloquence, all it tells of his actions and attitudes during the Cinnan years is that he concentrated on his studies, wishing to perfect his oratorical talents before commencing his public life. He is more explicit about his political position toward the end of the decade, when the inevitable confrontation between Sulla and the Cinnan faction began to develop. In his speech for Roscius he repeatedly asserts that his sympathies lay with Sulla's cause, which he equates with the *causa nobilitatis*, and he claims that, when his primary wish for a peaceful resolution of the crisis proved vain, he worked, though without taking up arms, for the victory of that cause.[57]

This skeletal description of Cicero's responses to the political oscillations of the eighties can be supplemented by the numerous general allusions to the period and its principal figures scattered throughout his writings. While most of these allusions, as in the case of Cicero's remarks on 88, are later than the events they describe, their congruity with what Cicero relates of his actions during those events, and their uniformity of tone and substance, despite the wide variety of contexts and situations in which they occur, attest their reliability as evidence of Cicero's thinking in the eighties and leave small grounds for suppositions of significant *ex post facto* revisions or reversals.

Cicero's analyses of the *Cinnanum tempus* reveal a fundamental antagonism to the goals and methods of Cinna and his supporters, an antagonism that provoked a simplified and one-sided judgment of Cinna's concerns and circumstances and precluded recognition of any benefits from the regime for the *respublica*.

The war of 87 Cicero blames entirely on the intransigence of Cinna in the matter of the voting rights of the new citizens.[58] Cinna's victory in that war he regards as a triumph of the *improbi* and *perditi* which led to the ruthless extermination of the state's leading luminaries. He makes Cinna chiefly responsible for the proscriptions of 87 and presents the killings as a purge of *principes* which was followed by the rule of the *indigni*. Under this *improborum dominatus*, Cicero believed, the workings of the *respublica* were interrupted in essential ways. *Dignitas*, a primary prop of the ascendancy of the hereditary *nobilitas* of the

57. *Brut.* 308–12. *Rosc.* 135–42.
58. *Phil.* 13.2; 8.7.

middle and late Republic and, in Cicero's thinking, the crucial modifier of egalitarian notions of *libertas* and the guarantor of an equitable allocation of *gradus* and *honos*, was overwhelmed by *humilitas*. [59] Worse still, Cinna's power, greater than that of the entire state, was incompatible with the principles of freedom on which the republic was founded. His rule constituted *regnum*, and reduced the operation of the laws and the courts to an idle charade. Cicero mentions only one beneficial aspect of the *Cinnanum tempus*—the city was *sine armis*; there was *otium*, but the price was too high, for it was *otium sine dignitate*. [60]

Strikingly similar charges and criticisms recur in Cicero's denunciations of political conditions under Caesar in 46 and 45, and the remarkable parallelism in language and sentiments between his many and vehement indictments of Caesar's regime and his strictures on Cinna further clarify and emphasize the depth and basic character of his objections to the rule of the latter.

As in the case of Cinna, Cicero saw Caesar as the leader of the *improbi* and the *perditi* and the foe of the *causa bonorum*, which he equated with the *causa reipublicae*. [61] He expected, if Caesar won, the same slaughter of leading *boni* perpetrated by Cinna; he expected other dire consequences also, many of them likewise concomitants of Cinna's victory. [62] Caesar belied some of these predictions and won Cicero's gratitude and regard for his general magnanimity in dealing with his enemies and for his particular generosity and kindness toward Cicero himself. But despite a position of considerable favor under Caesar's regime, despite a certain respect and liking for Caesar himself, and despite the internal peace which he admitted Caesar had established, the *status reipublicae* in 46 and 45 made Cicero's life increasingly

59. *Fam.* 1.9.11. *Phil.* 8.7; 11.1. *De Or.* 3.8–12. *Cat.* 3.24. *Vat.* 23. *Att.* 7.7.7; 9.10.3. *N.D.* 3.80–81. *Tusc.* 5.55. *Rosc.* 135–37. *Verr.* 2.1.37. *Sen.* 9. *Brut.* 227. Cf. *Rep.* 1.43, 53.

60. *Cat.* 3.9. *Dom.* 83. *Har. Resp.* 54. *Brut.* 227, 308, 311. *Phil.* 2.108; 5.17. On the incompatibility of great power in the hands of an individual and *honestum otium* cf. *Fam.* 5.21.2; 7.3.5. On Cicero's use of the term *regnum* cf. W. Allen, Jr., "Caesar's *Regnum*" *TAPA* 84 (1953), 227–36.

61. *Att.* 7.3.5; 7.20.2; 8.3.4; 9.2a.2; 9.5.1; 9.18.2; 9.19.1; 10.1.2; 10.41; 10.7.1; 10.8.3, 8; 12.21.5; 13.40.1. *Fam.* 5.15.4; 6.18.1; 15.19.3. Caelius viewed Caesar's side similarly. Cf. *Fam.* 8.13.2; 8.14.3; 8.17.1.

62. *Att.* 7.7.7; 9.2a.2; 10.4.8; 10.8.2; 10.10.5; 10.13.1.

intolerable in all its aspects, generated *summum odium temporum, hominum, fori, curiae*, and moved him to indulge in unrestrained exultation when Caesar was murdered in March 44.[63]

The political maladies which Cicero saw in the government of Caesar and which inspired these intense reactions were, in the final analysis, essentially the same as those he attributed to the Cinnan era. Like Cinna, Caesar won with the help of the *improbi* and could not deny them a share in the political ascendancy achieved by his victory. Like Cinna, Caesar possessed more power than the entire state and used it to govern as he wished, in effect suspending the rule of law, destroying the *membra reipublicae* on which *honestum otium* was founded, and precluding any meaningful role for those whom *virtus* and *industria* had endowed with *dignitas* and the right to rule.[64]

In brief, the victories of Caesar and Cinna both brought peace, but both also brought the same intolerable disfigurements of republicanism —perversion of the natural political order by the elevation of the unworthy to positions of prominence, and abrogation, through an excess of power in the hands of an individual, of fundamental precepts of *libertas* and of long-standing traditions of the *vetus respublica.*

Cicero reacted to Caesar's ascendancy in the forties by withdrawing, to the extent possible, from any association with or participation in his regime. He refused to lend his approval to Caesar's rule even after the latter's victories removed any hope for the restoration of the *vetus respublica*, and he participated in public life only to the degree compatible with his understanding of the laws of political necessity.[65] This stance immediately recalls his avoidance of any involvement in public life under Cinna and immediately prompts the conclusion that such similar noninvolvement under a regime which he similarly disapproved was dictated by similar reasons.

63. *Fam.* 4.4.4; 4.8.2; 4.13.2; 6.6.8–13; 6.13.2; 9.17.2. *Marc.* passim. *Deiot.* 34. On Cicero's favored position with Caesar and the Caesarians cf. *Fam.* 6.7.5; 6.10a.2; 6.12.2; 7.24.1; 9.16.3–4; 9.20.2–4. On his unhappiness with political conditions cf. *Att.* 12.21.5; 12.23.1; 13.10.1. *Fam.* 4.6.2; 4.13.3; 5.13.4; 5.15.4; 5.16.3–4; 6.13.4; 6.14.2; 7.28.3; 9.20.3; 9.26.1; 15.18.1. *Tusc.* 1.84. On Cicero's reaction to Caesar's death cf. *Fam.* 6.15. *Att.* 14.4.2; 14.6.1. *Phil.* 2.30–33.

64. Cf. *Fam.* 4.9.3; 9.17.3; 12.18.2. On Caesar's autocratic rule and the end of *honestum otium, dignitas*, and the rule of law cf. *Fam.* 4.9.2; 4.14.1; 5.13.3; 5.21.2; 6.18.1; 6.21.1; 9.16.3; 9.18.1; 12.18.2. *Att.* 12.49.2; 13.10.1.

65. Cf. *Att.* 9.4; 9.15.2–3; 9.17.1; 10.1.3; 10.3a.2; 12.51.2; 13.42.3. *Fam.* 4.4.4; 4.8.2; 4.9.2–4; 7.3.4; 9.16.5; 13.77.1.

The insufficiency of Cicero's nonpolitical explanation of his quiescence in the eighties put forward in the *Brutus* has been mentioned earlier. Lengthy seclusion in study was a most unusual course for an ambitious *iuvenis* who badly needed to prove his *virtus* and *industria*, and even in the *Brutus* there is some indication that it was not entirely unconnected with the *status reipublicae*. In describing his association with Philo of Larisa, which began in 88, he acknowledges that he was moved to concentrate all his energies on the Academician's teachings not only by interest in philosophy but also by the seemingly permanent breakdown of law and order in the state, a condition which he repeatedly asserts prevailed throughout the *Cinnae dominatio*. There was an open field for talented young orators in the eighties due to the death or absence of the forum's older luminaries. Close associates of Cicero were taking advantage of it to build their reputations. Cicero's failure to exploit such an opportunity can only be explained as a political decision dictated by a desire to avoid any association with the *Cinnani* and their brand of government.[66]

His failure to take arms or to commit himself actively to the overthrow of the *Cinnani* after Sulla's return from the East does not conflict with these many indications of his deep-seated aversion to the Cinnan faction. His decision to remain *inermis* and his desire for peace closely match once again his reaction in the forties when war erupted between Caesar and Pompey. Then too he disavowed violence as a solution to political problems and refrained from taking arms, searching for a peaceful solution to the crisis.[67] He adopted this policy even though his opposition to Caesar could not have been more bitter or more basic, and he saw no ambiguity or inconsistency in such a course. When criticized for his conciliatory stand he vigorously denied that he was ever more friendly toward Caesar than those who rushed into armed opposition, or they more friendly toward the state than he. Both had

---

66. *Brut.* 236, 307 ff. For allusions to lawlessness under Cinna cf. *Brut.* 227. *Dom.* 83. *Quinct.* 69. Cf. Plutarch, *Cicero* 3.2.

67. *Att.* 7.17.4; 8.11d.6; 9.7.2–3; 9.10.3; 9.11a. *Fam.* 2.16.3; 4.1.5; 4.3.2; 4.7.2; 4.9.3; 5.21.2; 6.1.5; 6.6.6; 9.6.3; 15.15.1; 16.11.2; 16.12.2. Cicero finally left Italy in 49, driven by a sense of personal obligation to Pompey, but he never took an active part in the fighting. *Att.* 8.3.2; 9.1.4; 9.2a.2; 9.5.3; 9.7.3–4; 9.13.3; 9.19.2; 10.7.1. *Marc.* 14.

essentially the same concerns and objectives; they differed only on the most expedient means to their common ends.[68]

Cicero's position was founded on the belief that reliance on force in disputes that involved powerful leaders or *partes* was necessarily detrimental to the cause of republicanism, its risks and evils prohibitive regardless of the ends being sought or of the benefits that would accrue from their accomplishment.[69] He saw *auctoritas* and *consilium* as the only sane and proper weapons for the settlement of deep-seated disputes *de iure publico*, and he argued that to submit such disputes to settlement by arms was to bring catastrophic devastation on the state, to invite cruelty and arrogance from the victors, whoever they might be, and to risk a measure of tyrannical government even when victory fell to the *meliores*. Amid the many uncertainties of large-scale internal violence Cicero saw only one certainty: the *respublica* could not emerge a winner.[70]

His pacifistic posture in the late eighties, in a war which involved basic ideological issues and in which Cicero admitted there were many who did not choose the side of Sulla, no more signified ambivalence in his political sympathies or in his attitude toward the warring parties than did his similar stand in the conflict of 49. His repeated statements of his partiality for the Sullan side, confidently asserted at the trial of Roscius, can be confidently accepted as genuine, and they are consistent with his every subsequent allusion to Sulla's cause throughout his varied writings.

He invariably portrays Sulla's side as the side of the *respublica* and the side of the *nobilitas*, and its goals as the overthrow of the *indigni* and the reestablishment of the institutions of republicanism. The phrase *rempublicam reciperare* constantly recurs in one form or another in his references to the enterprise of Sulla and his supporters in 83 and 82. He presents recovery of the Republic not only as the purpose of their efforts, but also as the effect of their victory, and he accounts all who

68. *Att.* 8.11d.7–8. On his attitude toward Caesar's cause cf. *Att.* 7.11.1; 7.13.1; 7.18.2; 10.4.2; 10.7.1; 10.8.2. *Phil.* 2.53.
69. Cf. above, pp. 66 ff. Cicero took a different attitude with regard to the use of force in curbing those he regarded as aberrant extremists and self-seeking *seditiosi*, the *audaces* and *perditi* present in every society.
70. Cf. *Fam.* 4.4.2; 4.9.4; 6.1.5; 6.21.1; 9.17.1; 16.12.2.

contributed to that victory deserving of honor as benefactors of the state.[71]

He does express severe criticism of Sulla himself and of many aspects of his behavior in the late eighties, but this criticism does not extend in any way to the ideals and objectives of the cause Sulla led. It refers, as in the case of Cicero's objections to Sulla's handling of the Sulpician crisis, only to the general's immoderate and vengeful use of victory and to the flaws of character that provoked such conduct.

Cicero had neither regard nor respect for Sulla the man, whom he calls a master of *luxuria, avaritia*, and *crudelitas*, ready to stoop to the basest tactics to achieve his ends. In specific allusions to his leadership in the late eighties he charges him with defiling a noble undertaking by extremism, cruelty, and disregard for life and property, with establishing killing and plundering as the standard sequel to victory in civil war, and with sowing in the process the seeds of later wars and similar atrocities.[72]

These are, of course, mostly judgments of hindsight, products of Sullan abuses after victory and of their ruinous consequences for the state, but even from this harsh perspective Cicero's insistence on the righteousness of Sulla's cause never wavers. In the *De Officiis*, with the unhappy record of forty years of post-Sullan history before his eyes, and with the recognition that many of the calamities of those years were attributable to Sullan precedents, he still asserts that Sulla's *causa* was *honesta*. [73] The faults he perceived in the leadership of Sulla, like the faults he perceived in the leadership of Pompey in 49, did not make more acceptable the alternative prospect of a permanent despotism of the *improbi*. He may have seen no ideal choice in 83 or 49, but in neither of those two crises, which coincided respectively with the opening and closing stages of his political career, did he have any doubts as to where the cause of the traditionalists lay, and on both occasions, whatever his reservations concerning the worth and wisdom of its

71. *Rosc.* 135, 141. *Dom.* 79. *Har. Resp.* 54. *Brut.* 311. *De Or.* 3.12. *Verr.* 2.1.35–37. *Man.* 8, 30. *Phil.* 5.43; 8.7. *Att.* 11.21.3; 9.7.4. On the ideological issues at stake in the war cf. *Phil.* 5.43; 12.27. *Font.* 6.

72. *Fam.* 4.3.1. *Att.* 7.7.7; 9.10.3 *Leg. Agr.* 2.81. *Caec.* 95. *Cat.* 2.20. *Mur.* 49. *Sulla* 72. *Dom.* 43. *Lig.* 12. *Fin.* 3.75. *Off.* 1.43, 109; 2.27–29.

73. *Off.* 2.27.

leaders and their policies, his loyalties lay with that cause against the forces of what he considered destructive change.

The implications of Cicero's reactions to the *Cinnae dominatio* and ensuing civil war in terms of his political ideas and affiliations become still clearer when his behavior is compared with that of a distinguished senior statesman and Cicero's principal mentor in the eighties, Scaevola Pontifex. A close correspondence between Cicero's posture and Scaevola's becomes quickly obvious and points to the not surprising conclusion that Cicero's political outlook and actions in this period were to a very great degree inspired by his eminent patron, a statesman whom he greatly admired and who was linked by ties of friendship and ideology to the men who had dominated Cicero's life in the nineties.

Scaevola survived the massacre of 87, in which several of his friends and political allies perished, and he stayed in Rome throughout the *Cinnae dominatio.* It is evident, however, that he was no friend of the *Cinnani* and that his decision to live under Cinna's government did not extend to cooperation with it or to participation in its functioning.

According to Cicero, Scaevola's sole reason for standing his ground after Cinna's victory was an aversion to civil war, a determination, whatever the evils besetting the state, not to bear arms against it. Cicero draws a clear distinction between this *ratio* and that of another *consularis*, Marcius Philippus, who similarly remained in Rome under Cinna but whose motivation was a belief that one must bow to circumstances and make the most of them. [74] Philippus's *ratio* entailed acceptance of Cinna's regime; the point of Cicero's distinction between that *ratio* and Scaevola's is that the latter's entailed no such acceptance. This was a wide difference in the political outlook of the two *consulares* at the outset of the *Cinnanum tempus*, and it manifested itself in widely different political behavior throughout Cinna's ascendancy.

Philippus did not hesitate to cooperate with the ruling faction and to participate fully in the public life of the state. He continued to plead in the lawcourts and held an important office, the censorship, in 86. [75] Scaevola on the other hand, though a prestigious senior statesman, a

---

74. *Att.* 8.3.6. Two other *consulares*, L. Valerius Flaccus and M. Perperna, also remained in Rome. Cicero says nothing of their *rationes*, but there are indications that both had Marian connections, and both cooperated with Cinna's government. Cf. Badian, *Studies*, 55, 217.

75. *Brut.* 308. Cf. Broughton, *MRR*, 2.54.

respected orator, and a noted jurist, at the peak of his abilities and *auctoritas* when demands on his services would have been greatest, shunned the lawcourts entirely during the Cinnan years. The indications are that he similarly withdrew from other areas of public life. He held no public office or commission in this period, nor is there any record that he attended the senate until the eve of Sulla's return brought the opportunity to work for peace.[76]

Furthermore, there are clear signs that Scaevola's relationship with the *Cinnani* was unequivocally antagonistic throughout. The antagonism was advertised early in 86 by one of the most trusted adherents of Marius and Cinna, Flavius Fimbria, when he instigated an attempt on Scaevola's life at the funeral of Marius and made no secret of his desire to rid the state of the distinguished *consularis.* The attack cannot be dismissed as an isolated incident generated by private enmity or aberrant extremism. Fimbria was soon afterwards assigned a prominent place in the crucial eastern expedition, his standing with the *Cinnani* obviously undiminished, and Scaevola continued to fear other attacks and to express the belief that his stance under Cinna would cost him his life. There was no Cinnan vendetta against *boni*. Cinna's concern was to rule with the approval and support of the aristocracy. The hostility which Scaevola encountered and which gave rise to his continuing fears for his safety can therefore only have resulted from the pontiff's own refusal to reach accommodation with the regime and take a place in it.[77]

When civil war drew closer with Sulla's impending return, Scaevola persisted in his determination not to bear arms, but he did become active in the search for peace. It is quite evident, however, that as in the case of Cicero in 49 this stance in no way precluded partisanship or indicated lukewarmness in his political sympathies. Scaevola remained as unambiguously at odds with the ruling faction in his advocacy of peace as in his quiescence, and he paid for it with his life. He was murdered by the Marian praetor, Brutus Damasippus, in 81, one of four

76. Cf. *Brut.* 308. *Rosc.* 33.

77. *Rosc.* 33. Val. Max. 9.11.2. Livy, *Per.* 80. Orosius 5.20; 6.2. Fimbria had served as the envoy of Marius and Cinna on a crucial mission to the Samnites in 87. Gran. Lic. 29b. Appian, *BC* 1.68. On Fimbria's position in the eastern expedition cf. A. W. Lintott, "The Offices of C. Flavius Fimbria in 86-85 B.C." *Historia* 20 (1971), 696-701. On Scaevola's fears for his safety cf. *Att.* 8.3.6.

recorded leaders singled out for execution. The ancient tradition, including Cicero, is undivided on the questions of his political sympathies and the reason for his death; Scaevola was a *Sullanus* who refused to cooperate with the opposing *partes* and fell victim to the vengeance of a crumbling regime.[78]

Cicero, sheltered by insignificance, did not share his patron's fate or danger, but, in view of the exact correspondence between his behavior and Scaevola's at every major turn of events, there can be little doubt that he shared the pontiff's political views and closely followed his lead throughout the successive crises of this tumultuous decade.[79]

In Grief, the record of Cicero's political actions and attitudes throughout these eight unsettled years of his early political life reveals a continuing commitment to the *fundamenta* of the *vetus respublica* and a continuing attachment to the persons and policies of *principes* dedicated to their preservation. His actions were modelled on the conduct of one of Rome's most authoritative adherents of the *via optimas*, his attitudes founded on basic precepts of oligarchic ideology. He had full justification in advancing at the end of the period a claim of unwavering allegiance to the *causa nobilitatis*.[80]

Cicero's entry into the political limelight after Sulla's victory was quick and indicative of his optimate leanings and associations. In the year 80, Sextus Roscius, a native of the *municipium* of Ameria, was accused of the murder of his father in a prosecution instigated by a favored freedman of Sulla, Chrysogonus. The murder had actually been

78. Sources in Broughton, *MRR,* 2.73. Cf. *Att.* 9.15.2, where Cicero clearly implies that Scaevola died because of a refusal to cooperate with the *Cinnani.*

79. There are even verbal similarities in Cicero's description of their respective stands. *Rosc.* 33, 136. In 49, when he followed a similar course, Cicero explicitly appealed to Scaevola's example. *Att.* 8.3.6. That the position of Scaevola and Cicero was representative of the outlook of the *boni* as a whole can hardly be doubted. Badian (*Studies,* 206-34) has argued that the bulk of the *nobilitas* did not favor Sulla, did not see him as the champion of their cause, and only rallied to him after it became evident that he was going to win; but the view has not won wide acceptance, and, when one considers the evidence of Cicero and the other ancient sources (however tendentious some of it may be), the stance of a *consularis* like Scaevola, the ideological issues dividing Cinna and the oligarchy, the overall character of Cinna's regime, the tenacity of the *boni* in defending in earlier crises the *vetus respublica* and their privileged place in it, it is a view difficult to maintain. Cf. Balsdon, *JRS* 55 (1965), 229-32. Gruen, *Roman Politics,* 238. Meier, *Res Publica Amissa,* 229. B. W. Frier, *AJP* 92 (1971), 585-604.

80. *Rosc.* 135.

committed by kinsmen of the victim, who subsequently entered into a conspiracy with Chrysogonus to gain possession of the dead man's property by entering his name on the lists of the proscribed and purchasing for nominal sums his goods, which would become forfeit to the state as a result of the outlawry. This was successfully accomplished, and a scheme was then devised to get rid of the rightful heir by accusing him of the death of his father.[81]

The case had political ramifications of great importance. The family of Roscius had for long enjoyed the friendship of several of Rome's most influential noble houses. Cicero lists the Metelli, the Servilii, and the Scipiones among the defendant's patrons. The attempt of a freedman to destroy by a most brazen form of despotic intrigue a *cliens* of leading *nobiles*, using one of the major props of Sulla's new political order, the recently established *quaestiones perpetuae*, was a crucial test of the genuineness and solidity of Sulla's design for a revitalized *respublica* and an ascendant *nobilitas* to guide it.

The affirmation of the need to suppress Chrysogonus, his breed, and his methods without indicting Sulla himself and his management of public affairs was the delicate task assigned to Cicero by a *nobilitas* which was still uncertain of Sulla's temper and intentions and whose leading members were unwilling to risk confrontation by even implied criticism of the dictator. Cicero, sufficiently obscure but sufficiently well connected, could convey the message with less risk of personal reprisals or of political complications. Emphasizing that the new judicial system must demonstrate its independence and integrity, and isolating Chrysogonus as a rapacious opportunist covertly exploiting the *gratia* and *potentia* flowing from association with a great leader and portraying him as the meanest representative of the *humiles* whose elimination from public life was the primary objective of the *Sullani*, Cicero accomplished his task with skill and vigor and won his case and instant fame.[82]

81. *Rosc.* 15-29 and passim. Plutarch, *Cicero* 3. Gellius 15.28.5. Quintilian 12.6.4. Cicero had pleaded other cases before undertaking the defense of Roscius. The one best known to us is the civil suit in which he represented a certain C. Quinctius in 81, a case sometimes given unwarranted political importance. Cf. E. S. Gruen, "The Dolabellae and Sulla" *AJP* 87 (1966), 394.

82. *Rosc.* 11-12, 28, 136-42. Cf. Gruen, *Roman Politics,* 265 ff. Badian, *Foreign Clientelae*, 249 ff. Carcopino, *Sylla ou la monarchie manquée,* 155 ff. T. E. Kinsey, "Dates of the *Pro Roscio* and *Pro Quinctio*" *Mn* 20 (1967), 61-67.

His political debut as a spokesman and defender of vital oligarchic interests further advertised and cemented his ties to the *boni.* It was a fitting sequel to his youthful association with leading noble houses and to his lengthy apprenticeship as the loyal disciple of an eminent optimate. As he moved toward his first candidacy he had strong claims through his conduct and connections on the goodwill and support of the conservative *nobilitas.*

Stockton, *Cicero*, 8 ff. A. Afzelius, "Zwei Episoden aus dem Leben Ciceros" *CM* 5 (1942), 209–17. M. Gelzer, "Review of Carcopino, *Sylla ou la monarchie manquée*" *Gnomon* 8 (1932), 605–07. V. Buchheit, "Ciceros Kritik an Sulla in der Rede für Roscius aus Ameria" *Historia* 24 (1975), 570–91. Gabba, *ASNP* 33 (1964), 1–15.

3: CICERO THE CANDIDATE

Cicero's successful defense of Roscius in 80 was followed by many other cases on which he expended the greatest care and which further enhanced his reputation as an advocate. But the pressure of work and success, coupled with the strain of an exacting mode of delivery, took a heavy physical toll, and, concerned for his health, Cicero decided about the middle of 79 to take an extended trip to Greece and Asia Minor to seek to strengthen his voice and lungs and to refine his style of speaking to a manner more suited to his delicate physique.[1]

He spent six months at Athens, where he studied with the Academician Antiochus and the rhetorician Demetrius, traveled throughout Asia Minor in the company of its leading orators, stopped off at Rhodes to become once again the student of Molo, and returned to Rome about the middle of 77 strengthened in body and cured of the excessive exuberance that had marked his language and delivery.[2] He was

1. *Brut.* 312 ff. Plutarch, *Cicero* 4. Quintilian, *Inst. Or.* 12.6.7. The chronology of Cicero's forensic activity in this period clearly shows that Plutarch's statement that Cicero left Rome out of fear of Sulla is without foundation. The trial of Roscius took place early in 80. It was 79 before Cicero left the capital, and in between he pleaded many other cases and at least one in which he again risked offending Sulla—the case of the woman of Arretium, whose freedom Cicero defended, in the process contesting the attempt of Sulla to disenfranchise the citizens of this *municipium*. Cf. Kinsey, *Mn* 20 (1967), 61–67.

2. *Brut.* 315 ff. Plutarch records that Cicero was unwilling to enter public life on his return from the East, but this is clearly contradicted by the account of the *Brutus* and by Cicero's determined efforts while abroad to perfect his oratorical skills, efforts obviously designed to prepare him for a busy life in the forum.

now approaching the minimum age at which he could seek election to public office and was preparing to begin the long climb up the Roman political ladder toward the ultimate *honor*, the consulship. He would devote most of his energies during the next fourteen years to the effort to reach that political pinnacle.

Cicero faced serious obstacles in his quest for high political distinction. Few new men from families that had not previously participated in Roman politics had ever in the history of the Republic succeeded in reaching the top of the *cursus honorum.* Aristocratic domination, particularly of the higher magistracies, was more pronounced than ever in the wake of the Sullan settlement and was firmly founded on a firm command of the main components of electoral success.

These components, according to the ancient evidence, consisted of *amici* and *popularis voluntas.* [3] A candidate, especially a candidate for the high offices, needed an elaborate nexus of friends, drawn from all segments of the society. He needed friends among the ruling class for the benefits of their influence and to add credibility and luster to his campaign; he needed friends among the *iuventus* and the *equester ordo* to secure the votes of the eighteen centuries of *equites*; he needed friends among the *principes* of the *collegia, pagi, vicinitates,* men who were often of humble rank but who had the *industria* and *gratia* to deliver the votes of their friends and neighbors; finally, he needed friends in the *municipia, coloniae,* and *praefecturae* of Italy to act as surrogate candidates in areas where little personal canvassing could be managed. The number and variety of friends needed were matched by the number and variety of ways to acquire them. They came from inherited clients and connections; from ties with other families based on *adfinitas* or straightforward political alliances; from associations formed in the course of military service or political apprenticeships;

3. The principal ancient sources for Roman elections are the *Commentariolum Petitionis*, and the *Pro Murena* and *Pro Plancio* of Cicero. Cf. Gelzer, *Roman Nobility.* T. P. Wiseman, *New Men in the Roman Senate* (Oxford 1971). Taylor, *Party Politics.* R. Syme, *The Roman Revolution* (Oxford 1939). The authenticity of the *Com. Pet.* continues to be questioned, but no conclusive arguments have been produced to prove that it is spurious. For a recent discussion with full bibliography see "Le *Commentariolum Petitionis* de Quintus Cicéron," with sections by J.-M. David, S. Demougin, E. Deniaux, D. Ferey, J.-M. Flambard, C. Nicolet, in *Aufstieg und Niedergang der römischen Welt* 1.3 (Berlin 1973), 239–77.

from *gratia* procured by favors rendered or anticipated; and from genuine goodwill.[4]

Popularis voluntas was also won by a variety of means: brilliant achievements, particularly in the military and oratorical fields; assiduous canvassing to make personal contact with as many people as possible; generosity with goods and services, which included the provision of banquets, games, and shows, or seats at such entertainments, and the furnishing of practical aid or the promise of it; projection of the image of a winner, which helped guarantee the bandwagon effect and which was achieved by advertising the nature and magnitude of one's support, by the number of *salutatores*, by the size of the escort to the forum and on the canvass, and by the splendor and optimistic enthusiasm of the campaign. Finally, goodwill was achieved by creating favorable expectations of one's statesmanship. To this end a candidate was advised to shun political controversy and avoid taking stands on political issues, lest any segment should lose its hope in him as a champion of its views and interests.[5]

In this electoral world, in which success was won, not by persuasive advocacy of attractive programs or ideas or by the ready-made resources of an organized political party, but by a network of private friendships and personal goodwill, the advantages of the *nobilis* were various and of pivotal importance. He had the benefit of inherited clients, friends, and connections and of all the accumulated *potentia* on which earlier family successes had been based. He generally had considerable wealth with which to secure the rewards of *liberalitas*, and he had the standing and influence that generated fresh opportunities for the exercise of the many forms of patronage, with a resulting increase in his store of *gratia*.

The most formidable advantage of the *nobilis*, however, was not his command of the material sources of political power, which by the late Republic were no longer totally monopolized by the aristocracy, but the pronounced partiality for high birth which pervaded Roman society throughout its history. The aristocratic instinct of the Romans is reflected in the republican constitution and is well attested in the writings of Cicero and of the ancient historians. The progress toward

4. Cf. *Com. Pet.* 16–40. *Mur.* 18–30, 37–40, 43–53, 69–77. *Planc.* 18–30, 44–48.
5. *Com. Pet.* 40–53. Cf. *Off.* 2.58 for various forms of legitimate *liberalitas*. Cf. Taylor, *Party Politics*, 63 ff.

democratization in the development of the republican system and the search for a satisfactory definition of *libertas* which would identify the civic rights belonging equally to all members of the state, stopped far short of egalitarian notions that presupposed an equal share for all in the exercise of political power and identified popular sovereignty with popular rule. The *aequabilitas* underlying the Roman concept of *libertas* postulated for all citizens equality before the law, *iura paria* in their relations with one another, and equality of basic political rights. But in the sphere of the exercise of political power, the demands of *libertas* were met by an *aequabilitas quaedam magna* which would guarantee to all some say in the management of the *respublica*. [6]

But the extent of that say was linked to what the Romans termed *dignitas*. Derived from the adjective *dignus*, the word basically meant worthiness, but it came to represent the reputation and respect procured by that quality. It summed up an individual's prestige and the esteem in which he was held because of the *virtus* which was believed to exist in him. Roman thinking on the relationship of *dignitas* to the *constitutio reipublicae* is epitomized in Cicero's assertion that *aequabilitas* in the area of government which fails to recognize *gradus dignitatis* is *iniqua*. Recognition of such *gradus* meant bestowal of greater political power on those who were perceived to have the greater capacity to exercise it, and it meant for Rome a political system which, while it insisted on the principle of popular sovereignty, concentrated power in the hands of the executive officials and their advisory council, the senate. [7]

The aristocratic instinct of the Romans, however, resulted in acceptance not only of the idea that a few should govern but also of the idea that in choosing those few preference should normally be given to representatives of families that had achieved political distinction and demonstrated political *virtus*. In other words, *dignitas* came to be regarded as inheritable and was derived not simply from an individual's personal worth and prestige but from the reputation and standing of his family as well. The political *virtus* of the *nobilis* was thus largely

6. Cf. *Rep.* 1.49, 69. Livy 4.5.5; 38.50.8. Wirszubski, *Libertas*, 9–15.
7. *Rep.* 1.43, 53. Cf. *Phil.* 1.34. For the meaning and importance of *dignitas* cf. esp. *Mur.* 76. *Planc.* 7, 50. *Sest.* 128–29. *Dom.* 9, 14, 86. *Phil.* 2.38. *Att.* 7.11.1. Hellegouarc'h, *Vocabulaire latin des relations et des partis politiques sous la république*. Wirszubski, *Libertas*, 36 ff.

assumed. He claimed public office as his birthright, and before a receptive public he flaunted his name, pedigree, and ancestral busts, symbols of his family's political triumphs, as pledges of his competence and trustworthiness. *Nobilitas* continued as a *blanda conciliatricula* of public sentiment throughout the Republic, readying the way for the accumulation of *amici* and of *popularis voluntas*, and even Cicero saw merit in this captivation of the public by the illustrious name.[8]

The *novus homo* on the other hand had to prove his *virtus*, and to an often unsympathetic and begrudging citizenry, for *novitas* meant both the absence of the benefits of inherited *dignitas* and the presence of an antagonism characteristic of the class-conscious society toward those seeking to rise above their station. The prejudice and resentment increased markedly the closer the new man came to the consulship. The general public grew less well disposed; *consulares* received him as an intruder whose success would sully or diminish the distinction they had achieved; faltering *nobiles*, striving in a fiercely competitive, overcrowded profession to increase, or at least maintain, the *dignitas* of their families, resented above all the prospect of being surpassed by a parvenu, and even the lower echelons of the senate begrudged success where they had failed. Goodwill was a scarce commodity, and friends were hard-earned.[9]

Cicero, as noted in our discussion of his family's standing in Roman society, did not labor under all the drawbacks of *novitas* in their severest form. His legacy of noble connections and his affiliations with leading *boni* in the eighties were important assets which would blunt aristocratic *invidia* and hostility and provide him with some contacts within the main power structure. Nonetheless, as he began his life as a candidate, he was entering an unequal contest, lacking the distinguished pedigree and its benefits, and lacking many of the varied political resources inherited by most of those with whom he would compete. His years as a candidate also coincided with an intensification of the scramble for office, a consequence of the sharp increase in the number

8. Cf. *Cat.* 4.23. *Mur.* 15 ff. *Sest.* 21. *Planc.* 18, 59, 67. *Man.* 1 ff. *Leg. Agr.* 2.1 ff., 100. *Verr.* 5.80. *Pis.* 2. *Cat.* 4.23. Livy 4.44.2. Sallust, *Jug.* 63.6; 85.23, 29; *Catiline* 23.6. Cf. Gelzer, *Roman Nobility,* 28. Wirszubski, *Libertas*, 37.

9. *Com. Pet.* 2, 4, 7, 13–15. *Verr.* 2.3.7. *Cat.* 1.28. Cf. preceding note; also Wiseman, *New Men,* 100 ff. The difficulties facing *novi homines* in politics are best illustrated by the fact that in the period 366–63 B.C. only fifteen new men reached the consulship. Cf. Gelzer, *Roman Nobility,* 50 ff.

of candidates which resulted from Sulla's enlargement of the senate and of the college of quaestors, from the removal in 75 of the restrictions on the eligibility of tribunes for higher office, and from the expulsion of sixty-four senators in 70, most of whom immediately set about regaining their status with all possible speed by securing again the offices they had previously held. The increased competition brought into play the full weaponry of wealth and influence and produced an upsurge in electoral corruption, further compounding the difficulties of newcomers, especially of those who, like Cicero, lacked both the will and the means to cross the shadowy line between *liberalitas* and *ambitus*.[10]

Cicero overcame these many obstacles, gained each office, including the consulship, at the earliest possible age, and consistently headed the poll, a unique achievement for a new man. It is the purpose of the present chapter to examine the political craftsmanship that engineered his success and to explore the political ideas and methods that directed his actions and affiliations.

Cicero's Work in the Courts

Cicero's principal objective during his life as a candidate is clearly spelled out by himself in his many references to his early career and triumphs at the polls. From the beginning of his public life he set before himself the task of building among all segments of the electorate, by *privata officia* and *ingenii laus*, accruing primarily from work in the courts, the reputation and the network of clients and *amici* which his birth had not given him and on which electoral success at Rome so largely depended. It was a strategy modeled on the political course pursued by his patron, L. Licinius Crassus, and it was to his diligent pursuit of it that he attributed the greater part of his remarkable political success.[11]

Immediately on his return to Rome in 77, he embarked upon this

10. Dio 36.38.2. *Cluent.* 120. Nepos, *Att.* 6.2. Cf. Wiseman, *New Men*, 164–65. E. S. Gruen, *The Last Generation of the Roman Republic* (Berkeley 1974), 213. M. Griffin, "The Tribunate of Cornelius" *JRS* 63 (1973), 200.

11. *De Or.* 3.7. *Off.* 2.47. *Brut.* 159, 242, 319–21. *Div. in Caec.* 40–41. *Man.* 1 ff. *Cluent.* 149, 157. *Rab.* 1. *Mur.* 8. *Planc.* 66, 84. *Sulla* 5, 26. *Com. Pet.* 3, 20, 21.

design of winning a political following based on personal contacts. He resumed his work in the courts with renewed vigor and set his sights on outstripping his chief forensic rivals, C. Aurelius Cotta and Q. Hortensius. About the same time he married into the distinguished *gens Terentia.* Not much is known about his wife's immediate family, but it can be said definitely that she was wealthy and well born, half sister of a Vestal Virgin who belonged to the patrician house of the Fabii.[12] Cicero had carefully used the important political resource of marriage to improve his social standing and expand his connections within the aristocracy.

In 76 he sought his first political office, the quaestorship, and was elected *in primis.* The office was not a major political prize, and, in view of Cicero's oratorical achievements and high connections, his easy victory at this initial stage of the *cursus honorum* needs no explanation. He was assigned by lot to serve under the governor of Sicily, Sextus Peducaeus, as the governor's quaestor in the western half of the province. Cicero took his first public office very seriously. He viewed it as his opportunity to prove his *virtus* and demonstrate to the Roman people his worthiness for higher distinctions. He oversaw the shipping to Rome of great quantities of grain at a time of very high prices; he treated merchants, businessmen, and tax collectors with fairness and friendliness; he refrained from any wrongful gains at the expense of the Sicilians and carried out his every function with the utmost diligence. His high hopes for quick recognition in Roman politics were not met, however. He did succeed in winning the lasting friendship of his superior, Peducaeus, who belonged to a senatorial, but not a consular or praetorian, family; he made friends of some young *nobiles* whom he defended before the governor on charges of dereliction of duty; he doubtless won the approval of the business interests in the province; and he gained a considerable reputation and many friends and clients among the Sicilians. But he was soon to learn that Rome was little touched by routine happenings in the provinces, and, on his own

12. *Brut.* 317–18. Plutarch, *Cicero* 8.2. Asconius 91, Clark. The *gens Terentia* was distinguished, and one branch of it, the Terentii Varrones, was consular. There were close ties between Cicero's family and this branch, and there was the additional bond of *vicinitas*; it seems not improbable that Terentia belonged to the family of the Varrones. Cf. Wiseman, *New Men*, 49, 55.

testimony, the impact of his quaestorship on his reputation and standing in the capital was minimal.[13]

Cicero never forgot this indifference to his provincial labors, and its lesson that political influence and éclat came chiefly to those who exercised their talents and industry in the limelight of Rome. During the remainder of his life as a candidate he stayed close to the capital and sought to live in its limelight by ceaseless activity in the courts, as he continued to pursue his principal goal of acquiring a substantial body of personal supporters throughout the electorate.[14]

He concentrated his efforts particularly on developing support and contacts among the great nonsenatorial upper class to which his birth and background gave him special ties. This class was loosely termed the *ordo equester*, and it comprised two principal segments: the business community, of which the *publicani* formed the major part, and the aristocracies of the *municipia* of Italy. From an early stage Cicero sought to present himself as a special defender of the rights and interests of members of this entire order, and he worked hard to build connections within each of its major groups.[15]

By 70 he could already claim that he had spent a great deal of his life engaged *in causis publicanorum.* One such case was that of C. Mustius, a well-connected *publicanus* whom Cicero defended sometime in the late seventies.[16] Another case in which the *publicani* took a keen interest was that of M. Fonteius, who had governed Transalpine Gaul for three years in the latter part of the seventies and whom Cicero defended on a charge of extortion in 69. Whatever injustices Fonteius had perpetrated on the Gauls, he had carefully safeguarded the interests of Roman businessmen in his province, and they conspicuously rallied to his defense. Cicero does not appear to have had a good case, and the result is uncertain, but he worked hard for a friend of the *publicani* and rendered another *beneficium* to the *ordo*. About the same time he

13. *Verr.* 2.3.182; 2.5.35. *Pis.* 2. *Planc.* 64–66. Plutarch, *Cicero* 6. He might have said of his quaestorship what he said of those of Murena and Sulpicius: *consedit nomen in quaestura. Mur.* 18. On Peducaeus cf. *Verr.* 2.2.138; 2.3.156, 216; 2.4.142. *Sen.* 21. *Att.* 1.5.4; 10.1.1; 13.1.3.

14. *Planc.* 66. *Brut.* 318. Cf. *Fam.* 2.12.2: *omnis peregrinatio, quod ego ab adulescentia iudicavi, obscura et sordida est iis, quorum industria Romae potest illustris esse.*

15. *Verr.* 2.2.181. *Man.* 4. *Rab. Post.* 15. *Phil.* 6.13. *Fam.* 13.9.2; 13.10.2. Cf. Wiseman, *New Men*, 69, 136. Taylor, *Party Politics*, 64.

16. *Verr.* 2.1.139. Mustius was a close friend of Domitius Ahenobarbus.

defended P. Oppius, who had served as proquaestor under M. Cotta in Bithynia. Oppius had quarreled with Cotta, who dismissed him, and later accused him by letter of mutiny and attempted murder. There is no evidence that Oppius had particular connections with the *publicani*, but he was a *novus homo* of equestrian origins, and the case provided Cicero, who made much of Oppius's background in his speech for the defense, with another opportunity to show himself the special defender of all members of this class. In 66 he extended his services to the business community from the courts to the purely political arena when, as the chosen champion of the *publicani* with interests in Asia, he argued in his speech for the Manilian law the need for decisive action by the government to safeguard the property and investments of businessmen in this province.[17]

His labors were well rewarded. The *Commentariolum Petitionis* repeatedly states that he had the full backing of the *publicani*, and Cicero himself confirms this by numerous acknowledgments throughout his writings of consistent support from the financiers and of his great political debt to the entire *ordo publicanorum*.[18]

He worked equally hard and with equal success to gain the friendship of leading figures in the *municipia* of Italy. As a native of a *municipium* he had an advantage in this endeavor over *nobiles* of the capital because of his greater knowledge of those communities and because of the predisposition of Italians to favor one of their own. The native town of a *municipalis* seeking to climb the political ladder at Rome could be counted upon to provide zealous support. So, generally, could neighboring communities, honoring the obligations of *vicinitas*, an important concept in Roman social and political history, which created ties as strong and sacred as those of *amicitia, clientela,* or *hospitium*, and usually guaranteed support at elections.[19]

17. *Font.* 13-15, 32. *Man.* 4. Dio 36.40.3. Quintilian, *Inst. Or.* 5.10.69; 5.13.20-21. Sallust, *Hist.* 3.59-60, Maur. Cf. E. S. Gruen, "Pompey, Metellus Pius, and the Trials of 70-69 B.C.: The Perils of Schematism" *AJP* 92 (1971), 12-16. Gruen refutes an unlikely hypothesis advanced by A. M. Ward, "Cicero's Support of Pompey in the Trials of Fonteius and Oppius" *Latomus* 27 (1968), 802-05, that the trials represented an ongoing struggle between Pompeian and Metellan factions.

18. *Com. Pet.* 3, 33. *Q.F.* 1.1.6, 32, 35. *Prov. Cons.* 10. Cf. *Sest.* 26-28. *Pis.* 41.

19. *Planc.* 19-22. *Cluent.* 197, 202. *Sest.* 10. *Com. Pet.* 17, 31. Cf. Wiseman, *New Men*, 31 ff., 47 ff., 137. *Com. Pet.* 24 stresses the importance of cultivating men who are *in suis vicinitatibus et municipiis gratiosi.*

There is plenty of evidence to show that Cicero enjoyed the goodwill and secured the full electoral backing of the *municipia* surrounding his native Arpinum. Friendship with the leading men of one of them, Aletrium, is directly attested by himself and illustrated by their request in 74 that he defend a certain Scamander, a freedman of one of their townsmen, Fabricius, accused of attempting to poison Cluentius. Cicero took the case to oblige them, although Scamander was patently guilty and was in fact condemned. Friendly relations with another neighboring community, Atina, a populous and prestigious *municipium*, is indicated by Cicero's references in the *Pro Plancio* to his long-term and close relationship with the family of his client, particularly with the Elder Plancius, one of Atina's most influential citizens. In the same speech he goes on at length about the neighborly spirit of this district of Italy and its diligent efforts to advance Plancius's political career, and he explicitly states that he himself experienced the same vigorous support from this entire area. It was an important region politically, thickly populated and not far from Rome, but, more important, most of its major *municipia* were in different tribes. Arpinum itself was in the tribe *Cornelia*, Aletrium in the *Poblilia*, Atina in the *Teretina.* Of the other *municipia finitima,* Aquinum was in the *Oufentina*, Fabrateria in the *Tromentina*, and Sora in the *Romilia.* [20]

But Cicero's municipal contacts extended well beyond Arpinum and its neighbors. His work in the courts enabled him to establish ties with many other *municipia* in many different areas, and, through those ties, to gain a foothold in a very large number of tribes. His defense of Roscius in 80 brought him the friendship of a prominent citizen of Ameria, which was situated in southern Umbria and belonged to the tribe *Clustumina.* He expanded his contacts in this area by his defense of Varenus of Fulginiae sometime in the early post-Sullan period. Fulginiae was in Cicero's own tribe, the *Cornelia.* [21] In 80 or 79 he defended the freedom of a woman from Arretium, an Etruscan town in the tribe *Pomptina*,

20. *Cluent.* 49. *Planc.* 20–25. Cf. L. R. Taylor, *The Voting Districts of the Roman Republic* (Rome 1960).

21. On Roscius cf. ch. 2, nn. 81–82, above. For Roscius's influence cf. *Rosc.* 15. On Varenus cf. Quintilian, *Inst. Or.* 4.1.74; 4.2.26; 5.10.69; 5.13.28; 7.1.9; 7.2.22; 7.2.36; 9.2.56. Priscian 7.14.70; 12.6.29. Cicero was also patron of Reate in Sabine country in the tribe *Quirina (Scaur.* 27), though the date at which he assumed that position cannot be established.

and in the process successfully challenged the validity of Sulla's attempts to disenfranchise this and another Etruscan *municipium*, Volaterrae, and thus rendered an outstanding service to both communities. Volaterrae was not far from Arretium and was in the tribe *Sabatina*, a small tribe dominated by the Volaterrani. Cicero strengthened his ties to this important town in 69 when he appeared in a civil suit on behalf of its best-known citizen, A. Caecina, a valuable political ally, described by Cicero as *in parte Italiae minime contemnenda facile omnium nobilissimus.* There are other indications of *necessitudo* between Cicero and the aristocracies of Arretium and Volaterrae, and the relationship endured to the end of his life.[22]

In 69, also, he added another important municipal contact by his defense of Fonteius. The Fonteii came from Tusculum, which was in the tribe *Papiria*, and were a well-established family which had won an unbroken succession of praetorships at Rome. By 68 Cicero had also acquired a villa at Tusculum, which increased his opportunities to make friends in this community and added to his claims on its political support. Another villa, acquired near Formiae before 66, gave him a base in the tribe *Aemilia.*[23]

In 66 he defended A. Cluentius Habitus, a native of Larinum in eastern Samnium. Larinum belonged partly to the tribe *Clustumina* and partly to the *Voltinia*, and was surrounded by a group of towns all of which were in different tribes and all of which sent leading citizens to Rome to aid in the defense of Cluentius, who was obviously a popular and influential figure throughout the region. Cicero made the most of the occasion to identify himself socially and culturally with Cluentius and his supporters, and his successful defense made him valuable friends in another politically powerful district.[24]

The bulk of Cicero's known contacts with the Italian aristocracy were

22. *Caec.* 97. *Fam.* 6.6.9. *Att.* 1.19.4. *Fam.* 13.4.1–2. Cf. Wiseman, *New Men,* 141. The case of Caecina again challenged the validity of Sulla's disenfranchisement of the Volaterrani. Cf. W. V. Harris, *Rome in Etruria and Umbria* (Oxford 1971), 276–84.

23. *Font.* 41. *Att.* 1.4.3; 1.5.7; 1.6.2. Cf. J. Carcopino, *Cicero: The Secrets of His Correspondence,* trans. E. O. Lorimer (London 1951), 1.43 ff.

24. *Cluent.* 197. Of the towns that sent supporters, Teanum was in the *Cornelia,* Luceria in the *Claudia*, Bovianum in the *Voltinia.* On the tribe of Larinum itself cf. Taylor, *Voting Districts,* 321. For Cicero's defense of the rights of *equites* cf. *Cluent.* 151 ff.

in northern and central Italy, but there are indications that he also had friends in the south. He indicates that he had outstanding support from the *municipium* of Atella, which was situated in Campania and belonged to the tribe *Falerna*, in all the vicissitudes of his career. In the late seventies he appeared in a civil case on behalf of M. Tullius of Thurii, which was in the tribe *Aemilia*. When he describes his journey into exile in the *Pro Plancio* he states that all the *municipia* between Vibo and Brundisium were *in fide* and gave him protection. Elsewhere he specifically claims the Locrians as *clientes.* [25]

The majority of the cases defended by Cicero during his years as a candidate have gone unrecorded, but even on the basis of those known to us it is clear that he built considerable political support among the aristocracies of the towns of Italy and secured a foothold in a significant number of the thirty-one rural tribes. The support of a large section of this element combined with broad support from the *publicani*, gave Cicero a formidable political following. Each of these groups wielded considerable political influence, particularly in the *Comitia Centuriata.* The *publicani*, whose political importance is repeatedly stressed by Cicero, drew strength from a high level of cohesiveness derived from their common interests, were all members of the first class, whose vote generally determined the outcome of elections in the *Comitia Centuriata*, and possessed in abundance the material sources of political power. In addition, they had a dominant impact on the votes of the eighteen centuries of *equites*, in which they were strongly represented.[26] The municipal aristocracies were also a force to be reckoned with in the *Comitia Centuriata* following the census of 70, in which they secured proper registration for the first time. All would have qualified easily for membership in the first class. The midsummer elections which Sulla established as the regular practice made it easier for them to exercise their new power, and there are many indications that large numbers did assemble for the elections, especially from the populous central regions of Italy in which the great majority of the tribes

25. *Fam.* 13.7.4. *Tull.* 14, 39. *Planc.* 97. *Leg.* 2.15. He was also a patron of Cales (*Fam.* 9.13.3) and of Capua (*Sest.* 9), though the relationship may not have predated his consulship.

26. On the political importance of the *publicani* cf. *Planc.* 23. *Att.* 1.17.8–9; 1.18.7; 2.1.8; 2.16.4. *Fam.* 1.9.26; *Q.F.* 1.1.32. *Off.* 3.88. Cf. P. A. Brunt, "The *Equites* in the Late Republic" *Second International Conference of Economic History, 1962* (Paris 1965), 1.123 ff.

were represented. It is clear that the *ordo equester* had the capacity, if united, to influence strongly decisions of the *Comitia Centuriata*, and Cicero's diligent and successful cultivation of the two major segments of the order gave him a power base that offset some of the most serious drawbacks of his *novitas*. [27]

He did not, however, ignore other sections of the electorate and other sources of political influence in his quest for friends and supporters. He used his forensic talents to win *gratia* in diverse places. *Nobiles* are attested among his clients, as are members of the lower orders; a passage in the *Pro Cluentio* describes his pleading on behalf of a humble *scriba*, Matrinius. [28] He also sought support from two forms of organization that were achieving increasing political importance, *collegia* and *sodalitates*. *Collegia* were basically trade or religious clubs, comprising artisans and shopkeepers, and by the late Republic significant numbers of freedmen and slaves. They became increasingly active politically in the sixties and, in effect, controlled the votes of the four urban tribes. The *Commentariolum Petitionis* stresses their importance and testifies to Cicero's influence with several of them. [29]

Sodalitates were associations, social or religious, of the upper classes, which, like the *collegia*, began to play an active part in politics in the sixties and acted as pressure groups at elections and at trials involving their members or friends. In the mid-sixties Cicero defended prominent members of no less than four such *sodalitates*, and he received an explicit commitment in each case that the *sodalitas* would repay his service with its political support. [30]

27. Cf. *Sulla* 24. Wiseman, *New Men*, 124. Also T. P. Wiseman, "The Census in the First Century B.C." *JRS* 59 (1969), 65 ff. Taylor, *Party Politics*, 52, 56–57. Cicero was later to claim that *cuncta Italia* elected him to the consulship. *Pis.* 3.

28. *Cluent.* 126. *Com. Pet.* 3 asserts that he defended men from all orders and implies that *consulares* were among his clients. Only one *nobilis*, however, occurs among those who can be named as clients of Cicero during his years as a candidate, a Mucius Orestinus, presumably an Aurelius Orestes adopted by the Mucii. Asconius 86, Clark. Cf. Gruen, *Last Generation*, 183 n. 74.

29. *Com. Pet.* 3. Cf. ibid. 29–30, where the importance of *urbani, industrii,* and *libertini* in Rome is stressed. On *collegia* in general cf. S. Treggiari, *Roman Freedmen during the Late Republic* (Oxford 1969), 168–77. A. W. Lintott, *Violence in Republican Rome* (Oxford 1968), 78–83.

30. *Com. Pet.* 19. The defendants were C. Fundanius; Q. Gallius, praetor in 65, defended on a charge of bribery in 64 (Asconius 88, Clark); C. Cornelius, tribune in 67; and C. Orchivius, praetor in 66.

But Cicero's public life could not be confined entirely to the law-courts and, particularly as he climbed toward the higher offices, he had to consider in his electoral planning what place he wished to assume in the political spectrum, and what position he wished to adopt on the varied political issues and disputes of the time. It is this aspect of his life as a candidate that has provoked the greatest controversy and has produced, especially since the time of Drumann and Mommsen, the common conclusion that, in his early life, he was essentially a political trimmer with varying political loyalties and convictions, a characterization epitomized in Syme's pithy description of him as a politician "who, after espousing various popular causes and supporting the grant of an extraordinary command to Pompey, from honest persuasion or for political advancement, afterwards became more conservative when he gained the consulate and entered the ranks of the governing oligarchy." This view, which has been fostered to some degree by simple prejudice against a man who lacked the obstinacy of a Cato or the ruthless drive and determination of a Caesar, and who had little permanent effect on the course of politics in his day, constitutes a serious misrepresentation of Cicero's political posture prior to his consulship. It draws supporting evidence mainly from the taunts of contemporary enemies of Cicero, from remarks of later hostile historians, notably Dio Cassius, and from the uncertain evidence of criminal trials and the equally dubious testimony of forensic speeches. But there is a great variety of more reliable data on Cicero's early political life which presents a different picture and plainly shows that Cicero's political course as a candidate, while marked by the pragmatism and flexibility of an astute politician, was basically directed by a deep commitment to the ideals of traditional republicanism with which his conservative heritage had imbued him.[31]

31. Syme, *Roman Revolution*, 137. Cf. J. P. V. D. Balsdon, "Cicero the Man" in *Cicero,* ed. T. A. Dorey (London 1964), 179. Reaction against the view has come from R. Heinze, "Ciceros politische Anfänge" *Abh Leipz* 27 (1909), 945–1010; K. Büchner, *Cicero: Bestand und Wandel seiner geistigen Welt* (Heidelberg 1964). Cf. A. E. Douglas, *Cicero* (Oxford 1968), 7 ff. For ancient allegations of political trimming by Cicero cf. *Vat.* 5. Dio 36.43–44. Dio's prejudice against Cicero is discussed by F. Millar, *A Study of Cassius Dio* (Oxford 1964), 46 ff.

Cicero and Verres

The action which perhaps has been most responsible for the failure to recognize the essential conservatism of Cicero's early political career, and for the image of him as an early espouser of popular causes, is the one prosecution he conducted during his years as a candidate, the famous case of Verres in 70, undertaken by Cicero at the urgent request of the Sicilians, whom Verres had governed with unusual cruelty and rapacity from 73 through 71.

Extortion trials were a common feature of Roman life, but a number of factors combined to bring unusual public attention to this one. Verres' corruption was notorius, and had been well advertised by repeated complaints from the Sicilians extending back to 73. Furthermore, the trial took place at a time when Rome was thronged with crowds from all over Italy who had come for the elections, the census, and games which Pompey was sponsoring in connection with his triumph. Additional interest came from the fact that, although Verres was not of distinguished lineage, he had staunch friends in high places, chief among them Q. Hortensius and Q. Caecilius Metellus, both of whom were candidates for the consulship of 69 and both of whom gained election before the trial actually took place. Hortensius headed the defense, and Cicero found himself facing what he called a *certamen maximum*, as he pitted his skills in a cause célèbre against the *potentia* of preeminent *nobiles* and the talents of Rome's most famous pleader.[32]

The initial strategy of the defense was to postpone or prolong the trial beyond the middle of August, when a series of festivals would suspend judicial proceedings for most of the remainder of the year and allow extension of the case into 69. By then Verres' friends would be in office, and he would be able to capitalize more fully on their favor. Cicero frustrated this design by a procedural innovation which omitted the customary lengthy opening speeches by prosecution and defense, and, after a short introductory address, he went directly to the hearing of witnesses and documents, substantially shortening the entire process and reducing opportunities for dilatory tactics. Hortensius was

---

32. *Brut.* 319. *Verr.* 1.54. On the complaints of the Sicilians cf. *Verr.* 2.1.122; 2.2.83–118; 2.3.45, 204; 2.4.41. That the case attracted much attention is attested in *Div. in Caec.* 42. *Verr.* 1.1.4.

outmaneuvered; Cicero presented a mountain of irrefutable evidence, and Verres withdrew into exile midway through the trial.[33]

Cicero subsequently published the brief speech he had actually delivered to the jury, and he added to it five other orations which he would have delivered, if Verres had not abandoned his defense. They comprised a detailed exposition of the charges and evidence, masterfully organized and argued, a rhetorical tour de force which would further publicize his achievement and demonstrate the industry and oratorical skill which circumstances had prevented him from exhibiting in full measure at the trial.

The Verrines enshrined a victory which greatly enhanced Cicero's reputation and strengthened his credentials as an aspiring statesman. Historians, however, have tended to find in the case a far wider political significance than the contribution it made to Cicero's eminence and political status. A long-standing and widely held view depicts the trial as an important event in a classic political confrontation in the late seventies, in which defenders of the status quo were ranged against reformist elements which had secured the powerful support of Pompey in 71 and which were intent on dismantling the primary props of Sulla's constitution by achieving in particular the restoration of the powers of tribunes and an end to the senate's exclusive control of the courts. The prosecution of the notorious Verres is seen as a boon to the reformers in that it provided an opportunity for a telling exposé of the senatorial misgovernment and judicial corruption which spawned extreme abuses such as Verres had perpetrated, an opportunity which was fully exploited by Cicero.[34]

More recent analyses, which view the dynamics of late republican politics in terms of factional rivalries rather than political collisions between traditionalists and reformers, redirect the political import of the trial to some degree, perceiving it primarily as a factional clash between Pompey, who needed to protect his Sicilian clients, and for

33. If the trial went into 69 it would have to begin all over again and, by a strange coincidence, would be presided over by M. Metellus, brother of Quintus. Cf. *Verr.* 1.18 ff., 21, 30 ff.; 2.1.16. Ps. Asconius 185, 205, 212, 223, Stangl.

34. This view occurs in such important works as *Cambridge Ancient History*, 9.336 ff.; H. H. Scullard, *From the Gracchi to Nero* (London 1959), 98; W. E. Heitland, *The Roman Republic* 3 (Cambridge 1923), 18–19; J. L. Strachan-Davidson, *Cicero and the Fall of the Roman Republic* (London 1898), 55 ff.

this and other reasons of political inclination and expediency espoused Verres' opponents and their program of reform, and a leading faction of *nobiles* centered around the Metelli, who were friends of Verres, foes of reform, and bitter rivals of Pompey. Cicero is thus variously associated with a reform movement backed by Pompey and opposed to the dominance of the oligarchy, or more directly linked to Pompey, and through him to the reformist cause, in a largely factional struggle with a dominant oligarchic *factio* headed by the Metelli.[35]

These magnifications of an extortion trial into an event of major political significance with resultant major implications for Cicero's political role, sympathies, and associations in this period, deserve to be viewed with the greatest skepticism. They are founded on highly questionable conceptions of the patterns of political strife that prevailed in the seventies, and they suffer from the shortcomings of the testimony of trials and from a common distorting effect of Ciceronian evidence, particularly the evidence of forensic speeches, which, besides being artful special pleading, tends, by simply dramatizing and voluminously treating a particular event, to project, amid a frequent dearth of information on other happenings, an exaggerated image of the true significance of that event. It will be argued in the following pages that the case had no particular political importance, and that Cicero, in prosecuting it, was merely seeking to enhance his reputation and assist his Sicilian clients and was not espousing any reformist cause or aligning himself with any individual or faction. The discussion will require a detailed analysis of political events in the seventies and of the role in them of the decade's foremost figure, Pompey.

As in the case of other periods, the evidence for the politics of the seventies does not readily fit the mold of an ideological dichotomy of liberals and conservatives, or the equally schematic concept of organized factions of *nobiles* maneuvering for political supremacy. The decade

35. Cf. Badian, *Foreign Clientelae,* 278 ff. A. M. Ward, "Cicero and Pompey in 75 and 70 B.C." *Latomus* 29 (1970), 58–71. J. Van Ooteghem, "Verres et les Metelli" *Mélanges Piganiol* (1966), 2.827–35. B. A. Marshall, "Q. Cicero, Hortensius, and the *Lex Aurelia*" *RhM* 118 (1975), 147. Some dissent has come from Gruen, *AJP* 92 (1971), 1 ff., and B. Twyman, "The Metelli, Pompeius, and Prosopography" *Aufstieg und Niedergang der römischen Welt* 1.1 (Berlin 1972), 817–74. Another variation on the trial's importance occurs in Taylor, *Party Politics,* 103 ff., where it is suggested that Pompey and the *populares* wished for Verres' acquittal to bolster their case against the senatorial courts.

was marked by a high level of internal unrest and by a measure of personal feuding and political intrigue. But the unrest of the seventies was not generated or promoted by any ideological rift or significant division over political goals and methods among a *nobilitas* revitalized and solidified by victory and the Sullan settlement; neither did personal rivalries or enmities spill over into political disputes or confrontations over major domestic or foreign issues, and nowhere, either in the movement for change or in the scramble for power and prominence, can defined, continuous groups be discerned in sustained opposition or competition. Above all, the evidence does not support the notion that Pompey headed a reform party or a Pompeian faction in the late seventies in general opposition to the oligarchy or in specific opposition to one of its foremost families, the Metelli.

The first domestic crisis of the seventies was precipitated in 78 by the consul M. Aemilius Lepidus, a political opportunist eager to exploit the grievances of the many victims of Sulla's vengeance. His program offered to reinstate the grain dole, recall exiles, restore their property to the dispossessed and their political rights to the disenfranchised. An outbreak of violence in Etruria, where evicted landholders took arms against Sullan settlers, forced him to choose between suppressing the rebels and undermining his position as a leader of the aggrieved or siding with them at the risk of provoking an armed clash with his consular colleague, Lutatius Catulus. He chose the latter course, and sought to broaden the appeal of his movement by advocating restoration of the powers of tribunes. The senate, understandably anxious to avoid another civil war, at first attempted to negotiate with him and even summoned him to preside over the consular elections for 77. But Lepidus refused to be separated from his army by returning to Rome; 77 began without consuls, and Lepidus took over as governor of Transalpine Gaul clearly intent on enforcing his wishes on the state.

The oligarchy moved quickly and decisively, once the design of Lepidus became fully apparent. The *senatus consultum ultimum* was passed in the early days of 77, and Catulus and the *interrex* Appius Claudius were instructed to protect the state. Pompey was appointed a *legatus* to Catulus, and by the middle of 77 he and Catulus had separately and soundly defeated the forces of Lepidus.[36]

36. Sources in Broughton, *MRR*, 2.85, 89. Cf. T. Rice Holmes, *The Roman Republic* 1 (Oxford 1923), 363–69. N. Criniti, "M. Aemilius Q. F. M. N. Lepidus

The revolt represented a final effort by the anti-Sullan forces to reverse Sulla's victory and its political consequences. It had the support of the politically disaffected and disadvantaged and of the economically downtrodden, including some notable names prominent in the Marian cause in the eighties: a Cornelius Cinna, a Junius Brutus, a Scipio, a Perperna. But aside from predictable deféctions by such longtime *inimici* of Sulla, the *nobilitas* stood solidly together in the face of a serious threat to its ascendancy. Marcius Philippus, who in earlier days had been more tolerant than most of the designs of Marius and Cinna, was the author of the *consultum ultimum.* His proposal conferred the chief military authority on Catulus, with whose family he had deep and long-term differences. Pompey, earlier a political ally of Lepidus and no friend of Catulus, accepted a command under the latter and played a major role in the suppression of his former friend. The consuls elected to lead the state at the height of the crisis in 77, D. Junius Brutus and Mam. Aemilius Lepidus, bore the names of the two leading rebels, a coincidence seemingly aided by the oligarchy, presumably in order to advertise the isolation of the insurgent commanders, and made possible only by an unusual spirit of cooperation which saw a prominent and popular *Sullanus*, Scribonius Curio, voluntarily withdraw his candidacy. Overall, the senatorial effort against Lepidus was vigorous and concerted, unimpeded either by ideological divisions or factional rivalries, a notable illustration of the essential cohesiveness of the post-Sullan oligarchy.[37]

Senatorial solidarity is likewise evident in subsequent political crises in the decade. That is not to assert that the senate or the *nobilitas* was devoid of differences or divisions. Evidence of bitter antagonisms and sharp rivalries abounds. More than twenty criminal trials can be definitely assigned to the decade, and several show leading families of the

---

'ut ignis in stipula'" *Mem Ist Lomb* 30 (1969), 319–460. J. E. Neunheuser, *M. Aemilius Lepidus* (Münster 1902). L. Hayne "M. Lepidus (cos. 78): A Re-Appraisal" *Historia* 21 (1972), 661–68. M. Gelzer, *Pompeius* (Munich 1949), 49. Gruen, *Last Generation*, 12–16. Twyman, *ANRW* 1.1, 820 ff., 837 ff. Cf. n. 65, below, on Pompey's commission.

37. Suetonius, *Julius* 5. Plutarch, *Pompey* 16.2; *Brut.* 4.1. Livy, *Per.* 90. Orosius 5.22.17. Appian, *BC* 1.107. Exsup. 7. On Philippus and his role cf. Sallust, *Hist.* 1.77, Maur. Florus 2.11.23. J. Van Ooteghem, *L. Marcius Philippus et sa famille* (Brussels 1961). On the consuls of 77 cf. Sallust, *Hist.* 1.86, Maur. Gruen, *Last Generation*, 123; *AJP* 1971, 3–5. G. V. Sumner, "Manius or Mamercus" *JRS* 54 (1964), 41–48. Twyman, *ANRW* 1.1, 845 ff.

aristocracy in collision and leading *Sullani* suffering conviction. On a more directly political level there were sharp contests for major military and provincial assignments. The enlarged Sullan senate, more cumbersome and heterogeneous, made the means to control of its decisions more varied and tenuous and gave added scope for the machinations of the skilled political operator. The best example of the greater complexity of senatorial politics and of the keenness of senatorial rivalries is provided by the oft-quoted intrigues of P. Cornelius Cethegus, a Marian turncoat who never held high office, but who thoroughly understood the workings of politics and as a result had built influence in the senate equal to that of a *consularis* and was courted by the senate's *principes* with presents and visits in the night. Among those who sought his services and benefited from his support were two recipients of important *imperia extraordinaria* in 74, the praetor M. Antonius and the consul L. Licinius Lucullus, the latter, at least, no admirer of Cethegus, sharing an apparently general aristocratic disdain for the upstart renegade, but forced to sue for his favor in the rough-and-tumble of post-Sullan senatorial power jousts. There was no easy agreement among the oligarchy on the distribution of *honores*, and the road to preeminence was not smooth even for the distinguished.[38]

But neither the accounts of political intrigue nor the array of prosecutors, defendants, and advocates in the criminal trials permit the identification of any continuous political groups or of any divisions extending to the basic institutions of the Sullan system. They reveal instead haphazard, changeable coalitions, products of the unpredictable promptings of personal loyalties, strategies, and ambitions, which displayed a characteristic willingness to answer the demands of *amicitia* and *inimicitia* and to grapple for political advancement, but not, in this period, to the degree of assailing the existing social or political order. In matters related to the preservation of the status quo, the *nobilitas* of the seventies managed to maintain basic unity. Political unrest developed

38. Most noteworthy are the trials of the Dolabellae and C. Antonius in the early seventies and of P. Gabinius and A. Terentius Varro in the latter half of the decade. Cf. Gruen, *Last Generation,* 32, 38–39. On Cethegus and the commands of Antonius and Lucullus, cf. Appian, *BC* 1.60, 62, 80. Plutarch, *Marius* 40.2; *Lucullus* 5–6. Val. Max. 9.2.1. *Acad.* 2.1.1. *Brut.* 178. *Par. St.* 5.40. Sallust, *Hist.* 1.77.20, Maur. Ps. Asconius 259, Stangl. Cf. A. E. R. Boak, "The Extraordinary Commands from 80 to 48 B.C." *AHR* 24 (1918), 1–25.

and persisted throughout the decade and forced major refinements of the Sullan system, but the unrest was not instigated or led by any dissentient alliance within the oligarchy, and change took the form of a conciliatory series of concessions implemented by leading *nobiles* with general senatorial consent.[39]

The roots of the internal troubles of the middle and late seventies were economic rather than political. By the middle of the decade piracy had again become a critical problem for Rome, seriously disrupting Italian shipping and causing food shortages and soaring prices. Costly wars in Spain and Thrace were draining an already depleted treasury and putting severe strains on Roman manpower. The outbreak of the Mithridatic war in 74 and of the slave war in 73 brought further economic disruption and hardship and heightened the apprehensions of the public and its disenchantment with senatorial rule. A succession of tribunes took advantage of the public mood to assail the oligarchy and the Sullan settlement which had entrenched its hold on power and wealth. The agitation was begun in 76 by the tribune Sicinius, who called for restoration of the powers of tribunes, and bitingly criticized the *nobilitas*.[40] In 75 the tribune Opimius attempted to defy the limitations imposed by Sulla on the tribunician veto and continued the attacks on the senate's leadership.[41] In 74 L. Quinctius resurrected the tribunician *contio*, and he used it to pillory Sulla's constitutional arrangements and to intensify the clamor for restoration of tribunician prerogatives. Later in the year he made use of a scandal in the courts to sharpen and expand his attacks on the status quo. A man named Statius Albius Oppianicus was convicted on a charge of poisoning, amid rumors of wholesale bribery of the jury. Quinctius, who had defended Oppianicus, seized on the rumors to raise the specter of oppression through judicial murder, dramatizing in the process the need for the protective office of the tribunate and reopening the old and contentious question

39. Cf. Gruen, *Last Generation*, 38. The difficulties of constructing defined, stable factions is well illustrated by the varied and fanciful groupings that emerge from attempts to discern such factions. Cf. Twyman, *ANRW* 1.1, 832–74, the most recent lengthy analysis of factions in the seventies, which has added yet another new factional alignment of the politicians of the decade.

40. Sallust, *Hist.* 2.45, 47; 3.48.8, 10, Maur. *Planc.* 64. *Verr.* 2.3.215. Ps. Asconius 189, Stangl. *Brut.* 216–17. Quinctilian, *Inst. Or.* 11.3.129. Plutarch, *Crassus* 7.9.

41. *Verr.* 2.1.155–56. Ps. Asconius 255, Stangl.

of who should comprise the juries in the criminal courts.[42] In 73 Licinius Macer continued to hold *contiones*, and to harp on the tribunician question and denounce the tyrannical rule of the oligarchy and the inequalities in powers, burdens, and rewards in the post-Sullan system. There was an apparent lull in tribunician agitation in 72, as the threat of Spartacus superseded domestic disputes, but in 71 the tribune Lollius Palicanus returned to the attack, sounding again the twin themes of tribunician powers and court reform.[43]

These several tribunes who advertised popular grievances in the seventies and initiated demands for political change were relatively obscure politicians with few resources or connections. Sicinius, Opimius, and Licinius Macer could claim distinguished ancestors, but none for several generations; Quinctius and Palicanus were the first members of their families to win office in Rome.[44] All of them worked in apparent isolation; no links can be established between them; they headed no particular group, nor were they agents of any. All that gave continuity and strength to their cause was the continuity and strength of the public discontent, which they had the skill and initiative to exploit, using their office, as it had often been used before, to overcome obscurity and to wring political advantage from public disillusionment with senatorial government. In brief, the agitation for change in the latter half of the seventies was an amorphous and disjointed movement, fed by hard times and governmental failures and promoted by a discrete series of political outsiders in search of a constituency.

The response of the oligarchy throughout the period was a concerted and consistent two-pronged effort to discredit or suppress the dissident leaders and to placate their supporters by such concessions as seemed necessary. The earliest tribunician agitation in 76 was met with a hardline policy of repression by the consul Scribonius Curio, but by 75 mounting public anger at the oligarchy, which brought attacks on magistrates in the streets, forced the consul C. Aurelius Cotta to adopt

42. Sallust, *Hist.* 3.48.11, Maur. Plutarch, *Lucullus* 5.4. Ps. Asconius 189, 206, 216, 255, Stangl. *Verr.* 2.1.157. *Cluent.* 72–96, 103–16, 119, 136–38. Quintilian, *Inst. Or.* 5.13.39.

43. Sallust, *Hist.* 3.48; 4.43, Maur. Ps. Asconius, 189, 220, 328, Stangl. *Brut.* 223. *Verr.* 1.45; 2.2.95–100. Plutarch, *Pompey* 21.4. Appian, *BC* 1.121.

44. Palicanus was from Picenum and may have been a protégé of Pompey, though the evidence for it is slight, and in 60 we find him daily abusing Pompey's henchman, the consul L. Afranius. *Att.* 1.18.5.

a more conciliatory stand and to sponsor, in cooperation with the leading agitator, Opimius, a bill making tribunes eligible to stand for other
offices. Opimius, however, quickly paid for the concession he had
helped to exact. Soon after leaving office he was successfully prosecuted
by leading *nobiles* on a charge of having illegally used his veto, and he
was stripped of all his possessions.[45]

Cotta's bill, according to Cicero and Asconius, displeased some of the
senate's *principes*, but it is clear that the consul acted as a proponent,
not an opponent, of the *via optimas*, and that he carried the great
majority of the senate with him in a policy of conciliation designed to
alleviate massive public discontent. Sallust, in a speech attributed to
Licinius Macer, describes him as a consul from the heart of the *factio*,
a contemptuous label for the Sullan oligarchy; associates him with
Catulus, Curio, and Lucullus, who are presented as leading foes of the
people's interests; and explicitly portrays his bill as a concession dictated by fear. It is likely that Macer's speech contains some distortions,
but its remarks on the consul of 75 are essentially borne out by the
evidence of Cicero and by other ancient testimony for Cotta's political
affiliations. A nephew of the upright and rigidly conservative Rutilius
Rufus, and a member of the prestigious and traditionally conservative
college of pontiffs, Cotta served his political apprenticeship in the
nineties in the company of the decade's leading *optimates*, L. Licinius
Crassus, M. Antonius, Lutatius Catulus, and the Mucii Scaevolae.
Forced into exile by the Varian commission, he returned high in the
graces of Sulla after the latter's victory and quickly made his way to
the consulship, an office reserved almost exclusively in the seventies for
leading *Sullani.* There were few who could more truly be called *ex fac-
tione media consul,* and there is no indication that his behavior in 75 in
any sense constituted a volte-face or to any degree diminished his standing, or the standing of his family, with the Sullan establishment. In that
same year his brother Marcus was elected to the consulship and in 74
was appointed by the senate to an important command in the war
against Mithridates as governor of the newly acquired province of
Bithynia. Continuing friendship between the family and the Antonii

45. Cf. nn. 40 and 41, above. Palicanus did not immediately suffer, but in 67
his candidacy for the consulship was rejected by the optimate consul, Calpurnius
Piso. Val. Max. 3.8.3. The oligarchy had not forgotten.

and Lutatii Catuli is attested, and that Cotta himself retained the goodwill of the oligarchy as a whole is amply illustrated by the fact that, after his governorship of Cisalpine Gaul, he was awarded a triumph by the senate in 73 for extremely modest successes over a largely imaginary foe.[46]

Further proof that Cotta's stance was in harmony rather than in conflict with the senate's thinking emerges from the strategy of the oligarchy over the following two years, a strategy which essentially repeated the pattern of 75, combining prudent mollification of the public and partial satisfaction of its grievances with obstruction and defamation of the men who aired them. In 74 Quinctius suffered sustained harassment, but, to offset the public *invidia* he was arousing against the *pauci*, the senate passed a stern resolution ordering the establishment of a special commission to investigate his charge of judicial corruption. In 73 Licinius Macer was greeted with organized attempts to disrupt his meetings, and with a variety of measures designed to erode his following and undermine his case against the Sullan oligarchy. The *principes* attempted to portray themselves as *vindices libertatis*; the consuls passed a grain law; consuls and senate signaled repudiation of Sullan excesses by attempting to extract money owed to the state by Sullan *possessores*; further *delenimenta* were promised and it was implied that major reforms would be implemented after Pompey returned from the Sertorian war. Pompey was back in Rome in 71 and secured election to the consulship. After his election he publicly declared his support for proposals to restore the powers of tribunes and reform the jury system, and soon after entering office he sponsored a bill restoring in full the traditional tribunician prerogatives.[47]

46. Asconius 67, 78, Clark. Sallust, *Hist.* 3.48.8–11, Maur. *De Or.* 1.25; 3.11. *N.D.* 3.80–81. *Brut.* 305. On M. Cotta cf. Broughton, *MRR*, 2.101. Marcus supported the appointment of M. Antonius, an *adfinis* of Catulus, to an extraordinary command in 74. Ps. Asconius 259, Stangl. On Gaius's triumph cf. *Pis.* 62. Asconius 14, Clark. Cf. L. R. Taylor, "Caesar's Colleagues in the Pontifical College" *AJP* 63 (1942), 385–412. Badian, *Studies*, 36 ff.

47. Cf. nn. 42 and 43 above. Cf. also *Verr.* 3.81, 163; 5.52. Sallust, *Hist.* 4.1, Maur. We know of two optimate politicians who made private distributions of cheap grain in 75 and 74: L. Hortensius and M. Seius. Such largesse would obviously increase their personal popularity, but it would also help to lessen hostility toward the ruling class as a whole. *Verr.* 2.3.215. *Off.* 2.58. Pliny, *NH* 15.2; 18.16. Expectations were clearly created that major reforms would follow Pompey's return. Cf. *Verr.* 1.44. Sallust, *Hist.* 3.48.21, Maur. On the significance of this passage in Sallust cf. Twyman, *ANRW* 1.1, 852, with bibliography.

The tribunician bill was the most far-reaching in its consequences of all the reforms of the seventies, seriously undermining the stability of the Sullan constitution and paving the way for a renewal of destructive demagoguery and anarchical conflict between the powers of senate and people. But all of these consequences cannot have been evident in 70, and the political context of the bill, the accounts of its implementation, and the political stance and affiliations of its sponsor all point to the conclusion that the measure continued the pattern of reform of the preceding years and was enacted, not by senatorial foes over senatorial opposition, but by a consul firmly linked to the senate's *principes* and acting with general senatorial consent.

The bill fits into the strategy of concession and conciliation initiated by the oligarchy itself in 75 and sustained by its leading members in succeeding years in what was obviously seen as a necessary course to contain burgeoning public discontent with senatorial government. The level of that discontent had not abated by the time of Pompey's return in 71; the tribunician question continued to be its focal point; there were expectations of action by Pompey, partly generated, if one may believe Sallust, by the senate's leadership itself. There is every indication that those same leaders were fully aware of the gathering momentum toward final resolution of the tribunician question, that they remained convinced of the necessity of continuing the conciliatory course of the preceding years, and, in consequence, cooperated with Pompey in harmonious implementation of an unavoidable concession.

The senate had the opportunity to discuss and judge the proposal. No outcry or opposition from any segment is reported. In an allusion to the debate Cicero implies that no less stalwart a guardian of the *via optimas* than Catulus himself accepted the reform as inevitable in view of the public mood. Pompey's own handling of the bill also rules out any idea that in sponsoring it he was playing the part of a *popularis* and pursuing a course seriously at variance with the wishes and perceived interests of the oligarchy. There is no need to doubt that, as Plutarch asserts, he recognized the depth of the public feeling underlying the clamor for restoration of the powers of tribunes, and that, with typical opportunism, he was eager to reap the political benefits of implementing so popular a reform. But it is clear that he hoped and aimed to do so without provoking the hostility of the oligarchy, and in the capacity of the senate's representative rather than its opponent. He did not attempt to exploit the tribunician issue in his bid for the consulship, nor did he engage in any of the polemical rhetoric associated with calls for change in the preceding years. In fact, he made no public comment at all on any political controversy while a candidate, and he avoided addressing a *contio* until after his election. When he did put forward a proposal he first laid it before the senate in accordance with strict republican tradition. He was carefully avoiding any appearance of the style of the *popularis*, and he made clear that he viewed his role in the affair as that of a conciliator and unifier, doing what was necessary to achieve harmony between *plebs* and *patres*. [48]

A revealing discussion of the tribunate by Cicero in the *De Legibus* would seem to confirm that there was no serious conflict or basic disagreement between Pompey and the senate over the tribunician bill. Although writing almost twenty years later, when he no longer held Pompey's statesmanship in high regard, and when devising a constitution designed to entrench senatorial supremacy and the optimate ideal of government, Cicero defends Pompey's law in unequivocal terms and retains the tribunate with all of its traditional powers in his own ideal system. He presents the office as the most innocuous method of assigning to the people a share of power and liberty, and as a treasured symbol of political equality whose loss the people would not long endure. Pompey's action, whatever undesirable consequences might on occasion result from it, was therefore a practical necessity, the action of a prudent statesman promoting an insuppressible and unharmful cause so as to avoid the harm of its abandonment to the *popularis*. Thoroughly oligarchic in tone and spirit, Cicero's remarks disclose that Pompey's measure was not necessarily incompatible with the concerns and outlook of the oligarchy, and echoing as they do the apparent attitude of Catulus, the stance of Pompey himself, and the spirit of compromise

48. *Verr.* 1.44. Ps. Asconius 220, Stangl. Plutarch, *Pompey* 21. *Verr.* 1.45. Sallust, *Hist.* 4.45, Maur. Pompey gave private assurances to the tribunes that he favored their cause (Appian, *BC* 1.121), but clearly he avoided public statements on the matter. A good indication of his eagerness to avoid in any way offending the senate is the report of Gellius (14.7) that he asked Varro to write him a handbook on senatorial procedure. It remains uncertain whether Crassus co-sponsored the tribunician bill. Neither Cicero nor Plutarch states or implies that he did. The Epitome of Livy, making a brief, vague statement about the reform, remains the only ancient source to link Crassus's name to it. Cf. W. C. McDermott, "*Lex de tribunicia potestate* (70 B.C.)" *CP* 72 (1977), 49–52.

visible in the senatorial response to popular demands throughout the latter part of the seventies, they would seem accurately to reflect the prevailing oligarchic attitude in 70 toward Pompey's legislation.[49]

Pompey's place and posture in the political history of the seventies as a whole are no bar to this interpretation. Modern scholarship has tended to single out Pompey as the primary threat to the unity and supremacy of the Sullan oligarchy and to portray him as an inveterate power-builder whose career in the late eighties and seventies represents a continuous tug-of-war with a *nobilitas* striving to contain him or with a leading faction striving to outrival him. But the view is largely a product of an anachronistic overemphasis on the role of the military in the politics of the early post-Sullan era, and it seriously distorts, if not Pompey's goal of power, at least the manner of his pursuit of it in this period.[50]

Pompey's ambition and political craftiness cannot be denied. For more than thirty years he maintained a leading position in a complex and often turbulent political world, and in pursuit of preeminence he was seldom deterred by considerations of principle or consistency from the employment of any ally or resource that seemed necessary or expedient. His desire for power and primacy and his adroit opportunism are clearly visible in the record of his behavior in the late eighties and seventies, as in other periods, but in these years they moved him toward a traditional mode of power-building through alignment with leading members of the Sullan oligarchy.

Pompey had dramatically committed himself to the Sullan side in 83 by raising a private army to fight the *Cinnani*, with whom he had managed to coexist comfortably until events declared the likelihood of a Sullan victory. Following that victory he had moved quickly to maximize the benefits of his timely tergiversation by abruptly divorcing his wife, Antistia, in 82 and marrying Aemilia, the stepdaughter of Sulla.

49. *Leg.* 3.19 ff. Cf. U. Laffi, "Il Mito di Silla" *Athenaeum* 45 (1967), 177–213. Gruen, *Last Generation,* 28. The contention of these scholars that the reforms of 70 did not seriously undermine the Sullan system is, however, unconvincing.

50. Cf. Badian, *Foreign Clientelae,* 267–84. Gabba, *Athenaeum* 32 (1954), 323–32. M. Gelzer, "Das erste Consulat des Pompeius" *Kleine Schriften* 2 (1963), 146–89. Syme, *Roman Revolution,* 28–46. D. Stockton, "The First Consulship of Pompey" *Historia* 22 (1973), 205–18. Dissent has come from A. N. Sherwin-White, "Violence in Roman Politics" *JRS* 46 (1956), 1–9, and Gruen *AJP* 92 (1971), 1–16, and the present account is indebted to their contributions.

He had thus skillfully threaded his way through the treacherous political tangles of the eighties, to emerge in a prominent position on the winning side as a favored *adfinis* of Sulla and conspicuous defender of the *causa nobilitatis*. The position had been daringly sought and the evidence indicates that it was safeguarded with care throughout the seventies and for as long as the favor of the oligarchy remained a necessary and sufficient condition for political success.

Soon after his marriage with Aemilia in 82, Pompey was dispatched by senatorial decree to Sicily to confront the Marian generals, Perperna and Carbo. He quickly recovered the island, and immediately received a fresh senatorial commission to proceed against the forces of another Marian supporter, Domitius Ahenobarbus, in Africa. He successfully completed his campaign against Domitius early in 81 and was then instructed by Sulla to disband five of his six legions and await the arrival of a new governor for Africa. Pompey was privately indignant at the order, according to Plutarch, and his soldiers openly expressed their dissatisfaction and refused to leave without their commander. Finally, after unsuccessfully attempting to dispel their mutinous mood, Pompey returned with them to Italy. Soon afterwards he asked for a triumph, and, despite initial reluctance on the part of Sulla and the senate, he eventually received it.[51]

Pompey's behavior in returning to Italy with his troops and in pressing his claims to a triumph has often been viewed as outright insubordination, involving the illegal retention of an army and the extortion under its shadow of a personal benefit—the first in a series of quasi-revolutionary exploitations of military power by Pompey for private advantage.[52] Substantiation of illegality or of military intimidation, however, is difficult to find. The only deviation by Pompey from Sulla's directive which is documented in the sources is his departure from Africa before the arrival of his successor, a not unheard of action for which Pompey had a strong justification in this instance in the temper of his troops. That he retained his soldiers under arms after reaching Italy,

51. Plutarch, *Pompey* 4–14; *Sulla* 33.3. Cf. Broughton, *MRR*, 2.64, 70.
52. Cf. R. E. Smith, "Pompey's Conduct in 80 and 77 B.C." *Phoenix* 14 (1960), 1–13. Badian, *Foreign Clientelae,* 273–75. C. Lanzani, "Silla e Pompeo. La Spedizione di Sicilia e d'Africa." *Historia* 7 (1933), 343–62. Gelzer, "Cn. Pompeius Strabo und der Aufstieg seines Sohnes Magnus" *Kleine Schriften*, 2.130–38.

however, or used them in any way to extort a triumph is neither stated nor implied in any ancient account or reference, a strange omission if Pompey thus openly and with impunity defied the law and a powerful and uncompromising dictator. Not even Plutarch, with his fondness for anachronistically dramatizing the menace of the military in the political history of the late Republic, suggests that on this occasion Pompey engaged in such a perilous game of military brinksmanship. On the contrary, his account would seem to refute any contention that Pompey was insubordinate. He relates that Sulla first heard that Pompey was in revolt, and thought he would have to fight him, but on learning the truth he welcomed him with warmth and acclaim.[53] The truth that turned Sulla's mind from fighting to friendly welcome obviously did not spell military mutiny. The only evidence which might possibly suggest that the African legions remained intact after their return to Italy occurs in allusions to Pompey's triumph, where the soldiers are described as creating a disturbance because they had not received as much as they expected. But their presence at the triumph is no proof that the troops had been retained under arms, since the participation of at least part of a victorious army in a triumphal celebration was an essential feature of the proceedings, and disbanded troops were customarily reassembled for such an occasion.[54]

Besides, the idea that Pompey invited a military confrontation with Sulla in Italy in pursuit of a triumph is inherently implausible. If his indignation at his recall had moved him seriously to contemplate

53. Plutarch, *Pompey* 13.3–5. For Plutarch's fondness for emphasizing the threat of the military cf. *Sulla* 12.8–9; *Lucullus* 5.2; *Pompey* 21.3, 43.1. A fragment of Sallust (*Hist.* 2.21, Maur.): *Nam Sullam consulem de reditu eius legem ferentem ex composito tribunus plebis C. Herennius prohibuerat*, is commonly taken to mean that Sulla, anxious to avoid a confrontation with Pompey, passed a *privilegium* dispensing him from the *Lex Cornelia de provinciis ordinandis.* The objections to this interpretation are many, not least the fact that it goes against the account of Plutarch, which indicates that Sulla did not know Pompey's intentions until the latter reached Italy. It also assumes that Sulla's legislative program had been at least partly enacted by early 81. Badian (*Hermes* 83 [1955], 107 ff.) argues plausibly that the fragment refers to 88 and to Pompey's father. The fact that Sulla cut Pompey out of his will is sometimes adduced as proof that the latter was insubordinate in 81. But there is at least one other action of Pompey that could account for Sulla's displeasure, namely his support of Lepidus for the consulship of 78. Cf. Plutarch, *Sulla* 38.1; *Pompey* 15.1–2.

54. Frontinus, *Strategemata* 4.5.1. Plutarch, *Pompey* 14.5. Cf. Badian, *Hermes* 83 (1955), 116.

unlawfully using his army, surely he would have remained in Africa, where he could have represented a significant military threat, and he would have sought not the grant of a mere honor but a reversal of Sulla's unwelcome order. Once he landed in Italy and severed himself from potential allies in Africa and Sicily, he no longer had any reasonable hope of challenging Sulla's military might. His army was vastly outnumbered by the more than twenty-three legions Sulla had at his disposal. Even if these legions had been largely disbanded by the time of Pompey's return, which must remain doubtful, they remained a willing, readily available, and formidable fighting force for Sulla. They were strategically located throughout the peninsula, their loyalty fortified by generous grants of land and by their stake in the survival of the regime which would protect their rights to their new possessions. Sulla's veteran settlements provided strong and continuing insurance of his military supremacy in Italy.[55] The difficulties involved in assuming that Pompey attempted any form of military intimidation in those circumstances, or that Sulla, intent on reconstituting a *respublica* secure from such threats, meekly yielded to the pressure with the odds so strongly in his favor, or that Pompey's soldiers, whose chief concern all along was the size of their benefits, backed so rash a venture, are self-evident and overwhelming.

The story of Pompey's insubordination in the late eighties is a modern myth. Sulla's order to him had entailed two principal consequences: the disbandment of most of his army and his own return to the status of a *privatus*. Pompey was naturally displeased by the directive, but in bringing home his troops to Italy he in effect accepted both of its consequences and implemented the substance of its instructions.

As for his triumph, it is clear that the opposition to it was overcome not by threats of force but by a thoroughly traditional and respectable form of political machination, the forging of a political alliance with the powerful through a marriage connection. Aemilia had died in childbirth during Pompey's absence. He now married Mucia, uterine sister of Metellus Celer and Metellus Nepos and stepdaughter of Metellus Nepos

55. The idea that Pompey had to lead back his troops to qualify for a triumph has been shown to be groundless. Cf. Smith, *Phoenix* 14 (1960), 3 ff. On Sulla's legions, their numbers and loyalty, cf. Appian *BC* 1.96, 100. For their settlement in colonies cf. Gabba, *Athenaeum* 29 (1951), 270. Brunt, *Italian Manpower*, 300-12.

the Elder, consul of 98. The marriage linked him to the prestigious Metellan clan and also to a number of other prominent *nobiles*, notably Appius Claudius and Servilius Vatia, both soon to be consuls in 79. The consequences of the linkage are plainly illustrated in the stance of Servilius, initially a leading opponent of the triumph but, by the time of its celebration, Pompey's enthusiastic admirer.[56] Pompey had disarmed his opposition and strengthened his political position by the weapons of *amicitia*, and the entire process, which saw a young politician of remarkable talent and achievements seek and secure the favor and friendship of the inner circle of the *nobilitas*, was typical of the dynastic workings of oligarchic politics and needs no theories of fear or coercion to explain it.

In brief, Pompey, by his victories in the Sicilian and African campaigns, had once again rendered signal service to the Sullan oligarchy and had once again sought to capitalize on his success, not by intimidating the *principes* of the cause he served, but by increasing, through conventional political means, his connections with them and his identification with their interests. Pliny the Elder, in describing Pompey's achievements in this period, aptly speaks of his emergence as a *Sullanus in reipublicae causa.*[57]

The revolt of Lepidus brought a further demonstration of Pompey's commitment to the Sullan oligarchy and of his prominent status within it. He had backed the candidacy of Lepidus, who was a longtime *amicus* and, before 78, to all appearances a confirmed *Sullanus*; but, when the consul revealed his radical designs, Pompey unhesitatingly turned against him and was unhesitatingly assigned by the senate an important role in his suppression. He carried out his task with ruthless efficiency. He was later branded an *adulescentulus carnifex* for his actions in this war and in the late eighties, a title not totally undeserved, but won solely in the eradication of foes of the Sullan system.[58]

56. Plutarch, *Pompey* 14. Frontinus, *Strategemata* 4.5.1. *Fam.* 5.2.6. Pompey's marriage established links with the Metelli, Servilius Vatia, Appius Claudius, and Philippus, a brother-in-law of Appius and an old *amicus* of Pompey. Cf. Twyman, *ANRW* 1.1, 836. Gruen, *Roman Politics,* 274. On the date of Pompey's triumph cf. Badian, *Hermes* 83 (1955), 107–18; *Hermes* 89 (1961), 254–56. Gelzer, *Kleine Schriften,* 2.127–28. Despite Plutarch's dramatic tale of Sulla's change of heart on Pompey's triumph, it seems very likely that the dictator's stance was primarily influenced by Pompey's marriage and new allies.

57. Pliny, *NH* 7.96.

58. Cf. n. 36, above. Plutarch, *Pompey* 15.1. *Rab.* 21. Lepidus had served on

After the war with Lepidus, Pompey sought and obtained from the senate a proconsular command in Nearer Spain to aid Metellus Pius, proconsul in Farther Spain, in the war against Sertorius. It was an unusual commission for a *privatus* who had not yet even entered the senate, and modern analyses, beguiled again by the image of Pompey as a master manipulator of military power, frequently portray it as another instance of covert military extortion, this time aided, in the opinion of some scholars, by an eagerness on the part of factional foes of the Metelli in the senate to diminish the power and status of Pius by sending him a commander of equal rank.[59]

A review of the Spanish situation in 77 and of the senate's response to it quickly reveals the weakness of these hypotheses. The war was going badly. Metellus was in serious straits. To make matters worse Sertorius had just been, or was about to be, reinforced by the remnants of Lepidus's forces, led by Perperna. There was genuine alarm in the senate, and it was thought that an invasion of Italy was likely. The evidence indicates that the senate responded to the crisis by designating Nearer Spain, from which the propraetor, Q. Calidius, had recently returned, a consular province, for which the consuls of 77 were to draw lots. But both consuls declined the post, and no other eligible senator seemed anxious for the assignment. It was at this point that Pompey offered his services and secured the command.[60]

There is little room for theories of factional intrigue or military intimidation in this sequence of events. The senate's decision to send a second proconsular commander to Spain was a standard response to such military situations; it was demanded by the military news from

---

the *consilium* of Pompey's father in 89. Cf. Cichorius, *Rom. Stud.*, 147. He had sided with Sulla and received a praetorship in 81, and he had governed Sicily in 80. Cf. Sallust, *Hist.* 1.55.18, Maur. Broughton, *MRR*, 2.80. Pompey opposed his efforts to disrupt Sulla's funeral early in 78 (Plutarch, *Pompey* 15.3; *Sulla* 38.1). Sources for Pompey's conduct of the war in Broughton, *MRR*, 2.90. Cf. Gelzer, *Pompeius*, 49. Val. Max. 6.2.8.

59. Cf. Badian, *Foreign Clientelae*, 278. Smith, *Phoenix* 14 (1960), 9 ff. Sumner, *JRS* 54 (1964), 46.

60. Sources for Metellus's Spanish campaigns in Broughton, *MRR*, 2.83. Appian (*BC* 1.108) relates that Perperna had reinforced Sertorius before Pompey's appointment, and he emphasizes the alarm in the senate. Florus (2.10.5), and Orosius (5.23.8–9) also emphasize that there was fear of Sertorius in the senate. Dio (36.25) states that Pompey claimed he went to Spain after all others refused to go.

Spain and was reached without recorded dissension in a body presided over and dominated by men commonly regarded as friends of the Metelli. There is no trace of factional wrangling, and no reason to assume there was any. The *dignitas* of Metellus Pius was not at stake. The issue was not his replacement but his reinforcement, and the filling of a vacant governorship in the war zone in the face of a deteriorating military situation. Nearer Spain had already had a proconsular governor during Metellus's tenure of the farther province, and, in any event, a proconsular appointment to aid a beleaguered commander in an escalating war was no attack on the latter's position or prestige. Metellus certainly showed no reluctance to share the war with proconsular colleagues. He had welcomed the collaboration of Domitius Calvinus, proconsul in Nearer Spain in 79, and in the following year he had used the assistance of L. Manlius, proconsul in Transalpine Gaul. Faced with increasing prospects of total defeat, Metellus needed and wanted the largest reinforcement possible, and it is evident that for some time he had been sending that message to Rome.[61]

The unwillingness of the consuls and of other senior senators to accept the command, which is frequently attributed to factional fidelity or regard for Metellus, clearly had no such basis and can be readily explained as an understandable reluctance on the part of men of limited military ability and experience to undertake the formidable task of confronting the wily Sertorius, who had been building his strength in Spain for more than half a decade and had harassed and humiliated a succession of Sullan generals.[62] Pompey too, it should be emphasized, belonged to the Metellan circle, and if his dispatch to Spain represented an attack on Metellan interests, it seems highly improbable that he would have so eagerly exchanged his carefully cultivated friendship with the powerful clan for the dubious benefits of leading a war against a seemingly insuperable foe.

61. Sources for the governorships of Domitius Calvinus and L. Manlius in Broughton, *MRR*, 2.84, 87. Sallust (*Hist.* 2.32, Maur.) shows Metellus anxiously awaiting help. There was nothing unusual about a commander in trouble seeking reinforcement at the highest level. Cf. Crassus's request in 72 for the help of the proconsuls Pompey and Lucullus. Plutarch, *Crassus* 11.2.

62. Cf. n. 37, above, for bibliography on the consuls of 77 and their reasons for declining the Spanish command. Such refusals were not uncommon. Cf. Hortensius's refusal of a command against the Cretans in 69. *Schol. Bob.* 96, Stangl.

In seeking the Spanish command Pompey was not entering a factional fight or promoting a course unwelcome to any segment of the oligarchy. He was merely offering to implement a course fully agreed to be necessary and already determined without division or disagreement well before his name entered the debate. Nor was he pressing a demand which was likely from any aspect to generate wide opposition or to require the persuasion of arms for its acceptance. He was not displacing any other contenders, but simply stepping into a vacuum of leadership. His connections were sufficiently high to blunt the force of aristocratic *invidia* and guarantee a sympathetic hearing from at least some of the senate's *principes.* His proven military skill and impressive record as a destroyer of Marian generals left no doubt of his capacity for the task. The one objection that could be raised was his ineligibility for the commission under the *leges annales*, but there was ample precedent for such elevation of *privati*, and the senate seldom scrupled to disregard the requirements of the *cursus honorum* when it suited its purposes.[63]

The actual accounts of Pompey's appointment confirm the absence of serious opposition and of any grounds for assuming the use of military intimidation. The proposal to appoint him was made by the prestigious senior *consularis* Philippus, a most unlikely pawn in a power play by an upstart *iuvenis*. Philippus was playing the role he had so vigorously assumed in 78, rallying the senate to action against military threats to the Sullan system, and it is clear that he marshaled equal support on this occasion to meet an equally serious danger. The only recorded objection dealt with the obvious difficulty of Pompey's status as a *privatus*, but even on this issue the question raised concerned not whether Pompey should be sent but whether he should be given a rank as high as proconsul. Philippus dismissed that demurral with his pungent rejoinder that he was proposing to send Pompey *non pro consule sed pro consulibus.* The senators understood the import of Philippus's pun and the need of the state so pointedly summarized in it. Even Catulus apparently voted for the proposal. The only compulsion involved in the appointment was the fear of an impending military catastrophe and the lack of adequate military leadership to forestall it.[64]

63. Scipio Africanus's appointment to Spain in 210 provided a clear precedent. Pompey's own earlier command in Africa provided another.

64. Plutarch, *Pompey* 17.4. *Phil.* 11.18. *Man.* 62. Whatever his earlier connections, Philippus emerged in the seventies as a stalwart optimate, closely linked

There is one further serious difficulty with the notion that force was a factor in the senate's decision. It concerns Pompey's capacity to exert any significant military pressure in 77. There is cogent evidence to indicate that he was not given an independent command in the war against Lepidus but served as a *legatus* under Catulus. His name was not included among those summoned to take action against Lepidus in the *senatus consultum ultimum* moved by Philippus. Cicero, in recounting in the Eleventh Philippic instances of extraordinary grants of *imperium* to *privati*, mentions Pompey's Sertorian assignment, but he makes no reference to a command against Lepidus. Still more significant, when he lists all of Pompey's military commissions in his speech for the Manilian law, where his purpose is to magnify their number and scope, he again makes no mention of an extraordinary command in 77. These repeated omissions cannot easily be explained, and, in the absence of any clear evidence to the contrary, compel the conclusion that Pompey, though assigned a high responsibility in the war against Lepidus, was nonetheless in rank only a *legatus* to Catulus.[65] It cannot, therefore, be assumed, as it sometimes is, that Pompey was commissioned to levy his own army and that he raised it, after the fashion of the times, from among his clients and supporters. Once this assumption is discarded, it seems necessary to discard also any idea that Pompey could have successfully engaged in military coercion in 77 with troops that had sworn their oath of allegiance to a higher commander, and one whose success in the recent war had equaled Pompey's own. In addition, Catulus had himself directly under his command the army that had defeated Lepidus's main force, a further discouragement to any mutinous enterprise and a weapon which Catulus and the senate, after successfully resisting the demands of Lepidus as consul and proconsul, would hardly have hesitated to use if confronted by threatening gestures from a *legatus*.[66]

---

to the leading *Sullani* and at war with those who would threaten the Sullan system. Cicero's allusions to the appointment indicate that the debate concerned Pompey's rank, not whether he should be sent, and they imply that the command was approved by Catulus and the other *principes* of the senate.

65. Sallust, *Hist.* 1.77.22, Maur. *Phil.* 11.18. *Man.* 61–62. Cf. Smith, *Phoenix* 14 (1960), 9 ff. Twyman, *ANRW* 1.1, 821. Smith makes the point that if Pompey had been an independent commander, Catulus would have had no authority to order him to disband his army.

66. Cf. Badian, *Foreign Clientelae*, 277. Catulus was not readily intimidated. In 78 the senate had felt it necessary to pass a decree restraining him from engaging in hostilities with Lepidus. Gran. Lic. 35, Flem. Appian, *BC* 1.107. Mam. Lepidus may also have had an army in 77. *Cluent.* 99.

There is altogether only one modicum of evidence to associate Pompey's army with the senate's decision to send him to Spain, namely a statement by Plutarch to the effect that Pompey found excuses during the senate's deliberations for not disbanding his troops, though he had been ordered to do so by Catulus. But this remark, whose reliability in light of Plutarch's constant preoccupation with Pompey's military power and its potential abuse is not above suspicion, says far less than modern reconstructions have extracted from it. It does not allege any attempt at intimidation nor link Pompey's failure to disband his troops to the senate's approval of his appointment, and it is hardly a sufficient basis on which to build a theory of coercion that runs directly counter to all other evidence relating to the Spanish debate and the circumstances surrounding it.[67]

The record of Pompey's career during the remainder of the seventies further belies the view that he went to Spain as a consequence of factional maneuvering or raw power politics. His relations with Metellus Pius and with the oligarchy as a whole show no tensions or signs of bitterness or antagonism. He and Metellus conducted the war against Sertorius in a spirit of cooperation and mutual respect, a spirit which endured well beyond the war's end.[68] Pompey did have difficulty in securing adequate supplies and reinforcements from the senate, but the reasons cannot be ascribed to personal or factional enmity. The senate's concern about this war and its high stake in successfully concluding it at a time when its management of affairs was under heavy attack in Rome sharply contradicts any idea that its decisions in regard to it sacrificed victory to indulge personal antagonisms or narrow factional interests. Besides, Metellus had fared no better than Pompey in the matter of supplies, though his need was equally great. The senate's stinginess was nonpartisan and was occasioned simply by a depleted treasury and a public already loudly protesting economic conditions and the burdens of protracted warfare. Pompey got all he wanted, promptly and without dissent, as soon as he convinced the oligarchy

67. Plutarch, *Pompey* 17.3.
68. Plutarch, *Pompey* 19.1–5; *Sertorius* 19.6; 21.2. Appian, *BC* 1.110–12. After the death of Sertorius, Metellus allowed Pompey to finish the war by himself. Appian, *BC* 1.115. Pompey was later to insist on postponing his triumph until Metellus's return so that they could celebrate a joint triumph, and the agrarian law of 70 provided for Metellus's as well as for Pompey's veterans. Appian, *BC* 1.121. Dio 38.5.1. Cf. Gruen, *AJP* 92 (1971), 7–9.

in a stern letter in 74 of the disastrous consequences of further delay in strengthening the military effort against Sertorius.[69]

His reinforcement was followed by other and more unequivocal expressions of senatorial support and goodwill. A consular law of 72, moved in accordance with a resolution of the senate, conferred upon him the right to grant citizenship to individual Spaniards, a most important privilege, the basis for the building of an influential *clientela* in the Spanish provinces.[70] Not long afterwards he received a fresh senatorial assignment which commissioned him to return to Italy with his army to assist in the suppression of Spartacus. The new command gave him the right to retain and use his army in Italy, the one authority the oligarchy would have been careful to withhold from him if it had experienced or if it feared abuse of his military power. No threat of force can this time be offered to explain the senate's bestowal of this additional, critical authority on Pompey, and its action is compelling evidence of the general's continuing high position of trust and influence within the Sullan oligarchy.[71]

After aiding in the liquidation of the last remnants of Spartacus's forces, Pompey proceeded to Rome with his army, where he was awarded a triumph for his victory in Spain and an exemption from the *leges annales* to enable him to stand for the consulship of 70. The pattern of Pompey seeking and securing extraordinary powers or privileges from the senate while leading a victorious army was repeated for the third time, and the event is commonly portrayed as the third and most glaring instance of an unconstitutional grab for power by Pompey through the politics of force. The view is beset by difficulties similar to those that marked the theories of coercion applied to earlier dealings between Pompey and the senate. It lacks solid support in the sources, it imagines a senate intimidated by the very weapon it had itself voluntarily placed

69. Sallust, *Hist.* 2.98, Maur. Plutarch, *Pompey* 20.1; *Sertorius* 21.5; *Lucullus* 5.2. Cf. Sallust, *Hist.* 2.47.6, Maur. Appian, *BC* 1.111.

70. The law was sponsored by the consuls L. Gellius Publicola and Cn. Cornelius Lentulus, both commonly regarded, and perhaps correctly, as friends of Pompey. But the law was not the work of a Pompeian faction. It was enacted on instructions from the senate, a body not controlled by the consuls of 72, as their recall from the war against Spartacus later in the year well illustrates. Besides, the law gave Metellus the same right as Pompey. Sources in Broughton, *MRR*, 2.116. For Metellus's right to grant citizenship cf. *Arch.* 26.

71. Sources in Broughton, *MRR*, 2.124.

in Pompey's hand only months earlier, and it ignores the fact that there were three other armies in or near Italy to deter or to thwart any attempt at military intimidation of the government. Finally, it assumes a need for force where none is apparent. Exemptions from the *leges annales*, and indeed from other laws as well, were commonplace and readily available to friends of the senate's dominant *pauci*. Pompey was not without influence with the senate's potentates, and in addition his unique achievements and status as a proconsul of six years standing left little room for argument.[72]

It should now be sufficiently clear that the preponderance of the evidence for Pompey's career in the late eighties and seventies affirms the view that, throughout the period, he worked for and within the Sullan system and in general harmony with its principal proponents. He ambitiously sought and achieved a leading place, but his rapid rise to military prominence and to the political pinnacle of the consulship was due, not to revolutionary exploitation of the military legacy of Marius and Sulla, but to extraordinary initiative and military ability, aided by troubled times and a political sagacity that coupled military success with shrewd manipulation of traditional modes of political power-building. He had little reason as consul-elect or as consul to break the connections or abandon the strategy which had brought him his remarkable success. The oligarchy, though beleaguered, continued to dominate the course of political events, and Pompey continued to safeguard the high place in its favor which the efforts of a decade had secured him. The time had not yet come when it was necessary or expedient for him to woo support outside the senate at the risk of forfeiting his influence within it.

The other legislative enactments of 70 provide additional indications that Pompey did not play the role of anti-senatorial reformer in his consulship, and that his tribunician bill was not a *popularis* blow at the Sullan settlement, but another in a series of constitutional modifications of that system induced by public pressure and implemented with the general consent of the oligarchy. The latter half of the year brought

72. Cf. H. Last, *CAH* 9, 332 ff. Syme, *Roman Revolution*, 29. M. Lucullus returned to Italy from Macedonia in 71, and Metellus Pius was on his way from Spain. Sources in Broughton, *MRR*, 2.123–24. Exemptions from the laws were so common that the tribune Cornelius attempted to restrict the practice in 67. Cf. Sherwin-White, *JRS* 46 (1956), 7.

a resolution of the second major controversy of the late seventies, and with it a second major reversal of Sulla's constitutional arrangements. A judiciary law was enacted which deprived the senate of its monopoly of the courts and prescribed that juries should consist of equal numbers of senators, *equites*, and *tribuni aerarii*. It is significant that the name of Pompey cannot be associated in any way with this important reform. As consul-elect he had expressed general support for the idea of a change in the jury system, but during the first seven months of his consulship he made no move to implement a change and apparently took no active role in the conception or implementation of the measure which was finally promulgated in August. The senate's exclusive control of the courts had become a major issue in the internal conflicts of the late seventies, an explosive controversy which had thoroughly aroused the public, and Pompey's failure to exploit it or to garner from it the popular acclaim which would accrue from the abolition of a prime symbol of oligarchic domination would seem to belie any assumption that he was an aggressive advocate or architect of change in 70, embarked on a course of extra-senatorial power-building at the expense of the Sullan oligarchy.[73]

Nor was the judiciary law the work of any Pompeian lackey or the product of the tribunician powers Pompey had lately helped to restore. The bill bore the name of a *nobilissimus*, L. Aurelius Cotta, a praetor in 70 and brother of the consuls of 75 and 74, and, by all indications, a man similarly committed to the cause of the conservatives and held in similar high regard by the conservative *principes* of the senate. The evidence for his subsequent political career shows continuing *gratia* in high places and consistent conservatism. He was consul in 65, and he won the unusual distinction of election to the censorship for the very next year. He strongly supported Cicero in the Catilinarian crisis in 63, moved the proposal for a public thanksgiving in Cicero's honor, and advocated the death penalty for the conspirators. He worked hard for Cicero's restoration in 57, and he was one of the few *consulares* who won Cicero's commendation for his resistance to Clodius and refusal to acknowledge the validity of the latter's legislation. Although a relative

---

73. *Verr.* 1.45. Cicero emphasizes that the judiciary law was Cotta's brainchild. *Verr.* 2.2.174. Plutarch pointedly remarks that Pompey allowed the bill to go forward. He suggests no active role for the general. *Pompey* 22.3. For other references to Cotta's bill cf. Broughton, *MRR,* 2.127.

of Caesar, he refused to take his side in the civil war of 49 and settled for a form of neutrality. He still had Cicero's high regard and friendship in late 44, and together they lamented the state of the *respublica* and participated as little as possible in its operations.[74]

The judiciary bill of 70 was therefore conceived and sponsored by a loyal adherent of the views and ideals of the traditionalists. It was further enacted with no recorded opposition from conservative leaders, both of which facts plainly attest that once again the oligarchy itself took the initiative in implementing a widely desired reform, continuing a sustained policy of compromise and conciliation receptive even to major change under threat of its imposition, with more drastic consequences, by public pressure or demagogic dissidents.

Two additional laws can be assigned to 70, both of them sponsored by the tribune Plautius. One restored citizenship to the followers of Lepidus and Sertorius, the other provided land for the Spanish veterans of Metellus Pius and Pompey. Both were welcome to Pompey, and both had the full approval of the senate, further evidence of harmonious

74. *Verr.* 2.2.174. *Phil.* 2.13. *Dom.* 68, 84. *Sest.* 73. *Leg.* 3.45. *Fam.* 12.2.3; 13.40.1. Some scholars, e.g., Stockton (*Historia* 22 [1973], 216 ff.), advance the view that Cotta's bill was a late compromise, either somehow forced upon him or made acceptable by him to the oligarchy in preference to a total transfer of the courts to the *equites.* The evidence for such a view is some allusions by Cicero in the Verrines to proposals to turn over the courts to the *equites.* But Cicero was interested in magnifying the proposed change and, besides, such language could be loosely used to describe even a partial transfer of control to the *equites*, and it is in fact so used by Tacitus in a reference to the *Lex Aurelia* in *Ann.* 11.12. Cf. *Verr.* 2.3.2, 23; 2.5.177. *Schol. Gron.* (328–29, Stangl) indicate that Cotta's bill was along the lines demanded in preceding years, and there is no convincing evidence that a more radical reform of the jury system was ever sought in the late seventies. Certainly Cotta is unlikely to have promoted a radical demand for an outright transfer of the courts to the *equites*, and the absence of any record of public agitation over the courts in 70 also makes it unlikely that such a demand was being pressed by any element in that year, or that any fundamental disagreement on the judiciary issue still remained. For discussions of the *Lex Aurelia* cf. Gelzer, *Klein Schriften*, 2.158; *Cicero*, 41 ff. Ciaceri, *Cicerone*, 1.83 ff. A. Garzetti, "M. Licinio Crasso" *Athenaeum* 20 (1942), 19. Taylor, *Party Politics*, 106. H. Hill, *The Roman Middle Class in the Republican Period* (Oxford 1952), 156. R. F. Rossi, "Sulla lotta politica in Roma dopo la morte di Silla" *PP* 20 (1965), 134–41. Ward, *Latomus* 29 (1970), 63 ff. Marshall, *RhM* 118 (1975), 145 ff. Laffi, *Athenaeum* 45 (1967), 195 ff. Gruen, *Last Generation,* 28 ff. Laffi and Gruen argue persuasively that the law was not enacted over the opposition of the senate, but their view that the reform was not a major concession by the oligarchy is difficult to maintain in light of the history of the jury question at Rome.

relations between consul and senate, and further evidence of the senate's continuing desire for *concordia* and continuing willingness to make concessions to secure it.[75]

In summary, the latter part of the seventies brought a series of conciliatory decrees, laws, and pledges from the ruling oligarchy, climaxed by the major constitutional reforms of 70. The concessions were primarily a product of deep public discontent with the senate's leadership, sparked by the economic hardships and military burdens of the middle and later years of the decade. They were pressed by a succession of activist tribunes capitalizing on the public mood, but they were formulated and implemented with the cooperation and concurrence of the bulk of the oligarchy itself, which, faced with a growing threat to its ascendancy, saw greater wisdom in accommodation than in confrontation. In the internal history of those years, Pompey stands alongside other prominent *nobiles* as one of several *Sullani* who led this process of adjustment; his role was not unique nor his actions seriously in conflict with the overall direction of contemporary senatorial policies.

This is the background against which the political significance of the trial of Verres must be weighed, and once it is separated from schematic preconceptions of the structure of politics in the period and from obvious and understandable exaggerations of its importance by Cicero, it is difficult to find any reason to attribute to it any major political significance or role in the shaping of the political events of the late seventies. Rome was racked by no serious factional feuds in the period, and by the time Verres came to trial the political disputes of the preceding half-decade were essentially at an end, defused by a policy of appeasement on the part of the oligarchy, which was itself taking the lead in instituting the desired reforms. The tribunician bill had been passed in

75. Suetonius, *Julius* 5. Gellius 13.3.5. Sallust, *Hist.* 3.47, Maur. Dio 38.5.1; 44.47.4. *Att.* 1.18.6. Plutarch, *Lucullus* 34.3–4. *Verr.* 2.5.151–52. Cf. R. E. Smith, "The *Lex Plotia Agraria* and Pompey's Spanish Veterans" *CQ* 7 (1957), 82–85. E. Gabba, "*Lex Plotia Agraria*" *PP* 13 (1950), 66–68. Gruen, *Last Generation*, 37. The censorship was also revived in 70, another concession to popular demands. Cf. *Div. in Caec.* 8. There is no evidence, however, to support the common view that the revival was another Pompeian scheme to build power or that the senate was opposed to it. Cf. Gruen, *Last Generation*, 44 and n. 135. A final indication that 70 was not a year of reformist victories and senatorial defeats is provided by the consular elections, which brought victory to two stalwart conservatives, Q. Hortensius and Q. Metellus. The oligarchy was still in control of the course of political events.

an atmosphere of conciliation, and little doubt can have remained that a settlement of the closely related issue of the courts was also at hand. Pompey had long ago declared his approval of a change in the jury panels, and that other leaders of the oligarchy had accepted the idea in principle is clear from Catulus's admission in his speech on the tribunician bill that reform was warranted. The formulation of the specific nature of the change was doubtless a lengthy and complicated matter, requiring negotiation and persuasion, but the process was orchestrated from within the oligarchy and clearly to the satisfaction of the popular elements, as is amply attested by the absence of any measure of tribunician agitation in 70 and of any effort to bring into action the newly restored powers of the office. By early August, when the trial of Verres commenced, proposals were ready to be made public and were soon afterwards promulgated. The crucial decisions had already been taken, and the issue was moving toward its final resolution. There remained no grounds for conflict, no opposition to overcome, no need for further public ventilation of this moribund dispute.[76]

The only ancient evidence to imply the contrary is Cicero's attempts in the Verrines themselves to link the trial to the judiciary dispute by presenting it as a vital test of senatorial integrity and a golden opportunity for the jury of senators to vindicate their order and stave off the impending threat to the senate's monopoly of the courts. But this line of argument was of obvious benefit to Cicero's case, and he was himself later frankly to admit that, in making it, he was exploiting the license given to advocates to shape the truth to meet the exigencies of the moment. No other ancient writer even remotely suggests that the trial had any effect on the dispute over juries, nor did Cicero himself ever again in his many references to the prosecution and to his political achievements attribute to it any political importance other than its effects on his own career, a significant silence when one recalls his penchant for magnifying his *res gestae*.[77]

76. It is significant that there was no tribunician agitation or rush to use the newly restored legislative power. Only one tribune for the year is known, Plautius, and, as already indicated, his activities had the full approval of the senate. *Verr.* 1.1 indicates that the proposals for a change in jurors were ready for public airing at the time the trial began, and, as already noted, there is no reason to believe that these proposals were different from those soon afterwards implemented. Cf. n. 74, above.

77. Cf. *Verr.* 1.1–3. *Cluent.* 139. In the *actio secunda* (5.178), Cicero claims that the promulgation of the *Lex Aurelia* was a direct consequence of the belief

There are other grounds also for disputing Cicero's assertions of the trial's political implications. The judicial question involved in it, namely the senate's capacity to convict a notoriously guilty but wealthy and influential associate, was peripheral to the central issue underlying the campaign for jury reform. That campaign was part of a long-standing conflict surrounding the criminal courts in late republican politics, a conflict whose principal and persistent concern was not unjust acquittals such as a Verres might procure through political camaraderie or plain purchase, but unjust convictions and threats to the lives and liberties of citizens through judicial oppression.[78]

The issue first arose in the latter half of the second century as a concomitant of increasing political polarization and with the realization that control of inappellable *quaestiones* bestowed an important power that could be used as a weapon of intimidation or repression for personal or political ends. The senate brought the problem to light in 132 when it established a special senatorial *quaestio* headed by the consuls, which brought to trial the followers of Tiberius Gracchus and condemned large numbers to death or exile. Reaction came ten years later when Gaius Gracchus attempted to limit the criminal jurisdiction of senate and magistrates and to curb their brand of partisan justice by outlawing all *quaestiones* dealing with capital crimes which were not authorized by vote of the people and by making conspiracy by senators to secure an unjust conviction a criminal offense.[79] The anti-senatorial leaders who followed him went much further and sought to turn the tables on the *nobilitas* by excluding senators entirely from the ranks of jurors and by endeavoring to convert the system of *quaestiones* to their

---

that Verres would be acquitted. But this claim is obviously as fictitious as the proceedings at which it was supposed to have been made. Cicero simply used his imagination to recreate circumstances in which he would have had to deliver the speeches of the *actio secunda*, and his remark is obviously irrelevant to any discussion of the trial's political importance.

78. In fact, although bribery to secure acquittal was a common feature of jury courts in all periods, irrespective of the composition of the courts, the issue never seems to have greatly aroused either Roman politicians or public, and, aside from the ineffective *Lex Acilia* and the abortive judiciary legislation of Livius Drusus, no effort to deal with the problem can be documented before Sulla, who incorporated into his extortion law a clause that provided for prosecution of venal jurors. Cf. Appian, *BC* 1.22.35. Ewins, *JRS* 50 (1960), 95 ff. A. N. Sherwin-White, "The Extortion Procedure Again" *JRS* 42 (1952), 43 ff.

79. Sources in Broughton, *MRR*, 1.497–98, 513–18. Cf. Ewins, *JRS* 50 (1960), 101 ff. Weinrib, *Historia* 19 (1970), 422 ff.

own anti-senatorial ends. The result was an intermittent struggle, spanning three decades, for the critical political power embodied in control of the criminal courts, a struggle which the senate mostly lost until Sulla's victory restored senatorial supremacy, and with it senatorial dominion over the jury courts.[80]

Such was the history and nature of the dispute which was reopened by Quinctius in 74, and it is clear that it continued to focus not on the form of judicial corruption in question in the trial of Verres, but on the narrower and more political issue of judicial oppression. All types of judicial abuse naturally entered the debate, and all instances of judicial improprieties by senators were naturally cited to buttress the case for change, but lax enforcement of the law and trafficking in favorable verdicts cannot be shown to have been a particular problem of the seventies nor the particular grievance of the advocates of reform in that decade. The immediate cause of the reappearance of the judiciary dispute in 74 was an alleged conspiracy to convict an innocent man, a charge which was followed by other allegations of judicial murder. The issue was also closely linked to the demands for a restoration of the powers of tribunes and to calls for a revival of the censorship. In brief, the debate was centered on tyrannical use of the courts and was fitted into a campaign with a single theme—the repressive character of the Sullan system—and a single goal—refinement of the system through protective curbs and a more equitable distribution of power.[81]

The terms of the *Lex Aurelia* would seem to confirm that the vital concern in the dispute which the bill resolved was the danger of unjust convictions. The law, by distributing power between three distinct elements, took effective steps to lessen the threat of easy coalitions

80. The main developments in this conflict were: the Mamilian commission of 109, the *Lex Servilia Caepionis* of 106, the *Lex Appuleia* of 103, the *Lex Servilia Glauciae* of 101, the judiciary proposals of Livius Drusus in 91, the Varian commission of 90, the *Lex Plotia* of 89. Cf. Ewins, *JRS* 50 (1960), 103–04. M. Griffin, "Pre-Sullan *leges iudiciariae*" *CQ* 67 (1973), 108–26.

81. On corruption in the seventies cf. Gruen, *Last Generation*, 30 ff. Unjust convictions were alleged in the cases of Oppianicus, Opimius, and Calidius. *Cluent.* 77 ff. *Verr.* 2.1.155. *Verr.* 1.38; 2.3.63. Ps. Asconius 219, Stangl. On the close connection between the issue of the courts and the tribunician question cf. *Div. in Caec.* 8. *Verr.* 1.44. Palicanus also apparently seized on Verres' repressive administration of justice in 74 and used it to argue for restoration of tribunes' powers and possibly for a change in jurors. *Verr.* 2.1.122; 2.2.100. Ps. Asconius 250, Stangl.

likely to misuse the courts to intimidate or dispose of personal or political opponents, but it did nothing to counteract plain venality. In fact, by failing to extend to nonsenators the existing laws against the acceptance of bribes by jurors, it created courts in which two-thirds of the members could peddle their ballots with impunity.[82] It was not a measure that could claim to have ended or lessened the danger of a Verres going free, nor can that consideration have been of critical importance either in the bill's conception or implementation.

There is one additional fact which further diminishes the credibility of Cicero's version of the trial's political importance. Verres was forced into exile and condemned, yet it was almost simultaneously with this demonstration of effective law enforcement that the threatened change in jurors was enacted. There could not have been a more inauspicious time for the introduction of the reform if the case was being viewed as a critical test of senatorial integrity, and the coincidence surely shows the utter irrelevance of the trial and its outcome to both the terms and timing of the *Lex Aurelia*.[83]

As for the common notion that the trial aided the cause of reform by presenting in the crimes of Verres a devastating indictment of senatorial government and the *mores* of its leadership, it evokes several objections, even if one assumes that the question of a change in the jury system was still in doubt or in dispute at the time the case came to trial. The view lacks even the support of Cicero's evidence which, as already indicated, presents the political significance of the case in wholly different terms. Further, as an exposé of corruption, the trial was abortive. Only the *actio prima*, in which Cicero refrained from a full-scale rhetorical exposition of Verres' iniquities, took place. The complete tale of

82. Equestrian jurors were exempt both from the *Lex Sempronia ne quis iudicio circumveniatur*, which had been incorporated into Sulla's *Lex de sicariis*, and from Sulla's law on the acceptance of bribes by jurors. *Cluent*. 144, 148–58. *Rab. Post*. 15–16.
83. Those who believe that the trial affected the terms of the *Lex Aurelia* get around this difficulty by positing that the bill was a compromise forced upon the reformers by increased respect for the senate following Verres' condemnation. But, aside from the lack of convincing evidence to show that the bill was a compromise, it is difficult to see why the condemnation of a notoriously guilty criminal should have had such an impact on the senate's standing, especially since there were other extortion trials in the period in which senatorial juries convicted men who were both less blatantly guilty and more closely associated with the oligarchy, e.g., the trial of P. Gabinius. *Div. in Caec*. 64. *Arch*. 9.

cruelty and rapacity, related with such telling effect in the four orations of the *actio secunda*, was never heard in the forum and stood revealed only after publication of those speeches, an event which certainly came too late to affect the *Lex Aurelia*, even assuming that a significant segment of the Roman public read and digested such productions.[84]

Finally, Verres was no central pillar or guiding luminary of the aristocracy whose misdeeds could be represented as typifying the moral and political standards of senatorial government, nor did the oligarchy as a whole identify itself with his person or his practices by rising to defend him.

Verres was the son of a senator who, according to Cicero, had been a bribery agent and a thief, and who was very likely one of the *novi homines* elevated to the senate by Cinna in the mid-eighties.[85] Verres himself began his public life as a *Marianus*, and in 84 he was elected quaestor and assigned to the consul Papirius Carbo. He soon deserted him for Sulla, however, taking with him the funds which had been allotted for Carbo's army. He was later to increase his loot when he received from Sulla the property of certain proscribed persons in the region of Beneventum. His next public assignment came in 80 when he served as *legatus* to Cn. Dolabella, proconsul in Cilicia, who it appears was, like Verres himself, a Marian renegade. Dolabella was prosecuted for extortion on his return to Rome by Aemilius Scaurus, a stepson of Sulla, was abandoned, to all appearances, by the leaders of the oligarchy, and convicted. Verres, who was his close associate and had eagerly shared in the spoils of his corrupt regime, was in danger of sharing his fate, but for the second time he nimbly abandoned a faltering superior and rescued himself from prosecution by agreeing to testify against his former commander. Nothing more is known of his career until 74, when he held the office of *praetor urbanus*, after which he governed Sicily until the end of 71.[86]

84. Cicero indicates that the *Lex Aurelia* was promulgated in the interval between the *actio prima* and the *actio secunda*. *Verr.* 2.5.178. He cannot have published the Verrines before Verres' official condemnation, which came after the latter's failure to appear for the *actio secunda*, and it is obvious therefore that the speeches appeared too late to affect public opinion on the judiciary issue.

85. *Verr.* 2.3.161. In *Verr.* 2.1.35, Cicero implies that Verres belonged with the *novi*, who were a prominent part of the following of Marius and Cinna. Cf. ch. 2, n. 59, above.

86. *Verr.* 2.1.34–37. *Schol. Gron.* 329, Stangl. Cf. Gruen, *AJP* 87 (1966), 395–97. F. H. Cowles, *Gaius Verres: An Historical Study* (Ithaca 1917).

Verres had fared well in the civil war of the late eighties and in the political conditions that followed it, and it is clear that he possessed considerable political influence. He had a valuable resource in his father, who had practiced a profession which, though not highly regarded, brought contacts and knowledge of the mechanics of political intrigue and who seems to have possessed some of the skills and power of a Cethegus. His particular expertise in tribal bribery appears to have been put to good use by Verres, who had accumulated sufficient wealth in the civil war and in Cilicia and Sicily to exploit extensively this increasingly important variety of power building.[87]

Verres had also managed to forge links with a number of distinguished aristocrats and he was able to rally their support in 70. Chief among them was, of course, the celebrated orator Q. Hortensius, who was the leading advocate of the day, a brother-in-law of Catulus, a close friend of the Luculli, and a leading bulwark of the *via optimas* in the seventies and sixties. Cicero indicates in the Verrines and elsewhere that there were close ties between Hortensius and Verres. Their friendship may have resulted in part from the trial of Opimius in 74, at which Verres, who was president of the court, cooperated with the prosecutors Hortensius, Catulus, and Scribonius Curio in dispensing harsh and hasty justice to the former tribune. Cicero supplies a further explanation of their association, however, when more than once he broadly hints that Hortensius's support was sustained by bribes, a credible charge against a man well known for his luxurious tastes and little known for his integrity.[88]

Verres also enjoyed the friendship and active support in 70 of three Metellan brothers, Quintus, Marcus, and Lucius, grandsons of the great Metellus Macedonicus and sons of Metellus Caprarius, consul of 113. Quintus was elected to the consulship in 70, Marcus to the praetorship,

87. On *divisores* cf. Taylor, *Party Politics*, 63, 67. Wiseman, *New Men*, 83. Verres' father was able more than once to prevent senatorial action against his son. *Verr.* 2.2.95–96, 102. On Verres' use of *divisores* and bribery cf. *Verr.* 1.22; 2.4.45.

88. For Hortensius's career cf. *De Or.* 3.228; *Brut.* 1–6, 229–30, 301–04, 308, 317–29. On his relations with Verres cf. *Div. in Caec.* 23. *Orator* 129. On the trial of Opimius cf. Ps. Asconius 255, Stangl; *Schol. Gron.* 341, Stangl. Hints of bribery and charges of improper behavior occur in *Div. in Caec.* 24. *Verr.* 1.25, 40; 2.2.192; 2.3.9. *Cluent.* 130. Ps. Asconius 193–94, Stangl. Pliny, *NH* 34.48. Plutarch, *Cicero* 6.6. For Hortensius's luxurious tastes cf. Varro, *De Re Rustica* 3.13.2; 3.17.5–8. Pliny, *NH* 35, 130.

and Lucius was governor of Sicily and soon to be consul in 68. There was some form of *cognatio* between Verres' family and this branch of the Metellan clan, but an equally important reason for their efforts on Verres' behalf seems to have been the latter's generous use of his money and other political resources in the electoral campaigns of Quintus and Marcus.[89]

Two other politicians of note are attested as *amici* of Verres and appeared in his defense, P. Scipio Nasica, a cousin of the Metellan brothers and an *adulescens* of the highest nobility, and L. Cornelius Sisenna, who had held the praetorship in 78 and governed Sicily in 77, and who was later to serve as a *legatus* of Pompey in the pirate war. He was a man of many friends from varying backgrounds, among them Hortensius, L. Lucullus, A. Gabinius, author of the *Lex Gabinia* of 67, and Licinius Macer.[90]

But despite these indications of Verres' political influence and high connections, it would be a gross distortion to conclude that he was a favored member of the ruling elite or that he was identified or identifiable with that exclusive *factio* mentioned by Sallust which was the object of the attacks of dissidents in the late seventies. Verres' birth and political background gave him few optimate credentials and were powerful obstacles to any lasting or broad-based friendship with the potentates of the Sullan oligarchy. His checkered career, marked by perfidy, opportunism, and greed, did little to remove any of these impediments to his acceptance into the inner circle of the conservative *nobilitas*. It won him a measure of *potentia* and some isolated friendships in high places, but the aristocracy as a whole profoundly loathed his breed and abhorred the political conditions that gave such men the room to prosper.[91]

There is abundant evidence of the limited nature of the goodwill and influence Verres enjoyed within the oligarchy. All of his known *legati* in Sicily were *novi homines*, a significant indication of the sparseness of

89. Cf. *Verr.* 1.21, 26–29, 31; 2.2.63–64, 138–140, 164; 2.3.122–23, 152–53.

90. On P. Scipio cf. *Verr.* 2.4.80–81. Douglas, *M. Tulli Ciceronis Brutus*, 153–54. On Sisenna cf. *Verr.* 2.2.110; 2.4.43. *Brut.* 228. *Leg.* 1.7. Appian, *Mith.* 95. Dio 36.18–19. Plutarch, *Lucullus* 5. Sallust, *Jug.* 95.2.

91. The *nobilitas* seldom welcomed renegades. Carbo, the consul of 120; Catiline, another early Marian; Cethegus; Cn. Dolabella, the praetor of 81; Lepidus, the consul of 78; and Lucretius Ofella provide examples of men who switched to the optimate side but never won the goodwill of the oligarchy. Cf. Gruen, *AJP* 87 (1966), 392 ff. Badian, *Studies*, 229–30.

his aristocratic friendships.[92] He had made some powerful enemies among the *nobilitas* during his praetorship in 74, and in the following years his general lack of support in the senate was frequently illustrated. He would have been recalled after his first year in Sicily except for the fact that the war against Spartacus required the services of his successor, Q. Arrius. Complaints from prominent Sicilians repeatedly found a sympathetic hearing at Rome during his governorship, and in 72 both consuls and the bulk of the senate were ready to turn against him in the affair of Sthenius, and a resolution blocking his prosecution of the latter was prevented only by a filibuster and his father's exertions. Not long afterwards all ten tribunes for 71 officially registered their disapproval of his behavior in this same case by refusing to recognize the validity of his verdict.[93]

But the clearest evidence of his lack of fellowship and association with the aristocracy as a whole is in the record of his trial itself, which reveals a long parade of leading senators working for his conviction. Prominent among them were two brothers of the Claudii Marcelli, Marcus and Gaius, the former an aedile in 91 and father of the consuls of 51 and 49, the latter a praetor in 80, a revered governor of Sicily in 79 and father of the consul of 50. The family had had special connections with Sicily since the Second Punic War and had received repeated calls for help from the Sicilians in 71 and 70. Marcus had an additional reason for backing the prosecution in that a ward of his, Publius Junius, had suffered an injustice at the hands of Verres during the latter's praetorship in 74. Another member of the *gens* of the Claudii Marcelli, Cn. Lentulus Marcellinus, the future consul of 56, who was similarly a special patron of the Sicilians, took a leading part in promoting the prosecution and gave evidence against Verres at the trial itself.[94]

92. *Verr.* 2.2.49; 2.5.63, 114. Cf. Gruen, *Last Generation*, 203.

93. L. Piso, a distinguished *nobilis*, grandson of the author of the first extortion law and a cousin of the consul of 67, was a determined opponent of Verres in 74. *Verr.* 2.1.119; 2.4.56. Verres had also antagonized, when praetor, L. Gellius, consul in 72 and censor in 70, by an unfair judgment in an inheritance case against Gellius's client, a senator named M. Octavius Ligus, and Domitius Ahenobarbus and M. Marcellus by a decision defrauding the ward M. Junius. *Verr.* 2.1.125, 135, 139, 144, 153. On Q. Arrius cf. *Verr.* 2.2.37. *Schol. Gron.* 324, Stangl. B. A. Marshall and R. J. Baker, "The Aspirations of Q. Arrius" *Historia* 24 (1975), 221–31. For response to complaints of the Sicilians cf. *Verr.* 2.2.95, 100; 2.3.18, 132; 2.4.41.

94. *Div. in Caec.* 13. *Verr.* 2.1.135, 144, 153; 2.2.8, 36, 51, 110, 122; 2.3.45, 212; 2.4.37, 86. On Marcellinus cf. *Div. in Caec.* 13. *Verr.* 2.2.103; 2.4.53.

Also testifying for the prosecution were: Cn. Cornelius Lentulus Clodianus, consul in 72 and censor in 70, who gave evidence on behalf of an *eques*, Gaius Matrinius, who had been cheated by Verres; both consuls of 73, M. Terentius Varro Lucullus, who appeared in support of an injured client, Dio of Halaesa, and C. Cassius Longinus, whose wife's farm at Leontini had been plundered by Verres' tithe collectors; C. Licinius Sacerdos, praetor in 75, Verres' immediate predecessor as governor of Sicily and later a *legatus* of Quintus Metellus in Crete, who testified about bribes accepted by Verres for favorable verdicts; L. Domitius Ahenobarbus, son of the consul of 96, cousin of Catulus, brother-in-law of Cato, a haughty aristocrat and from his youth a dogged foe of *populares*, who gave evidence in the matter of Verres' defrauding of the young Publius Junius; C. Visellius Varro, Cicero's cousin, who had apparently been adopted by Cicero's uncle from the family of the Terentii Varrones, and who had served as a military tribune under Claudius Nero in Asia in 80 and had been witness to some of Verres' transgressions while he was *legatus* under Dolabella in Cilicia.[95]

The list, which dwarfs Verres' modest retinue of defending notables and contains many of the foremost figures of the seventies and representatives of leading families of the old *nobilitas*, is surely sufficient to dispel any notion that Verres was, or was seen to be, an inside member of the oligarchy or an important representative of Sulla's ruling elite. A low-born Marian renegade, profiteer of civil war, political machinator, indiscriminate pursuer of personal gain, he had singularly little to recommend him to that exclusive *factio*, and predictably he found scant favor with the bulk of its *principes*. He was a poor instrument with which to seek to tarnish a *nobilitas* from which he had not come and within which he had found little acceptance, his aberrations more an argument for the tradition of aristocratic rule than a threat to it.[96]

95. On Lentulus cf. *Verr.* 2.5.15; Lucullus 2.2.23; 2.4.49; Cassius Longinus 2.3.97; Sacerdos 2.2.119. *Planc.* 27; Domitius Ahenobarbus *Verr.* 2.1.139; Varro 2.1.71. M'. Acilius Glabrio, president of the court, was also clearly no friend of Verres. Cf. L. Hayne, "The Politics of M'. Glabrio, Cos. 67" *CP* 69 (1974), 280–82. Verres had clashed with many other, lesser-known senators, several of whom also appeared against him. Cf. *Verr.* 2.1.10; 2.2.23, 102, 119; 2.3.93–94, 152; 2.4.42–43. Many supposed friends he could not trust to support him. Cf. *Verr.* 2.1.18, 128; 2.5.114.

96. It was a basic justification of aristocratic government that members of old political families were more likely to rule with wisdom and integrity. Cf. *Sest.* 21. Wirszubski, *Libertas*, 35–38.

In fact, on many counts the senate came well out of his prosecution. It provided the members of the court which was responsible for the selection of a vigorous prosecutor and for expediting the procedure of the trial to forestall the dilatory maneuvers of the defense, and it provided a succession of prestigious witnesses to expose and, in the process, disavow Verres' wrongdoing and help insure his conviction. There was nothing here with which to impugn either the senate's government or its administration of justice.

The foregoing review of the supporters and opponents of Verres also reveals the implausibility of any attempt to present the trial in terms of factional feuding. Each participant had an unambiguously personal reason for the part he played in the case and was clearly following one of the best attested and most copiously documented practices of republican politics, whereby men appeared as defenders or accusers in the criminal courts primarily in response to the personal demands of *amicitia* and *patrocinium*, and generally without regard to whether such action arrayed them with their political friends or enemies.[97]

In addition, the list of those involved in the case is a singularly intractable one on which to impose a factional dichotomy, and to seek to do so is to ignore the obvious personal motivation of the trial's participants and to extend further the prosopographical schematism and subtlety which have bedevilled so many political analyses of the seventies. The supporters of Verres, while they were possibly friends of one another, can hardly be shown to have comprised a formal faction or to be obvious leaders or spokesmen of any. The same may be said of the roster of opposing witnesses, which shows still less cohesiveness as a group and contains in addition many who were demonstrably not personal or political antagonists of Verres' supporters but, on the contrary, friends and political allies.[98]

Further difficulties arise when the person of Pompey is injected as the leader of the accusing *factio*, for not only do the opponents and supporters of Verres not translate into friends and foes of Pompey, but all direct evidence for the trial indicates that the latter refrained from any involvement whatever in the case. It is true that appeals were made

97. Cf. Gelzer, *Roman Nobility*, 70 ff. Brunt, *PCPS* 11 (1965), 13 ff.
98. Lucullus and Domitius Ahenobarbus certainly belonged to the political circle of Hortensius, and in the following year Licinius Sacerdos served as a *legatus* of Q. Metellus in Crete. *Planc.* 27.

to him as consul-elect and as consul by deputations of Sicilians, but similar appeals were made by the energetic and determined victims of Verres to all who might aid their case, and Pompey's position and connections with Sicily naturally made him an object of this concentrated lobbying. There is no indication, however, that he took any positive action in response to the pleas of the Sicilians, and his name in the Verrines is chiefly conspicuous by its absence. Apart from some fleeting references to him which have no connection with the trial, Cicero mentions his name in only five passages, and then very briefly. While he expands on the achievements of the Marcelli and of Scipio Africanus and on their benefactions to the Sicilians, he says almost nothing of Pompey's Sicilian exploits and of his reorganization of the island in 82. When he mentions clients of Pompey who have been injured by Verres, he cannot add any supportive statement from Pompey such as other patrons of the Sicilians produced on behalf of other victims.[99]

Cicero's sparing use of Pompey's name is extremely significant. One of the most highly valued and exploited weapons of the advocate was the *gratia* and *auctoritas* of himself and of others on his side in a case. Examples of the exploitation and potency of this artifice abound in the history of Roman criminal trials. Cicero had learned its worth at an early stage from his mentor, M. Antonius, and there was no one who better understood its uses. He could never hope for a forensic ally more prestigious than was Pompey in 70, and his failure to capitalize on the general's power and popularity is a sure indication that the latter was taking no part whatever in the prosecution of Verres.[100]

Further, Cicero never subsequently stated or implied that in taking the Verrine case he acted as the ally or agent of Pompey. Even when he carefully recounts his benefits to the latter, he never mentions the trial of Verres.[101] It is in fact apparent that there was little contact and

99. There were friends of Pompey such as Sisenna among the defenders, and enemies such as Domitius Ahenobarbus among the accusers. Appeals to Pompey by the Sicilians are mentioned in *Verr.* 2.3.45, 204. The only other references of note to Pompey in the speeches are *Verr.* 1.44–45; 2.2.113; 2.5.153. Cf. Gruen, *AJP* 92 (1971), 9 ff.

100. On the importance of *auctoritas* in trials cf. *Mur.* 2, 59, 86. *Sulla* 2, 10, 21–22. *Cluent.* 57, 93 ff. Gelzer, *Roman Nobility*, 75 ff. Brunt, *PCPS* 11 (1965), 15.

101. Cf. *Att.* 2.9.1. *Fam.* 1.9.6. *Q.F.* 3.4.2.

no political cooperation between Cicero and Pompey before 66. Attempts to link them through common membership of the *consilium* of Pompey's father in 89 have already been shown to be without foundation. During the Cinnan years, when Cicero pursued a deliberate policy of quiescence, and Pompey made his peace with the *Cinnani* and even joined Cinna's army in 84, they had little in common, either in their interests or in their political sympathies, on which to build a friendship. Afterwards the manner of their public lives sharply diverged and provided little opportunity for contact. Cicero concentrated his energies on the law courts, and it was through his forensic and rhetorical labors that he became acquainted with many of his distinguished contemporaries, including Julius Caesar. He had no such occasion to come to know Pompey, whose career was almost exclusively military and who had no need or desire to seek advancement through the courts, and significantly Cicero does not claim with him the early association and friendship that he does, for instance, with Caesar.[102] Furthermore, Cicero was out of Rome for two years in the early seventies, the period during which he would have had the best opportunity to lay the foundations of *amicitia* with Pompey. By the time he returned the latter was about to depart for Spain, and he was not to see Rome again until almost the middle of 71.

There are also some positive indications in Cicero's writings that he was not closely allied with Pompey before 66. In his famous letter to Lentulus Spinther in 54, in which he attempts to justify his capitulation to the triumvirs after the conference at Luca in April of 56 and to emphasize his ties to Pompey, the most he can say is that he was Pompey's *fautor ab adulescentia* and his *adiutor in praetura autem et in consulatu*. A sudden beginning in 66 for their cooperation and friendship is also suggested by a passage in the second of Cicero's speeches against the land law of Rullus in 63 in which he insists that he had zealously guarded Pompey's interests during the preceding two years though he had not the stimulus of *familiaritas* to impel him to do so. It would be rash indeed to seek to stretch Cicero's connections and cooperation with Pompey beyond the limits claimed by Cicero himself, and those limits would seem positively to preclude the proposition that

102. He alludes to early friendship with Caesar in *Fam.* 1.9.12. *Prov. Cons.* 40. *Lig.* 30.

he was acting on Pompey's behalf or in alliance with him in the prosecution of Verres in 70.[103]

In the final analysis, apart from the fanciful hypothesis that all public events of the period were dominated by persistent feuding between Pompeian and Metellan factions, the only reason to connect Pompey's name to the trial is the fact that some of his Sicilian clients, notably Sthenius of Thermae, had suffered injustice at the hands of Verres. But if Pompey felt compelled to stand forth as the champion of his provincial *clientelae* it remains to be explained why his support was silent, why he entered no deposition on behalf of those clients as, for example, M. Lucullus did on behalf of Dio, and why there was no explicit indication of his sympathies in the trial as there was in the case of so many other *nobiles*.[104] It further remains to be explained, if vindication of injured provincial *clientelae* is to be taken as a sufficient reason for assuming automatic hostility to Verres, how the latter secured the support of Hortensius, whose friend Dio had been robbed of a legacy; of Q. Metellus, the man who had conferred citizenship on Dio; of P. Scipio, whose family's *clientes* in Segesta came to Rome to testify for the prosecution; of Sisenna who, like Pompey, was a friend of Sthenius and of many other Sicilians who had suffered from Verres' extortions.[105] It is clear that the claims of provincial clients were not always paramount in the complicated personal world of Roman politics.

In summary, once the trial of Verres is separated from excessively rigid conceptions of the dynamics of political change and of the patterns of political division in the seventies, and from the special pleading of Cicero himself in the Verrines, it emerges simply as another in the endless series of arraignments of provincial governors which marked the late Republic, differing, if at all, only in the dramatic qualities imparted to it by extended publicity and the well-known oratorical prowess of the opposing advocates. Neither the timing nor the issues of the trial nor the stature and influence of the defendant were such as to lend it particular political significance, and those who participated in it

103. *Fam.* 1.9.11. *Leg. Agr.* 2.49. Cf. *Dom.* 27–30, where in speaking of his friendship with Pompey he does not go back beyond the sixties. It is worth noting also that the *Com. Pet.* makes no reference to the prosecution of Verres in listing Cicero's popular actions and favors to Pompey.

104. *Verr.* 2.2.23.

105. *Verr.* 2.2.23–24, 110; 2.4.43, 80.

were motivated, as was usual, by the purely personal demands imposed by the varied forms of personal ties and obligations which governed much of the life of every Roman politician.

Cicero's reasons for taking the case are clear and are clearly stated by Cicero himself. He was pursuing a time-honored practice of Roman politics whereby younger politicians undertook the rigors of an *illustris accusatio* to prove their *virtus* and *industria* and their capacity for political life. Many of Rome's most illustrious statesmen, including Cicero's patrons and oratorical idols, L. Licinius Crassus and M. Antonius, had first won the attention of the public and recognition of their talents in this way. It was a means to *laus* and *gloria* for aspiring orators which was fully accepted and indeed commended, perceived as a healthy outlet for the energies and ambition of the rising generation.[106]

The case of Verres provided Cicero with a particularly good opportunity to exploit the benefits of the *illustris accusatio*, and he was well aware of all the political gains to be extracted from it. He was pursuing a man who had no great popularity and whose downfall would be welcomed by a sizable segment of the *nobilitas*. He was standing forth as the champion of the provincials and of the enlightened empire of more virtuous times and fulfilling specific pledges to his friends and clients in Sicily. Best of all he was undertaking a well-publicized case and confronting Rome's best-known advocate, the ideal circumstances and the ideal antagonist for an ambitious orator intent on displaying his ability and building reputation and influence through the courts. Success would bring substantial *gloria* and that *popularis voluntas* in which the circumstances of his birth had left him especially lacking.[107]

Cicero's purposes extended no further. In undertaking the prosecution he was not embracing any reformist movement or aligning himself with any anti-senatorial faction. Nor in his arguments or in the general presentation of his case did he seek to indicate sympathy for such a movement or faction or to emerge as a critic of the Sullan system and its leadership. On the contrary, he is at pains throughout the Verrines

106. In addition to Crassus and Antonius, Sulpicius, the Luculli, Julius Caesar, and M. Caelius Rufus provide examples of other politicians who conducted prosecutions at the beginning of their careers. Cf. *Off.* 2.49 ff. *Cael.* 47, 73–74. *Pis.* 82. *Div. in Caec.* 70. *Verr.* 2.3.1 ff.

107. Cicero frequently lists his motives for prosecuting. Cf. *Div. in Caec.* 2, 66, 72. *Verr.* 2.1.21; 2.2.117; 2.3.3, 6. On how *popularis voluntas* could be won by *fama* and oratorical brilliance cf. *Off.* 2.32, 48. *Com. Pet.* 55.

to present himself as an ally of the senate and a champion of the keystone of Sulla's constitution, senatorial supremacy. He speaks as a senator whose concern is to restore the order's *gratia* and *auctoritas* and to deprive its critics of any basis on which to challenge its fitness to govern. He laces the speeches with laudatory references to the great figures of the heyday of the senate's ascendancy and to the virtues they practiced. Nowhere does he imply support for a diminution of the senate's powers and prerogatives.[108]

He does deplore the power wielded by Sulla and the excesses of his regime, but so would most of the *nobilitas.* He seems to approve the restoration of the powers of tribunes, but that was hardly a radical stand in August of 70. He magnifies the corruption of senatorial juries, but such emphasis on lapses of the past was an obvious ploy to convince the jury of the necessity of voting for conviction in the present instance. He sharply criticizes the supporters of Verres, notably Hortensius, and speaks of his *intolerabilis potentia* and *regia dominatio*; but attacks on the opposing advocate and efforts to undermine his credibility and *auctoritas* were as common and acceptable as efforts to enhance the credibility and *auctoritas* of one's own side. He denounces the unprincipled *pauci* whose *improbitas* and *audacia* were defaming the senate and threatening its control; but this was a favorite form of Ciceronian invective against men like Verres, and it would be foolish indeed to interpret such language, which in all other contexts is reserved for criminals or enemies of the status quo, as referring in this instance to the leaders of the oligarchy, many of whom are, besides, lavishly praised in these same speeches. Finally, he attacks aristocratic prejudices against new men, but this was another favorite topic of Cicero's orations in all periods, designed to magnify *virtus* prevailing over the *potentia* of a partisan elite, a fertile political theme and a conventional one for the *novus homo.* Its exploitation should in no way be equated with serious personal or political antagonism between Cicero and the leading families of the *nobilitas.*[109]

108. *Verr.* 1.1; 2.1.4–5, 21; 2.2.117. For appeals to leaders of the past cf. *Div. in Caec.* 66 ff. *Verr.* 2.2.28, 87; 2.3.209; 2.4.73, 81; 2.5.180.
109. *Verr.* 2.3.81; 2.5.175. Criticism of Hortensius occurs in *Verr.* 1.35; 2.3.7 ff.; 2.5.175, 181. Cf. the attacks of the prosecutor Torquatus on Cicero in the trial of Sulla. *Sulla* 2 ff., 21 ff. In *Verr.* 1.36 Cicero speaks of the *improbitas* of the *pauci* and in *Verr.* 2.3.7 ff. and 2.5.180 ff. of the exclusiveness of the

There is one other consideration which should further discourage any deduction from these passages that Cicero was an opponent of the conservative *nobilitas* in the late seventies, namely the obvious hazards of constructing a political posture on the evidence of a forensic speech. The rules of advocacy clearly prescribed that the primary task of the forensic orator was the discovery and presentation of arguments likely to persuade the jury. To an even greater extent than usual this was Cicero's concern in the trial of Verres, where his ability and industry were being tested as never before. It was not a time for political manifestos but for rhetorical virtuosity, and it is a safe assumption that such statements as those discussed above, all of which fit well the needs of the case and the occasion, were dictated primarily by those needs. His contemporaries would have well understood the concerns and constraints that lay behind his pleading, and it is doubtful if many would have probed the speeches for serious indications of his political sympathies and ideas.[110]

In brief, Cicero's prosecution of Verres was a routine and fully acceptable step in the career of an ascending statesman. The chief effect it sought and achieved was the boosting of his reputation as an advocate and thereby the furtherance of his principal political objective of power-building through the courts. It did not involve him in any political controversy or identify him with any political faction or persuasion, and it provides no basis for assuming that he was sympathetic to popular movements for change in the late seventies.

Cicero's Political Posture as a Candidate

All other evidence for Cicero's political actions in this period supports these conclusions and reveals that he carefully kept his distance from all opponents of the Sullan oligarchy. He was sufficiently shrewd and sufficiently schooled in the realities of republican politics to recognize fully the limitations of his *novitas* and the need to overcome them by careful cultivation of individual friendships and general goodwill; but

---

nobilitas. Cicero was fond of emphasizing his *novitas* and of identifying it with *prisca virtus*, a conventional practice. Cf. Wiseman, *New Men,* 109. It should be emphasized again that most of these statements were never spoken.

110. Cf. *Cluent.* 139. Sentiments were dictated by *causae* and *tempora.* Cf. Brunt, *PCPS* 11 (1965), 15.

the means he chose for the procurement of influence and political supporters was a time-honored one, fully in keeping with the tenets of
traditional republicanism, which lauded *virtus* and *industria* as the rightful foundations of political success.

He avoided with a persistence indicative of deep conservatism the
alternative route to prominence and political influence, much in vogue
in post-Gracchan politics, which sought publicity and mass appeal by
demagogic exploitation of popular grievances, or by *largitio*, or by
attacks on conservative leaders of the *nobilitas*.[111]

Cicero's determination to avoid this form of politicking is well illustrated by his decision not to seek the tribunate. This was the office that
most of all provided younger politicians with the opportunity to bring
and keep their names before the public through vetoes, *contiones*, and
even legislation, an office often exploited even by basically conservative
young *nobiles* willing to flirt with popular programs to establish reputations, and one which the *novus homo*, seriously in need of opportunities to win publicity and popularity, could rarely afford to bypass.
Cicero would normally have held the post in 73, two years after the
quaestorship, the time when the political controversies centering around
the tribunate were at their height, and his decision to avoid the office
and embroilment in those controversies should in itself be sufficient to
lay to rest any idea that he was an espouser of popular causes in his
early political life. He might still have sought the tribunate after the settlement of 70, but instead he contented himself with the plebeian aedileship, and even in that office he refrained from the customary campaign
for fame and favor through lavish expenditure on the public games.[112]

Cicero also omitted until after his election to the praetorship another
important means of self-advertisement and mass appeal, the *contio*. The
volatile issues of the powers of tribunes and the composition of juries,
the proposals of the tribunes Cornelius and Gabinius in 67—all of these
he let pass without seeking to secure the sizable political benefits a
popular stand would have brought, particularly to a new man.[113] Most

111. Cf. *Sest.* 136–37, 139. *Planc.* 66–67. *Cluent.* 111–12.
112. Cf. Dio 36.43. *Off.* 2.56–59. Taylor, *Party Politics,* 30 ff. Wiseman, *New Men*, 159 ff.
113. Cf. *Att.* 1.11.3. Cicero registers disgust at the state of things in 67. Julius Caesar presents a strong contrast, speaking out on all the major political issues of the period. Cf. below, p. 168.

significant of all was his failure to support the Gabinian law, which gave Pompey his extraordinary command against the pirates, a measure which enjoyed wide support among the *equites* and the general public.

The problem of piracy had been growing in the Mediterranean since the middle of the second century, when the Cilician coast, left without a strong ruling authority by the decline of the Seleucid dynasty, became a stronghold of brigands. The senate made some halfhearted attempts to deal with the problem, beginning at the end of the second century, but it was not moved to decisive action until 74, when the threat of a coalition between the pirates and Mithridates developed. A special command was created in that year to combat pirates everywhere and, after much senatorial intrigue, was entrusted to a praetor, M. Antonius. Antonius's campaigns, which lasted until his death in 71, had little effect beyond the alienation of the communities of Crete, a development which led to a full-scale war with the island in 69.[114] Meantime, the activities of the pirates continued undiminished, making all sailing hazardous, threatening the coasts and harbors of Italy, and, most serious of all, hindering commerce and the operations of the *publicani* and disrupting the food supply of Rome. There was growing discontent, and finally in 67 an activist tribune, A. Gabinius, a friend of Pompey, introduced a sweeping measure which proposed that an ex-consul be given *imperium* for three years over the entire Mediterranean and *imperium* equal to that of the provincial governors for fifty miles inland, together with fifteen *legati* with *imperium pro praetore* and a vast quantity of ships, men, and money. Pompey was not named in the bill, but he was immediately seen as the unchallengeable candidate for the position.[115]

The proposal was solidly supported by the *equites* and the general public and strongly opposed by the senate's leadership. The objections of the oligarchy were numerous and concerned issues of fundamental importance. It was opposed to tribunician interference in the bestowal of commands; it was opposed to the creation of so vast an *imperium*, far greater than that entrusted to Antonius in 74; it was opposed to the

114. Cf. the account of D. Magie, *Roman Rule in Asia Minor* (Princeton 1950), 1.278–98.
115. Cf. *Man.* 31, 34, 44, 54. Plutarch, *Pompey* 24–25. Appian, *Mith.* 91–93. Rice Holmes, *Roman Republic*, 1.168. Sources for the Gabinian law in Broughton, *MRR*, 2.144–45.

bestowal of such a power on a *privatus*, always viewed by the conservatives as the most dangerous of precedents and invariably resisted by them; above all it was opposed to the bestowal of such a power on Pompey, already dangerously preeminent, and now subject to the *invidia* which was the lot of all who flew too high. But the oratory and *auctoritas* of the senate's most prestigious *principes*, and even their efforts to employ a tribunician veto, all proved futile; the measure was passed and Pompey was appointed.[116]

All of this took place early in 67 when Cicero was launching his campaign for the praetorship, his first election in the *comitia centuriata* and a crucial test of his political strength. Only two out of every five new senators could reach the praetorship in the post-Sullan period, and the competition was further sharpened in the sixties by the efforts of those ejected from the senate in 70 to stage a quick comeback. The Gabinian proposal provided Cicero with a tempting opportunity to gather behind him in this important election the enormous *potentia* of Pompey, and his failure to do so is strong evidence of the value he placed on friendship with leaders of the *nobilitas* and of the confidence he had in their support. He did not miscalculate. He was elected at the top of the poll, ahead of such formidable competitors as the patrician P. Sulpicius Galba, the plebeian *nobiles* C. Antonius and L. Cassius Longinus, and C. Aquillius Gallus, who came from a praetorian family. His success undoubtedly reflects the many friends and contacts he had built among all classes, but it must also be attributed to a considerable degree of support from the *nobilitas*, whose power in the *comitia centuriata* remained formidable in the sixties.[117]

Up to this point, Cicero, treading gingerly in a political world in which goodwill for the *novus homo* was as easily dissipated as it was difficult to acquire, had kept clear of open involvement in major political disputes, avoiding mass alienation of any segment and keeping faith with his political principles and ideals by careful disassociation from those whose policies and methods ran counter to them. After his election to the praetorship, however, his rank and *auctoritas* no longer made it possible for him to continue such a course, and over the

116. Optimate objections are spelled out in the speech of Catulus in Dio 36.31–36. Cf. Velleius 2.32.

117. *Man.* 1–2. *Pis.* 2. Plutarch, *Cicero* 9.1. Cf. Wiseman, *New Men*, 163–64. For Cicero's colleagues in the praetorship cf. Broughton, *MRR*, 2.151–52.

remaining three years of his life as a candidate he became more openly involved in the political clashes and controversies of the period and was forced to define more clearly his affiliations and beliefs. There resulted occasionally some difficulty in reconciling the *honestum* with the *utile*, and some equivocation in his public expressions of support for the oligarchy, but he was never to take a stand likely to alienate the conservative *nobilitas* as a whole or likely to prove detrimental to its interests, and he strongly supported its leaders and their causes whenever such a posture was compatible with his political survival.

His first speech at a *contio* was delivered early in 66 in a debate on the proposal of the tribune Manilius that Pompey's *imperium* under the Gabinian law be extended to all of Asia Minor and that he be given command of the armies in that area and of the war against Mithridates. Dio, writing two and a half centuries later, termed Cicero's action in supporting the bill a desertion of the optimate cause, but there is no reason to believe that anyone so viewed his behavior at the time, and a review of the background of the law and of the circumstances of its passage should dispel any notion that Cicero's speech for it involved abandonment of the *causa nobilitatis* or rejection of its ideals.[118]

The Mithridatic war had been in progress for almost eight years when Manilius introduced his proposal. Roman fortunes in the war had fluctuated greatly in that period. L. Licinius Lucullus, the first Roman commander, had initially been very successful, and by 70 he had gained control of Pontus and had driven Mithridates to seek refuge with his son-in-law Tigranes, king of Armenia. In 69 Lucullus invaded Armenia, defeated Tigranes, and took his capital of Tigranocerta. In 68 he advanced farther into Armenia and again defeated the forces of Tigranes and Mithridates, but his success in this year was marred by a mutiny of his troops and by a resurgence of Mithridates' military power in Pontus.[119] By then Lucullus was also in political trouble at Rome. He had outraged the *publicani* by financial reforms in Asia in 71 and 70, and they used their political influence with politicians in their debt and with tribunes to initiate agitation for his recall, on the grounds that he was needlessly prolonging the war. These pressures, coupled no doubt with an element of *invidia* among his peers, caused the senate to withdraw

118. Dio 36.42–43. Plutarch, *Pompey* 30. Appian, *Mith.* 97. Velleius 2.33.1.
119. Sources in Broughton, *MRR*, 2.101, 111, 118, 123, 129. Cf. Magie, *Roman Rule in Asia Minor,* 1.321–50.

Asia from Lucullus's control in 69. In 68 came a further diminution of his command when Cilicia was given to the consul of that year, Marcius Rex, an *adfinis* of Lucullus. Support for Lucullus in the senate was clearly ebbing, as the wisdom of his campaigns in Armenia and his ability to control his troops came into question. The end of the year brought the final blow, when Gabinius passed a bill bestowing the province of Bithynia and command of Lucullus's army on the consul of 67, M'. Acilius Glabrio. The law, which brought tribunes back into the area of foreign affairs, cannot have been entirely pleasing to the leaders of the senate, but there is no indication that any of them tried to prevent its passage. The mutinies and the revival of Mithridates' strength in Pontus gave Lucullus's enemies their opportunity, and it was evidently the feeling of the oligarchy that he had commanded long enough.[120]

In the course of 67, while Lucullus stood helpless with an army that refused to obey him, and while his successor remained in Bithynia, Mithridates recovered Pontus and Tigranes took control of Cappadocia.[121] This was the status of the war when Manilius introduced his measure early in 66. Opposition to the proposal was small, the circumstances entirely different from those surrounding the *Lex Gabinia* of the year before. Pompey was no longer a *privatus*; he had been spectacularly successful against the pirates and had vindicated the advocates of extraordinary commands; he was wintering in the eastern Mediterranean and was ideally situated to take over command. From every

120. Plutarch, *Lucullus* 20, 24, 33. Dio 36.2. Appian, *Mith.* 90. *Man.* 24 ff. Cf. Magie, *Roman Rule in Asia Minor*, 1.345 ff. Brunt, *Second International Conference of Economic History*, 1.148. Twyman, *ANRW* 1.1, 683–870. The figure of Pompey is often seen behind the series of developments that ended Lucullus's command, but without justification. Neither Marcius Rex nor Acilius Glabrio, obvious choices as consuls for the commissions given them, can be shown to have been friends of Pompey. Such evidence as there is points the other way. Besides, at the time of their appointment, the war in the East must have been seen as virtually at an end. Cf. Dio 36.17. Glabrio hoped for an easy triumph. It was only subsequent developments in 67 that made the military situation serious again and warranted the command proposed by Manilius. Pompey cannot have foreseen these developments in 68 or believed that there was much scope for his military talents in the eastern war. It is far more likely that he was concentrating his efforts on securing a command against the pirates, an assignment everyone believed would take several years.

121. Plutarch, *Lucullus* 35.1–6. Appian, *Mith.* 88–90. Dio 36.14–17. *Man.* 5, 12, 26. Cf. Magie, *Roman Rule in Asia Minor*, 1.348–49.

aspect it made sense to use his skill and victorious forces to end the long and costly eastern war.

Furthermore, Pompey had played his political cards in 67 with his customary skill and had disarmed many of his aristocratic opponents. He worked hard to minimize oligarchic resentment at his elevation to a great command through tribunician legislation by avoiding any involvement in the passage of the bill, and by ostentatiously feigning reluctance to accept the commission. After his appointment he worked harder still to conciliate the *nobilitas* by associating as many of them as possible with him in his power and glory. Pompey chose the bulk of his *legati* from the inner circle of the aristocracy. The position, which carried with it *imperium pro praetore*, was highly desirable. His known *legati* in 67 included Metellus Nepos, son of the consul of 98; Cn. Cornelius Lentulus and L. Gellius Publicola, consuls in 72 and censors in 70; Cn. Cornelius Lentulus Marcellinus, the future consul of 56; M. Pupius Piso, future consul of 61; L. Cornelius Sisenna, M. Terentius Varro, a Claudius Nero, two Manlii Torquati, and an Octavius. Pompey made no effort to cement his power by surrounding himself with henchmen. The oligarchy was offered and accepted a major part in the massive military operation authorized by Gabinius's law.[122]

It is not surprising, therefore, that the extension of that operation as proposed by Manilius evoked little oligarchic opposition. Four distinguished *consulares* actually spoke in favor of the bill: P. Servilius Vatia, consul in 79 and a leading *Sullanus*; C. Scribonius Curio, consul in 76 and one of the foremost conservative politicians of the seventies; C. Cassius Longinus and Cn. Lentulus Clodianus, consuls in 73 and 72 respectively. Many other *nobiles* were soon to benefit from the law. Metellus Celer, another son of the consul of 98, a Valerius Flaccus, an Aemilius Scaurus, and Faustus Sulla, son of the dictator, all appear as *legati* of Pompey in the following years. There can be little doubt that some resentment of Pompey's growing power continued among the *nobilitas*, but most preferred to share that power rather than uselessly to oppose it, and only the most diehard of the conservatives, Catulus

122. Cf. Dio 36.24 ff. When the consul Piso attempted to interfere with Pompey's operations and Gabinius was about to introduce a bill to depose him, Pompey prevented any hostile actions against the consul. Plutarch, *Pompey* 27.1. For Pompey's *legati* cf. Broughton, *MRR*, 2.148–49. E. S. Gruen, "Pompey, the Roman Aristocracy and the Conference at Luca" *Historia* 18 (1969), 75 ff.

and Hortensius, are known to have opposed the proposal openly. A final factor that lessened opposition was the fact that the two men being replaced by Pompey, Marcius Rex and Acilius Glabrio, had both failed miserably and, by all indications, commanded little support or sympathy in the senate.[123]

It is against this background that the political significance of Cicero's support of the Manilian law must be considered. On this occasion Cicero could make a bid for the political benefits of supporting so influential a figure and so popular a proposal without standing in opposition to the policies and perceived interests of the oligarchy as a whole. In speaking for the bill he was joining a bandwagon containing many *nobiles* and associating himself with a man in whose service were many of Rome's leading citizens, and whose goodwill the bulk of the senate's *principes* were intent on safeguarding. It was not a stand calculated or likely to alienate the oligarchy, nor did it involve any rejection of optimate associations or any assault on optimate ideology. The speech is devoid of any personal attacks or *popularis* sentiments. He treats the bill's opponents with the utmost respect and presents them as sincere and worthy statesmen, and argues convincingly that the proposal was well precedented and fully in keeping with the best practice of traditional republicanism.[124]

Later in 66, in his second known speech at a *contio*, Cicero stood unequivocally on the side of the oligarchy in a dispute *de Sullae bonis*. Faustus Sulla, son of the dictator, was indicted by a tribune for possession of property allegedly appropriated wrongfully by his father. The case was an outgrowth of a recurring, deep-rooted concern in this period to withdraw some of the ill-gotten gains of the years of Sulla's dictatorship and to punish the more extreme perpetrators of the many injustices of that era. A depleted treasury helped sharpen these feelings in the sixties. The oligarchy showed itself prepared to take limited steps to meet the public mood and redress some of the grievances. Reference has already been made to the efforts of the consuls of 72 to recover money owed to the state by Sullan *possessores*. In 64 Cato, as quaestor,

123. *Man.* 68. Plutarch, *Pompey* 30. Dio 36.43. Cf. Broughton, *MRR*, 2.156, 159, 170. Marcius Rex waited for years outside Rome seeking a triumph and may never have got it. Sallust, *Catiline* 30.3–4. Cicero treats Glabrio with scant respect in *Man.* 5, 12, a significant indication that Glabrio had few supporters.
124. *Man.* 51–66.

took measures to force repayment of money disbursed for assassination of those proscribed by Sulla. Prosecutions for such murders followed Cato's action, and there were many convictions. But the oligarchy as a whole was deeply concerned to contain this issue within narrow limits and prevent any large-scale challenging of Sulla's assignations and arrangements. The attack on Faustus, which was initiated by a tribune and which was later linked by Cicero to the backers of Rullus, was resisted by the senate's *principes*, who obviously viewed it as a partisan move and likely to lead to dangerous questioning of other Sullan *acta*. The trial was eventually halted, a course which Cicero strongly advocated at a *contio*. His action in speaking openly for the optimate view on this volatile issue was a noteworthy public identification with the *Sullani*.[125]

Not long afterwards he became involved in two trials, both of which had political overtones and both of which have contributed to the common view that he frequently espoused popular leaders and causes on his way to the consulship. In the last days of December 66, Manilius, lately out of office, was indicted in the extortion court, of which Cicero served as president during his praetorship. That the trial was an optimate attempt to have revenge on the radical tribune is attested both by the ancient sources and by the public support for Manilius that quickly showed itself. Manilius asked for time to prepare his defense, but Cicero allowed him only one day. The tribunes immediately took up the matter and denounced this decision at a *contio*. Cicero attempted to defend his action by saying it was designed to help Manilius by having his case heard before a well-disposed president. He then agreed to defend Manilius, thus reversing his decision and allowing the case to go into the following year.[126]

125. Asconius 73, Clark. *Cluent.* 94. *Leg. Agr.* 1.12. Plutarch, *Cato Min.* 17.4. Dio 37.10.2. *Lig.* 12. *Schol. Gron.* 293, Stangl. Suetonius, *Julius* 11. Cf. E. S. Gruen, "Some Criminal Trials of the Late Republic: Political and Prosopographical Problems" *Athenaeum* 49 (1971), 56–58. There are no grounds for the suggestion sometimes advanced that the prosecution of Faustus was an indirect attack on Pompey. The oligarchy and Cicero were to resist further attempts in 63 to reverse *acta* of Sulla, when it was proposed to restore political rights to sons of the proscribed. Quintilian 11.1.85. Dio 37.25.3. Plutarch, *Cicero* 12.1. Pliny, *NH* 7.117. *Att.* 2.1.3. *Pis.* 4.

126. Plutarch, *Cicero* 9. Dio 36.44. Cf. *Leg. Agr.* 2.49, which probably refers to Cicero's speech at the *contio*. Cf. B. Rawson, "*De Lege Agraria* 2.49" *CP* 66 (1971), 26–29.

Cicero's explanation of his behavior has often been taken at face value, but it is an extremely implausible *apologia*. Both Plutarch and Dio, who provide the two principal ancient accounts of the affair, make clear that Manilius wanted more time and that Cicero refused him. If Cicero were seeking to help Manilius, surely the latter would have known about it and would not have tried to thwart Cicero's friendly purpose by an application for delay. Neither would he have allowed friendly tribunes to protest a ruling designed to benefit him. There are other reasons also for doubting Cicero's protestations of friendship toward Manilius. Early in his tribunate the latter had attempted to force enactment of legislation giving freedmen the right to vote with those who had freed them. The measure, anathema to the oligarchy, was violently resisted, the forces of opposition being led by Domitius Ahenobarbus, who is also attested as the leading figure behind Manilius's prosecution. Domitius was a particular friend of Cicero, and Cicero himself affirms that he shared Domitius's outrage at Manilius's measure and methods. It seems highly unlikely that he went to any unusual lengths to frustrate his friend's design to bring down a man for whom he had scant regard. These several considerations point to the conclusion that Cicero's refusal to grant Manilius the requested delay was not a friendly action, but either an attempt to escape being asked to defend the former tribune if the case went into 65 or an act of collusion with Manilius's enemies to insure a speedy conviction. Cicero misjudged, however, the power of Pompey's friendship and the public support it would generate for Manilius, and, to avoid appearing to repudiate his own newfound friendship with Pompey, he was forced into feeble pretexts, and into the position of having to defend Manilius, the position which it had probably been his primary purpose to avoid.[127]

He never had to conduct the unwanted defense, however. When the trial opened in 65 Manilius disrupted it with gangs, and when it reconvened

127. Asconius 45, 64–65, Clark. Dio 36.42.2. *Schol. Bob.* 119, Stangl. Cf. Gruen, *Last Generation*, 261 ff. E. J. Phillips, "Cicero and the Prosecution of C. Manilius" *Latomus* 29 (1970), 595–607. A. M. Ward, "Politics in the Trials of Manilius and Cornelius" *TAPA* 101 (1970), 545–56. Ciaceri, *Cicerone*, 1.153 ff. Gelzer, *Cicero*, 60 ff. As praetor Cicero also presided over the trial of Licinius Macer, who was accused of extortion. Macer, who was defended by Crassus and was still likely out of favor with the oligarchy, was condemned, and Cicero won acclaim for his handling of the case. The trial would not have damaged his standing with the oligarchy. *Att.* 1.4.2. Plutarch, *Cicero* 9.1–2. Val. Max. 9.12.7.

with the consuls present to prevent disorder, Manilius failed to appear and was condemned. The whole affair had been a trying experience for Cicero, as his subsequent allusions to it make clear, but it is doubtful if it cost him any friends among the oligarchy. Manilius's opponents, who knew Cicero's true sentiments, would have fully understood the constraints that had forced him into the role of Manilius's defender.[128]

It is unlikely that the second trial with political overtones from this period, in which Cicero defended a tribune of 67, C. Cornelius, cost him any oligarchic goodwill either, or marked him in the eyes of the conservative *nobilitas* as a friend of its challengers. Cornelius had introduced, as tribune, a series of measures designed to check certain abuses of power and common forms of corruption in Roman politics. His first proposal, which he brought before the senate, advocated an end to the lending of money to foreign envoys at Rome. The senate, which had already dealt with this question in a decree in 94, was unwilling to take further action. Cornelius was stung and criticized the senate's decision at a *contio*. He next introduced a bill forbidding the granting of exemptions from the laws except by decree of the people. The measure would have ended a practice long accepted as a senatorial right, and it was opposed by the senate's *potentissimi*, who found a tribune, P. Servilius Globulus, to obstruct the reading of the bill preceding the voting. Cornelius disregarded the intervention and began to read the bill himself. When the consul Calpurnius Piso protested that a tribunician veto was being set aside, he was attacked and had his *fasces* broken. Cornelius then dismissed the assembly and, during a heated senatorial debate which followed, submitted a compromise bill, which was accepted without protest by the senate and which continued the senate's right to grant exemptions from the laws, provided two hundred members were present.

Two other major proposals are known to have been put forward by Cornelius, one requiring praetors to administer the law in accordance with their edicts, which was implemented without objection, and one increasing the penalties for bribery, which was rejected by the senate as too severe. To replace it the senate drew up a more moderate measure and instructed the consuls to pass it into law, and, to enable it to be

128. Asconius 60, 66, Clark. Domitius Ahenobarbus certainly continued to be one of Cicero's strongest supporters.

enacted before the elections for 66, which by this time had already been announced, it exempted the consuls from the *Leges Aelia et Fufia*, which forbade the passage of legislation in the interval between the announcement of elections and the date on which they were held. Cornelius opposed the senatorial proposal on the grounds that it was ineffectual, since it contained no sanctions against *divisores*, and it was rejected. The consul Piso, who had assumed responsibility for the bill's enactment, revised it to include a provision dealing with the activities of *divisores*, but when he submitted the new version a demonstration by the bribery agents disrupted the proceedings. Finally, armed with a bodyguard and calling on the assistance of all patriotic citizens, Piso succeeded in having the revised proposal passed into law.

In 66 Cornelius was prosecuted *de maiestate*, a charge based on his efforts to bypass the tribunician veto of his *solutio* proposal. The president of the court failed to attend on the appointed day, and the prosecutors, the brothers P. and L. Cominius, were threatened by gangs and were in danger of being killed until rescued by the consuls, who had come to aid Cornelius. The court convened on the following day, but this time the prosecutors were absent and the case was dismissed.

P. Cominius, encouraged by the fate of Manilius, resumed the prosecution in 65 and was solidly backed by the senate's *principes*, five of whom, Hortensius, Catulus, Metellus Pius, M. Lucullus, and Mam. Lepidus, gave evidence against Cornelius. But the former tribune had confidence in his case. He took scrupulous care to avoid any interruption of the proceedings by his supporters and secured Cicero as chief defense counsel. The trial drew large crowds and caused great excitement. It lasted four days, and resulted in Cornelius's acquittal by a large majority.[129]

Several layers of obfuscation have been laid over Cornelius's tribunate and trial by the hypothesizing of modern scholars. His legislative proposals are often viewed as an ongoing effort by a Pompeian or popular party to extend the reformist concerns of 70 and further curtail the power of the ruling oligarchy. The trial, in consequence, tends to emerge as a contest between Pompeian or reformist elements and the

129. The story of Cornelius's tribunate is told by Asconius (57–62, Clark), and Dio (36.38–40). The version of Asconius is the one related above. Cf. Griffin, *JRS* 63 (1973), 196–203.

principes of the conservative *nobilitas.*[130] These hypotheses reproduce again schematic patterns of conflict in Roman politics and are again vitiated by oversimplification that ignores much of the evidence.

The association of Pompey with the proposals of Cornelius is predicated on the highly questionable view that the general did more in 70 than resolve the tribunician controversy, which was already nearing its climax, and that he stood in general opposition to the oligarchy. The association is further unsupported by any of the ancient sources. Cornelius was undoubtedly a friend of Pompey, having served as his quaestor in Spain. Asconius states that the connection helped him at the trial, and Quintilian records that Cicero included a eulogy of Pompey in his speech for the defense. Asconius does not suggest, however, that Cornelius's activities as tribune had anything to do with Pompey, and Quintilian emphasizes that Cicero's Pompeian excursus was an irrelevant digression. Nowhere is there any implication that Cornelius was Pompey's political agent. It is, besides, unlikely that in the very year when Pompey was angling for the command against the pirates and, on good evidence, was seeking to avoid undue antagonism of the senate's leadership, he attempted to promote a series of reforms likely to arouse those leaders. Finally, Cornelius, though acquitted, got no further in Roman politics, a poor reward if his efforts in 67 were undertaken on behalf of Pompey.[131]

It is equally difficult to sustain the view that Cornelius was the leader or representative of any broader popular movement. He was not known before his tribunate as a radical; in the vocabulary of the *optimates* he was *homo non improbus.* Nor was his program revolutionary or seriously at odds with the policies and interests of the oligarchy. His first proposal was not new and not unacceptable to the senate. His *solutio* measure did threaten a treasured power of the senate's leaders, but Cornelius compromised on the issue, and, according to Asconius, no one could deny that the modified bill was *pro senatus auctoritate.* Asconius says of his third law that it was unwelcome to *multi*, but he does not say that it was unwelcome to the *pauci*, and it is unlikely that

130. Cf. W. McDonald, "The Tribunate of Cornelius" *CQ* 23 (1929), 196-208. Ward, *TAPA* 101 (1970), 554-56. Griffin, *JRS* 63 (1973), 203-13. R. Seager, "The Tribunate of Cornelius. Some Ramifications" *Hommages à M. Renard* (1969), 2.680-86. Gruen, *Last Generation,* 262-65.
    131. Asconius 61, Clark. Quintilian, *Inst. Or.* 4.3.13; 9.2.55.

it was, for it ended a means to *gratia* most likely to be exploited by those who lacked the many more legitimate means to influence possessed by the *nobilis.* The one man known to have ignored his edict in the administration of justice was Verres, who was thwarted in this abuse by L. Piso, a *propinquus* of the consul of 67.[132] Similarly, Cornelius's final proposal to curb electoral corruption was at least as likely to inhibit foes as friends of the senate, and it should in no way be regarded as an attack on the *potentia* of the oligarchy.

It is apparent from the many efforts made to check electoral abuses in the sixties that the period witnessed a pronounced increase in bribery of various forms, induced, no doubt, by an increase in the number of candidates and by a greatly expanded electorate which gave greater opportunity and created a greater need for the exploitation of material political resources. But the attempts to deal with the problem were initiated for the most part by leading *nobiles* and plainly show that it was the oligarchy that was chiefly interested in suppressing electoral corruption. Wholesale bribery would throw into disarray the traditional modes of electoral control and introduce an anarchy into the political process unfavorable to those whose hold on power depended more on long-established social and political structures and conventions than on mere money. The *nobilitas* was interested in maintaining the common forms of generosity to the voters, which were traditionally classified as *liberalitas* rather than *ambitus*, and in preserving forms of canvassing which gave scope for the maximum utilization of clients and *amici*; however, it had no interest in protecting large-scale, direct purchasing of votes. Its differences with Cornelius on measures to curtail such trafficking concerned matters of scope and severity only, contentious questions which were often to produce dissension in subsequent debates on bribery legislation. There was no dispute about the need to check corruption, and no reluctance on the senate's part to take action, and in the end it approved a very severe bill and took unusual steps to insure that it would be applicable to the elections for 66.[133]

132. Asconius 57, 59, 61, Clark. It appears that Cornelius's final *solutio* bill made ratification of senatorial exemptions necessary, but it also forbade the use of *intercessio* at assemblies to consider such exemptions and thus insured that ratification would normally be the rule. For Piso's opposition to Verres cf. *Verr.* 2.1.119; Ps. Asconius 250, Stangl.

133. On electoral strife in the sixties cf. Dio 36.38. Wiseman, *JRS* 59 (1969), 65 ff. Sulla had given an indication of optimate attitudes toward *ambitus* when

Other efforts to eliminate corruption, mostly initiated by the senate, followed. A *Lex Fabia* limited the number of attendants that could accompany a candidate. Another law forbade the use of *nomenclatores.* A *senatus consultum* amended the *Lex Calpurnia* in 65, the year after the successful prosecution for bribery of the consuls-elect, P. Sulla and P. Autronius. Another decree in 64 abolished many *collegia*, which were becoming a potential source of disturbance and a weapon of electoral corruption. The senate also attempted in the same year to toughen further the laws on bribery, but its proposals were vetoed by the tribune Q. Mucius Orestinus. In 63 it turned back a determined effort by a tribune, L. Caecilius Rufus, to lessen penalties, and under pressure from Cato and Servius Sulpicius, who was then a candidate for the consulship, it strongly supported a bill sponsored by Cicero which again increased penalties and added to and defined more sharply the practices that constituted *ambitus.* Further efforts from within the oligarchy to close remaining loopholes in the bribery laws continued into 61. The record leaves no doubt that the conservative *nobilitas* of the sixties saw bribery as more likely to subvert than to strengthen its ascendancy.[134]

None of Cornelius's proposals in 67 can therefore be argued to have damaged the optimate cause or to have been designed to do so. He simply sought to remedy abuses where he saw them, and his only offense against the oligarchy was the pertinacity with which he pursued his goals and his willingness, whenever he failed to get his way inside the senate, to go outside it and seek to compel its compliance through popular pressures.

His methods won him the enmity of many of the senate's *principes*, and brought them out to testify against him. But no major ideological or partisan conflict was being played out in his trial, and Cornelius was by no means without friends and supporters among conservative politicians. The tribunes of 67, who included Globulus, whose attempted

---

he introduced the first bribery law in thirty years, excluding those convicted from seeking office for ten years. Clearly he did not see bribery as a weapon likely to confirm the hold of the oligarchy. For the distinction between *liberalitas* and *ambitus* cf. *Mur.* 68 ff. *Planc.* 45.

134. *Mur.* 71. Plutarch, *Cato Min.* 8.2. *Pis.* 8. *Asconius* 7, 69, 83, 85–86, 88, Clark. *Sulla* 63–64. *Mur.* 47, 67, 89. *Planc.* 83. *Sest.* 133. *Vat.* 37. Dio 37.29.1. *Schol. Bob.* 79, 140, 151, 166, Stangl. Cf. the detailed discussion of Gruen, *Last Generation*, 212–24.

veto was the basis for the charge against Cornelius, and L. Roscius and L. Trebellius, who had tried to block the Gabinian law, were solidly on Cornelius's side. The consuls of 66, Manius Lepidus and Volcatius Tullus, were also sympathetic, as were the senators on the jury who were not *familiares* of the *potentissimi*.[135]

Little political importance should be attached to Cicero's acceptance of such a case. No great political consequences hinged on the outcome of the prosecution, and, besides, Cornelius was an old friend of Cicero and as such had strong claims on the latter's help, whatever the circumstances under which he was being brought to trial. The ethics of the Roman bar placed few restrictions on an advocate's right to defend, and fewer still when the *caput* of an *amicus* was at stake. Antonius could defend without harm to his optimate friendships and standing the radical Norbanus, whose downfall was certainly no less desired by the conservative *nobilitas* than was that of Cornelius. Cicero himself, in his later career, often appeared for the defense in opposition to close friends, and in cases where vital interests of those friends were at issue. He never regarded such action as an infringement of *amicitia* of or political fellowship, and he even argued his right to oppose friends in court in defense of *alienissimi*.[136]

From the surviving passages of the speeches for Cornelius it is apparent that Cicero did criticize the motives of Cornelius's accusers and their alleged concern to preserve the *maiestas* of the tribunate, and did attempt to defend tribunician activism, and stressed the benefits the office had brought to the state. But it would be hazardous to conclude from these isolated fragments that he presented himself as an opponent of the senate's *potentissimi* and a champion of *popularis* policies and methods. The surest evidence of the tone and substance of his arguments remains the judgment of Asconius, who had the opportunity to read the entire defense, and who states that Cicero handled Cornelius's noble adversaries with great moderation and skillfully avoided any

135. Asconius 60–61, Clark. *Vat.* 5.
136. *De Or.* 2.89, 124, 198, 202. Cf. *Mur.* 7 ff. *Sulla* 6, 49. *Vat.* 5. *Planc.* 72. *Rab.* 1. *Fam.* 1.9.17. *De Or.* 1.184. *Att.* 2.1.9. Brunt, *PCPS* 11 (1965), 14 ff. Caelius did not lose Cicero's friendship when he appeared against him. *Cael.* 47. Cf. Calvus's defense of C. Cato in 54 against his good friend Asinius Pollio. Seneca, *Controv.* 7.4.7. *Att.* 4.15.4; 4.16.5. Cf. E. S. Gruen, "Cicero and Licinius Calvus" *HSCP* 71 (1966), 223 ff.

assault on their *dignitas*, while at the same time insuring that their *auctoritas* was not allowed to injure his client.[137]

In any event, the value of Cicero's pleading in the case as an indicator of his political views and place in the political spectrum in the mid-sixties is severely limited by the considerations already mentioned in relation to the Verrines. His defense of tribunician activism and presentation of the trial as an attempt by Cornelius's enemies to destroy rather than defend the tribunate were obvious modes of argument in the circumstances, and as always Cicero said whatever his ingenuity could contrive to sway the jury, exercising what Asconius calls *oratoriae calliditatis ius*, the well-accepted right of the advocate to use his craft to manipulate facts and fashion arguments appropriate to the needs of the moment. Antonius had gone so far in his defense of Norbanus as to exalt *seditio* and the sometimes salutary effects of popular movements. His friends on the opposing side did not deduce that he had suddenly changed his political creed, but simply saw his performance as a masterly display of the art of persuasion. Cicero's far more moderate handling of the same theme in a similar case would have been viewed no differently, and that it gave small offense to the oligarchy is amply illustrated by the fact that, not long after the trial, he held the offer of a *legatio* from none other than Cornelius's prime antagonist in 67, C. Calpurnius Piso, governor of Cisalpine and Transalpine Gaul in 66 and 65.[138]

Only one political speech by Cicero is recorded for 65, the *De Rege Alexandrino*, in which he vigorously opposed a proposal to make Egypt a tributary province. Egypt had allegedly been bequeathed to Rome by a will of Alexander I, who died in 87. The senate vot•d at the time to accept the bequest, but its resolution was vetoed. The matter continued to be raised periodically, but there were doubts about the authenticity of the will, and the senate, traditionally opposed to expansion and extension of administrative responsibilities, took no further action. When the question came up again in 65, and a motion to annex the kingdom was put forward, there was strong opposition, led by Catulus, and the proposal was rejected.[139]

137. Asconius 61, 76–77, 79–80, Clark.
138. Asconius 70, Clark. *De Or.* 2.124–25, 202 ff. *Att.* 1.1.2.
139. *Schol. Bob.* 91, Stangl. *Leg. Agr.* 1.1; 2.41, 44. Plutarch, *Crassus* 13.1–2. Suetonius, *Julius* 11. Cf. E. Badian, "The Testament of Ptolemy Alexander" *RhM* 110 (1967), 178–92.

The resistance in 65 would seem to have been intensified by the fact that the man behind the proposal was M. Crassus, one of the most powerful politicians of the period, but one who did not enjoy the goodwill of the oligarchy. Although he was the son of a distinguished optimate and had contributed significantly to Sulla's victory, Crassus pursued a political course and strategy which brought him no friendship from the conservative *nobilitas* and often ranged him with its foes. Unlike Pompey, he did not follow his service to the Sullan cause with any attempt to forge links with leading *Sullani*. Instead he concentrated on amassing wealth from the proscriptions, and in the process he won the hostility of Sulla and the disapproval of his peers. There is no sign that he ever improved his standing with the ruling elite or tried to do so. There are many references in the sources to his disagreements with prominent *nobiles*, such as Metellus Pius and Catulus, but evidence of friendship or cooperation with the leaders of the oligarchy is hard to find. Even his *legati* in his two major military undertakings, the slave war in 72 and the Parthian war in 54–53, were little known or came from little-known families. One of his sons did marry a daughter of Metellus Creticus in the mid-sixties, but this alliance may well have been prompted by the mutual hatred of the two families for Pompey, and in any event it did not lead to any broader friendship with the Metelli or their associates.[140]

Crassus preferred to build power outside the leading families of the oligarchy using all the political weapons of the post-Gracchan era. He purchased political followers by lending his money free of interest. He constantly worked to secure others by frequent pleading in the courts, by canvassing for candidates, and by making himself accessible to the

140. For Crassus's father cf. *De Or.* 3.10. *Tusc.* 1.81. Plutarch, *Crassus* 1. For Crassus's early career cf. Plutarch, *Crassus* 2.2, 4–6; clashes with Metellus Pius and Catulus, Plutarch, *Crassus* 6.2, 13.1. Dio 37.9; *legati,* Broughton, *MRR*, 2.119, 231–32. Plutarch, *Crassus* 10.1, 11.4, 31.2; marriage connection with Metellus Creticus, *ILS*, 881. Cf. F. E. Adcock, *Marcus Crassus, Millionaire* (Cambridge 1966). T. J. Cadoux, "Marcus Crassus. A Revaluation" *Greece and Rome* 3 (1956), 153–61. Gelzer, "Licinius" *RE*, 13.1, 295–331. A. Garzetti, "M. Licinio Crasso" *Athenaeum* 19 (1941), 1–37; 20 (1942), 12–40; 21 (1944–45), 1–61. Gruen, *Last Generation*, 66–74. E. Parrish, "Crassus' New Friends and Pompey's Return" *Phoenix* 27 (1973), 357–80. B. A. Marshall, *Crassus: A Political Biography* (Amsterdam 1976). A. M. Ward, *Marcus Crassus and the Late Roman Republic* (Columbia 1977).

general public and wooing its favor by affability and varied forms of *liberalitas*. His political stands also reflected his determination to cultivate a wide constituency. Though he was no leader of popular causes nor open advocate of popular reform, he was fond of befriending popular politicians and of staking a claim on the support of their followers. There is evidence that he was connected with activist tribunes such as Sicinius, Quinctius, Licinius Macer, and Manilius, and he was widely known as an opportunistic champion of radicals. Catiline may also safely be reckoned among his political associates in the mid-sixties. The evidence for the association is contaminated by propagandist writings of the fifties and by Cicero's defamatory and posthumously published *De Consiliis Suis*, but Cicero's allegations of an alliance between Crassus and Catiline went back at least as far as 64, and in 63 there were many senators who were ready to believe accusations that Crassus had some involvement in the revolutionary designs of Catiline. There is little doubt that the accusations were slanderous, but the suspicions of his contemporaries suggest that there was, or had been, some form of connection between him and Catiline. The suspicions also illustrate Crassus's distance from the *via optimas* and its guardians, as does the fact that soon afterwards he conspicuously absented himself from the senatorial debate on the fate of the leading conspirators in December 63, in which as a *consularis* and *censorius* he would have been called upon to play a major part.[141]

It is likely that by 65 he was also a friend and political ally of Julius Caesar, a rising political star, and a man of not dissimilar political

141. For Crassus's political techniques cf. Plutarch, *Crassus* 3, 6.7, 7.1–4, 12.2–3. *Att.* 1.18.6. *Brut.* 233. His power is noted in Plutarch, *Pompey* 22.1–3; *Cicero* 15.1. For his association with tribunes and radicals cf. Plutarch, *Crassus* 7.9, 11.4; *Cicero* 9.1–2. Frontinus, *Strategemata* 2.5.34. Dio 36.42.2–3. Sallust, *Catiline* 48.8. Crassus was certainly a friend of a close associate of Catiline, Cn. Piso, whom he helped secure an appointment as proquaestor to Nearer Spain in 65, and in 64 Cicero clearly indicated that he believed Crassus was behind Catiline also when he stated in his speech, *In Toga Candida*, that the latter's backers were the same men who engineered the dispatch of Piso to Spain. Asconius 66, 83, 92–93, Clark. Sallust, *Catiline* 19.1. Cf. Plutarch, *Crassus* 13, 2–3; *Cicero* 15.2. Sallust, *Catiline* 48.5. Dio 37.31.1. *Cat.* 4.10. Arguments against association between Crassus and Catiline are advanced by R. Seager, "The First Catilinarian Conspiracy" *Historia* 13 (1964), 346–47. E. S. Gruen, "Notes on the First Catilinarian Conspiracy" *CP* 64 (1969), 20–24. P. A. Brunt, "Three Passages from Asconius" *CR* 71 (1957), 193–95. For Crassus and the so-called First Catilinarian Conspiracy cf. ch. 4, pp. 223 ff.

methods, though a more open espouser of popular causes and a more conspicuous builder of extra-senatorial power. Caesar had friends and relatives within the *nobilitas*, and he was on good terms with leading *Sullani* in the early seventies; but as he approached his first candidacy he began to show his independence and his support for change and for *popularis* policies. He spoke in favor of the restoration of the powers of tribunes and of the amnesty bill of Plautius in 70, made the death of Marius's widow in 69 an occasion to glorify the general, championed the claims of the Transpadani when they agitated for citizenship in 68, supported the Gabinian law in 67 and the Manilian in 66, and used his aedileship in 65 to put on extravagant games and to reerect in the forum memorials of Marius's victories which had been dismantled by Sulla. By 65 he was clearly identified as an enemy of traditional republicanism and a threat to its survival, and was a special object of attack by Catulus.[142]

Caesar was the type of politican who attracted the patronage of Crassus, and that they were friends in the sixties is directly stated by Plutarch, who tells the story of Caesar's deliverance from his creditors in 62 by a pledge from Crassus to stand surety for his debts. It should be noted that Plutarch recounts the incident as an example of their friendship, not as its beginning, and there are many indications that the association in fact went back at least as far as 65. Crassus's first major undertaking in that year was an attempt as censor to include the Transpadani in the roll of citizens, a sudden espousal of a cause to which Caesar had already boldly committed himself and which he continued to champion until finally in 49 he succeeded in extending Roman citizenship to the whole of Cisalpine Gaul. Crassus's Egyptian proposal almost certainly commanded the support of Caesar also. Suetonius relates that, after conciliating the people with extravagant shows, Caesar attempted to secure

142. For Caesar's early career and connections cf. Suetonius, *Julius* 1.1-2, 5-6, 8, 10. Plutarch, *Caesar* 1.1-2, 5-6; *Pompey* 25.3. Dio 36.43; 37.8; 44.47.4. Velleius 2.43. Pliny, *NH* 33, 53. L. R. Taylor, "Caesar's Early Career" *CP* 36 (1941), 113-32; *AJP* 63 (1942), 385-412; "Caesar and the Roman Nobility" *TAPA* 73 (1942), 1-24. M. Gelzer, *Caesar,* trans. P. Needham (Oxford 1968), 27-42. H. Strasburger, *Caesars Eintritt in die Geschichte* (Munich 1938). There were many who believed that Caesar, like Crassus, was an associate of Catiline, and efforts were made to implicate him in the conspiracy in 63. Cf. Plutarch, *Cicero* 20.3-4; *Caesar* 8.1. *Off.* 2.84. Sallust, *Catiline* 49. Asconius 83, Clark. Suetonius, *Julius* 9.

through tribunician legislation an extraordinary command to implement the will of Alexander, and, though the account includes references to events that belong to the history of the early fifties and is less than trustworthy, it can hardly be dismissed entirely, and when combined with the evidence for Caesar's involvement in the Rullan agrarian proposal of 63, which most probably aimed at the incorporation of Egypt, the likelihood emerges that he was a party to Crassus's Egyptian policy and looked to involvement in its implementation as a means to political advancement. Catulus was Crassus's chief opponent in both the Transpadane and Egyptian disputes, and he indulged at the same time in vigorous denunciations of Caesar and his political designs, a coincidence that further betokens political collaboration between Caesar and Crassus in the latter's power-building schemes in 65. Finally, Caesar's rapid rise to prominence in the latter half of the sixties, dramatically illustrated in his victory as an *aedilicius* over none other than his archenemy, the venerable *consularis* and *censorius* Catulus, at the elections for the office of Pontifex Maximus in 63, is most readily explained if attributed to the formidable *potentia* of Crassus, who would certainly have relished Catulus's defeat, as well as to Caesar's own command of the electorate.[143]

In speaking out on the Egyptian question in 65, Cicero was therefore entering a dispute involving both partisanship and policy, opposing a measure unacceptable to the conservatives both on general principles and because of the person of its author, whose friends and methods placed him far outside the circle of the *boni* and marked him as one of the most formidable dissentient politicians of the sixties. The surviving fragments of Cicero's speech show that he aligned himself to the fullest degree with the opponents of the proposal, not only attacking the measure on its merits, but also denouncing the motives and methods of Crassus. His stand provided another clear affirmation of his continuing adherence to the *bonae partes* and its leaders.[144]

143. Plutarch, *Crassus* 7.6. Dio 37.9.3. Suetonius, *Julius* 11. *Leg. Agr.* 1.1; 2.44. For Catulus and Caesar and the pontifical election cf. Plutarch, *Caesar* 6.4; 7.1–4. Suetonius, *Julius* 13. Dio 37.37.1–3. Sallust, *Catiline* 49.2. Velleius 2.43.3. Friendship between Crassus and Caesar in the mid-sixties is doubted by G. V. Sumner, "Cicero, Pompey and Rullus" *TAPA* 97 (1966), 574 ff., but he ignores much of the evidence for it.

144. *Schol. Bob.* 92, Stangl. It is stated by Rice Holmes (*Roman Republic*, 1.227) that Cicero spoke in the interests of Pompey. I can find no evidence to support such a statement.

By the time of his election to the consulship Cicero's conservatism was so well recognized that the authors of the Rullan land law, convinced of his total opposition to any form of *largitio*, refused his offer to consult with them to try to frame a bill he could support. Later, in attempting to persuade the people that his opposition to Rullus's proposal was dictated by the people's interests, he was forced to admit that he had never been a *popularis* in the ordinary sense of the word. Numerous other comments on his political affiliations throughout his writings reiterate that he had always shunned the *popularis via*, and had ever been a *bonus civis* devoted *prima a parte iuventae* to the goals and ideals of the *bonae partes*.[145]

But the clearest evidence of Cicero's close personal and political relationship with the oligarchy is the number of conservative *nobiles* who can be adduced as his friends and likely political supporters in the sixties. Prominent among them is the name of the consul of 67, C. Calpurnius Piso, who as governor of the Gallic provinces offered Cicero a legateship in 65 and gave him the opportunity to canvass, from the authoritative position of friend and *legatus* of the governor, a most important district whose citizens were represented in a large number of tribes. Cicero also had links to other members of the family of the Pisones. C. Piso Frugi, probably a nephew of the consul of 67, and son of the praetor of 74 who had so vigorously opposed Verres, became engaged to Cicero's daughter, Tullia, in 67, and another Piso, M. Pupius, the future consul of 61, had been Cicero's companion in study in the eighties and a fellow student and friend at Athens in the early seventies.[146]

Another influential *nobilis* from whom Cicero drew strong support was the arch-conservative, L. Domitius Ahenobarbus. Described by Cicero in 70 as *princeps iuventutis*, Domitius was a man of the highest nobility, immensely rich, owner of large estates in Italy, possessed of the *dignitas* and *gratia* which made him, in Cicero's words, destined for

145. *Leg. Agr.* 1.23; 2.7, 9, 11–12. *Att.* 1.20.3; 2.3.4; 2.4.2; 2.19.2. *Q.F.* 1.2.16. *Fam.* 1.7.7; 1.8.2; 1.9.10; 13.29.7. *Brut.* 281. *Sulla* 21–25. *Prov. Cons.* 40. *Planc.* 93. *Phil.* 7.4.

146. *Att.* 1.1.2. *Phil.* 2.76. Cf. Taylor, *Party Politics*, 58. Wiseman, *New Men*, 140. Cicero mentions Tullia's engagement in *Att.* 1.3.3. For his friendship with Pupius Piso cf. *Brut.* 236, 310. *Fin.* 4.73. *N.D.* 1.16. Cf. E. S. Gruen, "Pompey and the Pisones" *CSCA* 1 (1968), 155–70.

the consulship from the day he was born, and which also made him a mainstay of Cicero's own hopes of reaching that office.[147]

Domitius's conservative and influential brother-in-law, M. Porcius Cato, can also be reckoned among Cicero's friends and supporters in the sixties. Friendship between Cicero's family and Cato's went back to the previous generation, and that it persisted is attested by Cicero himself, who also reveals that he was on intimate terms with Cato's half brother, Servilius Caepio, to whom Cato was greatly attached and who was the son of Q. Servilius Caepio and Livia, the sister of M. Livius Drusus. Cato was a powerful figure even in the sixties, with marriage links to several leading noble houses. In addition to the connection with Domitius, he had a half sister married to L. Lucullus, his half brother married to a daughter of Q. Hortensius, a daughter married to M. Calpurnius Bibulus, the future consul of 59, and he was himself married to a daughter of L. Marcius Philippus, the future consul of 56.[148]

The patrician house of the Cornelii Lentuli, which was returning to prominence in post-Sullan politics, provided Cicero with additional, valuable aristocratic support. As early as 66, Cicero claims particular friendship with Lentulus Clodianus, consul in 72 and censor in 70. He affirms that he had the support of Lentulus Spinther, the consul of 57, from the beginning of his career. He worked closely with Lentulus Marcellinus, the future consul of 56, at the trial of Verres, and later paid tribute to the remarkable goodwill the Marcellini always showed toward him. He described in similar terms his relationship with another important noble family, the Claudii Marcelli, who had also been prominent supporters of the prosecution of Verres and who were close political allies of the Cornelii Lentuli in this period.[149]

Early connections between Cicero and other less distinguished but nonetheless noble families can also be established. He had links to the

147. Cicero and Domitius had a mutual friend in the *publicanus* Mustius. *Verr.* 2.1.139. Cf. *Att.* 1.1.3–4; 4.8a.2. *Mil.* 22. *Brut.* 267. Caesar, *BC* 1.17. Dio 41.11.1–2. It might be noted that both Domitius and L. Piso were enemies of Pompey. Cicero's noble support had nothing to do with friendship with Pompey.

148. Plutarch, *Cato Min.* 1.1, 3.5, 11.2, 24.3, 25.2, 41.2, 54.1; *Lucullus* 38.1. *Fam.* 15.3.2; 15.4.13. *Brut.* 222. *Off.* 3.66. *Fin.* 3.8–9. *Att.* 2.1.8. Cato was one of the few *boni* Cicero never accused of *invidia* toward himself. Cf. *Sest.* 60–63. *Att.* 3.15.2. Cato was also a close friend of Atticus. Nepos, *Att.* 15.3. Cf. *Att.* 1.17.9; 2.1.8. Cf. Münzer, *Römische Adelsparteien und Adelsfamilien,* 342–47.

149. *Cluent.* 118. *Fam.* 1.7.8; 15.7; 15.8; 15.10.1–2. *Sulla* 19. *Brut.* 250–51. Cf. Gruen, *Last Generation,* 102.

Terentii Varrones through his longtime friendship with M. Terentius Varro of Reate, the great scholar and encyclopedist, through his cousin Visellius Varro, and very probably through his wife, Terentia. He was a friend from youth of the patrician Servius Sulpicius Rufus, the future consul of 51, an *adfinis* of the Marcelli and the Junii Bruti, and an eminent jurist. Cicero and Sulpicius were very close, their friendship similar to the relationship between Crassus and Scaevola.[150]

Cicero had a sizable following as well among the *adulescentes* of the *nobilitas*, who were attracted to him by his oratorical brilliance, and who made valuable allies both because of their general influence and because of their importance in the eighteen centuries of *equites*. Those who can be named among Cicero's admirers and likely supporters in this group include C. Scribonius Curio, L. Manlius Torquatus, M. Antonius, L. Aemilius Lepidus Paullus, M. Juventius Laterensis, C. Cassius Longinus, and M. Junius Brutus.[151]

Of the prominent *consulares* still living in the sixties only C. Piso can be positively said to have been a firm supporter of Cicero, but there are many grounds for believing that he secured the backing of at least some of the others. Both he and Atticus had been school friends of L. Manlius Torquatus, the consul of 65. Atticus formed a lasting friendship with Torquatus as a result, and it is likely that Cicero did also. He always speaks of Torquatus with the greatest admiration, and he presents him as a man of refinement, foresight, and unusual integrity. He was on intimate terms with his son, whose active and enthusiastic support he enjoyed from at least 66 onwards. When the Elder Torquatus returned from governing Macedonia in 63, Cicero used his influence as consul to secure him the title of *Imperator*, and later in the year he drew heavily on his advice in the Catilinarian crisis, a level of cooperation which suggests that Cicero had the friendship and support of the father as well as the son long before 63.[152]

The evidence for friendly relations with L. Lucullus prior to 63 is

150. For Cicero and Varro cf. *Att.* 2.20.1; 3.8.3; 3.15.1; 3.18.1; 4.2.5. *Fam.* 9.1–8. C. Kumaniecki, "Cicerone e Varrone, Storia di una Conoscenza" *Athenaeum* 40 (1962), 221–43. For his friendship with Sulpicius cf. *Brut.* 150–56. *Mur.* 7 ff. *Fam.* 4.1–6; 13.17–28b. *Phil.* 9.4, 6. Cf. Münzer, *Römische Adelsparteien und Adelsfamilien*, 407.

151. *Com. Pet.* 6, 33. *Fam.* 2.1.2; 2.2; 2.6.2; 2.7.4; 15.14.6. *Sulla* 11.34. *Phil.* 2.3. *Planc.* 2, 5.

152. Cf. *Sulla* 11, 34. *Fin.* 2.62. *Brut.* 239. *Pis.* 44, 47. *Nepos,* Att. 1.4.

equally convincing. There was an early link through the poet Archias, the special client of the Luculli and a tutor of Cicero in the nineties. Atticus, who had long-standing ties with L. Lucullus, provided Cicero with another avenue to the latter's friendship. Lucullus's marriage in the mid-sixties to Servilia, with whose family Cicero had many close connections, created yet another bond. Finally, it was through Cicero's efforts that Lucullus secured his long-awaited triumph in 63, a fact which, as in the case of Cicero's *beneficium* to Torquatus in the same year, betokens an existing *amicitia* and possibly a political debt. Any idea that Cicero incurred the enmity of Lucullus by his support of the Manilian law is groundless. Cicero paid Lucullus extravagant compliments in that speech, and since the latter had already been recalled long before the introduction of Manilius's bill, passage of the measure in no way affected his position or his *dignitas*.[153]

Hortensius and Catulus should probably be added also to the list of Cicero's noble supporters, though the evidence for their relationship with him is less clear. Cicero did publicly criticize their political posture on a couple of occasions, and it may well be to them that he refers at the beginning of his canvass for the consulship in 65 when he tells Atticus of a rumor that noble friends of the latter were going to oppose his election. But the overall evidence provides more reason to believe that they were friends than that they were enemies of Cicero. Hortensius and Cicero had an early inducement to friendship in a common association with Archias and with the circle of Crassus and Scaevola. Their rivalry as forensic orators was no impediment to the continuance of friendly relations, especially since they often appeared in court as allies not opponents. Cicero in fact explicitly affirms that the competition between them did not extend to the political sphere, and he states that on the contrary they helped each other's political careers *communicando et monendo et favendo*. Furthermore, they shared several close friends in the sixties, notably Atticus, whose relationship with Hortensius was the closest of all his many optimate friendships and who would have been a powerful influence in winning Hortensius's support for Cicero. Cato was another common *amicus*, and so was Cato's half brother Servilius Caepio, who was Hortensius's son-in-law, and who was

153. *Arch.* 5-6, 8, 11. *Acad.* 2.1-4, 62. *Fin.* 3.8-9. Plutarch, *Lucullus* 41.3. For Lucullus's friendship with Atticus cf. Nepos, *Att.* 5. *Att.* 1.19.10. Shackleton Bailey, *Cicero's Letters to Atticus,* 1.7 ff.

close enough to Cicero to make him the guardian of his son. There may have been a further connection between Cicero and Hortensius through Cicero's cousin Visellius Varro, believed by some to have been a son of A. Terentius Varro, the cousin of Hortensius.[154]

Cicero's relationship with Catulus is more difficult to determine with certainty. Cicero undoubtedly admired him more than any other politician of the post-Sullan era, and in all of his allusions to him, from the Verrines to the *De Officiis*, he speaks of him in glowing terms and presents him as an exemplary optimate statesman, great in his achievements and in his *auctoritas*, the undisputed leader of the senate and of the guardians of the *via optimas*, and, unlike so many of the fish-pond-loving *boni*, a tireless watchdog of the *respublica* and unwavering opponent of its enemies. Catulus's father had close connections with all of Cicero's noble patrons and may have been a friend of Cicero's father, so it is likely that Cicero had a friendly relationship with Catulus in the nineties, and likely too, in view of the high regard he expresses at all periods of his life for Catulus, that he afterwards did his best to maintain that relationship. The one occasion on which he crossed swords politically with him was in the debate on the Manilian law, but Cicero carefully tempered his opposition on that issue with extravagant compliments to Catulus's achievements and political standing, and in the following year he conspicuously took Catulus's side with his stand on the Egyptian question and his attack on Crassus. Cicero's friendship with Cato, Lucullus, and probably Hortensius, leading political associates of Catulus in the sixties, would have further inclined the latter to favor him. It is certain in any event that in 63 and in the years following Catulus was one of Cicero's staunchest allies and defenders, and while too much cannot be inferred from this about earlier associations, it does fortify other indications that, as in the case of so many other *nobiles*, Catulus's friendship with and support of Cicero well predated 63.[155]

Cicero's aristocratic support may safely be assumed to have extended well beyond the list of names that can be adduced from the scattered

154. *Att.* 1.2.2. *Arch.* 6. *De Or.* 3.228, 230. *Div. in Caec.* 44. *Brut.* 1–4, 229, 301–03, 317–30. For Hortensius's friendship with Atticus cf. *Nepos, Att.* 5.4. *Att.* 2.25; 5.2.1; 5.9.2. Cf. Wiseman, *New Men*, 55, 275.
155. *Verr.* 3.2.210. *Man.* 51, 59 ff. *Dom.* 113–14. *Sest.* 101, 122. *Pis.* 6. *Att.* 1.16.5; 1.20.3; 2.24.4. *Fam.* 9.15.3. *Off.* 1.109, 133. Next to L. Crassus, Catulus

evidence of a scanty record, and its scope can perhaps best be seen in a clear signal from the senate in 64 of its support for Cicero when it authorized a new bribery bill to curb the *audacia* of his competitors, Antonius and Catiline. The senate's action is often presented as a late rallying of the oligarchy behind a moderate newcomer, when alarm over the methods and designs of his rivals made their exclusion from the consulship more important than its preservation from contamination by a *novus*, but the evidence discussed above sufficiently demonstrates that support for Cicero among the *nobilitas* was strong and active well before 64, and it makes it far more likely that the extreme electoral tactics of his competitors were a consequence rather than a cause of oligarchic goodwill toward him.[156]

The bribery decree was vetoed, to the considerable anger of the senators, and Cicero responded to their mood with his speech *In Toga Candida*, a blistering invective against Antonius and Catiline, which also assailed certain *mali cives* allegedly backing them with revolutionary intent and pointed unmistakably to Crassus as the foremost figure among those sinister schemers. When the elections followed a few days later, Cicero was chosen consul *cum universi populi Romani summa voluntate, tum optimi cuiusque singulari studio.*[157]

It was a success which cannot be attributed simply to opportunistic vacillation between conflicting groups and ideologies or to the mere

receives the highest praise with the greatest consistency of all the statesmen of the late Republic. Catulus had been a friend of Catiline, but there is no evidence that he was supporting Catiline politically in 64. Cf. Sallust, *Catiline* 34.3–35.6. Orosius 6.3.1. *Schol. Bern.* Lucan, 2.173. There is some evidence to suggest that Cicero had the friendship of many other *nobiles* as well, notably L. Gellius, Servilius Vatia, Scribonius Curio, Metellus Celer, Aurelius Cotta. Cf. *Cluent.* 117. *Quir.* 17. *Dom.* 132. *Prov. Cons.* 1, 22. *Verr.* 1.18. *Att.* 1.16.13; 3.12.2. *Fam.* 2.1; 2.2; 5.1; 5.2. *Att.* 1.18.5; 2.1.4. For Cicero's relations with L. Cotta cf. n. 74, above. Cotta's family had close connections with the circle of Cicero's patrons, Crassus and Scaevola. Cf. *De Or.* 1.25; 3.11. The family of Servilius was one of those whom Cicero represented in his defense of Roscius in 80. *Rosc.* 15.

156. The view goes back to Sallust (*Catiline* 23.4), who was interested in magnifying both the exclusiveness of the oligarchy and the revolutionary designs of Catiline in 64. It is reechoed in Plutarch, *Cicero* 10-11, and reproduced in such modern works as Rice Holmes, *Roman Republic*, 1.236–41; E. Meyer, *Caesars Monarchie und das Principat des Pompeius* (Stuttgart 1922), 23–24; H. Haskell, *This Was Cicero* (London 1942), 166 ff.; T. Petersson, *Cicero, a Biography* (Berkeley 1920), 201 ff., and, most recently, E. Rawson, *Cicero* (London 1975), 58 ff.

157. Asconius 82-94, Clark. *Vat.* 6.

good fortune of being ranged against radical outcasts. It was due instead to the energetic employment of his oratorical talents in sustained pursuit of political influence through the agency of *gratia* and *popularis voluntas* and to a political posture that safeguarded inherited aristocratic connections and goodwill without antagonizing other segments of the electorate. It was a cautious posture, but it entailed no sacrifice of principle or consistency. In his early years as a candidate, when his rank made possible a strategy of silence, he refrained from any unnecessary advertisement of his views on political controversies. Later, when prudence or the pressure of circumstances dictated involvement, he sought to woo a broad constituency and to avoid being identified solely with the outlook and interests of the oligarchy; but, in doing so, he always stayed well within the boundaries of the conservative political path to which his background and political instincts directed him, and he never renounced the principles and practices fundamental to the survival of traditional republicanism.

4:CICERO THE CONSUL

The record of Cicero's consulship provides valuable evidence for his political ideas and practical statesmanship. Freed from the constraints of electoral politics and invested with the considerable powers of Rome's highest office, his term as consul provided him with the best opportunity of his career to declare his political ideals and work for their implementation. It was also a time which demanded strong stands and hard decisions, a turbulent year in which many of the woes and weaknesses of the *respublica* came to the surface, its beginning marked by a classic collision between the proponents of oligarchic rule and a coalition of dissentient politicians promoting popular reforms, its end by the more unusual and alarming phenomenon of an embittered patrician organizing the more desperate elements of the discontented in armed revolt. It is the purpose of the present chapter to examine Cicero's reactions and achievements as a chief executive in these testing circumstances, and the ideas of the state and of statesmanship that shaped his policies and actions.

The reasons for the discord and upheaval that afflicted the Roman state once more in 63 were multifarious. The general cohesiveness and political control that the Sullan oligarchy had managed to maintain in the seventies suffered quick erosion in the sixties. Partly responsible was the revitalized tribunate, which provided opportunity and inducement to those seeking change or advancement outside the senatorial power structure. There were other factors, however, of perhaps greater importance. Political rivalries sharpened markedly in the wake of the censorship of 70, which greatly complicated the political scene by the expulsion of sixty-four senators and the enrollment in tribes and classes of large numbers of Italians. There resulted increased competitiveness and more elaborate campaigns, which brought increased corruption and divisive debate on measures to control it, and, in the middle of the decade, the unedifying spectacle of two consuls-elect convicted of bribery and suffering the harsh penalties of the *Lex Calpurnia*.[1] The bitterness generated by such exercises is reflected in the rumors of plots and violence that followed the convictions and aroused public concern to the level where its alleviation was sought by recourse to the soothsayers of Etruria and expiatory rights.[2] Further problems arose from untended evils of the civil wars. Injustices of the Sullan years lingered and festered, as profiteers of the proscriptions continued to flourish and their victims to suffer economic deprivation and loss of political rights. The *Mariani* who had survived the wars against Lepidus and Sertorius had received amnesty in 70 but nothing more, and they constituted another pocket of citizens with little reason to feel any allegiance to the Sullan establishment. Even the veterans who had fought on the side of the government had a grievance, since the *Lex Plotia* of 70, which assigned them land, was apparently not implemented. A further source of contention and division lay in the problem of the Transpadani, who had been excluded from citizenship in Sulla's settlement of Italy, an exclusion dictated by administrative concerns and reluctance to extend the state, and lacking any ethnic or cultural foundation.[3]

But the greatest threat to harmony and stability in the sixties came from economic distress, which reached its peak about the time of Cicero's election to the consulship. The successive wars that had plagued the Roman state since 90 had left their mark on the economy. Rural Italy had been devastated by the civil conflicts of the late

1. Sources for the censorship of 70 and the consular elections of 66 in Broughton, *MRR*, 2.126–27, 157. Cf. Wiseman, *JRS* 59 (1969), 59–75. Griffin, *JRS* 63 (1973), 200.

2. *Cat.* 3.19. Dio 37.9. For a fuller discussion of these events cf. pp. 223 ff., below.

3. Sallust, *Hist.* 3.47, Maur. Suetonius, *Julius* 5. Dio 44.47.4. Gellius 13.3.5. *Verr.* 2.5.152. *Att.* 1.18.6. Dio 38.5. Cf. Gruen, *Last Generation*, 413. Brunt, *Italian Manpower*, 312. Gabba, *PP* 13 (1950), 66–68. Smith, *CQ* 7 (1957), 82–85. For the Transpadani cf. Asconius 3, Clark. Brunt, *Italian Manpower*, 168 ff.

eighties and the wars against Lepidus and Spartacus. Land was ruined and agriculture disrupted, a situation worsened by the depletion of the peasantry through conscription. The Mithridatic wars brought enormous losses of property, capital, and business opportunities to the financiers. The treasury suffered heavily from expanded military costs and the loss of revenues from Spain and Asia. The activities of the pirates disrupted commerce and increased the cost of shipping, and they had a particularly critical impact on the price of food.[4]

The economic depression, inflation, and shortage of money which resulted from these various circumstances caused widespread hardship and led in particular to an unusually high level of indebtedness among all classes. Indebtedness was a chronic condition of much of the ruling class, particularly of younger politicians, who tended to borrow freely to finance extravagant campaigns, hoping to recoup the costs from the provincial governorships which would follow political success. But the number of aristocrats heavily in debt in the sixties appears to have been much greater than usual, and the same situation prevailed in other sections of the society. In rural Italy many farmers in all parts of the peninsula were insolvent, the condition most common among the eighty thousand or more Sullan colonists for whom the problems of hard times were compounded by inefficiency, extravagance, and questionable titles, which made favorable terms of credit more difficult to secure. A depressed property market, an inevitable outgrowth of a shortage of money and uncertain times, further aggravated the problem, making it impossible or undesirable for bankrupt farmers to sell their land to discharge their debts.[5] In Rome the situation was as bad or worse for much of the *plebs urbana.* Sallust states that this entire

4. *Man.* 15, 19, 32–33, 38, 54–55. Plutarch, *Pompey* 24–25. Appian, *Mith.* 91–93. Dio 36.20–23. Cf. Brunt, *Italian Manpower*, 108, 285–89. For the problems of the treasury in this period cf. Sallust, *Hist.* 47.7, Maur. Asconius 73, Clark. The senate was compelled to authorize the sale of certain public properties in 81. *Leg. Agr.* 2.35.

5. *Cat.* 2.18–24. *Off.* 2.84. *Mur.* 50. *Att.* 2.1.11. *Q.F.* 1.1.6. *Fam.* 5.6.2. Plutarch, *Cicero* 10.4. Sallust, *Catiline* 12.2, 13.5, 14.2, 20–21, 35. Cf. B. D. Shaw, "Debt in Sallust" *Latomus* 34 (1975), 187–96. M. W. Frederiksen, "Caesar, Cicero and the Problem of Debt" *JRS* 56 (1966), 128–41. For the problem of debt in rural Italy cf. *Cat.* 2.8, 20. Sallust, *Catiline* 16.4, 33. Brunt, *Italian Manpower,* 108–09, 289, 309–12; "The Army and the Land in the Roman Revolution" *JRS* 52 (1962), 73. Gruen, *Last Generation,* 425 ff. Val. Max. 4.8.3 speaks of a depressed property market in 63.

segment of the society supported Catiline out of economic desperation, obviously attracted by his well-known promise to cancel debts.

The debt and desperation are easy to believe. Small shopkeepers would not have had the financial reserves to withstand a long and severe economic depression and would have had to resort to borrowing to remain in business. As for the lower levels of the urban proletariat, their economic condition was always precarious. They paid high rents to live in overcrowded, poorly built, fire-prone *insulae* and depended for a livelihood on patronage and casual employment in building or on the docks, or on seasonal labor on the land in the countryside around Rome. But in the seventies, and particularly in the sixties, with prices rising, opportunities for employment declining, and the numbers of the poor swelled by an influx of rural dwellers who had been dispossessed by Sulla, had lost their farms, or could no longer make a living in the country, ever-increasing numbers must have sunk into debt, no longer able to find the money to pay their high rents and other living costs.[6]

The situation became critical in the mid-sixties, when it appears credit tightened still further and creditors began to call in their debts, a development provoked by a continuing serious shortage of money and the growth of favorable opportunities for investment abroad following Pompey's pacification of the Mediterranean and conquest of Asia Minor. The consequences for the heavily indebted were grievous. Some faced political ruin and the loss of lands or other property; others, whose debts were greater than their assests, faced the grim penalties of Rome's draconian debt laws. All would be eager to find some avenue of escape from so precarious a predicament.[7]

As usual, there was no lack of politicians to highlight these varied political, social, and economic grievances and to champion the aggrieved.

6. Sallust, *Catiline* 37. Cf. Z. Yavetz, "The Living Conditions of the Urban *Plebs* in Republican Rome" *Latomus* 17 (1958), 500–17; "The Failure of Catiline's Conspiracy" *Historia* 12 (1963), 485–99. P. A. Brunt, "The Roman Mob" *Past and Present* 35 (1966), 11 ff.; *Social Conflicts in the Roman Republic* (New York 1971), 128–29. S. L. Mohler, "*Sentina reipublicae*. Campaign Issues, 63 B.C." *CW* 29 (1936), 81–84. W. Allen, Jr., "In Defence of Catiline" *CJ* 34 (1938), 70–85.

7. Cf. Val. Max. 4.8.3. *Cat.* 2.10. *Leg. Agr.* 2.8. Cicero records that the export of gold and silver had to be halted in *Flacc.* 67 and *Vat.* 12. For the harshness of the debt laws cf. Frederiksen, *JRS* 56 (1966), 128 ff.

In 66 two prominent *Sullani*, Faustus Sulla and M. Lucullus, were hauled into court by tribunes to answer charges of embezzlement during the Sullan years. There followed, in 64, prosecutions of those believed to have engaged in assassination of persons proscribed by Sulla. Julius Caesar was a leading *accusator*, and there were several convictions.[8] Caesar was also zealously and successfully wooing and rallying the *Mariani*, for whose return he had pleaded in 70 when he spoke in favor of the *Lex Plautia*. In 69 at the funeral of his aunt Julia, the widow of Marius, he displayed images of the general and his son, and in 65 he had the memorials of Marius's victories, which had been removed by Sulla, reerected in the forum, to the delight, openly expressed, of Marius's former partisans.[9] Caesar was active too in promoting the cause of the Transpadani, who commenced their agitation for citizenship in 68. In 65 they acquired an additional, powerful champion in Crassus, censor in that year, whose efforts on their behalf provoked a major confrontation with his colleague, Q. Catulus, and brought the resignation of both men from office. The seriousness of the Transpadane controversy and the degree of agitation it stirred is indicated by the passage in 65 of the *Lex Papia*, which ordered the expulsion from Rome of all aliens whose permanent domicile lay outside Italy, an obvious attempt by the oligarchy to bury this complaint by the primitive and drastic expedient of banishing the complainants out of sight and sound.[10]

These were sporadic airings of individual issues dividing Roman society in the sixties, but in 64 efforts to effect a broad range of reforms were launched simultaneously. Toward the end of the year a comprehensive set of proposals emerged from the tribunician college of 63, dealing with several major areas of discontent. The proposed legislation included measures to reduce the penalties of the *Lex Calpurnia* and restore their civil rights to the convicted consuls-elect of 65, P. Autronius Paetus and P. Cornelius Sulla; to purchase and distribute land in Italy on a massive scale to the poor; to restore their political rights to

---

8. *Cluent.* 94. *Leg. Agr.* 1.12. Asconius 73, Clark. Plutarch, *Lucullus* 37.1. *Lig.* 12. *Schol. Grov.* 293, Stangl. Dio 37.10.1. Suetonius, *Julius* 11. Cf. Gruen, *Athenaeum* 49 (1971), 56–58; *Last Generation*, 76–77.

9. Plutarch, *Caesar* 5–6. Suetonius, *Julius* 6.1, 11. Velleius 2.43.3.

10. Suetonius, *Julius* 8. Dio 37.9.3. Sources for the *Lex Papia* in Broughton, *MRR*, 2.158.

the sons of those proscribed by Sulla; and to alleviate the problem of
debt. Later, tribunician initiatives to curb the power of the oligarchy
were to emerge with a prosecution to challenge the extent to which a
senatus consultum ultimum justified supralegal action against citizens
and a bill restoring the elections of priests to the people in accordance
with the provisions of the *Lex Domitia* of 104.[11]

That this sudden and concentrated burst of tribunician activism was
the work of a single, organized, and powerfully backed reform movement seems certain, its timing dictated in part, no doubt, by the burgeoning economic discontent, but also, as I will argue later, by the
desire of ambitious men, as Pompey's eastern campaigns drew to a
close, to entrench their political position before the dominant figure
of the general reentered the political scene. Cicero asserts in the speeches
against Rullus that at the beginning of 63 there was a widespread belief
that a major movement was afoot to effect large-scale change and the
entrenchment of the political position of certain individuals. Cicero was
prone to exaggerate, and notably so in the Rullan speeches, but there
are good grounds for believing that, in this instance, his assertions had
some substance.

The simultaneous appearance of several complex and wide-ranging
proposals itself betokens an organized and single enterprise. Certainly
the entire tribunician board cooperated, initially at least, in the formulation and promotion of all the measures. Dio unquestioningly presents
the bills as a single program of a unified tribunician college. Confirmation of his testimony occurs in Plutarch and Cicero, who repeatedly
affirm that the most elaborate and important of the measures, the
Rullan land law, was a joint undertaking of all the tribunes. Later there
was a threatened veto by one of them, L. Caecilius Rufus, but this was
evidently a defection, possibly induced by the failure in the first days
of 63 of the bribery proposal, which Caecilius sponsored. There is no
other mention, however, of any vetoes in connection with tribunician
legislation throughout 63, a highly significant fact in view of the variety
and extensiveness of that legislation, and another strong indication that
the tribunes of the year were basically united and committed to common political ends.[12]

11. Dio 37.25. Plutarch, *Cicero* 12.
12. *Leg. Agr.* 1.26; 2.8-12, 22. *Fam.* 13.4.2. Dio 37.25. Plutarch, *Cicero*
12.1-2. The only tribunician veto recorded for 63 concerned Cicero's proposal
to abolish *liberae legationes. Leg.* 3.18.

The election of such a unified board was a most unusual phenomenon in Roman politics, and it required a political organization and political resources well beyond the capacity of the tribunes themselves. The names of the most active members of the college have been preserved, and they were all relatively obscure figures. L. Caecilius Rufus, who introduced the first tribunician legislation of the year, was a half brother of P. Cornelius Sulla, the consul-designate convicted of bribery in 66, but the fact that no other Caecilius Rufus appears in the lists of magistrates suggests that his immediate family was not distinguished. P. Servilius Rullus, the sponsor of the agrarian law, claimed to be a *nobilis*, but Cicero mocks the claim, which indicates at the very least that Rullus's *nobilitas* was not of the highest variety. The two other known tribunes of 63, T. Labienus and T. Ampius Balbus, were *novi homines*, and there is no evidence that they possessed any significant independent political influence.[13]

A broader *factio* behind the tribunician legislative program of 63 must be assumed, and indeed further evidence for it exists in the record of the political activity of Caesar and Crassus in this period. Caesar was aggressively charting a political course as a friend of the people and champion of popular interests in the sixties. His name is associated with almost every popular issue that surfaced in the decade, and his involvement in the tribunician proposals of 63 is clearly attested. He openly supported several of the measures, was a close friend of at least one of the tribunes, T. Labienus, and was himself later to implement many of the same reforms. His actions and political aspirations and concerns all link him to the *popularis* schemes of Cicero's consulship, and it is a safe conclusion that he played a leading part in the formulation of them and in the procurement of a tribunician college willing to promote them.[14]

That Crassus played a similar role can be affirmed with equal confidence. Cicero publicly and positively identified him as a leading force behind the Rullan land law when he alleged both in the senate and before the people that the proponents of the bill were the same men who had tried two years earlier to secure the annexation of Egypt.

13. *Sulla* 62. *Leg. Agr.* 2.19. Cf. R. Syme, "The Allegiance of Labienus" *JRS* 28 (1938), 113–21. Sumner, *TAPA* 97 (1966), 571–72. A. M. Ward, "Cicero's Fight against Crassus and Caesar in 65 and 63 B.C." *Historia* 21 (1972), 252–54.

14. Velleius 2.43.4. Dio 44.47.4; 37.37.1; 37.27.2; 37.21.4. *Off.* 2.84. Cf. ch. 3, n. 142, above. Plutarch, *Caesar* 37.1.

Cicero could hardly have made such a clear and public association between Crassus and the tribunes without some foundation, and his allegations are powerfully supported by the overall evidence for Crassus's allies, goals, and methods in the sixties and by his almost certain friendship with Caesar in this period. Crassus can also be linked to the tribunician activism of 63 through Cicero's consular colleague, C. Antonius, who was a leading ally and supporter of the tribunes until Cicero neutralized him about the middle of 63 by ceding him the province of Macedonia. Crassus, according to Cicero, had in 64 backed the candidacy of Antonius, and also of Antonius's electoral ally Catiline, with money and sinister designs, an allegation which, when considered in conjunction with Antonius's initial support of the tribunician program and the varied indications of Crassus's involvement in that program, becomes entirely credible. It also accords well with the several signs that a powerful *factio* was promoting the legislative initiatives of 63, and it indicates in addition that the preparation for their implementation was exceedingly elaborate, extending to the procurement of friendly consuls as well as tribunes.[15]

Cicero and the Rullan Land Law

The first of the tribunician proposals brought forward was the bill to amend the *Lex Calpurnia*, which was sponsored by Caecilius Rufus and laid before the senate in the last days of 64. The measure, which would not only bring a relaxation of the bribery laws unwelcome to the oligarchy, but would be applied retroactively to reinstate Autronius and Sulla, an action viewed as dangerous interference with a decision of the courts, drew strong opposition. The matter does not appear to have been pressed with much vigor, and it was abandoned at a meeting of the senate on January 1 without being brought to a vote.[16]

On the same day, however, the senate was presented with a bill of far more profound implications, a comprehensive agrarian law sponsored by P. Servilius Rullus. The terms of the bill have to be gleaned from Cicero's speeches in opposition to it, an obviously defective source, which has not surprisingly left some aspects of the proposal obscure

15. *Leg. Agr.* 1.1; 2.41 ff. *Sest.* 8. Plutarch, *Cicero* 12.3–4. Dio 37.25.3. Asconius 93, Clark. Cf. ch. 3, n. 141, above.
    16. *Sulla* 61–65.

and problematic. The main outlines of the bill can, however, be discerned clearly enough. It was proposed to settle colonies of needy citizens in Italy on the remaining public land, comprised mainly by the *Ager Campanus* and the *Campus Stellatis*, and on other land to be acquired by purchase from those willing to sell. Money for such purchase was to be raised by selling such public property as had been authorized for sale by *senatus consulta* passed since 81 but not implemented, and, if necessary, by disposing of state possessions outside Italy acquired since 88. In addition, certain specified *vectigalia* in various provinces were identified for definite sale, and a special tax was to be imposed on all other public land. Money was also to come from booty, spoils, or crown gold received by anyone other than Pompey and not paid into the treasury or spent on a memorial, and from all new revenues which accrued to the state after 63. The bill also aimed to settle any existing doubts or disputes about land titles in Italy by confirming as private property all land given, assigned, sold, or possessed since 82.[17]

To implement these proposals a commission of ten, aided by an extensive administrative staff, was to be established, to hold office with praetorian *imperium* for five years. They were to be elected by seventeen tribes chosen by lot from the full thirty-five and to have their power ratified by a *lex curiata*, the ratification procedure to be exempt from tribunician veto. All candidates for the office were required to hand in their names in person, and the entire electoral procedure was to be presided over by Rullus, who was also to have the right to stand for election himself.[18]

Cicero, while declaring his sympathy for sober and meaningful agrarian reform, vigorously opposed the proposal in two major speeches, one delivered in the senate and the other at a *contio*, and he gave two further, shorter addresses to the people, attacking particular aspects of the bill. The substance of his criticisms was as follows: the mode of electing the decemvirs was unprecedented and designed to insure the selection of Rullus and his backers and the exclusion of Pompey; the

17. *Leg. Agr.* 1.3–4, 10, 12–13, 20; 2.35–37, 47–57, 59–60, 62, 67, 73; 3.4–14. It is sometimes asserted that the bill authorized land for Pompey's veterans as well as for the poor, but there are no grounds for assuming that this was specifically stated in the bill. Cf. Gruen, *Last Generation*, 393.

18. *Leg. Agr.* 2.16–17, 20–22, 24, 26, 30, 32.

decemvirs were being constituted as lords of the world, immune from prosecution, accountable to no one, empowered to travel all over the empire arbitrarily deciding what was public property and salable, with no remedy or recourse for the victims of their decisions; public places and other valuable public possessions in Italy would be sold, while abroad whole provinces such as Asia and Bithynia might be disposed of. Egypt would be taken over, as would land in the war zone in the East, an affront and a threat to Pompey, to whom belonged jurisdiction in this area; the provision on booty, spoils, and crown gold would subject generals to undue harassment and had special targets in view, particularly Faustus Sulla; there would be endless scope for jobbery and favoritism in the purchase and colonization of land in Italy, and the result would be massive profiteering and the filling of Italy with henchmen of the decemvirs, garrisons to perpetuate decemviral domination; finally, the distribution of the *Ager Campanus* would bring the loss of safe and extensive revenues, the replacement of honest and industrious tenants by Rullus's minions, and the conversion of this area once more into a dangerous threat to the security of Rome.

Cicero's rhetorical onslaught had a telling effect. Public opinion turned against the proposal. A further blow was the defection of Caecilius, who, perhaps piqued by insufficient backing from his colleagues for his own proposal, threatened a veto. Certain to fail, the bill was withdrawn.[19]

The merits and purposes of the law and Cicero's presentation of it have been exhaustively examined, and with varying conclusions ranging from the view that it was a gigantic power play by Crassus and Caesar to combat Pompey, advanced by those who accept Cicero's denunciations at face value, to the idea that it was a sensible reform measure promoted in the interests of Pompey, advanced by those who react to Ciceronian rhetoric by seeking arguments for the opposite of all his contentions.[20]

19. *Att.* 2.1.3. *Leg. Agr.* 2.16–25, 32–34; 1.1–12; 2.36–58; 1.12–13; 2.59–62; 1.14–22; 2.63–99. Caecilius's threatened veto is noted in *Sulla* 65. The fate of the proposal is alluded to in *Rab.* 32. Plutarch, *Cicero* 12.5. Pliny, *NH* 7.117. It would be rash to conclude from the failure of the bill that the *plebs* had no interest in land. It is more likely that the bill failed because the public accepted Cicero's principal arguments that the measure would give too much power to the decemvirs and was aimed against Pompey.

20. Cf. E. G. Hardy, *Some Problems in Roman History* (Oxford 1924), 68–98. Ciaceri, *Cicerone*, 1.195–215. A. Afzelius, "Das Ackerverteilungsgesetz des P.

The overall evidence favors a more balanced evaluation of Cicero's criticisms and reveals a proposal of complex purpose, which, like other such measures in the past, pursued both social reform and the power that would come to the initiators and controllers of large-scale reallocation of the state's resources.

The speeches against Rullus are replete with the distortions and exaggerations of the masterful pleader. Cicero magnifies the powers and revolutionary capacity of the decemvirs, whose *imperium* was only praetorian, with no explicit evidence that it entitled them to the use of an army, without which there could be little threat of any coup d'etat. The *dominatio* he alleges they would achieve he bases on fanciful forecasts that they would be unscrupulous and power-mad *improbi* who would build a private army by packing the colonies they founded with loyal adherents. He also exaggerates the extent of the provincial lands authorized for sale, speaking of whole provinces where only *ager publicus* was in question and attempting to include within the bill's provisions the areas recovered as well as those acquired since 88, all the while accenting this hyperbole with lurid and wholly imaginary pictures of decemviral extremism and corruption in all of their operations in the provinces. He denies that the program of land allocation to the poor would benefit the *plebs urbana*, speculating gratuitously that the land distributed would be desolate, or unwanted Sullan confiscations, or would go only to friends of the decemvirs, and, demonstrating his own flair for demagoguery, he harangues his audience on the delights and diversions of urban living and urges them to cling to those enjoyments and to the political influence they wielded as residents of the city. He similarly obscures the merits of the provision to confirm in their titles those who had received or had taken possession of land confiscated by Sulla, exploiting the emotional aspects of this issue and deriding the provision as an attempt to give security to Rullus's land-grabbing father-in-law.[21]

Servilius Rullus" *CM* 3 (1940), 214–35. Meyer, *Caesars Monarchie,* 13–14. Gelzer, *Caesar*, 42–45. Rice Holmes, *Roman Republic*, 1.242–49. Ward, *Historia* 21 (1972), 251–59. Sumner (*TAPA* 97 [1966], 569–82) presents the view that the bill was a sensible proposal promoted in Pompey's interests, a view with which Gruen (*Last Generation*, 389–95) largely agrees.

21. Cicero does not claim that the decemvirs would have armed forces at their disposal, which is sufficient to prove they would not have military powers. For his most obvious exaggerations cf. *Leg. Agr.* 1.16–21; 2.15, 32–34, 39–40, 53–55,

The proposal of Rullus was not the extreme and blatant bid for control of Rome and the provinces alleged by Cicero, and the social and political advantages that would accrue from its implementation were considerable. Its land-distribution scheme addressed the problems of urban overpopulation and unemployment, problems sorely in need of a remedy. The continuing growth in Rome of a rootless, unpropertied, unemployed or underemployed proletariat was a threat to peace and stability of the most serious dimensions, particularly in the difficult economic circumstances that prevailed in the sixties, for it constituted not only an unhealthy economic imbalance, with concomitant dangers of unrest or violence, soon to be demonstrated in 63, but also a political menace of a special sort, as the influx of rural immigrants, with registration in rural tribes, gave ever greater control of the tribal assemblies to the *plebs urbana* and increased the scope for varied forms of bribery and demagoguery. In these circumstances more extreme forms of political manipulation, such as the recruitment of gangs or the mobilization of larger groups of hired, rowdy partisans, also became possible, practices that were to bring Rome to the brink of anarchy many times in the fifties.[22] The Rullan proposal would undoubtedly do much to obviate these political dangers and the social conditions that underlay them, and, in a predominantly agricultural society, some such program of agrarian resettlement provided the only obvious means to any lasting amelioration of Rome's urban woes.

The Rullan law would also help alleviate other internal difficulties of the period. Many of those dispossessed and reduced to poverty by Sulla would presumably receive land under the scheme, and Sullan colonists and *possessores* would be given the opportunity to sell their holdings in a favorable market or would be confirmed in their possession of them if they had the will and the resources to continue on the land. Several grievances and controversies left over from the Sullan years and some of the current economic distress of rural Italy would thus be lessened, important additional steps in the elimination of the many

68–71, 73–75; 3.4–14. He later admitted in 60 the desirability of draining off the *sentina urbis* and of confirming the Sullan *possessores* in their possessions. *Att.* 1.19.3.

22. Cf. Brunt, *Past and Present* 35 (1966), 3–27. Lintott, *Violence in Republican Rome*, 175–203. Gruen (*Last Generation,* 365) following Meier (*Res Publica Amissa,* 107–15) unduly discounts the danger from the urban *plebs.*

sources of disunity and unrest in this period. There was obviously a lot to commend in the land law of Rullus, and its attention to so wide a range of issues and the elaborate care and detail with which, in forty articles or more, it set forth proposals for dealing with them entitles it to be considered as a serious effort at genuine reform.

On the other hand the bill had several disquieting aspects which gave validity to many of Cicero's objections. Its scope was enormous, far exceeding that of the two other large-scale agrarian programs put forward in this period, the proposals of Flavius in 60 and of Caesar in 59, and its cost would have put intolerable strains on an already hard-pressed treasury. The distribution of the *Ager Campanus* would have ended an important source of income, as Cicero repeatedly emphasizes, his assertions supported by Caesar's reluctance to include this region in his agrarian program in 59 and by the objections centered upon loss of revenue which greeted him when he did, and which continued to be loudly voiced as late as 56. The loss of income resulting from the sale of extensive *vectigalia* abroad would have worsened the situation, and the fruits of Pompey's conquests, which were badly needed, and were no doubt being eagerly awaited to relieve existing financial difficulties, would provide no compensation, since they too were to be diverted to the land program.[23]

There were other drawbacks in the measure as well. The tenants who farmed the *Ager Campanus*, many of whom had held the land for generations, would be dispossessed, and there was no provision in the bill to provide them with any form of compensation for so abrupt a blow to their livelihood, or even for money invested in improvements to the land. Worse still, the bill threatened to dispossess the landholders of Arretium and Volaterrae, whose land had been confiscated by Sulla but had not been distributed. It stood in law, however, as *ager publicus*, and that it was earmarked for distribution in Rullus's bill is clearly indicated by Cicero in a letter written in 45 in which he recalls his opposition as consul to the iniquitous proposal of the tribunes concerning the

23. For the legislation of Flavius and Caesar cf. *Att.* 1.18.6; 1.19.4; 2.1.6; 2.16.1-2. Dio 37.49-50; 38.1; 38.7.3. Plutarch, *Caesar* 14.2-3; *Cato Min.* 31.4-32.6. Suetonius, *Julius* 20. For the importance of the *Ager Campanus* cf. *Leg. Agr.* 1.21; 2.80-83. *Att.* 2.16.1-2. *Pis.* 4. *Q.F.* 2.1.1; 2.5.1. The revenues from Pompey's conquests were to amount to 35 million *denarii* a year. Plutarch, *Pompey* 45.3.

lands of the Volaterrani, and his argument that those who had had the good fortune to escape the cruelty of the Sullan years should be left unharmed.

While some citizens thus stood to lose heavily as a result of the bill, others, who had land to sell, stood to gain from high prices or to make windfall profits from property which, for one reason or another, would be particularly needed, a situation inevitable in any such scheme of large-scale purchasing without price regulation or any form of constraint on the seller. Caesar was carefully to eliminate these last two serious flaws of the Rullan bill in his own agrarian legislation in 59, by exempting the land of the people of Arretium and Volaterrae from distribution and prescribing that the price paid for land would be determined by the valuation made by the censors.[24]

It is also clear that the bill had partisan motivations and aimed to secure for its backers the powers and varied political advantages which the program would bestow on its executors. The mode of election of the decemvirs strongly indicates as much. While precedents for its individual provisions may be discovered in earlier legislation, the high number of irregular features combined in it made the overall procedure unprecedented and raises grave doubts about its intent and the likelihood of impartiality in its operation.[25]

The use of an assembly of seventeen tribes evokes particular suspicion. This form of assembly had previously been used only for the elections to the priestly colleges and to the office of Pontifex Maximus, and it was employed in these elections for the special reason that religious usage prohibited the conferment of priesthoods by the people. It was reasoned, however, that if less than half the people participated in the electoral process, their decision could not be regarded as an act of the people and would not therefore constitute a violation of religious law. And so a minority assembly of seventeen tribes was instituted, a device specially conceived to circumvent a religious scruple and allow, to the degree possible, the participation of the people in the election of religious officials.[26]

---

24. *Leg. Agr.* 2.84. *Fam.* 13.4.1–2. Dio 38.1.4.
25. Gabba has examined precedents for Rullus's electoral procedure in "Nota sulla rogatio agraria di P. Servilio Rullo" *Mélanges Piganiol* (1966), 2.769–76.
26. Cf. L. R. Taylor, *Roman Voting Assemblies* (Ann Arbor 1966), 82. A. H. J. Greenidge, *Roman Public Life* (New York 1901), 254.

The proposed use of such a minority electoral body by Rullus outside of these special circumstances which gave it purpose and justification was therefore a radical innovation and a serious limitation of the democratic process. The move was obviously deliberate and dictated by some special concern, and the most likely explanation for it remains Cicero's contention that it was an effort to guarantee the election to the land commission of Rullus and his supporters. Modern speculation sometimes attributes more altruistic motives to the tribune, suggesting that his purpose was to lessen opportunities for bribery and other forms of electoral abuses by concealing the identity of the voters. But surely the drastic restriction of the right of franchise entailed in a minority assembly was an odd route to the achievement of a better and fairer democratic process, and, besides, as the campaign of Julius Caesar for the office of Pontifex Maximus in 63, which became notorious for the enormous sums he expended on bribery, dramatically demonstrates, the system did nothing to inhibit corrupt practices. In fact such a procedure could only serve to instigate more aggressive campaigning and wider use of illegal methods, since it required a candidate, if he wished to be sure of election, to secure the support of twenty-seven tribes, instead of the eighteen which gave a majority in the regular *comitia.*[27]

What the system did achieve was to make the task of insuring election more onerous and difficult for the general candidate, and both for him who planned to use illegal means and for him who did not. This did not hold true, however, for those who had charge of the election and their friends, for a second effect of the system was to give greater power, and with it greater opportunity for manipulation of the process, to the presiding officer, who together with his helpers would have charge of the casting of lots and would determine which tribes would vote. It was no doubt to guard against the possibilities of abuse contained in this power that the presiding officer at elections for the office of Pontifex Maximus was the newest member of the college, the one normally with least hope of election and therefore the one least likely to abuse his position. But in the case of the election of the land commissioners, it was specifically prescribed that the presiding officer should be none other than

27. *Leg. Agr.* 2.21-23. Cf. Gruen, *Last Generation*, 390. For Caesar's campaign for the office of Pontifex Maximus cf. Suetonius, *Julius* 13. Plutarch, *Caesar* 7.1-4. Dio 37.37.1-3.

the bill's *rogator*, Rullus himself, who would also be eligible to stand as a candidate. It is not surprising that Cicero loudly proclaimed that a rigged election was being orchestrated; the ideal conditions for it had been created.[28]

The clause requiring candidates to hand in their names in person smacks of political scheming also, and it makes it probable that a major element of the bill's political design was the counteraction of Pompey's enormous *potentia* and *auctoritas*, which, except in the unlikely event that he used them to alter radically the basic political structure, threatened not so much the collective supremacy of the oligarchy as the position of ambitious *populares*, whose ability to use the weapons of popular politics would be severely limited by Pompey's pervasive influence. *Professio* in person was not yet a requirement at Rome even for the regular magistracies, and there is no sign and little likelihood that it had previously been a requirement in elections for agrarian commissioners. The regulation was another new departure, and it is difficult to find any convincing reason for its introduction other than the exclusion of Pompey from the commission. Those who view the Rullan bill as designed to help rather than hurt Pompey's position speculate that it was included to prevent the election of enemies of the general, such as Lucullus and Metellus Creticus, who were outside Rome awaiting triumphs; but there would have been little point in excluding such men when there was an abundance of other equally well known and influential opponents of Pompey, such as Catulus and Hortensius, who would have been eligible for election.[29]

That Pompey was the target of the regulation has a far more compelling logic. His exclusion would not only remove his dominant influence from the workings of the commission and deprive him of a further opportunity to fortify his ascendancy, but it would also mean that his veterans, an important basis of his *potentia*, would look not to him but to the commissioners for the land that would constitute their principal

28. Livy 25.5. Cf. Greenidge, *Roman Public Life*, 254. Afzelius, *CM* 3 (1940), 224–26. Manipulation of the lots would not have been difficult. Cf. *Fam.* 5.2.3. Caesar was careful in 59 to make himself ineligible for election as a land commissioner. Dio 38.1.7.

29. *Leg. Agr.* 2.24 attests that *professio* in person was not yet a requirement for the regular magistracies. Sumner (*TAPA* 97 [1966], 581) and Gruen (*Last Generation*, 392) argue that the inclusion of such a requirement in Rullus's bill was not necessarily aimed against Pompey.

reward on discharge, and that the general would be displaced, to some degree at least, by the decemvirate as the soldiers' benefactor and patron. Such a consideration is often and plausibly regarded as an important motivation behind the agrarian legislation in 133 of Tiberius Gracchus, who, together with his supporters, was eager to counteract the power of Scipio Aemilianus, soon to return victorious from the Numantine war, and saw an agrarian program that would bring Scipio's veterans within the range of his patronage as an effective way to do it. It was an obvious device by which to divert some of the political benefits which the chaotic Roman system of rewards for discharged veterans normally enabled generals to secure through various forms of largesse to their soldiers, and it should cause no surprise that it was resorted to in the sixties in the case of an army as large as Pompey's.[30]

There were also other aspects of the bill which would adversely affect Pompey's interests and which further indicate a design to lessen his influence and to bid for some of the political dividends he might derive from his military success. The *vectigalia* from his new conquests, which he was to flaunt so ostentatiously at his triumph in 62, would go to benefit the *plebs* for the first five years, but under a program for which Pompey could claim no credit. The sponsors and administrators of the land law would again stand forth as the primary benefactors. Finally, the authority of the decemvirs to control and dispose of the vast estates of Mithridates in Pontus, Paphlagonia, and Cappadocia would enable them to invade another area of great potential power for Pompey and to secure some of the wealth and power which came from the settlement of overseas dominions. The exact extent of the land over which the decemvirs would have control is difficult to assess, but it would certainly be sufficient to allow substantial interference with the elaborate and detailed reorganization of Asia Minor being planned by Pompey.[31]

30. Cf. H. H. Scullard, "Scipio Aemilianus and Roman Politics" *JRS* 50 (1960), 73-74. A. E. Astin, *Scipio Aemilianus* (Oxford 1967), 200. Sumner's attempt to argue (*TAPA* 97 [1966], 581) that the timing of the bill shows it was designed in Pompey's interest, to insure that land would be available for his veterans, hardly needs detailed refutation. Three years were to elapse before Pompey attempted to secure land for his soldiers. Obviously he felt no urgency about the matter, and, in any event, he would not have covertly entrusted to others a task in which his personal involvement was of the greatest political importance.

31. Cf. Plutarch, *Pompey* 45. Appian, *Mith.* 116. Pliny, *NH* 7.95 ff. Dio 37.21. For Pompey's settlement of the East and the political benefits of such operations

The fact that some of the likely proponents of the bill, notably Julius Caesar, appear as supporters rather than opponents of Pompey in the sixties does not conflict with this analysis of the bill's anti-Pompeian design. It is true that Caesar was a consistent champion of Pompey's interests in the sixties. He spoke in favor of the Gabinian and Manilian laws, and in 63 he zealously supported a proposal by the tribunes T. Labienus and T. Ampius Balbus to bestow extravagant honors on Pompey in recognition of his military successes. In 62 he continued his pro-Pompeian posture, proposing that the job of restoring the temple of Jupiter on the Capitol should be transferred from Catulus to Pompey and supporting a bill put forward by the tribune Metellus Nepos to recall Pompey to Italy to restore order in the wake of the Catilinarian conspiracy.[32]

It would be naive, however, to assume that these efforts of a *popularis* to stand as the friend of Rome's most popular figure represented a genuine concern to enhance Pompey's power and position. Caesar's public support of the general in this period was simply part of his energetic drive to build popularity and influence by varied means. He knew well the political gains to be derived from championing a popular hero, and he pursued them with his customary boldness and vigor.

His support of the Rullan law and its design to limit and counteract the influence of Pompey was not incompatible with this stance and strategy, for the bill contained no overt attack on Pompey and invited no confrontation with him. On the contrary, it went to some lengths to appear to be safeguarding the general's interests and *dignitas*. Its political purposes were well disguised behind its ostensibly primary and thoroughly laudable concern to effect needed social reform, and, in promoting it, Caesar was able to pursue the political advantages the bill could bestow on its backers without revoking his public advocacy of Pompey or forfeiting its benefits.[33]

The clause on booty, spoils, and crown gold provides yet another

---

cf. Magie, *Roman Rule in Asia Minor*, 1.351-78. Badian, *Foreign Clientelae,* 154 ff., 263 ff.

32. Plutarch, *Pompey* 25.3. Dio 36.43.2-3; 37.21.4. Suetonius, *Julius* 15. Plutarch, *Cato Min.* 27. Dio 37.44. Cf. Dio 37.22.1.

33. E.g., Pompey was exempted from the provision requiring generals to account for the spoils of war. *Leg. Agr.* 1.13; 2.60. On Caesar's policy toward Pompey cf. Dio 37.22.1.

indication of partisan politics and *popularis* power-seeking in the framing of the bill. Though there was little to justify it as a money-raising expedient, the clause was made retroactive, and it would entitle the decemvirs to go back to the period of the civil wars and reopen the highly charged but politically fertile issues of profiteering and unjust appropriations during the Sullan years and to renew the attack on prominent *Sullani*, such as Faustus Sulla, whom popular politicians had unsuccessfully prosecuted in the regular courts a few years earlier. The ramifications of the clause were serious. The wrongs of the Sullan era were real and numerous, but, as was well appreciated by Cicero and the ruling oligarchy, attempts to reverse them, particularly in murkier areas such as military appropriations and the use of state funds, were fraught with the dangers of rekindling hatreds and divisions and fueling the politics of emotion to a degree which could threaten the peace and security of the state.[34]

The implications of the obviously partisan character of the law were rendered much more serious by the unusual opportunities for the accumulation of political influence which would be open to the bill's administrators. The sponsors and executors of all agrarian legislation stood to make substantial political gains from increased popularity with the masses and the enlistment as clients of those who received actual allotments. For the backers of the Rullan law, however, the extent of such gains would be greatly increased by the unprecedented scope of the proposed program and by the fact that it would involve the settlement of Pompey's veterans, who numbered in the region of thirty thousand men. Furthermore, the provisions dealing with the sale and taxation of public land in the provinces would open the way for the procurement of foreign *clientelae* all over the empire.[35] It is likely too that, as Cicero claimed, it was intended that Egypt would be annexed, in which case the commissioners would also gain control of that country's royal treasures and estates. The bill specified that any public property outside Italy acquired since 88 could be disposed of.

---

34. *Leg. Agr.* 1.12; 2.59. ff. The concern of the oligarchy to contain attempts to reverse Sullan injustices is illustrated by its reaction to the prosecution of Faustus Sulla in 66 and by Cicero's objections in 63 to restoration of their political rights to sons of the proscribed. Asconius 73, Clark. Quintilian 11.1.85. Pliny, *NH* 7.117. *Pis.* 4.

35. For the number of Pompey's veterans cf. Brunt, *Italian Manpower*, 460.

The date 88 was obviously not chosen at random, and it so happens that it was in that very year that Alexander I, by whose will it was alleged Egypt was bequeathed to Rome, was deposed and probably died. The coincidence is too striking to be accidental, particularly since no other reason for the selection of 88 can be discovered. It is not clear that the judicial powers of the decemvirs would have entitled them to decide the issue of the will on their own, but in any event they would have had little difficulty in securing a *plebiscitum* validating the bequest. The *plebs* were cooperative in ventures likely to benefit them. Clodius had no trouble enacting legislation to annex Cyprus in 58.[36]

The *factio* behind the Rullan law would not have achieved, and likely was not seeking, the means to *dominatio*, but its members would undoubtedly have been able to secure permanent and pivotal political resources, which would have insured, for the leaders at least, a prominent place in Roman politics and would also most likely have resulted in greater political polarization and factional strife.

It should now be clear that many of Cicero's charges concerning the purposes and consequences of the Rullan land law had considerable justification, though, in making them, he freely exercised his preeminent talent for hyperbole and misrepresentation. There can be no doubt, however, that he genuinely believed that the bill was pernicious and a danger to the state, his objections founded on a fundamental aversion to the goals and methods of the class of politicians he saw behind it, the class he denoted by the label *populares* or otherwise referred to by such derogatory catchwords as *improbi, audaces, perditi, mali, perniciosi.*[37] In his attacks on the Rullan law occur the first full expression of Cicero's vehement opposition to the politicians who promoted popular social or political change against the wishes of the senate, and the first clear statement of his conception of the social and political conflicts of the late Republic and how to confront them. He was to repeat and develop these political views and ideas first sounded

36. Cf. Badian, *RhM* 110 (1967), 178–92. Sumner, *TAPA* 97 (1966), 577. On Clodius and Cyprus cf. Broughton, *MRR*, 2.198. S. I. Oost, "Cato Uticensis and the Annexation of Cyprus" *CP* 50 (1955), 98–112. E. Badian, "M. Porcius Cato and the Annexation and Early Administration of Cyprus" *JRS* 55 (1965), 110–21.

37. Cf. *Leg. Agr.* 2.8, 10. *Cat.* 3.27–28. *Cat.* 4.22. *Sest.* 96, 99–100, 139. *Phil.* 7.4. C. Wirszubski, "*Audaces*: A Study in Political Phraseology" *JRS* 51 (1961), 12–22. R. Seager, "Cicero and the Word *Popularis*" *CQ* 22 (1972), 328–38.

in the Rullan speeches on many subsequent occasions and in varied writings; they contain the core of his vision of republicanism and its afflictions in his time, and, reflecting as they do the interests and policies of the oligarchy, they may also safely be regarded as representative of the outlook of the conservative *nobilitas* as a whole.

Cicero found the origins of the internal divisions and conflicts of the late Republic in the tribunates of the Gracchi, who, he considered, first sundered the political community into two segments and, by their turbulent methods and attacks on the state's *principes*, and on the treasury, and on the interests of the *locupletes*, disturbed *otium*, fostered *seditio* and *discordia*, and undermined the entire *status reipublicae*.[38] He also considered that they provided a model for a succession of later politicians, men who, led by *audacia* to an excessive lust for power, thought not of the *utilitas communis* but of their own political advantage and sought power and popularity by the political methods brought to light and shown effective in the Gracchan era. Their constituency he represents as the discontented elements present in every society: the criminals, the disgraced, the ne'er-do-wells, the debtors, and the *furiosi*, or chronic revolutionaries. Cicero adds also the *multitudo* which comprised the *plebs* and which was easily led to support those who offered to improve its lot.[39]

These elements so-called *populares* sought to rally by highlighting their grievances and dissatisfactions and promising political and economic change to better their condition. They posed as the champions of the rights and liberties of the masses, their protectors against oppression by the ruling elite, and the vindicators of their sovereign right to determine important matters of public policy. There resulted efforts to disrupt the courts, overturn legal decisions, recall exiles, restore the condemned; the introduction of such measures as ballot laws; and the submission to the people for decision of vital governmental questions. In the economic sphere they promoted programs that aimed to blind the minds of the people with the prospect of limitless *largitio*, and that

38. *Har. Resp.* 41–43. *Cat.* 1.3; 4.13. *Dom.* 24, 102. *Mil.* 72. *Sest.* 102–03. *De Or.* 1.38. *Brut.* 103. *Leg.* 3.20, 24. *Acad.* 2.15. *Fin.* 4.65. *Rep.* 1.31. *Tusc. Disp.* 3.48. *Am.* 37, 41. *Off.* 1.76; 2.43, 72, 80. Cf. R. J. Murray, "Cicero and the Gracchi" *TAPA* 97 (1966), 291–98.

39. *Sest.* 99, 103, 139. *Off.* 1.63–64. *Att.* 7.3.5; 7.7.6; 7.11.1; 8.11.2. *Leg. Agr.* 2.102.

comprised schemes such as land distribution or colonization, grain doles, and remission of debts.[40]

Such policies and the politicians who promoted them Cicero regarded as the primary cause of the problems of the *respublica* in his day and the primary threat to its survival. He emphasized that no external danger remained for Rome; the enemy was inside, in the opportunistic demagogues who thrived on sedition and sought profit from the polarization of the political community. He considered both their political and economic aims a negation of the fundamental principles on which the peace and stability of a political society depended, and certain to lead to the state's destruction. He pledged himself in the Rullan speeches to the defeat and suppression of such men and, in contrast to their seditious methods and programs for political and economic change, he offered and sought to arouse support for what he claimed were more truly *popularis* goals, namely *concordia*, and *otium*, and the preservation of the political and economic principles embodied in the institutions of traditional republicanism.[41]

Concordia meant harmony and agreement among the citizens of a state, the political contentment that came from the belief that the political system gave due recognition to the rights of all. *Otium* was the condition of peace and tranquillity that resulted from *concordia* when all civil strife or agitation was absent. The word was frequently linked with such terms as *pax, tranquillitas,* and *salus*, and opposed to *seditio* and *tumultus*.[42]

For Cicero, however, *otium* was a true political ideal only when combined with *dignitas.* He develops this idea particularly in the *Pro Sestio*, when he describes the goal of the good statesman as *cum dignitate otium.* The phrase has been the subject of numerous learned discussions, and has often been endowed with abstruse philosophical complexities which were surely never intended by Cicero in an address to a jury. The expression may well have been part of the political propaganda of the late Republic. In the speech attributed by Sallust to the

40. *Am.* 41. *Leg. Agr.* 2.8, 10, 102. *Sest.* 103, 139. *Acad.* 2.13. *Off.* 2.78. *Verr.* 2.5.12. *Att.* 7.11.1; 9.7.5. Cf. Seager, *CQ* 22 (1972), 331–32.

41. *Leg. Agr.* 1.26–27; 2.7–9, 101–03. *Rab.* 33. *Fam.* 1.9.12. *Sest.* 51. Cf. *Rep.* 1.69.

42. *Rep.* 1.49; 2.69. *Leg. Agr.* 1.23; 2–9. *Mur.* 78. *Quir.* 20. *Dom.* 15. *Pis.* 73. *Phil.* 5.41.

consul Lepidus in 78 occur the phrases *otium cum libertate* and *otium cum servitio*, describing respectively the *popularis* view of what was ideal and of what actually existed under a tyrannical Sullan oligarchy. There is a possibility that Sallust himself created the phrases as counters to Cicero's *cum dignitate otium*, but, in any event, the slogans indicate that Cicero's words had a straightforward political significance and represented an alternative to the insistence of *populares* on greater power for the people and an end to the domination of the oligarchy.[43]

Dignitas was a cardinal concept of conservative republicanism which asserted that, in politics as elsewhere, justice and common sense demanded that the inequalities between men should be recognized, and that *gradus dignitatis* should exist to reflect them. It was the precept that safeguarded republicanism against unjust ideas of social and political egalitarianism, allowed a hierarchical social structure, and gave *auctoritas* and control to those who, though *libertate pares ceteris*, were *principes dignitate*. This combination of equal liberty for all and *auctoritas* for those of greatest *dignitas* was, in Cicero's thinking, the ideal formula on which to build the balanced political system which would produce true *concordia* and *otium*. He further believed that the republican constitution was founded on such a formula, and that the preservation of its principles and institutions was therefore the means by which the good statesman could guide the ship of state into the haven of *otium* and *dignitas*.[44]

This meant for Cicero the preservation above all of that which he believed *populares* most wanted to destroy, the balance of power between the two main elements of the political community, the senate and the people. He carefully defines the place and powers of each. The senate he presents as a permanent council established by the founders of the Republic, intended to consist of those chosen by the people for their *virtus* and *industria* and designed to lead and protect the state and guide the magistrates, who were to serve as its *ministri* and the executors of its decisions. The people's role he saw defined by those powers necessary to guarantee *libertas*, namely the protective powers of tribunes and the powers entailed in the electoral, judicial, and legislative

43. *Sest.* 98–99. Cf. *Leg. Agr.* 1.23, 27. Sallust, *Hist.* 1.58.9, 25, Maur. C. Wirszubski, "Cicero's *Cum Dignitate Otium*: A Reconsideration" *JRS* 44 (1954), 1–13. J. P. V. D. Balsdon, "*Auctoritas, Dignitas, Otium*" *CQ* 54 (1960), 43–50.
44. *Rep.* 1.43, 53; 2.59. *Leg.* 3.28. *Phil.* 1.34. *Sest.* 99.

functions of the assemblies. This political structure, he maintained, achieved a *temperamentum*, otherwise described as *temperatio iuris*, in the state, whereby all matters of the greatest importance were controlled by those of the highest *dignitas*, while a certain equality of basic rights and liberties between all citizens was recognized, thus satisfying the claims of justice, efficiency, and political freedom and creating the stable and harmonious political society. Cicero takes great pains in the Rullan speeches to demonstrate to the people the extent of their freedoms and privileges under this, their traditional form of political organization.[45]

While the stability, harmony, and peace of such a society were powerfully safeguarded by the political justice on which it was founded, other safeguards were also necessary to protect it against the assaults of the *improbi*. Some of these Cicero found in the state's religious observances and in the auspices, in the laws, customs, and system of law enforcement, and in the provinces of the empire, the allies, and Rome's prestige and military strength. Public religion and the auspices were effective aids to the maintenance of an orderly and moral society and the restraint of dissidents; just laws and just enforcement of them constituted the impersonal and impartial guarantor of every citizen's *libertas*, the *vinculum dignitatis, fundamentum libertatis, fons aequitatis;* a secure empire, maintained in peace by Rome's prestige and military superiority, was vital to the achievement of tranquillity and prosperity.[46]

But next to the political justice manifested in its political institutions, Cicero believed that the most important safeguard of republicanism lay in adherence to the principles of economic justice, specifically in the recognition and protection of the rights of private property and free enterprise, the rights which he saw chiefly threatened by the Rullan land law and whose protection was his chief concern in his opposition to the bill. For Cicero, individuals have a right to private possessions,

---

45. *Sest.* 137. *Leg.* 3.10–11, 24, 28, 37. *Rep.* 2.56–59. *Leg. Agr.* 1.22–27; 2.1–16, 100–03. Cf. *Fam.* 4.1.2; 10.6.2.

46. *Sest.* 98. For the importance of religion and law cf. *Leg.* 2.26, 30 ff. *N.D.* 1.2 ff.; 2.153. *Leg.* 2.12. *Cluent.* 146. *Leg. Agr.* 2.102. *Par. St.* 27. *Att.* 9.7.5. The importance of a peaceful empire had been well illustrated in the sixties. Cf. *Man.* 14 ff.

a right to accumulate them, provided they do so honestly and without injury to anyone, and a right to use them for their own benefit, although they have a moral obligation to use them for the general good of society as well. He argued that it was chiefly to protect these rights that states were organized in the first place, and that statesmen therefore had a prime responsibility to see to it that no infringement of them occurred by act of the state, but that each citizen had free and untroubled control of what was his. The idea that the state should seek to equalize wealth or to aid to any degree the needy by taking from men of means he regarded as the most pernicious of social doctrines, analogous to one part of the body preying on another. It was a violation of the laws of nature and of nations and an assault on the chief bonds of society—*concordia*, which cannot exist when the state takes from one and gives to another, and *aequitas*, which is destroyed whenever a man is not allowed to possess his own.[47]

These beliefs led Cicero to oppose not only agrarian resettlement schemes affecting private land and other measures, such as property taxes and the reduction or cancellation of lawful debts, which directly interfered with private property, but also all programs that damaged or threatened to damage in any way the financial interests of any segment of the society. In the latter category came doles and agrarian proposals which were likely to lead to consequences such as the dispossession of long-term, productive tenants, the undermining of *fides*, that sense of confidence and good faith indispensable for the proper functioning of the state's financial life, or the draining of the treasury, whose problems would ultimately have to be resolved by taxes or some form of imposition on the rich. Measures that produced such effects violated economic justice equally with those which more directly attacked private property, since they benefited one segment of society at the expense of another.[48]

Cicero's public stand for what amounted to a doctrine of extreme laissez-faireism began with his attacks on the Rullan law and continued,

47. *Off.* 1.21, 25, 42, 51, 92; 2.72, 78–81; 3.21 ff. Cf. *Rep.* 2.69.

48. *Off.* 1.23; 2.72, 74, 78–84; 3.70. *Att.* 2.1.11; 6.6.2; 11.23.3. *Q.F.* 1.1.6. *Man.* 19. *Leg. Agr.* 1.23; 2.8, 10. *Sest.* 98. *Fam.* 4.1.2. *Pis.* 4. *Sulla* 65. Cicero even opposed the Flavian agrarian law sponsored by Pompey in 60, seeking the removal of all clauses damaging to any group of citizens, even though at the time he was eagerly courting Pompey's friendship. *Att.* 1.19.4–8; 1.17.8–10; 1.20.2; 2.1.6.

unaltered and undiluted, throughout the remainder of his life. He was not blind to the economic problems of Rome, nor to the political dangers attached to them, but he looked for a solution chiefly to patronage and the generosity of the affluent, a voluntary system of wealth distribution which he considered to have the merit both of helping the poor and of entrenching the political ascendancy of the upper class. Modest measures by the state in the form of doles or land distribution he was willing to approve on occasion for the relief of particular hardship, but he circumscribed all such programs of aid to the poor with the rigid stipulation that they must entail no adverse financial consequences for the rest of the community.[49]

Adherence to these economic principles, Cicero believed, would remove from the state the *discordia* that inevitably came from the inequity of taking from one to give to another and, in addition, would secure for it the united support of the *lauti et locupletes*, the great body of prosperous citizens who had a large stake in peace and stability and in the preservation of the system that guaranteed them the secure enjoyment of their prosperity. Such men, Cicero considered, were bound to the state by many pledges and were natural allies of the conservative *nobilitas* in the defense of traditional republicanism. He called this alliance of the well-to-do, in which he included self-supporting citizens from the lower levels of the society, such as *scribae* and *tabernarii*, *consensus bonorum* or, when he was thinking principally of cooperation between the ruling class and the upper stratum of the *locupletes*, the *equester ordo*, he termed it *concordia ordinum*. His belief in the ability of self-interest to bind such citizens into a powerful and active political force in support of the social and political status quo and its political champions constituted his main hope for the survival of the *respublica*. It was to them that he chiefly addressed his pledges in the Rullan speeches to work for *otium* and to end the fears and the general uncertainty induced by the schemes and pledges of *populares*. The rallying of this great constituency of the prosperous, which he was later to refer to as *noster exercitus*, remained a central goal of his entire consulship.[50]

49. In *Att.* 1.19.4 he admits the desirability of draining off the *sentina urbis*, and he was willing to support a modest agrarian law to do this. He also approved the small dole introduced by the tribune M. Octavius. *Off.* 2.72. On patronage and generosity by the rich cf. *Off.* 1.21 ff., 92. *Rep.* 2.59. *Sest.* 137. *Mur.* 70–71.
50. *Leg. Agr.* 1.22–27; 2.1–16, 102. *Cat.* 4.15, 22. *Har. Resp.* 60. *Pis.* 4, 7.

The limitations of Cicero's political ideas and prescriptions for the political and economic maladies of his time were many, and they were mostly illustrated in his own lifetime. Captivated by the success of a system designed for other days and other conditions and blinded by the prejudices of his elitist background and deeply conservative political upbringing, he clung to aristocratic political and economic doctrines and traditions which were a tissue of irrelevancies in the circumstances prevailing in the first century B.C. There was little room in the corrupt, increasingly competitive, and exclusive political world of the Ciceronian age for the true functioning of the concept of *dignitas* or for the emergence of the virtuous and benevolent ruling elite whose *auctoritas* would guarantee it political control and frustrate the designs of *improbi*. His hopes for a union of *boni*, and particularly for an alliance between the ruling and business classes, were equally illusory. The bulk of Rome's citizens, who lived in Italy, had little opportunity to participate in politics outside of elections and little interest in exerting themselves on behalf of traditional republicanism, as their quick support of Caesar in 49 was to demonstrate.[51] As for cooperation between the senate and the *equester ordo*, Cicero's faith in such an alliance was severely shaken soon after 63, as events revealed the inevitability of conflict between government, concerned with the common interest, and big business, concerned with its own. In the late sixties and fifties *concordia ordinum* appeared not as a natural and secure alliance of the upper classes cemented by mutual self-interest in the preservation of the status quo, but as a shaky coalition whose survival required endless concessions to the financiers, often amounting to open bribery.[52]

But the most fatal flaw in Cicero's political thinking was its failure to come to grips with the problems posed by the economic plight of the urban and rural poor, the chief cause of the internal unrest in post-Sullan Rome and a major contributor to the urban violence and

Phil. 10.3; 13.8, 16. *Att.* 1.14.4; 1.16.6–8; 1.17.8; 1.18.3; 1.19.4; 2.16.4; 6.1.16; 8.1.3. *Fam.* 1.9.12, 17; 5.21.2. *Off.* 3.88. *Rep.* 2.39. Cf. H. C. Boren, "Cicero's *Concordia* in Historical Perspective" *Studies in Memory of W. E. Caldwell* (Chapel Hill 1964), 51–62. H. Strasburger, *Concordia Ordinum, eine Untersuchung zur Politik Ciceros* (Amsterdam 1956).

51. Cicero was not totally unaware of the difficulties involved in achieving his ideal. Cf. *Leg.* 3.28–29. For the defection of the Italians to Caesar cf. *Att.* 8.13.2; 8.16.1.

52. Cf. *Att.* 1.17.8; 1.18.3, 7; 2.1.7–8. In *Q.F.* 1.1.32 Cicero acknowledges the fragility of the ideal of *concordia ordinum*.

breakdown of order which was relentlessly growing in the sixties and was destined repeatedly to create anarchic conditions in the capital in the fifties.[53] The massive economic gulf between the upper and lower classes which resulted from Rome's successful wars, whose burdens had been chiefly borne by the small property-holder and whose benefits had gone largely to the upper class, had destroyed the cohesiveness of the earlier society so warmly admired by Cicero, and with it the foundations of Cicero's entire political and economic structure. The enormity of the economic inequality which existed in Rome in the first century and the exploitation of the poor which inevitably accompanied the unregulated use of their wealth by the rich were producing an economic tyranny more threatening to *otium cum dignitate* than all the designs and schemes of so-called *populares*.[54] Talk of the people's political privileges and *libertas* under traditional republicanism had little meaning for those facing economic servitude, and, propertyless and indigent, and lacking the means to rise above their poverty, such citizens were even less likely to be persuaded and pacified by disquisitions on the sanctity of private property or the injustice of governmental regulation of the distribution of wealth.

But to all this Cicero was either blind or indifferent. Like Sallust, he could muster no sympathy for the poor or the unfortunate. The failures in society were contemptible parasites whose betterment could not be achieved at the expense of the successful and industrious. He continued to rely on private patronage to cope with a problem whose dimensions and causes demanded immediate and large-scale intervention by the state, and in the process he continued to provide his political foes with issues and followings and hooligan henchmen for their assaults on the status quo.[55]

Throughout his consulship Cicero pursued with energy the aims set forth in the Rullan speeches to defeat the designs of popular reformers

53. Cf. Brunt, *Past and Present* 35 (1966), 3–27; *Social Conflicts,* 127–40. Lintott, *Violence in Republican Rome*, 175–203. Yavetz, *Latomus* 17 (1958), 500–17.

54. In *Rep.* 2.59 Cicero shows awareness of the importance of balance in the distribution of wealth to the maintenance of a cohesive political society. On the economic inequality of the late Republic cf. Brunt, *Social Conflicts*, 40 ff.

55. Sallust gives a typically unsympathetic portrayal of the *plebs* in *Catiline* 37. Cf. *Att.* 1.19.4. *Flacc.* 15–18. *Sest.* 103–04, 139. *Mur.* 36. *Cluent.* 138. *Phil.* 7.4.

and to build *concordia* and support for his brand of republicanism. When, early in the year, public resentment over a law enacted by the tribune L. Roscius Otho in 67 reserving fourteen rows of seats in the theater for the *equites* erupted into an open demonstration, a development which most likely reflected growing hostility in hard times toward the moneylenders and financiers, he intervened promptly and successfully, summoning the people to a *contio* at the temple of Bellona and persuading them of the justice and merits of the law. The speech is lost, but no doubt it sounded the themes of *concordia* and *otium*, and the importance of the equestrian order to the prosperity and stability of the *respublica*.[56]

Cicero and the Senatus Consultum Ultimum

Not long after his defense of the *Lex Roscia* he faced a considerably more serious political storm. The aged and obscure senator, C. Rabirius, was put on trial by the tribune Labienus, acting in cooperation with Caesar, on a charge of *perduellio* arising out of Rabirius's alleged murder of Saturninus thirty-seven years earlier. Saturninus had been a tribune in 100, and, after he had resorted to violent methods to further his schemes, the senate passed a *consultum ultimum* calling on the consuls to save the state. Marius, consul at the time, armed the people; Saturninus fled to the Capitol with his followers. What ensued was not known precisely, but Saturninus was killed, and Labienus contended that he was murdered by Rabirius after he had surrendered and received a pledge of public safety from Marius, and when his death could no longer be said to be demanded by the public safety.[57]

The evidence for the sequence of events and for the procedures followed in the prosecution is unclear and contradictory, and it has resulted in a bewildering variety of reconstructions.[58] Certainty seems

56. Plutarch, *Cicero* 13.2–4. *Mur.* 40. Asconius 78–79, Clark. *Att.* 2.1.3. Cicero recounts the favorite themes of his speeches in this period in *Att.* 1.14.4. For a sample of his oratory on the importance of the *equester ordo* cf. *Man.* 17–20.

57. Sources in Broughton, *MRR*, 1.576. The accounts of the death of Saturninus are conflicting. Florus (2.4) and Appian (*BC* 1.32) report that he was killed as an unarmed prisoner, and this was apparently the version promoted by Labienus. *Rab.* 28.

58. Cf. Hardy, *Problems in Roman History*, 99–125. J. L. Strachan-Davidson,

unattainable, but the most persuasive hypothesis is that Labienus enacted a law authorizing the appointment of *duumviri* by the *praetor urbanus* to charge and pass sentence of death by scourging and crucifixion on Rabirius, in accordance with the obsolete procedure which had been used in cases of *perduellio* in the regal period. Caesar and his cousin, L. Julius Caesar, consul in 64, were selected as *duumviri* and duly carried out their assignment. But Cicero, again effectively using his oratorical power to marshall public opinion, brought sufficient pressure to bear on Labienus to force him to abandon his plans to go through with the execution.[59] The tribune then initiated a regular tribunician prosecution for *perduellio* before the *populus*, at which Cicero delivered his extant speech in defense of Rabirius. The trial ended without a decision, terminated by another piece of antiquarian machination, this time employed on behalf of the defendant. The praetor, Metellus Celer, had the red flag which flew over the Janiculum whenever the centuries met lowered. In ancient times, when Rome was liable to sudden attack from hostile neighbors, it was required that a guard be posted on the Janiculum whenever the *comitia centuriata* was in session, and the red flag indicated that the guard was in place. The removal of the flag signaled the departure of the guard and required the dismissal of the assembly. Roman reverence for tradition had preserved the practice of flying the flag, and with it the requirement that the assembly be dismissed whenever it was lowered. Metellus's action thus brought an immediate end to the proceedings against Rabirius, and Labienus then apparently decided to drop the prosecution.[60]

Problems of the Roman Criminal Law (Oxford 1912), 1.188–204. Meyer, *Caesars Monarchie*, 549–63. R. A. Bauman, *The* Duumviri *in the Roman Criminal Law and in the Horatius Legend* (Wiesbaden 1969), 9–21. Gelzer, *Cicero*, 76–79. Rice Holmes, *Roman Republic*, 1.452–55. A. W. Lintott, "*Provocatio.* From the Struggles of the Orders to the Principate" *Aufsteig und Niedergang der römischen Welt*, 1.2, 261–62. W. B. Tyrrell, "The Trial of C. Rabirius in 63 B.C." *Latomus* 32 (1973), 285–300. Gruen, *Last Generation*, 277–79. E. J. Phillips, "The Prosecution of C. Rabirius in 63 B.C." *Klio* 56 (1974), 87–101.

59. *Rab.* 6–8, 10–17, 28. *Pis.* 4. Dio 37.26–28; 33.37.2. Suetonius, *Julius* 12. Quintilian, *Inst. Or.* 5.13.20.

60. Dio 37.28. Metellus's sympathies in the affair remain obscure, but the indications are that he was on Cicero's side. He was no *popularis*, he was on good terms with Cicero in 63, and it was about the time of the trial of Rabirius that Cicero contrived to have the province of Cisalpine Gaul allotted to him. *Fam.* 5.2.3. *Pis.* 5.

The motives behind the attack on Rabirius were blatantly political. The charge was dug up from ancient history and concerned an event the true details of which were unknown and a defendant whose guilt was unproven. The whole affair was a transparent scheme to challenge the extent to which extralegal action could be taken against citizens in internal crises under the authority of the *senatus consultum ultimum.* The jeopardy in which the trial placed Rabirius thirty-seven years after his uncertain role in the death of Saturninus would serve as a memorable warning that the ultimate decree had narrow and controversial limits, and that anyone who ventured beyond well-precedented uses of it was liable to be called to a grim accounting. The revival of a barbarous ritual from the distant past would dramatize the proceedings and drive home the message of the trial.[61] The practices and assumptions of the status quo were again under challenge from the activist tribunes of 63 and their powerful backers, and once again Cicero stood forth as the foremost opponent of such agitators and the defender of the institutions of traditional republicanism. He repeated his warning that the threat to Rome's survival came not from any king, race, or nation, but from the internal plottings of turbulent revolutionaries, and he repeated his plea for resolute and unified resistance to them to preserve the *respublica* and its foundations of *dignitas* and *libertas.* He drew a stirring picture of the *consensio bonorum* which saw even the lame and crippled come forth in arms to suppress the *seditiosi* in response to the senate's decree in 100, and he urged the preservation of the machinery of the *consultum ultimum* which made possible such mobilization of the *boni* against men of violence, declaring his own readiness unhesitatingly to use the decree to destroy with arms those who would threaten with arms the safety of the state.[62]

His speech also contains an important statement of his views on the troublesome constitutional questions associated with the *consultum ultimum.* The decree was first issued against Gaius Gracchus in 121 B.C.[63] Gracchus, then a private citizen, had surrounded himself with

61. Cicero liked to portray the prosecution as an attack on the senate and an attempt to eliminate the *consultum ultimum.* Cf. *Pis.* 4. *Rab.* 2. *Orator* 102. It is clear, however, from *Rab.* 19 and 28 that Labienus did not challenge the legality of the decree itself but merely argued that its mandate had been exceeded.

62. *Rab.* 20–22, 27, 33–35.

63. It is sometimes argued that the decree was passed against Tiberius Gracchus in 133. Cf. K. von Fritz, "Emergency Powers in the Last Centuries of the

a bodyguard, and, in a fracas with partisans of the consul L. Opimius, one of the consul's servants was killed by Gracchus's men. The senate responded with a decree which, in the words of Cicero, ordered *uti L. Opimius consul videret ne quid respublica detrimenti caperet.* Acting on this decree Opimius called the senators and *equites* to arms. Gracchus reacted by seizing the Aventine, which was quickly captured by the consul. Three thousand people died in the affair, according to Plutarch, but not all of them in the fighting. Large numbers were executed by summary order of Opimius, or following some form of *quaestio* conducted by the consul, after the revolt had been crushed. This was a direct violation of the Porcian and Valerian laws and of the *Lex Sempronia* of 123, and Opimius was brought to trial *apud populum* by the tribune P. Decius in 120 on the charge that, in violation of the laws, he had executed Roman citizens without trial. Opimius did not deny that he had acted against the laws, but he pleaded that he was justified since he had done so in the interests of the state *ex senatus consulto.* He was acquitted.[64]

The question at issue in the trial, according to Cicero, was whether a defendant who had killed a citizen in violation of the laws, but in accordance with a decree of the senate and to protect the safety of his country, should be considered worthy of punishment. The verdict answered the question in the negative. The acquittal of Opimius therefore meant that a magistrate was justified in taking supralegal action when danger to the state created the need for it and when the senate had instructed him that such a need existed. This was, to some extent, an affirmation of an old principle of government later stated by Cicero in the precept *salus populi suprema lex esto.* But the principle was affirmed with a qualification. The exoneration of Opimius only vindicated the infringement of law in defense of the public safety *ex senatus consulto*, and indeed Opimius had not sought justification without reference to the senate's decree. Consequently, the senate was recognized to have a certain power of initiative in dangerous crises. The nature of this power and its effect on the legal position of magistrates

Roman Republic" *AHA* 3 (1942), 221–37. Plutarch (*Tiberius Gracchus* 19) shows, however, that no such decree was issued in 133. The term *consultum ultimum* is first found in Caesar, *BC* 1.5.3.

64. Plutarch, *Gaius Gracchus* 13–18. *Cat.* 1.3. *De Or.* 2.106, 132. *Part. Or.* 104, 106. Appian, *BC* 1.26. Sallust, *Jug.* 31.7. Livy, *Per.* 61.

to whom it gave instruction form the central problem connected with the *senatus consultum ultimum.*[65]

Did the acquittal of Opimius give the senate a constitutional right to decide that a particular situation was sufficiently dangerous to warrant the suspension of normal legal procedures in order to bring it under control, and to so instruct the magistrates? If so, to what extent did such instruction permit the magistrates to ignore regular processes of law in handling the situation, and how did it affect their responsibility for action taken? Or was the decree of the senate merely advice which the magistrate might accept or reject, and which could make no legal change in his normal powers or in his responsibility for the use of those powers?

These questions have been discussed in detail by numerous historians, notably by G. Plaumann, H. Last, and Mommsen.[66] Plaumann and Last essentially agree that the senate was at all times a mere advisory body, the *consilium* of the consuls, and that the ultimate decree had no effect on the legal powers of magistrates. The latter writes: "The *ultimum consultum* of the senate was in essence only an attempt to strengthen the resolution of the magistrates in face of a danger which might call for action of peculiar vigor and determination. It implied a promise of senatorial support; but neither in theory nor in fact did it add to the legal powers which they already had. It conferred on them no new authority nor did it even purport to remove any of the restrictions which were imposed by statute on the use of their *imperium.*"

Last believes, however, that, although from a legal standpoint the ultimate decree had no effect on a magistrate's position, in practice the effect was great, since, if a magistrate was prosecuted for illegal action taken under a *consultum ultimum,* the decree provided him with valuable evidence that the state had been confronted with a danger which justified nonlegal measures, on the old principle *salus populi suprema lex esto.* In short, the ultimate decree was merely advisory and did not

65. *De Or.* 2.132, 134. *Part. Or.* 104, 106. *Leg.* 3.8. *Phil.* 11.28.
66. Plaumann, *Klio* 13 (1913), 321–86. Last, *CAH* 9, 82 ff. T. Mommsen, *Römisches Staatsrecht* 3 (Leipzig 1888), 1240 ff. Cf. Wirszubski, *Libertas*, 55 ff. Strachan-Davidson, *Problems of the Roman Criminal Law,* 1.225–45. Mitchell, *Historia* 20 (1971), 47–61. Lintott, *Violence in Republican Rome*, 149–74. B. Rödl, *Das Senatus Consultum Ultimum und der Tod der Gracchen* (Bonn 1969). J. Ungern-Sternberg, *Untersuchungen zum spätrepublikanischen Notstandsrecht* (Munich 1970).

affect the legal responsibility of a magistrate, but it could be used to show that infringement of the law under its encouragement was justified by the gravity of the public danger.[67]

Mommsen's interpretation of the *consultum ultimum* is somewhat different. Whereas Last considers that the decree had no legal effect whatever on the duties, powers, or responsibilities of the magistrates, Mommsen believes that it created a state of war which empowered the magistrates to conduct acts of war against expressly designated persons or against those whom they saw to be the source of the disturbance. He argues that the right of the senate to establish a quasi-dictatorship of this type, legitimizing summary elimination of the source of danger to the state, was never seriously challenged in the last century of the Republic and must be admitted to have become constitutional. In other words, the effect of the decree was to establish the magistrates temporarily as the supreme power in the state and to permit them to deal with a particular situation free from the normal restrictions on their *imperium*.[68]

Cicero's concept of the decree, as indicated by his references to it in his defense of Rabirius and elsewhere, and by his use of it in the Catilinarian crisis later in 63, does not wholly agree with either of these interpretations. As already described in an earlier chapter, Cicero stood by the principle that the safety of the people was the highest law and that those who threatened it forfeited their rights as citizens and could legitimately be treated as *hostes*.[69] The *consultum ultimum* he viewed as a constitutional machinery for the controlled implementation of this doctrine, assigning to one organ of government, the senate, the power and responsibility to determine when the public safety was threatened and to authorize extraordinary measures to remove the threat. Passage of the decree was therefore an official declaration by an authorized body that a state of emergency existed, and for Cicero it had important effects on the constitution and on the legal position of the various elements of government.

These effects he spells out most clearly in the *Pro Rabirio*, where he presents a picture of the special cooperation which should exist in

67. Last, *CAH* 9, 84–85. Cf. von Fritz, *AHA* 3 (1942), 226.
68. *Römisches Staatsrecht,* 3.1240 ff.
69. Cf. ch. 2, n. 26, above.

dangerous domestic crises between *auctoritas senatus*, *consulare imperium*, and *consensio bonorum* to provide a defense against the *furor* and *audacia* of *improbi*. The senate in those circumstances must be considered to have *summum consilium*, the consuls *summum imperium*, and the people the duty to unite in full support of both. This can only mean that the senate becomes the state's supreme deliberative body, that the consuls are given unrestricted executive authority to implement the senate's directions, and that all necessity to consult or otherwise involve the people in decision-making is suspended. There is a clear distinction between the terms *consilium* and *imperium*, *consilium* signifying the power to formulate policy, *imperium* to execute it, a distinction maintained whenever Cicero juxtaposes these two words. Both powers became supreme following passage of the ultimate decree and left no role in government for the people who were required to accept without question the actions of senate and consuls. In abeyance, therefore, were the functions assigned to the people under such statutes as the Porcian and Valerian laws and the *Lex Sempronia* of 123. Cicero on several occasions explicitly affirms this fact, insisting that the decree empowered magistrates summarily to suppress, without regard for the normal processes of law or for the normal curbs on their *imperium*, those who were perceived to be endangering the *salus reipublicae*.[70]

He would not therefore agree with modern historians who hold that the ultimate decree had no effect on the laws of the state or on the legal position of those to whom it was addressed. Equally he would not agree with those who consider that the decree established a quasi-dictatorship in the persons of the magistrates. The role of the senate did not, in Cicero's view, end when it passed the *consultum ultimum*. It continued as the body with *summum consilium*, and consequently it continued as the director of the consul's subsequent actions, and a consul might act under authority of the decree only if he knew that he was carrying out the wishes of the senate, for it was the senate, and not the consuls, that was placed in supreme command as a result of the *consultum ultimum*.

This does not mean that Cicero would insist that the consuls should consult the senate about every step they proposed to take, for that

---

70. *Rab.* 2–4, 34. Cf. *Mil.* 70. *Cat.* 1.4. *Phil.* 5.34. *Att.* 10.8.8. For the contrast between *consilium* and *imperium* cf. *Leg.* 3.8–9. *Rep.* 2.50.

would destroy the advantages of swift action, which was the whole purpose of the decree. Normally the mandate from the senate ordering them to take whatever steps were necessary for the safety of the state would be a sufficient guide; Cicero would merely maintain that the senate remained the ultimate source of reference in situations that required deliberation.

In summary, Cicero held that the *senatus consultum ultimum* was an extraordinary machinery of government whereby, in dangerous internal crises, sovereign power in the state was temporarily assumed by the senate. This body issued a proclamation to the executive officers of the government empowering them to deal with the threat to the public safety unimpeded by the restrictions imposed by law on their *imperium*. The senate remained, however, the sovereign authority and the ultimate source of reference in situations that required deliberation. To it belonged the power and the duty of formulating policy, and, by the same token, to it belonged the responsibility for action taken under its direction.

That this represented Cicero's concept of the ultimate decree is confirmed by his actions in dealing with the Catilinarian conspirators in December 63. After obtaining documentary evidence of treasonable intent on the part of five leading conspirators, he had them arrested and brought before the senate. He presented irrefutable evidence that the prisoners were in alliance with Catiline, were planning murder and arson, and were inviting foreign troops to invade the country. The senate decreed thanks to him for having delivered the state from danger, voted a *supplicatio* to the gods, and ordered the prisoners kept in custody. Cicero, though he believed that the swift execution of the conspirators was essential to the safety of the state, decided to refer the question of their punishment to the senate, and he declared his intention of abiding by its judgment. The senate voted the death penalty and he had all five men executed.[71]

His action in consulting the senate is generally viewed as an attempt to lessen the risks of a controversial decision by sheltering behind the authority of that prestigious body, and it is argued to have in no way affected his legal responsibility for the executions, and by some possibly

71. *Cat.* 3.4–15; 4.6. Sallust, *Catiline* 40–54. Plutarch, *Cicero* 18–22. Dio 37.34–36. Appian, *BC* 2.4–6.

to have exposed him to charges of having violated the *Lex Sempronia*, since he could be said to have used the senate as a capital *iudicium*.[72] But, according to Cicero's concept of the decree, controversial decisions were the right and responsibility of the senate, the body with *summum consilium*, and consultation of it in the situation in which he found himself after the arrest of the conspirators was constitutionally the proper and necessary course. He had in custody the leaders of a dangerous plot, and he believed their execution to be necessary for its quick suppression. At the same time, extraordinary action under the authority of the ultimate decree had never been taken in the past against Roman citizens except when they had been caught in overt acts of hostility against the state. To execute citizens without trial merely for their intentions would constitute, in the words of Caesar, *genus poenae novum*.[73] On the other hand, to let them live might endanger the state. Cicero faced an unprecedented situation which required deliberation, and consequently he referred the matter for decision to the state's supreme deliberative body.

This is the reasoning that underlies all of his many subsequent allusions to his handling of the Catilinarian crisis. He insisted that the punishment and the sentencing of the conspirators were the duty of the senate, and that his role as consul was merely to implement the decisions of that body. He berated his enemies for the confusion of responsibility which they sought to create, and his position on that responsibility never varies. When Piso accused him of cruelty because of the executions he replied that the accusation was being leveled at the senate, not at the consul, who merely obeyed the senate: *nam relatio illa salutaris et diligens fuerat consulis, animadversio quidem et iudicium senatus.* He gave practically the same answer twelve years later to a similar charge by Antony: *nam comprehensio sontium mea, animadversio senatus fuit.*[74]

Cicero's interpretation of the *consultum ultimum* was in harmony

72. Cf. Strachan-Davidson, *Cicero*, 154–55. E. G. Hardy, *The Catilinarian Conspiracy in Its Context* (Oxford 1924), 85–111. F. F. Abbott, "The Constitutional Argument in the Fourth Catilinarian" *CJ* 2 (1906–07), 123–25. G. W. Botsford, "The Legality of the Trial and Condemnation of the Catilinarian Conspirators" *CW* 6 (1912–13), 130–32. Lintott, *Violence in Republican Rome*, 165.

73. Sallust, *Catiline* 51.18.

74. *Pis.* 14. *Phil.* 2.18. Cf. *Fam.* 5.2.8. *Sulla* 21. *Planc.* 89. *Sest.* 145.

with, and helps further to illustrate, his general belief that the senate should have control of decision-making in government, and that the magistrates should serve as its *ministri*. There is a good deal of evidence also that his view was not merely a subjective assessment of the decree derived from his general political theory, but was representative, as were so many of his views, of the common attitude of the bulk of the ruling class of his day. Sallust certainly believed that the decree had effects on the legal powers of magistrates; he presents it as a machinery whereby *potestas maxima* is entrusted to the magistrates *per senatum more Romano,* legitimizing actions otherwise forbidden unless approved by the people. In 58 Pompey declared his willingness to take arms against even a tribune if the consuls led the way backed by the authority of a *senatus consultum.* The *Cinnani* resorted to the decree against Sulla in 83, and no challenger of its use seems ever to have denied that it was a constitutionally valid proclamation of a state of emergency which legally entitled the magistrates to take extraordinary action against citizens in dealing with the danger.[75]

That the senate was also acknowledged to have a continuing and sovereign role in such emergencies is likewise strongly indicated in the ancient evidence. Frequently a *consultum ultimum* was later followed by another decree designating certain citizens as *hostes*, a declaration which legitimized summary extinction of those named and confiscation of their property. As in the case of the *consultum ultimum*, the validity of these declarations was never disputed, and they were employed by both foes and friends of the senate in the first century. Since the only conceivable purpose for such decrees after a *consultum ultimum* had been passed was to specify more precisely the source of the danger, or to clarify the status of *seditiosi* who had been defeated or captured and were no longer directly threatening the state, the practice clearly illustrates that the senate was viewed as the continuing ultimate decision-making body in situations where the course to be pursued was not indicated by the mandate of the ultimate decree.[76]

75. Sallust, *Catiline* 29.2–3, 51.25, 55.6. Caesar, *BC* 1.7.5. Cf. Gelzer, *Caesar,* 50–51.

76. *Hostis* declarations were made in 88, 87, 83, 77, 63, and 43. Cf. J. Bleicken, *Senatsgericht und Kaisergericht* (Göttingen 1962), 22 ff. R. A. Bauman, *Athenaeum* 52 (1974), 271–93. Lintott, *Violence in Republican Rome*, 155 ff. Not all of the *hostis* declarations were preceded by a *consultum ultimum,* a further indication that the senate was recognized to have the right to initiate supralegal action against citizens.

The record of the debate on the Catilinarian conspirators suggests the same conclusion. No questioning of the legality of Cicero's referral to the senate of the matter of the conspirators' fate and no questioning of the senate's right to decide the issue are reported. Cicero's handling of the affair won the approval of all the *consulares*, of the consuls-elect, and of the staunch constitutionalist, M. Cato. M. Brutus, nephew of Cato, when writing a biography of his uncle almost twenty years later, singled out Cicero's action in consulting the senate for special praise, and not long afterwards he again plainly set forth his view of the constitutional proprieties in such situations when, as proconsul of Macedonia, Achaea, and Illyricum, he refused to make any decision about the status or fate of C. Antonius, whom he had defeated and captured, and asserted, although the *consultum ultimum* had been passed and had clearly been directed primarily against the Antonii, that judgment on citizens who had escaped death in battle belonged either to the senate or the people.[77]

Even more significant, Caesar, the avowed *popularis* and opponent of senatorial supremacy, took a prominent part in the debate on the fate of the conspirators and made no protest about the senate's sitting in judgment on citizens accused of capital crimes and no suggestion that the matter should be referred to the criminal courts. Instead, he proposed that the property of the conspirators should be confiscated and they themselves imprisoned in the strongest of the muncipalities, and that no one should thereafter bring their case before senate or people under pain of being considered a public enemy. He argued for this penalty in preference to execution, not on strictly legal grounds, but for the reasons that the punishment of death was contrary to Roman practice and tradition, would provoke unhealthy reactions, and would set a dangerous precedent. His own proposal was in fact as plainly a violation of the laws as the death penalty, and his entire posture in the debate was a clear acknowledgment by him that the senate had sovereign power over citizens in such circumstances, and, as Cicero was careful to point out, an admission that laws protecting citizens' rights, such as the *Lex Sempronia*, did not apply.[78]

77. Sallust, *Catiline* 50–53. Plutarch, *Cicero* 20.3–21.4. Dio 37.35.4–36.3. Appian, *BC* 2.6. *Cat.* 4.10–12. *Att.* 12.21.1. *Phil.* 2.12–14. *Ad Brut.* 1.4.2. The *consultum ultimum* had been passed at the end of January 43. Dio 46.31.2.

78. Sallust, *Catiline* 51. *Cat.* 4.10. Dio 37.36. Plutarch, *Caesar* 7.5–8.2. Plutarch indicates that Caesar's proposal was meant as a temporary arrangement

Finally, the manner in which the *consultum ultimum* evolved would also seem to indicate that its designed effect was to give sovereign control of the state to the senate in situations of unusual danger. From the beginning of the Republic the Romans had believed in the need for some kind of extraordinary machinery of government which would go into operation in times of extreme emergency and permit quick, decisive action impossible under normal circumstances because of the restrictive laws by which their society protected itself against the unchecked and arbitrary use of power on the part of its rulers. Until the end of the third century B.C. this machinery was provided by an extraordinary magistracy—the dictatorship. This official, nominated by a consul to a six-month term when the state was seriously threatened by external wars or internal disorders, was exempt from many of the restrictions that limited the consular *imperium*; he had no colleague, was exempt, at least in the field, from *provocatio*, was in practice not subject to tribunician veto, and apparently could not be held accountable for his actions. Theoretically, the right to appoint a dictator belonged to the consuls, but eventually it became the regular and accepted practice for the senate to decide when a situation was grave enough to warrant the nomination of a dictator, and even to determine the nominee.[79]

But after the Second Punic War the dictatorship fell into disuse, and the senate sought other means of coping with serious domestic emergencies. The first expedient attempted was the establishment of special *quaestiones* headed by the consuls and endowed with inappellable jurisdiction to pass capital sentences on citizens, but this practice was terminated by the *Lex Sempronia* of 123, which forbade the establishment of any capital *quaestio* except by decree of the people.[80] Subsequently, the *consultum ultimum*, a far more drastic emergency measure which imparted *summum imperium* rather than *summum iudicium* to the magistrates, became the regular substitute for the dictatorship whenever

---

until the war against Catiline was ended, but this is plainly contradicted by the evidence of Cicero and Sallust. Cf. Gelzer, *Caesar*, 50 ff. Lintott, *Violence in Republican Rome*, 169 ff.

79. Later the dictator became subject to *provocatio* (Festus 216, Lindsay), and the tribunes also claimed the right to question his actions (Livy 27.6.5). Cf. Plaumann, *Klio* 13 (1913), 353 ff. Mommsen, *Römisches Staatsrecht*, 2.164.

80. Special *quaestiones* were set up in 186, 180, 138, and 132. Livy 39.8–19; 40.37. *Brut.* 85–88. *Am.* 37. Val. Max. 4.7.1.

a domestic crisis erupted which seemed to call for extraordinary measures.

The question which immediately suggests itself is why the senate abandoned completely the old, constitutionally defined institution of the dictatorship for the vague, constitutionally controversial machinery of the ultimate decree; and the obvious answer is that it was reluctant, once it gained a firm ascendancy, to endanger its control by creating a magistracy of such power and independence, just as it was reluctant to bestow any extraordinary commands which might produce an individual with the power or preeminence to threaten the collective supremacy of the *nobilitas*.[81] It is clear, therefore, that the *consultum ultimum* was not viewed as creating a quasi-dictatorship, but as a means whereby extraordinary measures could be taken in crises without the establishment of any supreme magistracy. The senate, by conferring unusual authority on the regular magistrates without giving them any new office with defined constitutional powers, made itself the sole source of the magistrates' added *potestas* and its mandate the sole justification for extraordinary magisterial action. The magistrates, in consequence, far from being sovereign, had no real independence in the use of their added power, since they could claim justification for activity normally beyond the jurisdiction of their office only in so far as they could show that they were acting as the senate's ministers and carrying out its orders. The senate had thus devised a means whereby unrestricted action was made possible in serious crises but under the direct control and supervision of itself.

The *consultum ultimum* would be an inexplicable development if its only effect was to produce the dictatorship in a new guise, and, even without the clear testimony of Cicero, it is apparent that the decree was designed from the beginning to substitute in times of danger the sovereignty of the senate for the sovereignty of individuals. It is apparent too that the majority of Romans viewed it in this way and accepted it as a valid constitutional weapon in the management of internal crises. No *lex* confirmed the senate's supremacy in such situations; the power was usurped, but since the usurpation was, to some degree at least, ratified by the acquittal of Opimius, and afterwards passed unchallenged, it

81. The senate's aversion to the bestowal of unusual *potestas* on individuals is well documented in the late Republic. Cf. Wirszubski, *Libertas as a Political Idea*, 61 ff. Velleius 2.28. Dio 36.34.

gradually became an accepted part of the *mos Romanus* and, in the manner of unwritten constitutions, assumed the force of law.

If, as seems likely, Cicero's listing of his consular speeches in a letter to Atticus in 60 presents them in chronological order, the next important political battle of his consulship after the trial of Rabirius concerned the tribunician proposal to restore their political rights to the sons of those proscribed by Sulla. The bill fitted well into the general design of tribunician enterprises in 63 to achieve reform and influence by discrediting the rule of the Sullan oligarchy and rallying the aggrieved or discontented, and it continued the several efforts of the preceding years to highlight wrongdoing in the Sullan era and injustices in Sulla's *acta*. The tribune who proposed the measure is not named in the sources, but Caesar, who in 64 had taken the lead in prosecuting *Sullani* accused of having assassinated citizens proscribed by Sulla, is not surprisingly mentioned as a leading supporter.[82]

Cicero took a firm stand in opposition to the proposal. His speech has been lost, but the spirit and substance of it have been preserved in allusions to it in Quintilian and Pliny the Elder. His tone was one of conciliation and entreaty. He freely admitted the justice of the measure, and the harshness of excluding from public office the children of distinguished men; but he argued that the constitution depended so essentially on Sulla's enactments that any interference with them would threaten the entire *respublica*, and that the general good of the state must prevail over even admittedly just claims of individual citizens. Cicero was once again walking the strictly conservative road, reiterating the sentiments of the oligarchy on the issue of Sulla's *acta* and the oft-proclaimed conservative doctrine that repeal of laws or reversal of legal decisions was a certain sign of political disintegration. Once again, also, he succeeded in isolating and defeating the advocates of change by combining sympathy for the aim of the reform with a basic plea for stability and peace through preservation of the status quo. The bill failed, though the manner of its demise is unrecorded. Pliny's allusion to it, however, implies that all support for it evaporated after Cicero's speech, and it is likely that it was withdrawn.[83]

82. *Att.* 2.1.3. Velleius 2.43.4. Cf. Gruen, *Last Generation*, 414 ff.

83. Quintilian 11.1.85. Pliny, *NH* 7.117. Dio 37.25.3. Plutarch, *Cicero* 12.1. *Pis.* 4. In the *In Pisonem* Cicero gives an additional reason for his opposition to the bill, the fear that opening the magistracies to embittered citizens would

The other recorded actions belonging to the first half of Cicero's consulship show a continuing close association with the conservative *nobilitas* and consistent and energetic pursuit of the aims set forth in the Rullan speeches to defeat the reformist *improbi* and preserve and revitalize the *vetus respublica.* He successfuly resisted efforts to reduce or cancel debts, successfully defended C. Calpurnius Piso, the consul of 67, accused of extortion in Gaul by Caesar, who was again advertising his sympathy for the Transpadani, helped secure his long-awaited triumph for Lucullus, and persuaded the senate to vote an unprecedented ten-day thanksgiving in honor of Pompey, following the latter's announcement of the death of Mithridates and the end of the Mithridatic war, a proposal fully supported by the oligarchy in an apparent effort to outdo the tribunes and Caesar, who were proposing to bestow a variety of extravagant honors on Pompey. Cicero also enacted one piece of legislation, a bribery bill increasing penalties and extending the range of activities that constituted *ambitus.* The law was strongly advocated by conservative elements in the senate, notably Cicero's close friend and a consular candidate in 63, Servius Sulpicius Rufus, and it was chiefly designed to curb the electoral tactics of Catiline, who was once again aggressively seeking the consulship.[84]

Cicero and Catiline

Catiline went down to defeat once more in 63 and proceeded to organize his celebrated conspiracy. His actions and designs were to occupy most of Cicero's attention during the remainder of his consulship. His confrontation with Catiline and his suppression of him and of his chief associates Cicero regarded as the highest achievement of his political life, a triumph of watchful energy and effective mobilization of *boni* against violent, revolutionary *improbi*, and the affair has obvious importance in any evaluation of Cicero's statesmanship in 63. The

---

endanger the constitution. For the conservative attitude toward the repeal of laws and legal decisions cf. *Leg. Agr.* 2.10. *Verr.* 2.5.12. *Sulla* 63.

84. *Off.* 2.84. *Cat.* 2.18. Dio 37.25. *Flacc.* 98. Sallust, *Catiline* 49.2. Plutarch, *Lucullus* 37.1–2; *Cato Min.* 29.3–4. *Mur.* 3, 5, 37, 47, 69, 89. *Acad.* 2.3. *Prov. Cons.* 27. Velleius 2.40.4. Dio 37.21.4. Cicero also attempted to implement a ban on *liberae legationes*, but the move was vetoed. A compromise was then worked out, limiting such appointments to one year. *Leg.* 3.18.

facts, however, are obscured by the tendentious nature of the evidence, which comes chiefly from Cicero himself, who excelled in vilification of his enemies and had a vested interest in magnifying the threat he had averted. The other major source for the conspiracy, the monograph of Sallust, is similarly suspect, written with the purpose of presenting Catiline as a memorable example of the moral degeneration of the late Republic and its doleful consequences. Modern historians have not surprisingly reacted to such a tradition with varying degrees of skepticism, and debate continues as to whether the affair was a broad-based plot which seriously threatened the *respublica* or a storm in a tea cup massively inflated by Cicero's powers of invective and penchant for self-glorification and hyperbole, and by Sallust's moralizing historiography. The following pages will reexamine the evidence and seek to determine in particular the dimensions and objectives of the conspiracy, and the political purposes and concerns that directed Cicero's handling of it.[85]

Accounts of the Catilinarian conspiracy generally and properly begin with an analysis of Catiline's political background and his early career and associations. The record is meager and unsatisfactory, but sufficient to rebut decisively Sallust's presentation of him as a man of unrelieved viciousness, afflicted with an inbred craving for the extreme and intent since the time of Sulla on seizing control of the state and establishing a *regnum.*[86]

Catiline belonged to a distinguished patrician *gens* which traced its ancestry back to a companion of Aeneas, and his family, though no member of it had reached the consulship in the late Republic, had remained active in politics and with considerable success.[87] Catiline

85. The bibliography on the conspiracy is very extensive. Some of the more important accounts are: C. John, "Die Entstehungsgeschichte der catilinarischen Verschworung" *Jahrb Cl Phil* Supp. 8 (1876), 703–819. Hardy, *Catilinarian Conspiracy.* Syme, *Sallust,* 60–137. Rice Holmes, *Roman Republic,* 1.253–83. A. Kaplan, *Catiline. The Man and His Role in the Roman Revolution* (New York 1968). Yavetz, *Historia* 12 (1963), 485–99. For a fuller bibliography cf. N. Criniti, "Studi recenti su Catilina e la sua congiura" *Aevum* 41 (1967), 370–95.
86. Sallust, *Catiline* 5.4–8.
87. Virgil, *Aen.* 5.121. Catiline's great-grandfather distinguished himself in the Second Punic War and reached the praetorship. His grandfather was a *legatus* of Aemilius Paullus and a commander at Pydna; his father held a quaestorship in the nineties but died soon afterwards. Pliny, *NH* 7.104–06. Livy 32.31.6; 33.21.9; 44.40.5. Cf. Broughton, *MRR,* 2.13.

himself began his public service as a member of the *consilium* of Pompeius Strabo in 89. He joined Sulla in the civil war of the late eighties and won his confidence and respect sufficiently to be awarded the high position of a *legatus*.[88] Subsequently, he embarked on a political career which, prior to his campaigns for the consulship, was by all indications devoid of extremist stands or radical associations and was pursued with reliance only on the conventional *opes* of the *nobilis*. No involvement in the constant and often turbulent agitation of the late seventies is alleged even by his most hostile traducers in the ancient tradition. The great purge of the senate by the censors of 70 did not include him, and in the very next year he won election to the praetorship. Cicero, in his well-known characterization of him in the *Pro Caelio*, presents him as a noted soldier, a man of initiative and industry, a charismatic figure who spared no effort to win *amici* and *gratia*, who professed devotion to the *boni* and had many of them as his friends. Cicero himself regarded him as a *bonus civis* in the mid-sixties and even contemplated defending him with a view to securing his political friendship.[89]

Catiline's *amicitia* with leading *boni* is also attested elsewhere, and it is not surprising in view of the antiquity and distinction of his family. Catulus came to his support in 73 when Clodius, who was launching a broad attack on Roman priests and priestesses, linked his name to charges of *incestum* being made against the Vestal Fabia. The consul L. Manlius Torquatus defended him in 65 in his trial for extortion as governor of Africa. Several unnamed *consulares* also appeared for him in the extortion case, as they did again in 64 when he was in court once more, this time on a murder charge associated with the Sullan proscriptions. He had also married well. His wife, Aurelia Orestilla, was a daughter of Aufidius Orestes, who came from a consular family and had himself achieved the consulship in 71.[90]

There was another side, however, to Catiline's character and to his

---

88. *ILS* 8888. Cf. Cichorius, *Römische Studien*, 172–74. Sallust, *Hist.* 1.46, Maur. Cf. Broughton, *MRR*, 2.72.

89. *Cael.* 10–14.

90. Asconius 87, 90–91, Clark. Orosius 6.3.1. Sallust, *Catiline* 15.1, 35.1. *Com. Pet.* 10. *Cat.* 3.9. Plutarch, *Cato Min.* 19.3. *Att.* 1.2.1; 1.16.9. *Cael.* 14. *Sulla* 81. *Pis.* 95. For Aurelia cf. Syme, *Sallust*, 85. B. A. Marshall, "The Date of Catiline's Marriage to Aurelia Orestilla" *Riv Fil* 105 (1977), 151–54. It does not appear that Catiline was formally charged with *incestum* in 73. Cf. Shackleton Bailey, *Letters to Atticus*, 1.319.

relationship with the aristocracy. It is clear that from an early stage he had a reputation for ruthlessness, rapacity, and immorality, and that there were narrow limits to the respect and support he commanded from the ruling class as a whole. Charges of cruelty and wanton killing in the civil war, of adultery and murder in his domestic life, of sacrilege and general debauchery abound in every ancient allusion to him, even in the *Pro Caelio*, where Cicero is concerned to emphasize the positive aspects of his character. Due allowance must, of course, be made for the distortions, exaggerations, and additions of the forensic and political invective which forms the foundation of the tradition, but even the allegations of invective, like all other forms of propaganda, must have some level of credibility to be effective, and all the varied charges of criminality and immorality, particularly those in sources such as the *In Toga Candida* and the *Commentariolum Petitionis*, which predate the conspiracy, can hardly be dismissed as total fabrications.[91]

Besides, the record of Catiline's various entanglements in scandals and criminal prosecutions affirms that there was some basis for at least some of the accusations commonly leveled against him. Whatever the truth of his alleged involvement with the Vestal Fabia, his accuser obviously saw him as a credible figure around whom to build charges of *incestum*. His trial in 64 indicates that there was at the least a prima facie case to substantiate the stories of his slaughtering of citizens in the civil war of the late eighties. Finally, his depredations in Africa, which led to his prosecution for extortion in 65 and which had brought protests to the senate from the Africans and senatorial censure of his behavior even before his term was over, were obviously of extreme dimensions and suggest a degree of unscrupulousness and greed well above the ordinary, even by the standards of the late Republic.[92]

It is further evident that Catiline was held in low esteem by many of his peers, and that, despite his associations with *boni* and *amicitia* with individual *nobiles*, he inspired little confidence and had little solid support among the aristocracy as a whole. The senate's willingness to heed the complaints of provincials and to condemn his behavior in Africa even before he left office is clear testimony that, by the mid-sixties at the latest, he had accumulated considerable distrust and

91. Asconius 83–93, Clark. *Com. Pet.* 9–10. Cf. *Cat.* 1.14. Sallust, *Catiline* 15. Broughton, *MRR*, 2.72.
92. Asconius 85, Clark.

disfavor within the senatorial order. Aristocratic *invidia* is manifest again in the action of the consul Volcacius Tullus in 66, who, after consultation with a *consilium* of *principes*, blocked Catiline's bid for the consulship of 65 by refusing to accept his *professio*, apparently giving as the reason impending charges of extortion. The decision of the consul and his *consilium* was a signal rebuke, and a serious political blow which not only prevented Catiline from standing for the consulship *suo anno*, but also closed to him a major avenue of escape from the threat of a conviction in the extortion court.[93]

The next important recorded development in Catiline's political career was the association of his name with the plot which has become known as the First Catilinarian Conspiracy. The affair is notoriously obscure and has been endlessly debated, with recent salutary tendencies to regard the varying and improbable accounts of it in the ancient sources as largely unfounded creations of invective and propaganda. Nothing happened and nothing was discovered to have been planned, and all that can be said about the matter with any certainty is that a rumor arose at the end of 66 that a plot had been hatched to murder the consuls and the *principes* of the senate on the first of January 65. The names linked to the conspiracy were Catiline, his close friend Cn. Piso, and P. Sulla and P. Autronius, the ousted consuls-elect of 65.[94]

93. Sallust, *Catiline* 18.2–3. Asconius 66, 85, 89, Clark. Debate continues as to whether Catiline sought to be a candidate at the original elections or at the second elections following the convictions of Autronius and Sulla. Sallust relates that he became a candidate only after the convictions, but his account, which presents Catiline as a *reus* and gives his failure to hand in his name in time as the unlikely reason for rejection of his *professio*, inspires little confidence, and it is not confirmed by Asconius, whose remarks imply that Catiline had sought to be a candidate at the regular elections. It seems most unlikely that Catiline, who had no guarantee that his term in Africa would be extended, and who was very eager to secure the consulship, would have decided not to seek the office *suo anno*, and, if he had made such a decision, it is difficult to explain why he would have abruptly changed his mind after the convictions. Sumner ("The Consular Elections for 66 B.C." *Phoenix* 19 [1965], 226–31) attempts an explanation, but it is not convincing. Cf. M. Mello, "Sallustio e le elezioni consolari del 66 a.C." *PP* 18 (1963), 36 ff.

94. Asconius 92, Clark. *Cat.* 1.15. *Mur.* 81. *Sulla* 10, 67–68, 81. Sallust, *Catiline* 18–19. Suetonius, *Julius* 9. Dio 36–44. The bibliography on this affair is very large; most noteworthy are the following: H. Frisch, "The First Catilinarian Conspiracy. A Study in Historical Conjecture" *CM* 9 (1948), 10–36. E. J. Phillips, "Asconius' *magni homines*" *RhM* 116 (1973), 353–57. Syme, *Sallust*, 86–101. Strasburger, *Caesars Eintritt*, 107–09. Ciaceri, *Cicerone*, 1.144–50. Rice Holmes,

The rumors were taken seriously by the leaders of the senate and pre-
cautionary and investigative steps were taken. It would appear that
there was a high level of nervousness in the state at the time, induced
no doubt by the divisive effects of sharply contested consular elections
in 66, followed by the indictment of the successful candidates on
charges of bribery and their conviction in a trial which was twice disrupted by serious violence. Many portents were reported in 65, according to Cicero, and the Etruscan soothsayers were consulted and predicted
murder, civil war, and the destruction of the city and the empire if the
gods were not placated. Games were held for ten days and various other
expiatory measures undertaken.[95]

It was a fertile atmosphere for rumors, but that no evidence of a
specific design by Catiline, Piso, and the convicted consuls-elect to
overthrow the government was uncovered and no credence whatever
given to the story is decisively attested by several factors. The consul
Torquatus and several *consulares*, prime targets of the alleged plot,
came to Catiline's defense in his trial for extortion in 65, and Torquatus

---

Roman Republic, 1.446–47. E. T. Salmon, "Catiline, Crassus, and Caesar" *AJP*
56 (1935), 302–16. Seager, *Historia* 13 (1964), 338–47. Gruen, *CP* 64 (1969),
20–24. Hardy, *Catilinarian Conspiracy*, 12–20. Phillips, *Latomus* 29 (1970), 601–
03. That the names of Catiline, Piso, Sulla, and Autronius were associated with
the plot from the beginning seems clear from *Sulla* 11, 67, 81. Cf. Asconius 92,
Clark. Sallust speaks of two plots, the second planned for February 5, but this
has no support in Cicero, who, in numerous allusions, never speaks of more than
one attempt at a coup in 66–65. Recently efforts have been made to connect the
story of the conspiracy to disturbances in late 66 and early 65 connected with
the trial of Manilius. The second plot reported by Sallust conceivably had its
origin in the disorders at Manilius's trial, but the main story cannot be explained
as an outgrowth of the protests in 66 surrounding Manilius's prosecution. No
ancient source makes such a connection. The *contio* at which the demonstrations
on behalf of Manilius took place probably was held earlier than December 29, the
day on which Catiline was alleged to have been seen armed in the forum preparing
for the murder of the consuls and *principes*. Further, if the rumors of plotting
were related in any way to that *contio*, Cicero would surely have been included
as one of its targets, and he would not have failed to mention that occasion in his
innumerable listings of the times Catiline had tried to kill him. That Catiline was
a friend of Manilius also remains doubtful, and it is certain that Catiline's chief
associate, Cn. Piso, was not. Piso was a notorious enemy of Pompey, and he had
prosecuted Manilius in 69 or 68. Val. Max. 6.2.4.

95. *Sulla* 10 ff., 15. *Cat.* 3.19. *Div.* 1.19. Dio 37.9. Dio relates that the consuls
were given a bodyguard (36.44.4–5). He also states that the senate proposed to
take further action against the conspirators, but was prevented by a veto. No
other source mentions this development, however, and its truth remains questionable.

indicated that he did not believe the rumors of Catiline's involvement in a conspiracy. Cicero contemplated defending Catiline in the same case, hoping to enlist his political support, and obviously not viewing him as a violent revolutionary. Hortensius, reportedly another prime target of the plotters and a leading figure in the deliberations which followed the reports of a conspiracy, defended P. Sulla in 62. Finally, Cn. Piso, in the very year of his alleged conspiratorial designs, and though he was only a quaestor, was dispatched by the senate with propraetorian *imperium* to govern Nearer Spain.[96]

The information about a conspiracy which was produced in 65 was obviously viewed with total skepticism even by those who had most reason to fear such plotting, and, as Cicero once remarked, the reports should not have been given more credence when old than they received when new. That they ever were seriously accepted was partly due to Cicero himself, who exploited them in his invectives against Catiline, and partly to the real conspiracy in 63, which resurrected and made more credible old accusations of extremism, and encouraged accretions.[97]

Catiline may safely be considered innocent of conspiratorial intrigue in 66–65, but the association of his name with the rumors of conspiracy points once more to estrangement from the senatorial establishment. His trial for extortion, which took place around August 65, adds further to the evidence for such estrangement. His noble friends came to his aid, as they were bound to do *in summis eius periculis*, but the senators on the jury voted solidly against him, and he managed to gain acquittal only through the purchased support of jurors from the *equites* and *tribuni aerarii.*[98]

Freed at last from the legal difficulties which had halted his political career for more than a year, Catiline became a candidate for the consulship of 63, and, in a course consistent with the many indications of continuing antagonism between him and much of the senatorial order, he moved decisively to build support for his candidacy outside the

96. *Sulla* 11 ff., 81. *Att.* 1.2.1. Sallust, *Catiline* 19.1. Asconius 92, Clark. Dio 36.44.5. Suetonius, *Julius* 9.3.

97. *Sulla* 81.

98. *Sulla* 81. Asconius 89, Clark. Metellus Pius testified against him. Asconius 87, Clark. Clodius is generally presented as a collusive prosecutor on the evidence of *Att.* 1.2.1, *Pis.* 23, *Har. Resp.* 42, and Asconius 87, Clark, and there seems little reason to dispute the ancient tradition. For an opposite view cf. Gruen, *Athenaeum* 49 (1971), 59–62.

senatorial power structure. He formed a *coitio* with the disreputable C. Antonius, who was chiefly known for his debts and depravity and had been expelled from the senate in 70, and, as already argued, they both became allies of Crassus and Caesar and conducted an aggressive campaign marked by audacious bribery.[99]

Catiline narrowly lost, and he proceeded to launch a fresh campaign for the consulship of 62. This time, impelled by the failure of his earlier efforts and by the particular embitterment of defeat at the hands of the man he liked to call an *inquilinus*, he adopted a far more extreme electoral strategy, assailing the Sullan oligarchy and their hold on wealth and power and proclaiming himself the leader of the *miseri*, dedicated to the alleviation of their grievances by radical transformation of the political and economic order.[100]

The constituency he appealed to and rallied was numerous and varied. He attracted the support of much of the *iuventus*, the *adulescentes* of the upper classes, who were very active in politics in the Ciceronian period. They tended to act together and, because of their influence in the equestrian centuries, they were valuable political allies. In general, they took liberal stands on political and social issues, and they were frequently at variance with the conservative *nobilitas* in the sixties and fifties. Cicero experienced their hostility immediately after his consulship in the controversy that arose over the execution of the Catilinarian conspirators; they rallied behind Clodius in 61 when the senate tried to secure his conviction for *incestum* after he was seen in the house of Caesar during celebration of the rites of the Bona Dea, and in 49 they once again showed disenchantment with the status quo and took the side of Caesar in large numbers. Financial troubles added to the willingness of many *iuvenes* to join Caesar, and similar difficulties may have won many of his youthful supporters for Catiline, but it is apparent that the latter's personality and assault on the privileged position of the *pauci* were also powerful lures.[101]

99. There is no convincing evidence that Catiline had revolutionary designs at this stage. That Sallust predated Catiline's plans for an armed coup is now generally agreed (cf. John, *Jahrb Cl Phil* Supp. 8 (1876), 763–77), and it can safely be assumed that Cicero's allegations in speeches such as the *In Toga Candida* were gross exaggerations.

100. Asconius 93–94, Clark. Appian, *BC* 2.2. Sallust, *Catiline* 21.2, 31.7. Plutarch, *Cicero* 14. *Cat.* 2.18. *Mur.* 49–51. *Off.* 2.84. Dio 37.30.2.

101. *Cael.* 10–12. *Mur.* 49. Sallust, *Catiline* 14.4, 17.6. On Caesar and the *iuventus* cf. *Att.* 7.3.5; 7.7.6. Even Quintus's son favored Caesar, as did the son of Hortensius and Cicero's son-in-law, Dolabella. *Att.* 10.4.6; 10.7.3; 7.14.3.

Catiline also secured adherents among ambitious politicians who had suffered affronts to their *dignitas* at the hands of the oligarchy, or who faced a bleak political future because of debts or insufficient material and political resources. Those who can be named include ten members of the senatorial order, six of them *nobiles*. Cicero's colleague, C. Antonius, remained a confidant and supporter of Catiline until Cicero won him over just before the elections in 63 by ceding him the province of Macedonia.[102] Other *nobiles* among Catiline's associates were P. Cornelius Lentulus Sura, C. Cornelius Cethegus, L. Cassius Longinus, and the brothers Publius and Servius Sulla. Lentulus had reached the consulship in 71, but he had been expelled from the senate in 70. By 63 he had managed to reach the praetorship once again, but, obsessed by a desire to emulate the achievements of the more famous members of his illustrious *gens*, he was not content to rely for the success he craved on his dubious standing within the Sullan oligarchy.[103] Cethegus, an ambitious activist, known for his rash and fiery temperament, had made little headway in electoral politics, failing, despite his patrician birth, to get past the quaestorship. Cassius Longinus had been a colleague of Cicero in the praetorship in 66, but his candidacy for the consulship of 63 had foundered early, revealing little likelihood of any further political advancement. The Sullan brothers, though presumably connected with the family of the dictator, had not, so far as is known, progressed beyond the quaestorship and were likely headed for an obscurity unacceptable to men of such distinguished lineage.[104]

The other known supporters of Catiline from the senatorial order were P. Autronius Paetus, of senatorial family, who had been convicted of bribery following his election to the consulship in 66; L. Vargunteius, of senatorial family, who had similarly been convicted of bribery sometime in the mid-sixties; Q. Curius, of senatorial family, who had been

102. Dio 37.25.3, 30.3. Plutarch, *Cicero* 12.3. *Mur.* 49. *Sest.* 8, 12. *Pis.* 5.
103. Plutarch, *Cicero* 17. *Cat.* 3.9–16. Cf. Broughton, *MRR*, 2.166.
104. For Cethegus cf. *Sulla* 70. *Cat.* 3.8, 10, 16; 4.11, 13. Sallust, *Catiline* 17.3, 32.2, 43.3–4, 50.2, 52.33. Plutarch, *Cicero* 19.1–2. For Cassius Longinus cf. *Cat.* 3.14; 4.13. *Sulla* 53, and for the Sullan brothers cf. *Sulla* 6. Sallust, *Catiline* 17.3, 47.1. Another *nobilis*, Calpurnius Bestia, a tribune in 62, is also included by Sallust (*Catiline* 17.3, 43.1) as one of Catiline's intimates and a participant in the later conspiracy. Appian also lists him among the conspirators (*BC* 2.2). Bestia became a leading critic of Cicero's handling of the conspiracy in 62, but Cicero never accused him of being involved in Catiline's schemes, and it seems unlikely that he was. Cf. *Sulla* 31. *Schol. Bob.* 82, 127. *Sest.* 11. Plutarch, *Cicero* 23.1. Syme, *Sallust,* 131 ff.

expelled from the senate in 70; and finally two senators about whom nothing is known aside from their involvement with Catiline, Q. Annius Chilo and M. Porcius Laeca.[105]

Four members of the equestrian order are also attested as leading Catilinarian associates: M. Fulvius Nobilior, of a once illustrious family which had faded into obscurity in the latter half of the second century; P. Gabinius Capito, whose family was praetorian; C. Cornelius, who likely belonged to a senatorial family; and L. Statilius, who was a prominent, activist figure among Catiline's adherents, but whose family background remains obscure.[106]

Such are the recorded names of Catiline's allies within the Roman upper class. They include, however, only those who, like Antonius, were particularly prominent or who later became leaders in the conspiracy, and undoubtedly Catiline had many other supporters among alienated, insolvent, or unsuccessful politicians who sympathized with his attacks on the *pauci* and his call for a more even distribution of wealth and power. Sallust indicates that *complures nobiles* were involved in his schemes, and that he had the sympathy of politicians who were outside the senate's inner circle and who preferred to see the state in turmoil than themselves without power.[107] Certainly Catiline was not afraid to voice his radical views and objectives in the senate itself, and he did so on separate occasions before the elections when attacked by Cato and Cicero, and without senatorial rebuke.[108] Long after the elections, when substantial evidence of a conspiracy was unfolding, Cicero continued to be worried by the number of Catiline's senatorial sympathizers, and in the Second Catilinarian he expressly identified ambitious politicians who were financially oppressed and politically frustrated as one of the major elements in Catiline's following. In his later life he always maintained that in suppressing Catiline

105. For Autronius cf. *Sulla* 7, 10, 17–18, 71. *Brut.* 241; for Vargunteius cf. Sallust, *Catiline* 17.3, 28.1. *Cat.* 1.9. *Sulla* 6, 67; for Curius cf. Sallust, *Catiline* 23.1, 26.3, 28.2; for Chilo cf. *Cat.* 3.14. Sallust, *Catiline* 17.3, 50.4, and for Laeca cf. *Cat.* 1.8; 2.13. *Sulla* 6, 52. Sallust, *Catiline* 17.3, 27.3–4. Florus 2.12.3.
106. *Cat.* 3.6, 9, 12, 14; 4.12, 14. *Sulla* 6, 18, 51–52. Sallust, *Catiline* 17.4, 28.1, 43.2, 47.4, 52.34.
107. Sallust, *Catiline* 17.5, 37.10. Cf. 52.35.
108. *Mur.* 49–51. Plutarch, *Cicero* 14.3–5. Cicero failed to persuade the senate to take any action against Catiline following these exchanges. Dio 37.29.3. Cf. *Cat.* 1.30. *Mur.* 51.

and his movement he had thwarted the designs of a large and formidable body of politicians, and that he genuinely believed the claim is
confirmed by the fact that he deeply feared the vengeance of these
improbi to the end of his life.[109]

Catiline's most numerous supporters, however, came not from the
ranks of faltering or disaffected politicians, but from two other elements, the victims of Sulla and the many in Italy and Rome who lived
continually on the verge of financial ruin, or who had been reduced to
that perilous state by the particularly severe economic problems of the
sixties. Both groups were vigorously in search of remedies in 64 and 63.

Sulla's vengeful and despotic use of victory in the late eighties had
afflicted many citizens. According to Valerius Maximus he proscribed
a total of 4,700 of his opponents, among them many wealthy and distinguished men from all over Italy. The property of the proscribed was
confiscated and their children, in addition to losing their patrimony,
were deprived of their political rights. But Sulla's oppression of his
enemies did not stop with the proscribed and their families. He needed
large areas of land for the settlement of his twenty-three legions, and in
large blocks since he planned to settle his soldiers in colonies. The
estates of the proscribed, which were scattered throughout Italy, went
chiefly to enrich Sulla himself and those who had contributed to his
victory, or they were retained as public land and occupied by the so-
called *possessores.* Sulla, therefore, had to look elsewhere for land for
his colonial settlements, and he found it by confiscating large tracts of
the territory of towns that had fought against him, creating in the
process a second sizable body of aggrieved and impoverished citizens.[110]

As already noted, several efforts were launched in the latter half of
the sixties to redress Sullan injustices, particularly in 63, when two
proposals were put forward—the Rullan land law and the bill to restore
their political rights to sons of the proscribed—which, if implemented,
would have done much to alleviate the major grievances of those who
had suffered ruin at the hands of Sulla. But both of these measures
failed in the first half of 63, and Catiline then became the hope of this
extensive group of frustrated *miseri.* Numbers of them became active

109. *Cat.* 1.30; 2.3, 5, 18–19; 4.6, 20. *Mur.* 79. Cf. *Fam.* 5.6.2. *Att.* 9.1.3;
8.3.5; 8.11d.7; 9.4.2. *Phil.* 2.1. *Sulla* 28–29.
110. Val. Max. 9.2.1. Plutarch, *Sulla* 21. Appian, *BC* 1.95–96. Cf. Brunt,
Italian Manpower, 300–12.

in his campaign for the consulship in 63 and became part of the *exercitus* which, according to Cicero, surrounded him as he conducted his canvass.[111]

Catiline's supporters among those in financial difficulties comprised a more varied and probably still more numerous group. Some of them were men of means, *locupletes* who owned considerable property, but who had accumulated large debts and were unwilling to part with any of their possessions to liquidate them. They supported Catiline in the hope that they could retain their property through the program of *tabulae novae* he was proposing. In this class should most likely be included the many prominent Italians who are attested as supporters of Catiline, the men whom Sallust described as *domi nobiles.*[112]

A second category of financially troubled citizens rallied by Catiline consisted of Sullan colonists and other *agrestes*, both small farmers and farm laborers, who were no longer able to make a living off the land. The indications are that the number of such men was high and that they were in a state of considerable desperation in 63. There is strong and consistent evidence that a high proportion of Sullan settlers failed as farmers, though the reasons were not simply incompetence or extravagance but small holdings, poor land, the devastation caused by the uprisings of Spartacus and Lepidus, conscription, and the general economic recession and scarcity of money which marked the sixties. These same conditions had brought ruin to many other small farmers in all parts of Italy and unemployment to farm laborers, creating a broad rural economic crisis by the time of Cicero's consulship.[113]

The predicament of the insolvent *agrestes* is well illustrated in Sallust's record of a letter which was sent in 63 by one of their leaders, a former Sullan centurion, C. Manlius, to the proconsul Marcius Rex, and which set forth the grievances of men who stood at the mercy of Rome's rigorous debt laws and faced not only the loss of their property

111. *Mur.* 49. Cf. Sallust, *Catiline* 28.4, 37.9.

112. *Cat.* 2.18. Sallust, *Catiline* 17.4. Some of the Italians can be named: the Campanian P. Sittius, the Camertine Septimius, M. Caeparius from Tarracina, T. Volturcius from Croton. Sallust, *Catiline* 21.3, 27.1, 44.3, 45.3–4, 46.3–4, 47.1. *Sulla* 56. *Cat.* 3.4, 8, 14; 4.5. Florus 2.12.9. Appian, *BC* 2.4.

113. Sallust, *Catiline* 16.4, 28.4, 52.15, 58.13. *Mur.* 49. *Cat.* 2.5, 8, 20; 4.6. *Leg. Agr.* 2.68. Appian, *BC* 2.2. There were outbreaks of violence, or threatened outbreaks, at many points throughout the peninsula later in 63. Cf. Brunt, *JRS* 52 (1962), 73; *Italian Manpower*, 310 ff.

but even the loss of their freedom. Catiline had no difficulty in attaching these *miseri* to his following, and his standing with them was, no doubt, greatly strengthened after proposals to alleviate the plight of debtors were rejected in the first half of 63. Etruria provided the most important support, where Manlius assembled groups from the colonies of Faesulae and Arretium and brought them to Rome to press for Catiline's election to the consulship.[114]

Finally, there was a third element which was moved by financial woes to favor Catiline, the *plebs urbana*, the motley mass of the urban lower class, inflated in the post-Sullan era by drifters from the country, and chiefly composed of *tabernarii*, artisans, laborers, and varied types of chronic ne'er-do-wells. All of them had small resources at the best of times, and all would have felt severely the impact of the general economic problems of the sixties. Catiline, foe of the oligarchy that had repeatedly shown its indifference to the tribulations of the urban proletariat and professed champion of the destitute, had an obvious appeal for the *plebs urbana*, and initially they followed him *en masse*, just as they followed Caesar in 49, hoping for relief from fear and from the oppression of poverty and indebtedness.[115]

Catiline's constituency of *iuvenes*, malcontent politicians, Sullan victims, and the several sizable groups in Rome and Italy afflicted by destitution and deep indebtedness was unquestionably broad-based and numerically formidable. Many elements of it, however, had little power in the timocratic *comitia centuriata*, a fact of which, no doubt, Catiline was well aware, and during his campaign he sought additional backers by resort to bribery on a scale which prompted yet another law on electoral malpractices and brought the threat of a prosecution from Cato. Surrounded by a band of *iuvenes* and by Manlius's battalions from Etruria, he also adopted a threatening pose in his rhetoric and in his dealings with critics and competitors, and it is not improbable that he was planning to use Manlius's men at the elections themselves to overawe his rivals and intimidate their supporters.[116]

114. Sallust, *Catiline* 21.4, 28.4, 33, 57.1. *Mur.* 49. *Cat.* 2.20; 3.14. Plutarch, *Cicero* 14. Appian, *BC* 2.2.
115. Sallust, *Catiline* 37.1, 48.1. *Cat.* 1.12; 2.7–8, 21. Cf. Yavetz, *Latomus* 17 (1958), 500–17; *Historia* 12 (1963), 485–99. For Caesar and the *plebs* cf. *Att.* 7.3.5. *Fam.* 8.13.2; 8.14.3; 8.17.2.
116. *Mur.* 49–51. Dio 37.29.1. Plutarch, *Cicero* 14. *Cat.* 1.11. *Sulla* 51. Sallust, *Catiline* 26.4. It does not follow, however, that he had formed any definite plans

Any coercive designs he may have entertained, however, were thwarted by Cicero, who, exercising his propagandist powers and the resources of the consulship, did much to damage Catiline's electoral prospects in general by a vigorous drive, just before the elections, designed both to undermine his following and to impede any attempt at intimidation of the voters. It was at this time that he neutralized Antonius, on whose support Catiline was counting heavily, by handing over to him the province of Macedonia, and he followed this arrangement with a public renunciation of the other consular province of Cisalpine Gaul, citing as the reason the critical state of the *respublica* and likely reiterating the declarations of the Rullan speeches, where he first announced that he would give up his right to a province to devote all his energies, without the need to conciliate those who might obstruct a provincial assignment, to the preservation of *otium* and the suppression of the *improbi* who threatened it. Soon afterwards, when rumors circulated of revolutionary pledges by Catiline to his followers and of threats against the state, he exploited them to the full and persuaded the senate to postpone the elections so that the reports could be discussed. He did not succeed in getting the senate to take any further action and the elections went ahead, but he continued his efforts to dramatize the extremism of Catiline and to forestall any danger from it by assembling a strong guard of *amici* and *clientes* and by ostentatiously wearing a breastplate when he presided over the *comitia.* He achieved all his objectives. There was no violence, no attempt at intimidation, and Catiline was again defeated.[117]

His second defeat ended Catiline's hopes of winning the consulship by constitutional means and turned his mind to the desperate expedient of an armed coup. To what extent he was forced into this extreme course by the militancy of some of his supporters can never definitely be determined, but it is clear that Manlius and many of his men were

---

at this stage for an armed coup, and in view of the length of time that elapsed between the elections and the first signs of a conspiracy, it is extremely unlikely that he had.

117. *Att.* 2.1.3. *Pis.* 5. *Mur.* 49. *Sulla* 51. *Cat.* 1.11. Dio 37.29. Plutarch, *Cicero* 12.4. Sallust, *Catiline* 26.4. There is some dispute about the exact time at which Cicero neutralized Antonius, but *Att.* 2.1.3 and *Pis.* 5, where he lists his consular achievements chronologically and in both passages places the arrangements about provinces just before the conspiracy, clearly indicate that it was about the middle of 63.

intent on bettering their condition by any means necessary, as were some of Catiline's associates in Rome, and that the decision to initiate an armed insurrection was not wholly Catiline's remains a distinct possibility. In any event, after the elections Manlius went back to Etruria to raise an army among Sullan settlers and Sullan victims, and also among the brigands who abounded in this area, remnants of the armies of the Marians and of Spartacus and Lepidus, who had taken to the *calles* of the Apennines and had never been rounded up.[118] Agents were also dispatched to organize resistance in other areas of Italy, particularly Picenum and Apulia. The first plan formulated called for Manlius to take the field on October 27, his action to be followed by a massacre of *optimates* on October 28. Manlius duly raised the standard of revolt on the appointed day, but the other part of the plan was foiled by Cicero, who, supplied with evidence of the conspirators' designs from letters received by Crassus warning the latter of the impending massacre of *principes*, and with reports of Manlius's activities in Etruria, and possibly with other information provided by a woman named Fulvia, who was the mistress of one of the conspirators, Q. Curius, and was to become an invaluable source of intelligence later in the crisis, he persuaded the senate to pass the *consultum ultimum* on October 21, and he immediately placed guards under the command of the minor magistrates all around the city.[119]

These precautions forced the postponement of the conspirators' plan for the takeover of Rome, and they next directed their efforts against one of the strongest cities in Latium, Praeneste, planning to seize it on November 1. But Cicero got forewarning of this endeavor also, and he forestalled it by placing a garrison in the town. Meanwhile, definite news that Manlius was in revolt in Etruria and reports of uprisings of slaves at Capua and in Apulia brought further senatorial action. Marcius Rex and Metellus Creticus, who were awaiting triumphs outside Rome, were dispatched to Etruria and Apulia respectively. Two praetors, Pompeius Rufus and Metellus Celer, were also given military assignments. Pompeius was sent to Capua and Metellus to Picenum,

118. Sallust, *Catiline* 28.4. On the extent of brigandage in Italy in this period cf. Brunt, *Italian Manpower*, 198, 291, 308–09, 557.

119. Sallust, *Catiline* 27–30. Plutarch, *Cicero* 15. Dio 37.30–31. *Cat.* 1.3, 7–8. Suetonius, *Julius* 17. Cf. Hardy, *Catilinarian Conspiracy*, 49–60.

and both were empowered to raise whatever number of troops was demanded by the emergency.[120]

In early November Catiline decided to take control of the military effort in Etruria, which apparently was making slow headway. At a meeting at the house of Porcius Laeca on November 6, he announced this decision, made arrangements regarding other operations in various parts of Italy, and finalized plans for the conspirators in Rome, where the overthrow of the government was to be accomplished with the aid of incendiarism as well as murder. He also advocated the immediate assassination of Cicero, and two *equites*, Cornelius and Vargunteius, agreed to attempt the murder of the consul at his house the following morning.[121]

Cicero immediately got word of the meeting and of the substance of its decisions from Fulvia and barred his house to the would-be assassins. On the same day he called a meeting of the senate to announce his latest intelligence of Catiline's intrigues. Catiline attended, and Cicero delivered the first of the Catilinarian orations, a vitriolic review and denunciation of Catiline's plans and actions, real and rumored, from 66 onwards, including a detailed description of the proceedings at the house of Laeca the night before. He did not, however, propose to take any action against Catiline himself, and he refused a direct challenge from the latter to lay a decree of banishment before the senate, merely demanding that Catiline leave the city and openly join the revolt in Etruria, of which Cicero asserted he was the real author.[122]

Cicero's strategy was shrewd and carefully calculated. Throughout his consulship, by tireless oratory, he had fought to defeat the purposes and diminish the following of popular leaders in general, and of Catiline in particular, and to gather goodwill and support for his brand of government by ascribing self-seeking and revolutionary motives to all dissentient politicians and by presenting traditional republicanism as the guarantor of peace and the true protector of the people's interests. The conspiracy of Catiline was a fulfillment of his direst predictions of the

120. *Cat.* 1.8. Sallust, *Catiline* 30.
121. *Cat.* 1.8–10; 2.12–13. *Sulla* 52. Plutarch, *Cicero* 16.2. Dio 37.32.3–33.1. Sallust, *Catiline* 27–28.3. R. Seager ("*Iusta Catilinae*" *Historia* 22 [1973], 241–45) doubts the entire story of the meeting at the house of Laeca, but for totally inadequate reasons.
122. Sallust, *Catiline* 31.6. Plutarch, *Cicero* 16.3. *Cat.* 1.20.

extremist aims of the enemies of the *vetus respublica*, an opportune vindication of the basic contentions of his political rhetoric, and he dealt with it carefully so as to extract from it the maximum benefit in his fight to cement *consensio bonorum* and to undermine the power-base of *populares*.

By November his evidence for a conspiracy in Rome still consisted only of rumor and unverifiable reports from unauthoritative sources. He was aware of broad skepticism, real or pretended, about Catiline's revolutionary intent and the danger from it, and, sensitive to the volatility of public opinion and the political hazards of any drastic response to unproven charges or of seemingly tyrannical tactics against a man who commanded the sympathy of a constituency as broad as Catiline's, he was determined to let the conspiracy develop until he could convince the public of its scope and purposes, and win from exposure of the danger and from its suppression the vindication of his beliefs and the entrenchment of his ideal of republicanism.[123]

Accordingly, despite passage of the *senatus consultum ultimum*, he took no unusual steps during October or November to nip the plotting in the bud; Catiline was left unmolested, no arrests were made, no repressive or supralegal measures adopted. Cicero was content to post guards and to wait, while exercising his rhetorical skills on each new report to bolster belief in the existence of a dangerous and vicious plot, and thereby to rally the great body of *boni*, silence the *improbi*, and trim the fringes of Catiline's support. The First Catilinarian was a major effort in this rhetorical offensive, and it had an important effect, as is explicitly stated by Sallust and indicated by the hostile reception which Catiline met from his peers and by his uncharacteristic failure to make any reply. He immediately left Rome, and Cicero continued his verbal attack on November 9 with an address to the people, which repeated the substance of his senatorial speech, exulted in the departure of Catiline, warned the latter's supporters in the city to join him or desist, and pledged easy defeat of all the designs of the conspirators.[124]

When news reached Rome that Catiline had joined Manlius, the

123. Cf. *Cat.* 1.12, 23, 30–32; 2.3–4, 6; 3.4, 27; 4.1, 9, 20 ff. *Sest.* 47.
124. Sallust, *Catiline* 31.6. *Cat.* 1.16; 2.12. Plutarch, *Cicero* 16.3. Sallust's report of a reply by Catiline, which is contradicted by the evidence of Cicero and Plutarch and which contains words spoken by Catiline on an earlier occasion (*Mur.* 51), can be discounted.

senate declared both of them *hostes*, ordered a regular levy, and directed Antonius to take command in Etruria. Little else of significance happened in the crisis during the remainder of November.[125] It is apparent that the military situation of the rebels in northern Italy was not sufficiently strong to enable Catiline to take any definite action. Manlius's army had not grown significantly, was poorly equipped, and had between it and Rome the growing forces of Antonius and Metellus. Uprisings which had developed in other parts of the peninsula were badly organized and easily contained, while in the capital the conspirators, led by the praetor Lentulus, though they had prepared a detailed plan of attack against the city, were clearly awaiting the approach of Catiline before making any move.[126]

Finally, at the end of November, matters came to a head when Lentulus made a critical mistake and attempted to enlist the aid of two envoys of the Gallic tribe of the Allobroges, who had come to Rome to complain of the misdoings of Roman officials and financiers among their people. The envoys reported the overtures to their Roman patron, who informed Cicero. Cicero instructed the envoys to pretend support for the conspiracy and to secure what proof they could of the conspirators' designs. The envoys complied and managed to obtain from Lentulus and two other leaders, Cethegus and Statilius, sealed pledges to take back to their government. They were to confirm the alliance by visiting Catiline on their way home, and Lentulus sent with them T. Volturcius with a letter for Catiline urging him to advance on Rome and to enlist the help of slaves. Cicero staged an arrest of the envoys as they left Rome early in the morning of December 3 and got possession of all the letters. He then had four of the conspirators—Gabinius, Statilius, Cethegus, and Lentulus—summoned to his house and arrested. Acting on information from the envoys, he also had the house of Cethegus searched, and he confiscated a stockpile of weapons which was found there. A meeting of the senate followed on the same day, at which Cicero first questioned Volturcius, who told what he knew, then

125. Sallust, *Catiline* 36.2–3. Plutarch, *Cicero* 16.3. Dio 37.33.3. In the latter part of November Cicero, anxious to have two consuls enter office for 62, successfully defended the consul-elect, L. Licinius Murena, who was accused of bribery by Cato and Sulpicius Rufus.

126. Sallust, *Catiline* 39.6, 42–43, 44.6, 56.1. Appian, *BC* 2.7. *Cat.* 3.10, 17. Plutarch, *Cicero* 18.1–2. Cf. Hardy, *Catilinarian Conspiracy*, 65, 72.

the Gallic envoys, and lastly the arrested conspirators, who, confronted with the letters and testimony of Volturcius and the Gauls, finally confessed. The senate decreed that Lentulus should resign his office, that he and eight other leading conspirators should be given into custody, and that a public thanksgiving should be held in honor of Cicero.[127]

Demonstrating once again his determination that the conspiracy should be exposed to the fullest possible extent, Cicero took unusual efforts to insure that the evidence placed before the senate should be unimpeachable and disseminated as widely as possible. He refused to open the letters taken from the envoys and Volturcius so that they could be presented to the senate with their seals unbroken; he commissioned four senators to make a verbatim record of the senatorial proceedings and had copies made for circulation throughout Italy; and, after the meeting of the senate was over, he again went before the people and delivered a triumphant speech in which he graphically related, to the enthusiastic response of the crowd, the events leading up to the arrest of the conspirators and the developments that had just transpired in the senate, and he dwelt upon the dread designs from which Rome had been delivered by divine favor and his own vigilance.[128]

On the following day a further meeting of the senate was held to consider the testimony of a man named L. Tarquinius, who had been arrested while trying to make his way to Catiline and who claimed that he had been sent by Crassus to encourage Catiline to hasten his advance on Rome. On the motion of Cicero, the senate decreed that the testimony of Tarquinius appeared to be false, and that he should be kept under guard until he disclosed who had prompted him to tell such lies. According to Sallust, Cicero also rejected repeated petitions from Catulus and C. Calpurnius Piso that he suborn witnesses to accuse Caesar of complicity in the conspiracy. However much he may have wished to discredit Crassus and Caesar and have been willing indirectly to tarnish them with the extremism of Catiline, he was not about to jeopardize his drive for *consensio* by inviting the division which would

127. *Cat.* 3.4–15; 4.5. Cf. Plutarch, *Cicero* 18.3–19.2. Sallust, *Catiline* 40–41, 44–47. Dio 37.34.
128. *Cat.* 3.7. *Sulla* 41–42. Plutarch, *Cicero* 19.3. Dio 37.34.3. Plutarch, *Cato Min.* 23.3.

result from any attempt openly to incriminate figures of such influence and resources.[129]

Meanwhile, reports were circulating that efforts were being made to organize a rescue of the arrested conspirators. Cicero placed a garrison, mainly of *equites*, in the forum and Capitol, and next day he made a general call for enlistments in case additional forces were required. There resulted a dramatic show of unity. *Equites, tribuni aerarii, iuvenes, scribae, tabernarii, libertini* came forward in numbers too great for the clerks to register. Cicero, as already described, then referred the question of the fate of the conspirators to the senate, which voted the death penalty. He had the verdict implemented that same evening and was escorted home in triumph by the state's *principes* through a throng which hailed him as the savior of his country.[130]

He had now achieved his dearest objective, the unification of honest citizens of all orders, classes, and ages under the respected leadership of the senate's *principes* in active defense of the *respublica* against the revolutionary schemes of the *perditi*. Since the arrest of the conspirators the senate had acted with an unusual degree of unity in acceding to the wishes of its leadership; the *equester ordo*, for long, as Cicero noted, at variance with the senate, rallied behind it in this crisis and provided valuable physical support in the effort to suppress the conspiracy; even the *iuventus* and *plebs*, both groups shortly before important sources of support for Catiline, zealously took the side of the consul and the senate after Cicero's revelations of the conspirators' intent. *Concordia ordinum* and the broader *consensio bonorum* had been, temporarily at least, established and had been shown in action.[131]

129. Sallust, *Catiline* 48.3–9, 49. Dio 37.35.1–2. Appian, *BC* 2.6. There is no evidence of political association between Catiline and Crassus or Caesar after the elections of 64. Cicero, who had clearly associated Crassus with Catiline's campaign for the consulship in 64, never tried to associate him with Catiline's campaign in 63. Nor is Catiline anywhere linked to the tribunician activism of 63. He was by then pursuing an independent course as the outspoken champion of the *miseri*, a more extreme course than suited the styles of Crassus and Caesar. Cicero's posthumously published work, *De Consiliis Suis*, which alleged the involvement of Crassus and Caesar in the conspiracy, is generally and rightly dismissed as a libelous invective. Cf. Dio 39.10.2. Syme, *Sallust*, 62–63.

130. *Att.* 2.1.7. *Sest.* 28. *Phil.* 2.16. *Sulla* 34. *Cat.* 4.14–18. *Flacc.* 96. *Sen.* 12. Sallust, *Catiline* 49.4. Dio 37.35.3–4.

131. *Sulla* 34. *Cat.* 4.14. Plutarch (*Cicero* 29.1) records that Clodius was one of Cicero's eager supporters. Sallust (*Catiline* 48.1) emphasizes the change of

The execution of the conspirators essentially ended the danger in Rome and also substantially lessened the threat from the rebels in Etruria, where news of the executions brought large-scale desertions. Catiline, no longer having any hope of being able to march on Rome, attempted to lead his men northward into Transalpine Gaul; but his way was blocked by the army of Metellus Celer and, unable to advance in any direction, he was forced to fight. He chose to make his stand at Pistoria, and against the army of Antonius, and in a single, bloody battle early in 62 he and his army of about three thousand men were annihilated.[132]

The conspiracy was thus quickly extinguished without any serious disruption of *otium* and without major cost to the state. At no stage had it come close to overthrowing the government or precipitating a dangerous civil war. Manlius had not succeeded in raising a formidable army in Etruria. The revolts in other parts of Italy had been fragmentary and mostly abortive. The initial schemes of the conspirators in Rome had been rendered harmless by premature disclosures of their plans, and, after Cicero had assembled his *praesidia*, it is doubtful that they ever again had the capacity to threaten seriously the security of the city.

It does not follow, however, that the conspiracy was a trifling episode. Its course and consequences could have been very different. Rome, in the absence of an organized police force, was extremely vulnerable to the form of sudden attack being planned by Catiline. There was no army in Italy to protect the state against a major uprising in the countryside. There was deep discontent both in the city and throughout Italy, and many of the discontented were aggressively pressing for redress of their grievances and had little reason to cherish the old order or to feel any loyalty to the Sullan oligarchy. If Cicero had not secured advance information of the conspirators' plans and had not acted promptly and effectively to forestall them, if he had not quickly moved the senate to dispatch commanders to threatened areas of Italy and to authorize the recruitment of troops, if he had not so

---

heart on the part of the *plebs*. For the *concordia* which Cicero believed he had established cf. *Cat.* 4.17–22. *Har. Resp.* 60. *Pis.* 4 ff. *Off.* 3.88. *Att.* 1.14.4; 1.16.9; 1.17.9–10; 1.18.3. *Fam.* 1.9.12, 17.

132. Sallust, *Catiline* 56–61. Dio 37.39–41. Plutarch, *Cicero* 22.5. Appian, *BC* 2.7.

effectively used his oratory to undermine Catiline's following and to rally the opponents of revolution, Catiline would have been able to take advantage of the vulnerability of Rome and Italy, and, if his enterprise had achieved any measure of success or showed any prospect of ultimate victory, there can be no doubt that much of the vast constituency which had supported him for the consulship in 63, and to which he represented the best hope for improvement of the lot of the *miseri*, would have taken his side and embroiled Italy in another major civil war. Cicero's monotonous and embroidered exaltations of his achievement in suppressing Catiline should not, of course, be swallowed whole, but neither should they be dismissed in irritation as the baseless rhetoric of a man who specialized in hyperbole and was incurably addicted to self-praise.[133] Conditions favorable to a revolutionary movement existed in Rome and Italy in 63, and that no large-scale upheaval resulted from the effort of a leader of Catiline's standing to launch an armed insurrection should be ascribed not to the absence of a significant revolutionary threat, but in the main to Cicero's skillful and effective leadership. His contemporaries acknowledged the gravity of the crisis, and no ancient commentator disputed his claim that he had delivered the state from a serious danger. He may have praised his consulship *sine fine*, but he did not praise it *sine causa*.[134]

For the remainder of his consulship Cicero basked in the glory he had won on the Nones of December. Further tributes were paid to him in the senate, where Catulus named him *parens patriae*, and L. Gellius, consul of 72, declared him worthy of a *civica corona*. Controversy over the executions did develop, promoted by two of the new tribunes, Metellus Nepos and Calpurnius Bestia, and when Cicero, as was customary, appeared before the people on the final day of December, Metellus prevented him from delivering an address, permitting him only to take the usual oath of outgoing magistrates, that he had upheld the laws. Cicero presented his own version of the oath, proclaiming that he had saved the city and the state. The crowd roared its approval and

---

133. The skeptical view has been argued most recently by K. H. Waters ("Cicero, Sallust, and Catiline" *Historia* 19 [1970], 195–215) and Seager (*Historia* 22 [1973], 240–48), and it has been countered by E. J. Phillips ("Catiline's Conspiracy" *Historia* 25 [1976], 441–48).
134. Cf. Seneca, *Dial.* 10.5.1.

again escorted him to his home, providing a triumphant conclusion to his eventful year at the helm of the Roman state.[135]

Cicero displayed in his consulship the full impact of his conservative heritage and of the influence of the oligarchic mentors of his youth, emerging as a vigorous and uncompromising proponent of the political and social values of the *vetus respublica* and an unrelenting foe of the forces of change. He also earned a place among the foremost *principes* of the conservative *nobilitas* as he pursued with striking success his goal of stabilizing the status quo through the forging of a great alliance of the *boni.* Working through the senate, and using his oratory to present himself as a consul of all the people and to exalt his ideal of senatorial rule and the tranquillity, prosperity, and glory it had achieved for Rome, he successfully resisted a succession of attempts to effect social or political reform, proved his determination and ability to protect the interests of the business class and of all *locupletes*, and, in the end, by exposing and suppressing the extremist schemes of Catiline and his associates, he evoked public demonstrations of support from all segments of the society. There was justice in his claims that he had established what he believed were the vital *firmamenta* of the *respublica*, *auctoritas senatus* and *concordia ordinum.*[136]

His consulship was the apogee of his remarkable ascent in Roman politics. The structure of harmony and unity that he built was unstable and soon to succumb to the stresses building in a society for which the ideals and institutions of the *respublica* were no longer adequate and from much of which they commanded little loyalty. Forces too strong for oratory or for the workings of *auctoritas* gained control of politics within a few years of Cicero's consulship and, aside from a few brief interludes, enforced upon him either silence or compromise. But his failure to envision a lasting remedy for the ills of the republic was a failure he shared with all his contemporaries, and it should not obscure the many enduring merits of the political ideal he so eloquently and, for a short period, so effectively promoted, an ideal which championed the basic principles of political liberty and private right and argued for their preservation in a rule of law and in a concept of statesmanship which saw the achievement of the *beata vita* for citizens as the primary

135. Plutarch, *Cicero* 23.1–2. Appian, *BC* 2.7. Pliny, *NH* 7.117. Gellius, 5.6.15. Dio 37.38. *Sulla* 34. *Rep.* 1.7. *Fam.* 5.2.6–7. *Pis.* 6–7. *Att.* 61.22. *Dom.* 94. 136. *Att.* 1.18.3.

goal of government.[137] Neither should the futility and sometimes faltering quality of his later statesmanship in an uncertain world dominated by the *potentia* of a few obscure the *virtus* and *industria* of his earlier life, which raised him from *novus* to *nobilis* and won him, for his administration of Rome's highest office, unprecedented honors from a begrudging aristocracy. The successes and achievements of Cicero's ascending years were rare and admirable by any measure of statesmanship, and they entitle him to a prominent place among the political leaders of the late Republic.

137. *Att.* 8.11.1.

BIBLIOGRAPHY

Abbott, F. F. "The Constitutional Argument in the Fourth Catilinarian." *CJ* 2 (1906–07), 123–25.

Adcock, F. E. *Marcus Crassus, Millionaire*. Cambridge, 1966.

Afzelius, A. "Das Ackerverteilungsgesetz des P. Servilius Rullus." *CM* 3 (1940), 214–35.

——. "Zwei Episoden aus dem Leben Ciceros." *CM* 5 (1942), 209–17.

Allen, W., Jr. "In Defense of Catiline." *CJ* 34 (1938), 70–85.

——. "Caesar's *Regnum*." *TAPA* 84 (1953), 227–36.

Astin, A. E. *Scipio Aemilianus*. Oxford, 1967.

Badian, E. "*Lex Acilia Repetundarum*." *AJP* 75 (1954), 374–84.

——. "The Date of Pompey's First Triumph." *Hermes* 83 (1955), 107–18.

——. "Q. Mucius Scaevola and the Province of Asia." *Athenaeum* 34 (1956), 104–23.

——. *Foreign Clientelae*. Oxford, 1958.

——. "Servilius and Pompey's First Triumph." *Hermes* 89 (1961), 254–56.

——. "From the Gracchi to Sulla (1940–1959)." *Historia* 11 (1962), 197–245.

——. *Studies in Greek and Roman History*. New York, 1964.

——. "Marius and the Nobles." *DUJ* 56 (1964), 141–54.

——. "M. Porcius Cato and the Annexation and Early Administration of Cyprus." *JRS* 55 (1965), 110–21.

——. "The Testament of Ptolemy Alexander." *RhM* 110 (1967), 178–92.

——. *Roman Imperialism in the Late Republic*. Oxford, 1968.

——. "*Quaestiones Variae.*" *Historia* 18 (1969), 447–91.

——. *Lucius Sulla, the Deadly Reformer.* Sydney, 1970.

——. "Two More Roman Non-entities." *Phoenix* 35 (1971), 135–44.

Balsdon, J. P. V. D. "Sulla Felix." *JRS* 41 (1951), 1–10.

——. "*Auctoritas, Dignitas, Otium.*" *CQ* 54 (1960), 43–50.

——. "Review of Badian, *Studies in Greek and Roman History.*" *JRS* 55 (1965), 229–32.

Bauman, R. A. *The* Duumviri *in the Roman Criminal Law and in the Horatius Legend.* Wiesbaden, 1969.

——. "The *Hostis* Declarations of 88 and 87 B.C." *Athenaeum* 52 (1974), 270–93.

Benario, H. W. "Cicero's *Marius* and Caesar." *CP* 52 (1957), 177–81.

Bennett, H. *Cinna and His Times.* Menasha, Wisc., 1923.

Bernardi, A. "La Guerra Sociale e le lotte dei partiti in Roma." *NRS* 28–29 (1944–45), 60–99.

Bicknell, P. "Marius, the Metelli, and the *Lex Maria Tabellaria.*" *Latomus* 28 (1969), 327–48.

Biscardi, A. "La questione italica e la tribu sopprannumerarie." *PP* 6 (1951), 241–56.

Bleicken, J. *Senatsgericht und Kaisergericht.* Göttingen, 1962.

Bloch, G. "M. Aemilius Scaurus." *Mélanges d'histoire ancienne* 25 (1909), 1–81.

Bloch, G. and Carcopino, J. *Histoire romaine.* Vol. 2. Paris, 1940.

Boak, A. E. R. "The Extraordinary Commands from 80 to 48 B.C." *AHR* 24 (1918), 1–25.

Boren, H. C. "Livius Drusus, T. P. 122, and His Anti-Gracchan Program." *CJ* 52 (1956), 27–36.

——. "Cicero's *Concordia* in Historical Perspective." *Studies in Memory of W. E. Caldwell.* Chapel Hill, 1964.

Botsford, G. W. "The Legality of the Trial and Condemnation of the Catilinarian Conspirators." *CW* 6 (1912–13), 130–32.

Broughton, T. R. S. "Notes on Roman Magistrates." *TAPA* 77 (1946), 35–43.

——. *The Magistrates of the Roman Republic.* 2 vols. New York, 1951–52.

Brunt, P. A. "Three Passages from Asconius." *CR* 71 (1957), 193–95.

——. "The Army and the Land in the Roman Revolution." *JRS* 52 (1962), 69–86.

——. "Italian Aims at the Time of the Social War." *JRS* 55 (1965), 90–109.

——. "The *Equites* in the Late Republic." *Second International*

Conference of Economic History, 1962. Vol. 1, Paris, 1965, 117-37.

——. "*Amicitia* in the Late Roman Republic." *PCPS* 11 (1965), 1-20.

——. "The Roman Mob." *Past and Present* 35 (1966), 3-27.

——. *Italian Manpower 225 B.C.-a.d. 14.* Oxford, 1971.

——. *Social Conflicts in the Roman Republic.* New York, 1971.

Buchheit, V. "Ciceros Kritik an Sulla in der Rede für Roscius aus Ameria." *Historia* 24 (1975), 570-91.

Büchner, K. *Cicero: Bestand und Wandel seiner geistigen Welt.* Heidelberg, 1964.

Bulst, C. M. "*Cinnanum Tempus.*" *Historia* 13 (1964), 307-37.

Cadoux, T. J. "Marcus Crassus. A Revaluation." *Greece and Rome* 3 (1956), 153-61.

Cambridge Ancient History. Vol. 9. Cambridge, 1932.

Carcopino, J. *Sylla ou la monarchie manquée.* Paris, 1931.

——. *Cicero: The Secrets of His Correspondence.* Translated by E. O. Lorimer. Vols. 1-2. London, 1951.

Carney, T. F. "Marius' Choice of Battlefield in the Campaign of 100." *Athenaeum* 36 (1958), 229-37.

——. "Cicero's Picture of Marius." *WS* 73 (1960), 83-122.

——. *A Biography of Marius.* Assen, 1961.

——. "The Picture of Marius in Valerius Maximus." *RhM* 105 (1962), 289-337.

Ciaceri, E. *Cicerone e i suoi tempi.* 2 vols. Milan, 1939, 1941.

Cichorius, C. *Römische Studien.* Leipzig and Berlin, 1922.

Clemente, Guido. *I Romani nella Gallia meridionale.* Bologna, 1974.

Cowles, F. H. *Gaius Verres: An Historical Study.* Ithaca, 1917.

Criniti, N. "Studi recenti su Catilina e la sua congiura." *Aevum* 41 (1967), 370-95.

——. "M. Aemilius Q.F.M.N. Lepidus '*ut ignis in stipula.*'" *Mem Ist Lomb* 30 (1969), 319-460.

——. *L'Epigrafe di Asculum di Cn. Pompeo Strabone.* Milan, 1970.

Dorey, T. A., ed. *Cicero.* London, 1964.

Douglas, A. E. *M. Tulli Ciceronis Brutus.* Oxford, 1966.

——. *Cicero.* Oxford, 1968.

Earl, D. C. "Sallust and the Senate's Numidian Policy." *Latomus* 24 (1965), 532-36.

Ewins, U. "*Ne Quis Iudicio Circumveniatur.*" *JRS* 50 (1960), 94-107.

Fraccaro, P. *Opuscula.* Vol. 2. Pavia, 1957.

Frank, T. *An Economic Survey of Ancient Rome.* Vol. 1. Baltimore, 1959.

Frederiksen, M. W. "Caesar, Cicero and the Problem of Debt." *JRS* 56 (1966), 128–41.

Frier, B. "Sulla's Propaganda: The Collapse of the Cinnan Republic." *AJP* 92 (1971), 585–604.

Frisch, H. "The First Catilinarian Conspiracy. A Study in Historical Conjecture." *CM* 9 (1948), 10–36.

Fritz, K. von. "Emergency Powers in the Last Century of the Roman Republic." *AHA* 3 (1942), 221–37.

Gabba, E. "Le origini dell' esercito professionale in Roma. I proletari e la reforma di Mario." *Athenaeum* 27 (1949), 173–209.

——. "*Lex Plotia Agraria.*" *PP* 13 (1950), 66–68.

——. "Ricerche su alcuni punti di storia Mariana." *Athenaeum* 29 (1951), 12–24.

——. "Ricerche sull' esercito professionale romano da Mario ad Augusto." *Athenaeum* 29 (1951), 171–272.

——. "Politica e cultura in Roma agli inizi del I secolo a.C." *Athenaeum* 31 (1953), 259–72.

——. "Le origini della guerra sociale e la vita politica romana dopo l'89 a.C." *Athenaeum* 32 (1954), 41–114, 293–345.

——. "Il ceto equestre e il Senato di Silla." *Athenaeum* 34 (1956), 124–38.

——. "Osservazioni sulla lege giudiziaria di M. Livio Druso (91 a.C.)." *PP* 11 (1956), 363–72.

——. "Review of Valgiglio, *Silla e la crisi repubblicana.*" *Athenaeum* 35 (1957), 138–41.

——. *Appiani Bellorum Civilium Liber Primus.* Florence, 1958.

——. "Review of Badian, *Foreign Clientelae.*" *RFIC* 37 (1959), 189–99.

——. "M. Livio Druso e le riforme di Silla." *ASNP* 33 (1964), 1–15.

——. "Nota sulla rogatio agraria di P. Servilio Rullo." *Mélanges Piganiol.* Vol. 2, Paris, 1966, 769–76.

Garzetti, A. "M. Licinio Crasso." *Athenaeum* 19 (1941), 1–37.

——. "M. Licinio Crasso." *Athenaeum* 20 (1942), 12–40.

——. "M. Licinio Crasso." *Athenaeum* 21 (1944–45), 1–61.

Gelzer, M. "Review of Carcopino, *Sylla ou la monarchie manquée. Gnomon* 8 (1932), 605–07.

——. *Pompeius.* Munich, 1949.

——. *Kleine Schriften.* Vols. 1–2. Wiesbaden, 1962.

——. *Caesar.* Translated by P. Needham. Oxford, 1968.

——. *Cicero: Ein Biographischer Versuch.* Wiesbaden, 1969.

——. *The Roman Nobility.* Translated by R. Seager. Oxford, 1969.

Gnauk, R. *Die Bedeutung des Marius und Cato Maior für Cicero.* Berlin, 1936.

Göhler, J. *Rom und Italien.* Breslau, 1939.

Greenidge, A. H. J. *Roman Public Life.* New York, 1901.

Griffin, M. "Pre-Sullan *leges iudiciariae.*" *CQ* 67 (1973), 108–26.

——. "The Tribunate of Cornelius." *JRS* 63 (1973), 196–213.

Gruen, E. S. "The *Lex Varia.*" *JRS* 55 (1965), 59–73.

——. "The Dolabellae and Sulla." *AJP* 87 (1966), 385–99.

——. "Political Prosecutions in the 90's B.C." *Historia* 15 (1966), 32–64.

——. "Cicero and Licinius Calvus." *HSCP* 71 (1966), 215–33.

——. *Roman Politics and the Criminal Courts.* Cambridge, Mass., 1968.

——. "Pompey and the Pisones." *CSCA* 1 (1968), 155–70.

——. "Antonius and the Trial of the Vestal Virgins." *RhM* 111 (1968), 59–63.

——. "Notes on the First Catilinarian Conspiracy." *CP* 64 (1969), 20–24.

——. "Pompey, the Roman Aristocracy, and the Conference at Luca." *Historia* 18 (1969), 71–108.

——. "Pompey, Metellus Pius, and the Trials of 70–69 B.C.: The Perils of Schematism." *AJP* 92 (1971), 1–16.

——. "Some Criminal Trials of the Late Republic: Political and Prosopographical Problems." *Athenaeum* 49 (1971), 54–69.

——. *The Last Generation of the Roman Republic.* Berkeley, 1974.

Hands, A. R. "Sallust and *Dissimulatio.*" *JRS* 49 (1959), 56–60.

——. "Livius Drusus and the Courts." *Phoenix* 26 (1972), 268–74.

Hardy, E. G. *The Catilinarian Conspiracy in Its Context.* Oxford, 1924.

——. *Some Problems in Roman History.* Oxford, 1924.

Harmand, J. *L'armée et le soldat à Rome de 107 à 50 avant notre ère.* Paris, 1967.

Harris, W. V. *Rome in Etruria and Umbria.* Oxford, 1971.

Haskell, H. *This was Cicero.* London, 1942.

Hassall, M.; Crawford, M.; and Reynolds, J. "Rome and the Eastern Provinces at the End of the Second Century B.C." *JRS* 64 (1974), 195–220.

Hayne, L. "M. Lepidus (cos. 78): A Re-Appraisal." *Historia* 21 (1972), 661–68.

——. "The Politics of M'. Glabrio, Cos. 67." *CP* 69 (1974), 280–82.

Heinze, R. "Ciceros politische Anfänge." *Abh Leipz* 27 (1909), 945–1010.

Heitland, W. E. *The Roman Republic.* Vol. 3. Cambridge, 1923.

Hellegouarc'h, J. *Vocabulaire latin des relations et des partis politiques sous la république.* Paris, 1963.

Hill, H. *The Roman Middle Class in the Republican Period.* Oxford, 1952.

Holmes, T. Rice. *The Roman Republic.* Vols. 1-2. Oxford, 1923.

Husband, R. W. "On the Expulsion of Foreigners from Rome." *CP* 11 (1916), 315-33.

John, C. "Die Entstehungsgeschichte der catilinarischen Verschworung." *Jahrb Cl Phil* Supp. 8 (1876), 703-819.

Kaplan, A. *Catiline. The Man and His Role in the Roman Revolution.* New York, 1968.

Katz, B. R. "The First Fruits of Sulla's March." *AC* 44 (1975), 100-25.
——. "Studies on the Period of Cinna and Sulla." *AC* 45 (1976), 497-549.

Kinsey, T. E. "Dates of the *Pro Roscio* and *Pro Quinctio.*" *Mn* 20 (1967), 61-67.

Kontchalovsky, D. "Recherches sur l'histoire du mouvement agraire des Gracques." *RH* 153 (1926), 161-86.

Kumaniecki, C. "Cicerone e Varrone, Storia di una Conoscenza." *Athenaeum* 40 (1962), 221-43.

Laffi, U. "Il Mito di Silla." *Athenaeum* 45 (1967), 177-213.

Lanzani, C. *Mario e Silla.* Catania, 1915.
——. "Silla e Pompeo. La Spedizione di Sicilia e d'Africa." *Historia* 7 (1933), 343-62.

Lavery, G. B. "Cicero's *Philarchia* and Marius." *Greece and Rome* 18 (1971), 133-42.

Levick, B. "Cicero, Brutus 43.159 ff., and the Foundation of Narbo Martius." *CQ* 31 (1971), 170-79.

Lintott, A. W. *Violence in Republican Rome.* Oxford, 1968.
——. "The Tribunate of P. Sulpicius Rufus." *CQ* 21 (1971), 442-53.
——. "The Offices of C. Flavius Fimbria in 86-85 B.C." *Historia* 20 (1971), 696-701.
——. "*Provocatio.* From the Struggles of the Orders to the Principate." *Aufstieg und Niedergang der römischen Welt* 1.2, Berlin, 1972, 226-67.

Luce, T. J. "Marius and the Mithridatic Command." *Historia* 19 (1970), 161-94.

McDermott, W. C. "*Lex de tribunicia potestate* (70 B.C.)." *CP* 72 (1977), 49-52.

McDonald, W. "The Tribunate of Cornelius." *CQ* 23 (1929), 196-208.

Magie, D. *Roman Rule in Asia Minor.* 2 vols. Princeton, 1950.

Marshall, B. A. "Q. Cicero, Hortensius, and the *Lex Aurelia.*" *RhM* 118 (1975), 136–52.

———. "The Date of Q. Mucius Scaevola's Governorship of Asia." *Athenaeum* 54 (1976), 117–30.

———. *Crassus: A Political Biography.* Amsterdam, 1976.

———. "The Date of Catiline's Marriage to Aurelia Orestilla." *Riv Fil* 105 (1977), 151–54.

Marshall, B. A., and Baker, R. J. "The Aspirations of Q. Arrius." *Historia* 24 (1975), 221–31.

Mattingly, H. B. "The Foundations of Narbo Martius." *Hommages Grenier.* Vol. 3, Brussels, 1962, 1159–71.

———. "The *Consilium* of Pompeius Strabo in 89 B.C." *Athenaeum* 53 (1975), 262–66.

Meier, C. "Review of Badian, *Foreign Clientelae.*" *BJ* 161 (1961), 503–14.

———. "Review of Carney, *A Biography of C. Marius.*" *Gnomon* 36 (1964), 64–70.

———. *Res Publica Amissa.* Wiesbaden, 1966.

Mello, M. "Sallustio e le elezioni consolari del 66 a.C." *PP* 18 (1963), 36 ff.

Meyer, E. *Caesars Monarchie und das Principat des Pompeius.* Stuttgart, 1922.

Michels, A. *The Calendar of the Roman Republic.* Princeton, 1967.

Millar, F. *A Study of Cassius Dio.* Oxford, 1964.

Mitchell, T. N. "Cicero and the *Senatus Consultum Ultimum.*" *Historia* 20 (1971), 47–61.

———. "Cicero, Pompey, and the Rise of the First Triumvirate." *Traditio* 29 (1973), 1–26.

———. "The Volte-Face of P. Sulpicius Rufus in 88." *CP* 70 (1975), 197–204.

Mohler, S. L. "*Sentina reipublicae.* Campaign Issues, 63 B.C." *CW* 29 (1936), 81–84.

Mommsen, T. *Römisches Staatsrecht.* 3 vols. Leipzig, 1887–88.

———. *Römisches Strafrecht.* Leipzig, 1899.

Münzer, F. *Römische Adelsparteien und Adelsfamilien.* Stuttgart, 1920.

Murray, R. J. "Cicero and the Gracchi." *TAPA* 97 (1966), 291–98.

Neunheuser, J. E. *M. Aemilius Lepidus.* Münster, 1902.

Niccolini, G. "Le leggi *de civitate Romana* durante la guerra sociale." *RAL* S.8.1. (1946), 110.

Nicolet, C. "Arpinum, Aemilius Scaurus et les Tullii Cicerones." *REL* 45 (1967), 276–304.

Oost, S. I. "Cato Uticensis and the Annexation of Cyprus." *CP* 50 (1955), 98–112.

Ooteghem, J. Van. *L. Marcius Philippus et sa famille.* Brussels, 1961.

——. *Caius Marius.* Brussels, 1964.

——. "Verres et les Metelli." *Mélanges Piganiol.* Vol. 2, Paris, 1966, 827–35.

Pareti, L. *Storia di Roma.* Vol. 3. Turin, 1953.

Parrish, E. "Crassus' New Friends and Pompey's Return." *Phoenix* 27 (1973), 357–80.

Passerini, A. "C. Mario come uomo politico." *Athenaeum* 12 (1934), 10–44, 109–43, 257–97, 348–80.

Petersson, T. *Cicero, a Biography.* Berkeley, 1920.

Phillips, E. J. "Cicero and the Prosecution of C. Manilius." *Latomus* 29 (1970), 595–607.

——. "Asconius' *magni homines.*" *RhM* 116 (1973), 353–57.

——. "The Prosecution of C. Rabirius in 63 B.C." *Klio* 56 (1974), 87–101.

——. "Catiline's Conspiracy." *Historia* 25 (1976), 441–48.

Plaumann, G. "Das sogennante *senatus consultum ultimum.*" *Klio* 13 (1913), 321–86.

Rambaud, M. *Cicéron et l'histoire romaine.* Paris, 1953.

Rawson, B. "*De Lege Agraria* 2.49." *CP* 66 (1971), 26–29.

Rawson, E. "Lucius Crassus and Cicero." *PCPS* 17 (1971), 75–88.

——. *Cicero.* London, 1975.

Rödl, B. *Das Senatus Consultum Ultimum und der Tod der Gracchen.* Bonn, 1969.

Rossi, R. F. "Sulla lotta politica in Roma dopo la morte di Silla." *PP* 20 (1965), 113–52.

Salmon, E. T. "Catiline, Crassus and Caesar." *AJP* 56 (1935), 302–16.

——. *Roman Colonization.* London, 1969.

Scholz, U. *Der Redner M. Antonius.* Erlangen, 1963.

Scullard, H. H. *Roman Politics 220–150 B.C.* Oxford, 1950.

——. *From the Gracchi to Nero.* London, 1959.

——. "Scipio Aemilianus and Roman Politics." *JRS* 50 (1960), 59–74.

Seager, R. "The First Catilinarian Conspiracy." *Historia* 13 (1964), 338–47.

——. "*Lex Varia de Maiestate.*" *Historia* 16 (1967), 37–43.

——. "The Tribunate of Cornelius. Some Ramifications." *Hommages à M. Renard.* Vol. 2, Brussels, 1969, 680–86.

——. "Cicero and the Word *Popularis.*" *CQ* 22 (1972), 328–38.

——. "*Iusta Catilinae.*" *Historia* 22 (1973), 240–48.

Seleckij, B. P. "Der Gesetzentwurf Drusus' des Jüngeren zur Gewährung der Bürgerrechte für die Italiker im Lichte der Schriften Ciceros (Q.fr.1.1; Att. 2.16)." *Klio* 58 (1976), 425–37.

Shackleton Bailey, D. R. "The Roman Nobility in the Second Civil War." *CQ* 10 (1960), 253–67.

———. *Cicero's Letters to Atticus.* 6 vols. Cambridge, 1965–68.

Shaw, B. D. "Debt in Sallust." *Latomus* 34 (1975), 187–96.

Sherwin-White, A. N. *The Roman Citizenship.* Oxford, 1939.

———. "The Extortion Procedure Again." *JRS* 42 (1952), 43–55.

———. "Violence in Roman Politics." *JRS* 46 (1956), 1–9.

Shochat, Y. "The *Lex Agraria* of 133 B.C. and the Italian Allies." *Athenaeum* 48 (1970), 25–45.

Siber, H. "*Provocatio.*" *ZSS* (1942), 376–91.

Smith, R. E. "The *Lex Plotia Agraria* and Pompey's Spanish Veterans." *CQ* 7 (1957), 82–85.

———. *Service in the Post-Marian Army.* Manchester, 1958.

———. "Pompey's Conduct in 80 and 77 B.C." *Phoenix* 14 (1960), 1–13.

Stockton, D. *Cicero, a Political Biography.* Oxford, 1971.

———. "The First Consulship of Pompey." *Historia* 22 (1973), 205–18.

Strachan-Davidson, J. L. *Cicero and the Fall of the Roman Republic.* London, 1898.

———. *Problems of the Roman Criminal Law.* Vol. 1. Oxford, 1912.

Strasburger, H. *Caesars Eintritt in die Geschichte.* Munich, 1938.

———. *Concordia Ordinum, eine Untersuchung zur Politik Ciceros.* Amsterdam, 1956.

Sumner, G. V. "Manius or Mamercus." *JRS* 54 (1964), 41–48.

———. "The Consular Elections for 66 B.C." *Phoenix* 19 (1965), 226–31.

———. "Cicero, Pompey, and Rullus." *TAPA* 97 (1966), 569–82.

Syme, R. "The Allegiance of Labienus." *JRS* 28 (1938), 113–21.

———. *The Roman Revolution.* Oxford, 1939.

———. "Review of Schur, *Zeitalter des Marius und Sulla.*" *JRS* 34 (1944), 103–09.

———. *Sallust.* Berkeley, 1964.

Taylor, L. R. "Caesar's Early Career." *CP* 36 (1941), 113–32.

———. "Caesar's Colleagues in the Pontifical College." *AJP* 63 (1942), 385–412.

———. "Caesar and the Roman Nobility." *TAPA* 73 (1942), 1–24.

———. *The Voting Districts of the Roman Republic.* Rome, 1960.

———. *Party Politics in the Age of Caesar.* Berkeley, 1964.

———. *Roman Voting Assemblies.* Ann Arbor, 1966.

Thompson, L. A. "The Relationship between Provincial Quaestors and Their Commanders-in-Chief." *Historia* 11 (1962), 339–55.

———. "Pompeius Strabo and the Trial of Albucius." *Latomus* 28 (1969), 1036–39.

Thomsen, R. "Das Jahr 91 v. Chr. und seine Voraussetzungen." *CM* 5 (1942), 13–47.

Treggiari, S. *Roman Freedmen during the Late Republic.* Oxford, 1969.

Twyman, B. "The Metelli, Pompeius, and Prosopography." *Aufstieg und Niedergang der römischen Welt* 1, Berlin, 1972, 817–74.

———. "The Date of Sulla's Abdication and the Chronology of the First Book of Appian's Civil Wars." *Athenaeum* 54 (1976), 77–97.

Tyrrell, W. B. "The Trial of C. Rabirius in 63 B.C." *Latomus* 32 (1973), 285–300.

Ungern-Sternberg, J. *Untersuchungen zum spätrepublikanischen Notstandsrecht.* Munich, 1970.

Valgiglio, E. *Silla e la crisi repubblicana.* Florence, 1956.

Ward, A. M. "Cicero's Support of Pompey in the Trials of Fonteius and Oppius." *Latomus* 27 (1968), 802–09.

———. "Cicero and Pompey in 75 and 70 B.C." *Latomus* 29 (1970), 58–71.

———. "Politics in the Trials of Manilius and Cornelius." *TAPA* 101 (1970), 545–56.

———. "Cicero's Fight Against Crassus and Caesar in 65 and 63 B.C." *Historia* 21 (1972), 244–58.

———. *Marcus Crassus and the Late Roman Republic.* Columbia, 1977.

Waters, K. H. "Cicero, Sallust, and Catiline." *Historia* 19 (1970), 195–215.

Weinrib, E. J. "The Prosecution of Roman Magistrates." *Phoenix* 22 (1968), 32–56.

———. "The Judiciary Law of M. Livius Drusus (tr. pl. 91 B.C.)." *Historia* 19 (1970), 414–43.

Wirszubski, C. "Cicero's *Cum Dignitate Otium*: A Reconsideration." *JRS* 44 (1954), 1–13.

———. *Libertas as a Political Idea at Rome.* Cambridge, 1960.

———. "*Audaces*: A Study in Political Phraseology." *JRS* 51 (1961), 12–22.

Wiseman, T. P. "The Census in the First Century B.C." *JRS* 59 (1969), 59–75.

———. *New Men in the Roman Senate.* Oxford, 1971.

Yavetz, Z. "The Living Conditions of the Urban *Plebs* in Republican Rome." *Latomus* 17 (1958), 500–17.

———. "The Failure of Catiline's Conspiracy." *Historia* 12 (1963), 485–99.

INDEX OF NAMES

INDEX OF SUBJECTS